W9-BBW-670

An Introduction to Educational Research

Michael Langenbach
University of Oklahoma

Courtney Vaughn
University of Oklahoma

Lola Aagaard
Appalachia Educational Laboratory

Allyn and Bacon
Boston • London • Toronto • Sydney • Tokyo • Singapore

We dedicate this book to students.

Editor in Chief, Education: Nancy Forsyth
Editorial Assistant: Christine Nelson
Production Administrator: Susan McIntyre
Editorial-Production Service: Ruttle, Shaw & Wetherill, Inc.
Composition Buyer: Linda Cox
Manufacturing Buyer: Megan Cochran

Copyright © 1994 by Allyn and Bacon
A Division of Simon & Schuster, Inc.
160 Gould Street
Needham Heights, MA 02194

Library of Congress Cataloging-in-Publication Data

Langenbach, Michael.
    An introduction to educational research / Michael Langenbach, Courtney Vaughn, Lola Aagaard.
        p.   cm.
    Includes bibliographical references and index.
    ISBN 0-205-13902-7
    1. Education—Research. I. Vaughn, Courtney.
II. Aagaard, Lola. III. Title.
LB1028.L27 1993
370'.78—dc20   93-22189
                                                                        CIP

Printed in the United States of America

10 9 8 7 6 5 4 3 2 1   98 97 96 95 94 93

Contents

Preface

This book is designed to acquaint the reader with the rudiments of educational research. It is intended for readers who have limited, if any, background in research. This group consists of educational faculty members whose training, background, and experience did not include much research-related activity; graduate students in education who are beginning to be engaged in research as part of their training; and prospective, as well as practicing, teachers and administrators who want to look behind the scenes of educational research.

We believe that by beginning with two important, but different views of reality, we can introduce the uninitiated to three basic elements of educational research: ontology, epistemology, and axiology. These are philosophical terms that mean, respectively, view of the world, nature of knowledge and how we know it, and values. Primarily we discuss truth-seeking and perspective-seeking views of the world; quantitative and qualitative sources of data and methods; and ideology and ethics (part of axiology) as they shape and form educational research. The subsequent topics are the same as those found in most texts, but their treatment will be within the context of the three elements. Whenever possible, examples are used to illustrate the variety of ontologies, types of data and methods, and ideologies. (Ideally, ethical standards should remain constant!)

We believe it is imperative that graduate students of education become familiar with educational research. Increased knowledge and understanding will help to make them discerning consumers and better producers of educational research.

Being an informed consumer of educational research is important. The criteria for judging research need to be broad enough to accommodate the different varieties of research. It is critical that consumers understand there are different views of the world from which research projects can be launched, different methods for data collection, and different ideologies that influence their conduct. Informed consumers of research need to understand the variety of legitimate options within the field of educational research.

Overview

Research is a way of knowing or understanding, just as insight, divine inspiration, and acceptance of authoritative declarations can be ways of knowing. One difference between research and other ways of knowing is that research requires reporting. Reporting is sharing the results of the research and the way the research was conducted with those who may have an interest in it. A research report can be written as a paper presented at a conference, included in a conference's proceedings, or published in a research journal. Whatever form is used, sharing means that the research is subject to scrutiny by others. And, just as might be expected when a number of people scrutinize something, research is judged on some sort of scale as being somewhere between very good and very bad. Certainly, according to our scales, all kinds of good and bad research are presented or published.

One major difficulty in discussing good and bad research is overcoming the myriad misunderstandings associated with research, especially the ways in which it is taught and written about. The assumptions made about reality, for example, underlie what some people even consider valid research. More than a few research textbooks boldly assume that there is just one reality, objective and knowable, and that the only reliable way to know it is through research. The specific problem with this approach is that it denies other views of reality and the appropriate ways to learn about them from which a multitude of research is conducted.

The Problem

At least three factors contribute to the difficulty most novices have with understanding educational research: vocabulary and symbols; a singular, systematic approach; and, especially for graduate students, a sacrosanct view of the master's project or thesis or doctoral dissertation.

Vocabulary and Symbols

The vocabulary problem is addressed in detail in this book, but suffice it to say here that many synonyms exist for nearly any term associated with research. The presence of synonyms is not unique to educational research, but the failure of most research texts to acknowledge the variety of terms often used to represent the same concept leaves many novices bewildered when they begin reading other sources. A case in point is the number of terms used synonymously to represent the conventional approach to research, such as *rationalism* and *positivism*. At the opposite end of the philosophical continuum one can find *naturalism* and *phenomonology*. Seldom, however, will an author espousing one pair of these even acknowledge that such synonyms exist. We are not making a brief for any of the terms being more descriptive than others—in fact, we select our terms more by default than anything else—but we do alert the reader that different words are used to mean approximately the same thing, and it is rare for writers of research texts to remind readers of this practice. To assist in understanding the vocabulary we have included a glossary of research-related terms.

Additional confounding occurs when the same terms are used to mean different things. Reading several research textbooks can be like reading a Russian novel, in which characters' names change without warning. We try to separate three important aspects of research: view of the world; method; and ideology; but we realize how difficult maintaining the separation becomes when researchers use terms like *phenomenology* to indicate a view of the world in one text and design or method in another.

Switching between specific meanings and general meanings, depending on the context, also confuses readers. *Quantitative methods,* for example, means a class of methods that uses numbers. However, to different writers, a quantitative study may mean a study that uses such methods, or it may mean the philosophical position on which the study is based. We try to be consistent in the use of terms, but warn the reader that not only may we slip, but also that other writers of books and articles on research show scant attention to these inconsistencies. To assist your understanding, we have placed in brackets terms that we have used in the chapters, next to certain research terms used by the authors of our readings.

Clarity seldom occurs even when authors move discussions to statistics, a branch of mathematics wherein one would hope for more uniformity. The use, for example, of Greek or English symbols varies, not by the concept being represented but by the proclivity of the particular statistician. One can take some comfort in the existence of such guides as the *APA Manual of Style*, in which at least a uniformity in writing is forged, but then there is the *Chicago Manual of Style*, not to mention Turabian's *A Manual for Writers* or the Modern Language Association's Handbook. All the manuals have their self-interests to serve and that rarely has anything to do with making content more understandable when different styles are encountered.

Singular, Systematic Approach

A singular, systematic approach to research creates confusion especially when novices begin their own projects. The singular approach so often promulgated as the only legitimate way to conduct research has really two strands of error. One reflects the conventional approach to research, that is, one particular view of the world and one preferred method, both of which are discussed in Chapter 2. The other strand represents an obsession with orderliness.

Research, like most other human activities, is messy. Yet accounts of it (i.e., research reports heard at conferences or read in journals) are routinely and traditionally clean, uncluttered, and always systematic. More is said about logic-in-use (what really happened) and reconstructed logic (what sounds and looks orderly) in Chapter 8. The point here is that, frequently, beginners are led astray by assuming that reports of research correspond almost exactly with the actual conduct of the research project.

It is not unusual for a research project to begin with a collection of data, requiring the researcher to work "backwards" through the procedures found in research reports. Purists may recoil in horror at the apparent violence done to systematic progress through step one, step two, and so on, but we have a growing suspicion that not many purists do research. Obviously one would not draw inferences or make conclusions before data are collected and analyzed, but short of that we maintain that the orderly sequencing of a research project seldom occurs in the real world of educational research.

Sacrosanct View of the Research Project

The sacrosanct view of the research project can have a devastating effect on graduate students. Because of the belief that such an important undertaking cannot be attempted until one is fully proficient in research, no other research can be attempted before the required research project. Undoubtedly some must believe that everyone has been allotted just one good research project, and consequently they ask, why spend it on anything but the required one—whether it be a master's project or thesis or dissertation? Far too many theses and dissertations represent the students' first attempt at research. And, for many, the thesis or dissertation, if completed, is also their last attempt at a research effort.

Any research project, whether it be for a master's or doctoral degree, is an important undertaking. A great deal of planning and careful procedures are indispensable to the successful completion of such a project. We believe, however, that the "final" project will be less intimidating and more competently pursued if it is the student's second, third, or fourth research project, instead of the first.

We are not advocating a multiple thesis or dissertation program for graduate students. We are claiming that research projects of a smaller scope can be accomplished by graduate students before the thesis or dissertation. A very small version of a research project, or any large study, is known as a *pilot study*. Pilot studies can be useful for checking out the logistics necessary for the main study, but pilot studies are seldom presented at conferences or published in journals. We advocate that graduate students engage in smaller scale studies before, and perhaps completely different from, the thesis or dissertation.

Working as a research assistant on a large-scale study can be a valuable experience in that it provides an opportunity to contribute to a research project. All too often, however, research assistants have rather meaningless chores and rarely are involved in the conceptualization, design, or write-up of a study. Experience as a research assistant is important, but actually conducting a research project, from start to finish, is a far more valuable experience.

Our experience has been that students can, with little help, plan and carry out a small-scale research project within a semester under the aegis of a research, statistics, or issues course. Submitting a research proposal or completed project to a research conference for presentation and having it accepted is an invaluable experience for graduate students. Significant, too, is attending, listening, and socializing at a research conference, be it local, state, regional, or national.

Our Solution

Undoubtedly, all textbook authors believe their book will dispel mystery and clarify, once and for all, the rudiments of their subject. We are no different. We intend to introduce educational research as an understandable endeavor. We do not intend to suggest that research is necessarily easy or that one can be cavalier in carrying it out. All too often, however, educational research has been unnecessarily shrouded in a kind of mystique that permits only a few to claim understanding. We hope to remove the shroud.

We begin with an entire chapter devoted to a definition of research. No one definition appears to work for all occasions; hence, we contrast research with journalism to illustrate the relevance of theory to research and research to theory. Broadly conceived, research is about asking and answering questions. The questions in education frequently are informed by related social sciences and humanities and a few are presented as examples.

Before proceeding with the role of theory, we interject what we consider the most useful tool (we call it a *scaffold* or *cube*) for understanding research. Chapter 2 describes our scaffold. Illustrations are presented for each of three dimensions: view of the world; method; and ideology.

Chapter 3 describes the role of theory and its relationship to philosophical design. Included within the chapter are examples of several theories and a discussion of descriptive and prescriptive theories. Sources for theory are also discussed.

Chapter 4 addresses various research designs, including theory-driven ones and descriptive, exploratory, and emergent designs.

Sources of both quantitative and qualitative data are included in Chapter 5. A discussion of data banks and data-gathering instruments such as surveys, standardized forms, and self-developed questionnaires are included in the quantitative section of the chapter. The qualitative side includes the use of archives, newspapers, personal papers, observations, and interviews.

Chapter 6 contrasts data analysis principles and procedures for quantitative and qualitative data.

Chapter 7 discusses ethics in research with examples of ethical problems encountered in various research designs and methods.

Chapter 8 describes writing research reports. Reconstructed logic and logic-in-use are discussed, as well as the conventional subtopics of research reports.

Beginning with Chapter 2 we have included readings that treat each chapter's topic in more depth. Some of the readings serve as examples or models of research, and others present points of view regarding research. The *Introduction to the Readings*, following Chapters 2 through 8, highlights the various points each of the readings brings out. Questions for discussion and suggestions for activities appear at the end of each chapter before the *Introduction to the Readings.*

Acknowledgments

We are greatly indebted to our students who have helped us understand and clarify the many varieties of educational research. Helpful, too, have been the reviewers of the book's manuscript: Richard G. Lomax, Boston College, Sandra L. Stein, Rider College, Edwin J. Cook, Russel Sage College, Susan M. Brookhart, Duquesne University, Richard F. Purnell, University of Rhode Island, Robert O'Neill, University of Oregon, and Jerome Popp, Southern Illinois University. We continue to learn about and appreciate more the different points of view held by our colleagues in the research community.

In any project of this magnitude, assistance comes from many sources. We gratefully acknowledge the authors of our readings and their publishers for granting permission to use their works. And we thank Susan Houck, whose competence in word processing is matched only by her ability to make order out of chaos.

Chapter *1*

What Is Research?

This chapter defines research, emphasizing its necessary connection to theory. Also it acquaints you with various academic fields in the social sciences and humanities from which educational research derived. In so doing it may help you begin to think in terms of asking questions that you might answer through some research project.

Research is difficult to define. One approach is to let researchers define the word by their activities. It is not enough, here, however, to say research is what researchers do. Too many people misuse the word. For example, some faculty colleagues claim to do research to prepare for a class, every week, no less. What they usually mean is they read or reread material that they will be presenting or discussing in class. Such a preparation may take time and effort, but it is not research.

Students frequently are assigned research papers, wherein they read from books and journals, usually in a library, and synthesize the material to form the research paper. The students would claim to be doing research, or at least library research. What they are doing is searching or reviewing the literature on a topic and writing about their findings. It is not research.

A journalist may systematically investigate an occurrence to find out why it happened, and the same journalist may indeed claim that what he or she is doing is research, but it is not. It is journalism.

Research is an activity that makes an impact on theory. In the absence of theory, the activity is not research. The activity may be preparing for a class, writing a paper, or developing a story, all honorable activities, but they are not research unless they have a connection with something theoretical.

The role of theory is to describe and explain a phenomenon. The presence of theory means the writer has gone beyond the local event and is trying to connect it with similar events or, more accurately, other descriptions or explanations that have served to describe or explain similar events. An example may illustrate the distinction we are trying to make.

A well-known college football coach resigns unexpectedly. A journalist writes about the event in very specific terms, that is, what preceded and possibly precipitated the resignation. The story seeks to describe and explain the event, but because there is no attempt to connect anything about the story to anything theoretical, it is journalism. If, on the other hand, the journalist had observed that the coach had been promoted originally from within the organization and the journalist had referred to organizational theory (a body of knowledge that explains human behavior within an organizational setting) that speaks to the possible consequences of promoting from within, which might include a number of predictable consequences, then the journalist is doing research, because the journalist is extending the story, or aspects of it, beyond the specifics of the local event. This extension makes it research.

It is important to note in the example used that including something theoretical, in this case, drawing on organizational theory, can be accomplished in a relatively thorough manner or simply superficially. One can cite a generalization or two from a book on organizational theory and claim to be doing research. A more thorough treatment, however, would be to look carefully for other explanations or other theoretical perspectives that might not be congruent with the first one found. The writer quickly gets into something of a conceptual quagmire when this is done, and just as quickly needs to begin to qualify the generalizations.

The original event and the interpretations of the many specifics surrounding it can be used to confirm or refute some of the theory that exists to explain similar events. Whenever the effort is made to be more theoretical about what one writes, it is incumbent upon the writer to seek competing theoretical positions and, when found, acknowledge them. In short, to be thorough, one needs to take some time and effort and realize the finished product may raise more questions than it answers. (The deadlines most journalists face preclude their doing very much research, as we define it. And when you think of local nightly television news, there is no doubt that thorough coverage often gives way to superficiality.)

We believe the theoretical component of research is what ought to determine most of the substance of course work at the graduate level. In this regard, students become steeped in the theory associated with an area (e.g., the organization and administration of public schools) sufficiently to be able to draw from the theory certain expectations that can be tested, confirmed, or made more or less credible by research. Gaps in the theory, those areas about which precious little is known, can be discovered and speculated about in terms of how subsequent contributions to the knowledge base could fill them. The primary value of course work, then, is to familiarize students with the various theories that abound in any particular field of interest (viz., school finance, teaching methods, and curriculum development, to name a few).

Asking Questions

Essentially, research is an attempt to answer questions. The answers, we insist, have to have some kind of theoretical importance. The answers may confirm or refute theory; make theory more or less credible; or develop theory where little or none exists. Surveys, evaluation reports, policy studies, or action research reports may come to mind as examples of research that are not necessarily related to anything theoretical. They are projects that administrators, teachers, or other educators conduct to solve a particular problem. Because they are so situation-specific they may not explicitly illustrate how their findings relate to anything theoretical, but certainly the consumers of such reports might take into account the extent to which the findings concur with other research in a particular field before making a policy or instructional decision based on them. Certainly such projects (e.g., the percentage of teachers with master's degrees or the various class sizes in schools serving high and low socioeconomic students) do get published, but we simply consider them to be what they are—surveys. Likewise, evaluation reports sometimes appear as research papers or articles, but, as in the case of surveys, if there is no explicit attempt to connect the findings and their analysis with theory, they too are not research. The kind of question that is asked will determine the kind of research that needs to be conducted.

Most conventional educational researchers insist that research questions deal with variables that can be observed and measured. These criteria make sense only when one is confined to quantitative methods and operating from a belief that constant, objective answers to research questions exist.

Methods of research can be qualitative (detecting patterns) in addition to quantitative (employing statistical calculations), and different views of the world can be used as a base for research. (We discuss the different views of the world in Chapter 2.) Consider, for example, the question, "To what extent, if any, are Euro-American, elementary school teachers biased toward nonwhite elementary students?" The conventional research approach would require some kind of quantitative measure of bias and some degree of representativeness of the sample measured, the latter for the purpose of generalizing back to the population of white, elementary school teachers. The validity and reliability of the instrument, used to measure bias, would be critical to the overall validity of the research project. Finding a valid and reliable measure of racial prejudice has eluded test makers for generations and probably always will. Thus, for many researchers, this would mean the end of the research project.

The idea can be investigated, however, if one had a different view of the world and were to use different methods. If the researcher were not interested in generalizing back to a larger population, but wanted mainly to find out what seems to be operating in this one situation, and the researcher were able to use another method for collecting data, the study could proceed.

Through the use of in-depth interviews, for example, and classroom observations, some insights about these elementary teachers' perceptions, feelings, or attitudes about unlike races or ethnic groups could be gained. The insights possibly would relate to theoretical statements (from the appropriate literature) regarding biases, either by confirming or refuting the statements. It is possible that in-depth interviewing and observations might yield information that does not appear to be addressed in theories about biases. That finding would lead the researcher to other theories that sought to describe or explain similar findings, but perhaps in different settings. Or it could lead to developing new theories.

Several important differences must be noted in the above example. A conventional study of elementary teachers' biases toward children of different races would involve a representative sample of elementary teachers, probably a sample size in excess of 30. Rather exact procedures exist to determine an optimum sample size. Some things, too, would have to be known about the instrument used to assess racial bias, if one were found, to compute the optimum sample size. Indeed, many specific rules must be followed when attempting to carry out a conventional research project. Examples appear in Chapter 4 and in the end-of-chapter readings throughout the text.

Research projects that are not based on the conventional view of the world and that use methods other than quantitative ones have different sets of more loosely constructed rules to follow. The greater variety of rules among types of qualitative research is a double-edged sword. One can be quite imaginative in one's approach with less fear of violating some prescription or proscription, but one has many qualitative research traditions from which to select procedures. This can be an intimidating experience, especially for novices. One solution to the problem is to become familiar with the procedures used in other studies. Studies based on different views of the world and using different methods are provided as examples at the end of Chapter 4.

The types of questions asked in educational research often have their roots in other social sciences or the humanities. A brief description of the salient questions asked in the academic disciplines of sociology, psychology, anthropology, history, and philosophy and how they apply to educational problems follows. The various perspectives provide insight into the ways educational practices can be seen and the various kinds of questions that can be asked.

Sociological Questions

Sociologists study formal and informal groups and the relationships between them and their members. General and specific interest in the relationship of the individual student, teacher, counselor, principal, superintendent, and parent, or groups of any of these to society at large or aspects of it constitute a major interest of the sociology of education. A few illustrative questions from sociology could be:

How do students relate to teachers?

What are the various purposes being served by this school or district?

What aspects of the formal organizational structure of a school or district are related to others or to the informal groups of the organization?

In what ways does schooling affect achievement, aspiration, or subsequent occupation?

How does the socioeconomic background of students and teachers relate to their other characteristics?

Psychological Questions

The field of psychology is concerned with the science of the mind and behavior. The field is broad in that it considers legitimate turf to be anything associated with human thought and every kind of animal and human behavior. The obvious links to education are psychology's interest in thinking, learning, memory, and the development of attitudes. Less obvious, but nonetheless important, are psychologists' studies of sensation, perception, and the various ways information is received, processed, and acted on. Illustrative questions from educational psychologists related to the above areas include:

> How are information, attitudes, beliefs, values, and physical skills taught and learned?
>
> What aspects of teaching are related to learning, memory, and the acquisition of problem-solving skills?
>
> How can tests or other instruments that measure intelligence, problem solving, or creativity be developed?
>
> What information gained from studying animals in a laboratory is applicable to students or teachers?
>
> What are the personality characteristics of effective teachers and administrators?

Anthropological Questions

Equally broad in scope and obviously overlapping with sociology and psychology is anthropology's devotion to the study of people. Culture, both material and nonmaterial, and people's relationship to it are grist for the anthropologist's mill. Organizations have their own cultures and subcultures that may or may not be congruent with one another and the larger culture in which they exist. Anthropologists interested in education do not automatically assume schools to be an educative element in students' lives. The kinds of questions anthropologists ask of education include:

> What relationship exists among the various educative elements in the culture?
>
> What effects does a family have on the total learning of a child in school?
>
> How does change occur in complex organizations?
>
> What elements of a particular setting are congruent with current understanding (theory) of these same elements in different settings?
>
> If values and behaviors of a subculture are different from the larger culture, what are the effects on inhabitants of both?

Historical Questions

In many respects the quest of an educational historian involves one or more of the sociologist's, psychologist's, and anthropologist's foci. Often taking a particular perspective, the historian examines the history of educational institutions, educators, students, potential students, movements, or learning itself in a given setting. As is often the case in other fields, a scholar's penchant for a historical school of thought may also guide the formation of research questions and subsequent design of the study. Illustrations from two extremes best illustrate the point. The more conservative historian might investigate the history of education from the top down, answering questions that complement American schooling in a given setting: How has American education served its citizens through a particular institution or movement? How has the liberal arts curriculum (perhaps in one particular school) evolved since the eighteenth century to serve a multicultural United States?

The more iconoclastic scholar reminds readers of the existence of conflict and the inadequacies of schooling in a given setting. Queries posed with this in mind might include: How has formal education failed to empower certain individuals, and what measure have they taken to create a divergent system that rivals the status quo? Did early twentieth century progressive education fulfill its promise to the American people?

Philosophical Questions

Philosophy is the oldest form of human inquiry which speaks to humankind's age-old search for answers to such questions as what, if anything, is real to all of us, and what things have meaning only to each person? Rather than focusing on traditional data (numbers or interviews, for example), philosophers analyze ideas, values, and their verbal and written expressions. They address pertinent issues such as the presence or absence of democracy in education. Various philosophical schools of thought in education range in ideology from the more conservative traditionalists to the more avant-garde existentialists. Philosophical questions might include:

> Does a given type of educational curriculum meet the needs of all students?
>
> How can we understand a particular culture by examining its advice literature?
>
> How does ideology inform theory and practice?

As you read Chapter 2 you might return to the above questions or consider others, deriving more specifically from your own field. Because questions drive research, restricting the types of queries asked will restrict the project that follows. Being aware of the broad scope of questions from which educational research emanates will enable you to understand the equally broad range of educational research. Thus, you can become the architect, not the victim, of your own research. Or, as a thoughtful consumer of other peoples' work, you can decipher the conscious or unconscious biases and limitations of other studies, enabling you to determine how much credence to give their conclusions.

Summary

This chapter has introduced you to the concept of research. We have provided only a beginning here, so do not despair if you are unclear as to what constitutes research. As we have pointed out, begin by trying to think of good research questions, perhaps unanswered queries from the graduate course work you have taken thus far.

Discussion Questions and Activities

1. Think about the way you have been taught (in college) to, in turn, instruct your own students. What kinds of questions did researchers ask that ultimately led to these established practices? Give specific examples.

2. Theories and schools of thought exist in almost every subject area. Find different theories or schools of thought that propose the "best" way to teach reading or some other skill.

3. Select a theory that competes with other theories either in explaining a phenomenon or in describing how to teach it. On what bases does the proponent of the explanation or description claim superiority over competing explanations or descriptions?

4. Locate and examine reports of surveys and speculate about the kinds of theories that might have been related to the surveys' findings.

5. Locate and examine reports of evaluation and speculate about the kinds of theories that might have been related to the evaluations' findings.

6. To which academic fields discussed in this chapter are your major educational interests related? Find two differences and similarities in a comparison of the research reports done in two of these disciplines.

7. In what ways can a researcher reveal his or her biases in a research report? Illustrate your claim with an example from an actual research report.

8. Make a list of journals that contain educationally relevant research reports.

Chapter 2

Varieties of Research

Many people are involved in what they call educational research, but if you take a close look at the studies being done you will notice wide variations among them. This chapter offers you a means to dissect a particular research project to determine just how it was conducted (i.e., what assumptions were made in designing it and what values may be imbedded within the findings). We also provide a conceptual cube that can serve as a visual scaffold within which you may plot a given research project, after having determined how it was designed and carried out.

A good example of the diversity in educational research can be found in the end-of-chapter reading by Firestone. He begins by explaining that an important unanswered question in educational research is: Can principals have a significant influence over student learning? The author goes on to describe two pieces of research that in different ways attempt to answer this question. (One study began by posing a question that was answered by testing an already existing body of knowledge that theorized about the relationship of principals' behavior on students. To test this theory the researchers then gathered and analyzed information deriving from a sample of several different settings. In so doing they followed a convergent or deductive line of reasoning—proceeding from the general to the specific. The other work focused on a single setting and proceeded to make a variety of observations and conclusions, thus following a divergent or inductive path—leading from the specific to the general.) (In Chapters 3, 4, and 5 we provide more details about the role of theory in educational research and for the blending of convergent and divergent designs.)

The studies cited in Firestone represent the two extremes, with diverse methods used and, very likely, different styles of reporting the results. (See Chapter 8 for further discussion of writing reports of research.) They may also have very diverse audiences, due in part to the nature of the research conducted. The fact remains, that as Baird (1988) states, the goal of educational research is to understand better some type of human behavior and thought. And, as Firestone suggests, we need to evaluate and consider all types of research when building theories that attempt to answer a particular question. In this chapter we provide a conceptual overview of what contributes to the different approaches taken to conduct an individual educational research project.

You already may have encountered descriptors of the two distinct types of research: the convergent one—an example of realism and empiricism, or rationalism and positivism, or quantitative—in contrast to the divergent one being an example of idealism and phenomenology, or naturalism and post-positivism, or qualitative (Lincoln & Guba, 1985; Cohen & Manion, 1980). These labels, and many others, have been used rather inconsistently to describe various approaches to and philosophies of research. In our Firestone reading and elsewhere, they have been called *paradigms* (Kuhn, 1970; Lincoln & Guba, 1989). To better facilitate an understanding of the basic concepts involved in consuming and conducting research, we use such terminology sparingly. And, throughout the book, in all of the readings we place those few terms that we employ or coin in brackets next to the various authors' terminology that is synonymous to our own.

Views of the World

In the course of your life so far you may have discovered that different people view the world differently. What you may not be aware of is that your world view can affect your approach to research, whether you are simply reading about or conducting it. Philosophers call this world view *ontology*.

When constructing a study, some researchers perceive of the world as a giant jigsaw puzzle to be solved (Agnew & Pyke, 1969). Such research originated with the natural sciences (e.g., biology, physics, chemistry). As explained by Kuhn (1970), questions in those fields ask: What are the fundamental entities of which the universe is composed: How do these interact with each other and with the senses: What questions may legitimately be asked about such entities and what techniques employed in seeking solutions? (pp. 4–5).

The jigsaw that promises to answer one of the above questions has only one correct configuration that enables you to see the overall picture, and it is determined by tedious piece-by-piece analysis. Assuming that no pieces are missing, it is theoretically possible to complete the puzzle eventually, even if there is no box-top picture to use as a guide. The researchers who hold this view are epitomized by the traditional natural scientists, who, often in highly controlled settings such as a laboratory, hope to discover another small piece of the puzzle or theory that explains some natural phenomenon. Thus, one of their major tasks is to simplify information—cutting off the corners that do not fit—until pieces can be placed somewhere in the uncompleted puzzle. Their ultimate goal is to see what the whole picture looks like.

Other researchers, usually working within the social sciences and humanities disciplines, may adopt a different ontological approach when conducting a study. Yet, their goal also is to better understand some human phenomenon. As Baird

(1988) explains, this type of researcher views the individual research project more as a riddle to be solved, posing a question and considering a multitude of ways to answer it. Riddles can have many different answers depending on who is telling them, the region of the country you are in, the age of the listener, ad infinitum. For example, we personally know of several variations on the answer to the old riddle, "Why did the chicken cross the road?" The answer many people will give you is: "To get to the other side." However, a regional interpretation in Oklahoma and Texas where roads feature "wildlife pancakes" is: "To show the armadillo it could be done." A southern Californian told us that in the late 1980s when there was much gunfire on the freeways the regional answer there was: "It was running from a sniper."

The riddle view of the world therefore questions the existence of a consistent way in which human beings might react to a particular situation. Ideally, to conduct such a research project one does not begin with an overall picture or theory in need of further testing. Again using Firestone's example of a divergent study, such researchers examine, often in one context, several possible answers to the question taken from the multiple perspectives of those involved. A simple characterization of the varieties of perceptions this researcher is forced to deal with would be two movie reviewers who both watch the same film, yet give completely opposite opinions about the movie—one thumb down, one thumb up. Those researchers whose projects encompass multiple views concerning the question to be answered tend to revel in its complexity and make only the slightest attempts to simplify the information they obtain in the course of their study. Their goal is not to discover one precise answer to the riddle but to collect as many answers as they can find and decide which one or which combination of answers is most appropriate for the setting being examined.

These two general views of the world may take many different labels depending on who is doing the labeling. Although others may disagree, we have chosen to label the puzzle concept position as *truth-seeking*. Other terms that you may encounter include *conventional* or *objective*. Actually, many educational researchers who view the world in this way understand that it has its origins in natural sciences research, and, thus, they do not really believe that the answers to their research questions will establish truth as in the existence of a physical reality. (In fact many natural scientists such as the quantum physicists even doubt the static quality of some physical particles.) Yet, educational researchers who accept a truth-seeking ontology generally contend that, ultimately, there are, with possible exceptions, truths about human behavior and thought. Because human behavior is often ephemeral, hard to simplify and comprehend, the truth sought in educational settings represents a less static truth than, for example, the physical fact that the earth revolves around the sun. Perhaps the types of answers sought by educational research questions represent a different level of truth (Ford, 1975) such as the one sought in Firestone's example of the convergent study that asks: Can a principal affect student learning?

We have labeled as perspective-seeking the riddle view of the world, but it has also been associated with (among other things) constructive or subjective research. Whether you or the work you read or produce takes a truth- or perspec-tive-seeking view, or some position in between (and there are many), your onto-logical perspective will influence a large portion of your research life. It may affect the kinds of questions that interest you, how you go about answering those questions, and what interpretation you make of the information you collect in the process.

There are aspects of each view that we are professionally drawn to in our own work. For example, the concept of a model (presented later in this chapter) in which you might plot a given research study is truth-seeking, because it envisions one reality, existing outside of the perceptions of those who are involved with it. Yet, we are also drawn to the perspective-seeking notion that to understand human behavior one must always be willing to recognize and examine multiple realities. To this end we have read and assessed hundreds of research studies, attempting to comprehend all of their varying constructions, before we ever proposed a model and we expect our conceptualization of research will continue to evolve.

Types of Data

Data are the facts and observations gathered to answer a research question. In a very simple manner they are examples of what philosophers call *epistemology*, the nature or type of knowledge. In educational research such data might represent peoples' perceptions in their own words or in the artifacts they have created, or data may take the form of some standard measurement, such as a number, that is often a compilation of one or many peoples' perceptions or reactions to some-thing (Coombs, 1964). In educational research, measurements of attitude, aca-demic achievements, and self-esteem are often represented in the form of numbers compiled from a relative scale and referred to as *quantitative data*. Arti-facts, newspaper clippings, diaries, taped interviews with people, or researchers' observations of a classroom also can provide data. Although in a given research study they may be presented as numbers, more often they are displayed as pictures or words and are considered *qualitative data*.

Because truth-seekers are interested in precision of information or data, their research often involves the use of quantitative or numerical data. As in Firestone's truth-seeking example, dealing with one number, like an average, is mathemati-cally easier than looking at each of the individual numbers that went to make up the average. These numbers are generally a measure of something (ability, atti-tude, anxiety, and so forth).

Perspective-seekers, on the other hand, often use qualitative data, because what they wish to understand are peoples' perceptions. And, so the argument goes, perceptions are best known through the most original source of informa-tion. For example the words (qualitative) of a person's diary promise more clearly to explain his or her thoughts than the number (quantitative) of times he or she refers to a particular topic. (See Chapter 5 for a discussion of data.)

Methods of Analysis

Truth-seekers often use quantitative methods or mathematical formulas which when applied to numbers help to explain what they mean and, thus, help to answer the research question. Perspective-seekers tend not to use quantification in their research because they believe that the complexity of the question asked by a particular study is better revealed by interviews, observations, old newspapers, diaries, and other forms of data that are not easily quantified. As noted above, like numbers, these types of information are also representations of peoples' perceptions or behaviors. Yet, the perspective-seeker may examine them in their most original form and look for patterns of response (qualitative methods) to help determine the answer to the research question. However, data analyzed in this way are also subject to some simplification when the researcher identifies patterns or themes, but the result is still much more complex than the simplicity achieved by calculating a mean.

Because those seeking truth, particularly in a quantitative study, want to find a piece of a certain puzzle, they attempt to isolate the piece of reality under scrutiny and understand the complex interactions among a set of variables, or numerical representations of human reactions. The researcher might go to one of the many books detailing experimental design to set up an experiment in which the researcher applies a treatment or intervention to one or more groups of subjects, or a study in which a researcher focuses on the interactions among people in some natural setting (applying numbers to those reactions and calling them variables). In either case this truth-seeking quantitative researcher would strive to control for all other outside influences or interventions that might affect the precise relationships he or she wished to examine. In so doing the researcher would be concerned with generalizability, how to select a sample that represents the population to which the results can be applied; validity, how to determine whether data authentically represent the human phenomenon under investigation; and reliability, how to ensure that if a study is repeated the same results will occur. All of these concepts (discussed in Chapters 5 and 6) are designed to ensure that the resultant research represents something objective, a true puzzle piece.

Those who seek different perspectives do not believe that a world jigsaw puzzle exists, and thereby have no wish to generalize in the same way as truth-seekers. Rather than inserting several levels of measurement tools between themselves and the subjects of their research, perspective-seeking qualitative researchers employ themselves as their primary research tool. They do, however, strive for awareness of how they and their sources of data might change over time (dependability). Perspective-seeking qualitative researchers also attempt to interpret data in a trustworthy manner. In other words, does the researcher truly understand what the data source intends to say (Lincoln & Guba, 1985)? When striving for trustworthiness of data some researchers rely literally on what, for example, an interviewee says, whereas another scholar reserves the right to interpret what an informant might subliminally believe. For instance, in one historical study of turn-of-the-twentieth-century women teachers, a woman who had a lifelong career as an educator said, "What's wrong with the world is working women." The researcher interpreted this statement to mean that the teacher believed that women who worked in traditional male fields were violating an established social order, but female nurses, social workers, and educators were acceptable to her (Vaughn-Roberson, 1984). Thus, if two perspective-seeking researchers study the same subject and derive different analyses, it does not pose the same problem that such a situation would present to researchers who are seeking truth. Generally the perspective-seekers consider it further evidence for the complex and subjective nature of the world.

Perspective-seekers may relate the results of their study to theory, which does involve moving from their specific data to a higher level of abstraction. However, they usually do not overtly say that the results of their study of a local situation are broadly applicable outside that situation. Nevertheless, generalizations are made by implication. For example, although Peshkin's (1978) perspective-seeking work is a contextual study of one community's relationship with its school system, he names the book *Growing Up American.* (For a good discussion of generalization in perspective-seeking research see Lincoln & Guba, 1985, Chapter 5.)

Once again, the purpose of your research may influence the view of the world you choose to adopt. If your job is to make broad policy decisions for many schools, then you might opt to read or conduct research from a truth-seeking position so that your decisions and research conclusions are considered applicable outside of one study. However, if you have no need to generalize from your study to a larger group, then you may be more likely to select the perspective-seeking approach. Also, the time frame for completion of your research may influence your means of gathering and analyzing data—in general, dealing with numbers (the method of choice for many truth-seekers) is quicker.

Thus far we have made the case that to answer a particular question, often truth-seeking researchers gather quantitative data and analyze them quantitatively, whereas perspective-seeking investigators compile qualitative data and analyze them qualitatively. Some observers maintain that these two combinations represent the only two appropriate means of conducting research (Hatch, 1985). This, however, is not always the case. Perspective-seeking researchers have collected quantitative data or analyzed data through quantitative means. For example, Peshkin (1978), in a well-known perspective-seeking study, gathered quantitative information with a survey that purported to measure one community's social attitudes. Salomon (1991), too, notes that some phenomenological (perspective-seeking) researchers in social psychology use quantitative methods (Kruglanski, 1989), whereas other researchers (Goldenberg, 1989) test models and hypotheses through qualitative means. Another example is a perspective-seeking researcher who uses numerical census data to hypothesize about teachers' motivations to enter the profession. (See the Vaughn & Liles reading in Chapter 4.) Usually, if quantitative means of analysis are used, the perspective-seeking ontology is blended with a truth-seeking one, the latter of which presumes the existence of one reality. As Firestone explains in the reading for this chapter, quantitative analysis involves an "abstraction process that directs attention from the total situation in a school to a set of variables [and] implies an almost physical connection between those variables." But when perspective-seekers use numbers to help illustrate the complexity of a situation, then they have remained true to the notion of multiple realities.

There are some truth-seekers who prefer qualitative data assessed through qualitative means. (See the Palmieri reading at the end of Chapter 5.) In the nineteenth century, Comte applied a positivistic or truth-seeking ontology to the study of history, which at the time relied on qualitative data and qualitative analysis (Barnes, 1963). Comte maintained that persistent historical investigations could unearth certain universal truths about humankind and the civilizations it has constructed. And many modern-day qualitative historians still hold to the same ontological assumption. (See, for example, Commager, 1965; Urban, 1982; Grob & Billias, 1992.)

When concerned with some type of objective truth, qualitative educational researchers spend a good deal of time establishing the *consistency* of data, a term which parallels *reliability* to some extent. (See Chapter 4 for more details.) Truth-seeking qualitative researchers also take great precautions to guard their data as much as possible against contamination and researcher subjectivity. For example, a researcher would be careful to note when interview data were paraphrased by the interviewer rather than represented as an original transcription of the interviewee's words. But this would be a concern for perspective-seeking qualitative researchers, as well. What makes truth-seeking researchers, who collect qualitative data or use qualitative means of analysis, different from perspective-seekers is truth-seekers' interpretation of the information they collect. Regardless of the type of data or means of analysis, a truth-seeker wishes to generalize from his or her research to a larger group (a population) that his or her sample of data represents. It may take more effort to simplify the data collected through qualitative means so that it fits somewhere, but that is the ultimate goal of the truth-seeking researchers, and some very helpful methods books have been written to assist them in this endeavor. (See, for example, Miles & Huberman, 1984; Goetz & LeCompte, 1984).

Ideology

Along with your view of the world (ontology) and types of data collected and methods of analysis (epistemology), there is another factor that affects your research: your values or *axiology*. Traditionally, philosophers break down axiology into ideology, ethics, and aesthetics. Because ethics play a crucial part in how you conduct, interpret, and evaluate research, we have devoted an entire chapter to the subject (Chapter 7). Aesthetics, dealing with what is pleasing and beautiful, can be related to educational research. For example, a research project in education may focus on students' appreciation of a certain genre of literature. In addition, you might construct an elegant research design and write very lucid prose when explaining the study. (Chapter 8 is devoted exclusively to writing.) In this chapter, however, we focus on defining ideology as one's political viewpoints and illustrating how they can influence educational research.

We have labeled the two extreme ideological views prevalent in the research community as *status quo* and *reform*. If a researcher accepts the world from a politically conservative position or as it seems to function, then his or her ideological view is status quo. Reformers, by contrast, want to create a totally different social or political situation in place of the one that currently exists. For example, in the United States reformers often challenge the dominant economic system of capitalism. Thus, there is a tendency to think of all reformers as neo-Marxist in political orientation. However, in the former Soviet Union some reformers were trying to replace communism or socialism (the former Soviet Union's status quo) with some aspects of capitalism. What makes someone a reformer is simply the desire to change the status quo from whatever it happens to be to something else. (Yet, as with seeking truth versus seeking perspective, intermediate positions exist.) For example, a researcher's work may recommend alterations in, but not the total dismantling of, a particular educational system or policy.

The two extreme ideological views are best illustrated by example. Imagine that two researchers are studying adult illiteracy. One researcher concludes after analyzing the data that the problem exists with the individual: somehow the illiterate person is learning disabled and this fact went unrecognized in the school system; or the individual is an underachiever and needs proper motivation; or the early family environment of the illiterate adult was dysfunctional; or all of the above. A solution to the illiteracy problem would then include better diagnostic procedures for learning disabilities and underachievement, increased emphasis on motivation for underachievers, and perhaps counseling intervention for dysfunctional families.

The second researcher offers a different type of conclusion: the illiterate adult is part of this country's under class, and the failure of the schools to recognize learning disabilities or to provide proper motivation is simply part of the deliberate plan by the ruling upper class for maintaining their elite position in society. With this scenario, the solution to illiteracy is empowerment of the lower class so that they can recognize the hegemony (domination) of the elite over all others in society and can unite against it.

The first researcher was not overtly political in his or her interpretation of the data, and therefore was oriented toward the status quo. The second researcher's highly political explanation moves into the realm of reform. Keep in mind that both researchers analyzed the same data through similar means and may even have the same view of the world—what differed were their ideologies.

Ideology can influence a study's theoretical considerations (Lincoln, 1988). (See Chapter 3.) For example, reform-minded theories in educational research (e.g., critical theory, action science, post-modernism, radical theory, feminist research) maintain that the social order should be changed in some fundamental way, and this belief is reflected in their research. Analyses that include the role of the political system in the situation being studied are common among reform researchers.

Similarly, as Lincoln (1988) explains, ideology is often inextricably woven into a project's view of the world (ontology). For example, a researcher may contend that a good form of government or organizational structure is one that is well controlled and functions with a defined set of policies. He or she may therefore prefer to conduct research from what Lincoln (1988) calls a conventional (truth-seeking) perspective. In addition, the researcher who tacitly accepts a truth-seeking ontology without question because he or she believes it to represent the only way in which research may be designed might also avoid questioning the appropriateness of the status quo (accepted policies, curricula, and so forth) of the entity to be investigated. Whether knowingly or not, the researcher has thus declared an ideological position, at least with regard to some aspect of the study.

Ideology might also influence the selection of types of data and methods of analysis used in a given study. For example, some neo-Marxists refuse to use quantitative methods, viewing them as the tool by which the ruling class has generated proof of Euro-American intellectual superiority (Berkhofer, 1983). The particular biases of a researcher could also play a part in studies that involve quantitative methodology.

When evaluating the many articles and books that you must read in the course of your studies, you will certainly view the worth of many research projects from your own ideological perspective. For example, you may believe that schools have failed in recent years because their disciplinary policies are not strict enough or that basic reading, writing, and arithmetic are not sufficiently stressed. Therefore you might be critical of a study concluding that many students who fail or drop out of schools do so because they are not given enough flexibility and intellectual freedom. We hope that after you read this book you will be able to critically analyze a piece of research so that you might be able to identify the role that research philosophy plays in the production and consumption of research.

The Cube

Complex research philosophies can be understood as composed of positions on each of the three dimensions that we have discussed: ontology, epistemology, and axiology. Because, as we have shown, the nature of the knowledge gathered to answer the research question(s) may, for example, be quantitative while the choice of methods may be qualitative, in this section we will deal only with the choice of methods when plotting a particular study. Nevertheless, any research design involves all aspects of epistemology. Also, our model has a continuum or plane that represents ideology alone. Entire books have been written to describe particular philosophies of research or research paradigms (Lincoln & Guba, 1985). However, they are difficult to understand if you do not have a firm grounding in philosophical terms.

As an aid to beginners, we have developed a scaffold for understanding the intersections of view of the world, data collection method, and ideology. The scaffold takes the form of a three-dimensional conceptual cube, and we will present it one dimension at a time.

The first dimension is that of your view of the world (Figure 2.1). We have presented this dimension as a continuum; perspective-seeking philosophical traditions (such as phenomenology) are found toward the left end and truth-seeking traditions (such as experimental and quasi-experimental design) taking their places toward the right end. (See Chapter 4 for other details of specific designs.) The dotted line drawn at right angles through the middle of the continuum is an indication of the many intermediate positions represented in existing educational research.

Adding the second dimension of data collection methods results in a four-celled box (Figure 2.2). The "objective" quantitative methods are found at the bottom of the method continuum, while the qualitative, "subjective" methods are found at the top. Thus, the bottom right-hand cell is truth-seeking and quantitative and would contain the bulk of traditional social science research. Such studies, often called rationalistic, are typically concerned with objective measurement, careful experimental or quasi-experimental design, and generalization from representative samples to like populations. (See Chapter 4 for details.) In the top left-hand cell (perspective-seeking and qualitative) would be found the typical naturalistic studies, which involve interviewing, observation, and other qualitative methods, and which are not concerned with generalization to larger populations but rather with detailed contextual description and analysis.

The existence of the other two cells (truth-seeking and qualitative, and perspective-seeking and quantitative) was alluded to earlier in this chapter. Some truth-seeking researchers prefer qualitative methods for some types of inquiries, but their wish to generalize keeps them in the right half of the big box. Likewise, some perspective-seeking researchers use quantitative methods on occasion, but the goal of their research is aimed toward understanding perspectives much more than generalization, and thus they remain in the left half of the box. The dotted lines in the middle again indicate the intermediate types of studies which are difficult to classify clearly in one cell or another.

With the addition of the third dimension of ideology, our box has become a three-dimensional cube (Figure 2.3 on p. 20). The third dimension signifies ideology. In the resulting cube, the entire back half would contain reform-oriented studies, irrespective of their view of the world or method of data analysis. Simi-

FIGURE 2.1   Conceptual Cube: First Dimension Alone

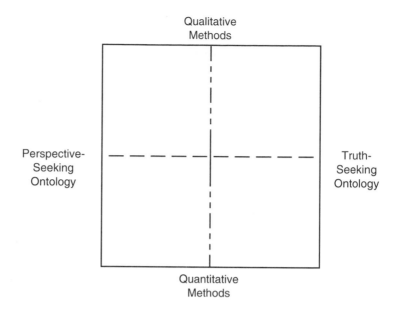

FIGURE 2.2   Conceptual Cube: Second Dimension Added

larly, status quo research of any world-view method combination would be found in the front half.

This cube can be useful in analyzing the perspectives of different research studies with which you are confronted even if they do not clearly indicate their world view, methodology, or ideology. (In Chapter 4 we plot the above descriptions and some specific research reports that appear as readings in this book.) By being attuned to these three aspects of research you may be able to place studies into general areas of the cube and perhaps thus not be shocked when studies with completely different approaches conclude the same thing, or when those with similar approaches result in entirely different interpretations of the phenomenon under study.

For example, say you are presented with a study in which the researcher investigated whether or not school children actually used the juvenile periodicals to which their school library subscribes and whether their use depended on the variety of periodicals available at school. Given only that much information, you have no idea where in the cube this study might be placed—it depends on how the study was designed and how the resultant data were interpreted.

To continue, imagine that the investigator had sampled 100 schools and had correlated the percentage of the library budget spent on periodicals with the number of checkouts accounted for by periodicals. This would be a terrible way to approach this subject for several reasons (e.g., libraries often do not circulate periodicals), but many studies you will read will be imperfect. You could now

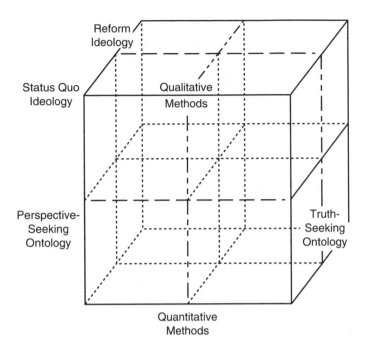

Reform/Ideology

Status Quo Ideology

Qualitative Methods

Perspective-Seeking Ontology

Truth-Seeking Ontology

Quantitative Methods

FIGURE 2.3   Conceptual Cube: All Three Dimensions

place this study in the quantitative half of the cube, but you still would not know enough to be more specific. (If you were observing children's interaction with periodicals and reporting the result in the form of descriptive vignettes, then you could place the study in the qualitative half.)

Continuing with the example, after obtaining the aforementioned correlation, the researcher generalized the result to all like schools, based on the random selection of the schools for the study. Now you have reason to place this study in the truth-seeking portion of the cube, because of the generalization involved. All that is left to question now is the ideological component.

If nothing overtly (or even implicitly) politically reform minded were contained in the study, then it would be placed in the status quo front half of the cube, down in the bottom right-hand corner. However, just for practice, let us assume that the researcher found a positive correlation between the two variables under study, which would mean that the larger the proportion of school library budget that was spent on periodicals the more use the periodicals received. Also, conversely, the smaller the proportion of the budget that was spent, the less use the periodicals received. This could be subject to a number of interpretations, the most obvious one being that there probably would be more periodicals in libraries that spent more of their budget on them, and thus more periodicals available to be checked out.

Let us imagine, however, that our hypothetical researcher did not see it that way. Instead, the researcher also found that the schools with larger budgets overall could afford to spend more on periodicals, while the poorer schools spent a smaller portion of their budget on periodical subscriptions. The researcher then chose to interpret these results as evidence that the relatively rich middle and upper class schools use the availability of periodicals in their libraries to perpetuate their students' status in a society that values reading and where reading current periodicals is a characteristic of the elite. On the other hand, the poorer schools that serve the lower class were denied adequate library acquisition funds, and thus their students were being denied the opportunity to cultivate the habit of reading periodicals that might eventually help them move out of their current social station. This interpretation clearly places the study in the reform back half of the cube.

As we mentioned before, few studies are this clear-cut—many are such a mix of world views, methods, and ideologies that an easy categorization is impossible. However, we believe that the conceptual scaffold the cube provides can help researchers, beginning and advanced alike, to be more sensitive to the different types of research studies and to the intersection of view of the world, method, and ideology that shapes every study.

Summary

In this chapter we explained how the variety of approaches to educational research can be understood largely as interactions among several components: the researcher's view of the world (ontology); method of data collection and analysis (epistemology); and social, moral, or political stance (axiology). As you read most research reports you should be able to get an idea of whether the research was conducted from a truth-seeking or perspective-seeking world view, used quantitative or qualitative methods, and made conclusions that imply that what exists is functioning rather well with suggestions only for modest change (status quo) or that an entire system or procedure needs to be dismantled and rebuilt (reform). The particular approach of any research study may be influenced by the purpose of the research, the need for generalization to other contexts, the amount of time available for study, and the ideological postures of the researcher.

Discussion Questions and Activities

1. What do you think might be some good educational research questions? Why?

2. How might the nature of these questions affect certain philosophical choices in how to conduct the study?

3. Give examples of how your own personal philosophy has an impact on the way you evaluate certain types of research.

4. Does your view of the world change, depending on the topic under investigation? Why or why not?

5. In what ways are quantitative and qualitative data different? Go to the library and find some research reports that use one type or another.

6. In what ways are quantitative and qualitative data alike?

7. If, in a research report, the current condition is not explicitly addressed, for example, the underfunding of many school districts that serve non-whites, does the research conducted in such settings support or challenge the status quo? Why or why not?

8. Locate two research articles and attempt to plot them on the cube.

Introduction to the Reading

Firestone's "Meaning in Method: The Rhetoric in Quantitative and Qualitative Research" is an excellent lead reading for our text. It not only assists us, generally, in introducing two major research philosophies, rationalism and naturalism, but it also contains a discussion of specific issues dealt with in other chapters throughout this book. For example, Firestone offers specific examples for the utility of quantitative and qualitative data, and he conceptually describes quantitative and qualitative data analysis. Finally, Firestone includes a content analysis of each section of the two different types of written reports, noting their differences and similarities.

Other researchers debate the utility or compatibility of what might be called *rationalistic* and *naturalistic* research philosophies. Qualitative as well as quantitative researchers of all kinds are becoming commonplace and feel less and less need to defend their positions so vehemently. There are still those on both sides who advocate separatism, but in our opinion they are being overwhelmed by the complementary forces. Practical considerations seem to have taken precedence over theoretical purity. If you attend the American Educational Research Association's annual meeting you will see an amazing mix of methods, ideologies, and perspectives—sometimes all within the same study! Some other excellent readings not included here are Eisner and Peshkin, 1990; Howe, 1990; and Smith, 1990.

Meaning in Method:
The Rhetoric of Quantitative and Qualitative Research[1]

William A. Firestone

Abstract

The current debate about quantitative and qualitative methods focuses on whether there is a necessary connection between method-type and research paradigm that makes the different approaches incompatible. This paper argues that the connection is not so much logical as rhetorical. Quantitative methods express the assumptions of a positivist [rationalistic] paradigm which holds that behavior can be explained through objective facts. Design and instrumentation persuade by showing how bias and error are eliminated. Qualitative methods express the assumptions of a phenomenological [naturalistic] paradigm that there are multiple realities which are socially defined. Rich description persuades by showing that the researcher was immersed in the setting and giving the reader enough detail to "make sense" of the situation. While rhetorically different, the results of the two methodologies can be complementary. Examples are drawn from two studies using different methodologies to study the same problem.

With the growing acceptance of qualitative methods in education (Shulman, 1981), the debate has shifted to what their relationship to quantitative methods should be. At the extremes are two groups (Rossman & Wilson, 1985). The purists (e.g., Smith & Heshusius, 1986; Guba, 1978) believe that the two method-types are based on paradigms that are necessarily in conflict. In choosing a method, the researcher makes a long-term value commitment that is difficult to change. Pragmatists argue that there is no necessary logical connection between paradigm and method-types (Reichardt & Cook, 1979). Method-types are mere collections of techniques that can be mixed and matched according to the specific problem.

An alternative view is suggested here, namely that the connection between method-type and paradigm is more aesthetic than logical. This view draws upon recent analyses of educational and social science research shaped by the study of the arts and literary criticism (Eisner, 1981; House, 1979; Gusfield, 1976). My suggestion is that qualitative and quantitative methods can be viewed as rhetorical devices. As such, each presents a different view of the phenomenon studied and uses different means to persuade the reader of the validity of the conclusions drawn. Yet, they are not antithetical. They present the reader with different kinds of information and can be used to triangulate to gain greater confidence in one's conclusions. This argument is advanced first in general terms and then illustrated by a comparison of two studies that use qualitative and quantitative methods to address the same issue.

Paradigms [Ontologies] and Methods

The purists assert that qualitative and quantitative methods are based in paradigms that make different assumptions about the social world and about how science should be conducted as well as what constitutes legitimate problems, solutions, and criteria of "proof" (Kuhn, 1970). These differences have been treated extensively, and there is considerable agreement on what they are (see Guba, 1978). Four differences are most relevant for this analysis:

1. *Assumptions about the world.* Quantitative research is based on a positivist philosophy which assumes that there are social facts with an objective reality apart from the beliefs of individuals. Qualitative research is rooted in a phenomenological paradigm which holds that reality is socially constructed through individual or collective definitions of the situation (Taylor & Bogdan, 1984).

2. *Purpose.* Quantitative research seeks to explain the causes of changes in social facts, primarily through objective measurement and quantitative analysis. Qualitative research is more concerned with understanding (*Verstehen*) the social phenomenon from the actors' perspectives through participation in the life of those actors (Taylor & Bogdan, 1984).

3. *Approach.* The quantitative researcher typically employs experimental or correlational designs to reduce error, bias and other noise that keeps one from clearly perceiving social facts (Cronbach, 1975). The prototypical qualitative study is the ethnography which helps the reader understand the definitions of the situation of those studied (Goodenough, 1971).

4. *Researcher role.* The ideal quantitative researcher is detached to avoid bias. The qualitative researcher becomes "immersed" in the phenomenon of interest (Powdermaker, 1966).

The pragmatists respond, however, that the relationship between method and philosophy [ontology, view of world] of science implied by the idea of paradigm is neither necessary nor logical. Reichardt and Cook (1979) present a number of examples that contradict expectations about differences between method-types that supposedly link them to paradigms. For instances, quantitative researchers use opinion polling to understand the perspectives of others and often immerse themselves in the situation during the planning and pretesting phases of their studies. On the other hand, Sanday (1979) links ethnography—the prototypical qualitative method—to three different paradigms in anthropology. While the semiotic, represented by the work of Geertz and Goodenough, approximates the phenomenological paradigm that educational researchers associate with qualitative methods, it has also been used to further a kind of behaviorism that is quite close to the positivist paradigm.

If the connection between method-types and paradigms is not logically necessary, there remains a correlation. Quantitative studies are typically more positivistic than most qualitative research (Reichardt & Cook, 1979). To understand why that is, it is helpful to understand some of the rhetorical devices of research.

The Rhetoric of Research

Rhetoric is the art of speaking or writing effectively. It refers generally to how language is employed, but has come to mean the insincere or even manipulative use of words. Technically, it includes the arts of persuasion and decoration or elaboration in literature (Frye, 1957). As such it is normally considered something to be avoided in research where the facts are supposed to "speak for themselves." Scientific writing is a stripped-down, cool style that avoids ornamentation, often stating conclusions as propositions or formulae. Forms of data presentation are supposed to be interchangeable. That is, the use of tables as opposed to charts should be immaterial. There is also a standardization of form—the theory-methods-findings-conclusion format—that is intended to limit rhetorical excess (Eisner, 1981).

This absence of style turns out to actually be a rhetorical device in its own right (Frye, 1957). The use of propositions, for instance, is a means to empty language of emotion and convince the reader of the writer's disengagement from the analysis. If one of the threats to the validity of a conclusion comes from the writer's own biases, as is considered to be the case in science, then any technique that projects a lack of emotion has considerable persuasive power. Thus, language does serve a persuasive function in research.

Elaboration also has a role in research. Without reference to some larger field of meaning, scientific propositions make no sense. The words of everyday language are rich in multiple meanings. Like other symbols, their power comes from the combination of meanings in a specific setting (Cohen, 1979). Scientific language ostensibly strips this multiplicity of meaning from words in the interest of precision. This is the reason why common terms are given "technical meanings" for scientific purposes (Durkheim, 1938). However, there can be a sort of subterfuge in this process (Polanyi & Prosch, 1975). While on the surface, meaning is reduced, scientific terms must rely on their suppressed definitions to attract the reader's interest and concern. For instance, behaviorist psychologists study only a limited range of forms of learning. However, their theories are valued because they make implicit reference to a wider range of situations that is suggested by the term "learning." Because scientific terms do have multiple meanings, the researcher must steer the reader's attention to specific ones. This is the work of demonstrating theoretical, policy, or practical relevance of the research that is accomplished in the introduction and the conclusion (Gusfield, 1976). It too requires rhetoric.

Recent attempts to understand the rhetoric of research have proceeded through the literary criticism of specific reports. Gusfield (1976) presents a masterful analysis of a quantitative study of drivers arrested for drinking. He shows how the study projects the image of the researcher as neutral, disengaged analyst (persuasion) at the same time that it presents a heavily value-laden interpretation of those who drink and drive and what to do about it (elaboration for meaning). House (1979) presents a similar analysis of an evaluation of an Upward Bound program.

Most analyses focus on the language of research and treat the data themselves as relatively neutral. Yet, the means of data collection, the results of those efforts, and the conventions about how to treat them can combine to create specific strategies for persuasion and project particular images of the research subject. These may vary systematically between [truth-seeking, quantitative] quantitative and [perspective-seeking, qualitative] qualitative studies. To explore this possibility, I turn now to a comparison of two studies.

Two Studies

The issue studied is whether leadership makes any difference in organizational outcomes. This issue was viewed as decided for schools in the 1960s when the effect of family background was found to be so strong that school-specific variables seemed to pale in comparison (see Parelius & Parelius, 1978). Researchers doubted that principals could have any significant influence on student learning (Boocock, 1972). The effective schools research which points to the importance of strong principal leadership has raised that issue (Edmonds, 1979).

Both studies described here examine the relative contributions of leadership and environment to organizational performance. The quantitative study addresses this issue by defining a specific set of variables and procedures for measuring them. The environmental variable is the family background of the students as indicated by the principal's report of the percent of students who receive free lunches (SES). There are two leadership variables: centralization of influence in the principal as opposed to decentralization to the teacher (CNT) and the extent of principal support for teaching (SPT). The outcome of interest is how much students learn (LRN). The initial theory assumes that the extent to which teachers work hard and try to teach all students in their class (TCH) mediates between the two leadership variables and student learning. The last four variables (CNT, SPT, TCH, and LRN) are all measured through a survey of teachers in the school. The analysis is guided by a theoretical model which proposes that levels of LRN are influenced by TCH, SPT and CNT, and SES and that leadership is influenced by

SES. Information comes from a national sample of 107 elementary and secondary schools (details of procedures are provided in Firestone & Wilson, 1986).

Two statistical analyses of the model are presented.[2] The first shows that SES has three times as much influence on LRN as the leadership variables. The second is a path analysis (Duncan, 1966) which verifies the existence of hypothesized relationships between variables. It shows that SES has a strong direct effect on LRN; increasing control reduces learning. The effect of SPT is indirect. Increasing SPT increases TCH which in turn increases LRN. Together the two analyses suggest that leadership does influence student learning although not to the extent that the environment does.

The qualitative study was part of a larger exploration of regional educational service agencies (RESAs), those agencies located midway between the state and local district. This project examined their contribution to research use in schools through training and dissemination activities. The study focused on pairs of Intermediate Units (IUs) in Pennsylvania and Education Improvement Centers (EICs) in New Jersey that were known to differ in the amount of training they offered. Data were collected using semi-structured interviews with agency directors and administrators, the training staff, and representatives of client districts. Interviews with state departments of education clarified the larger political context in which these agencies operated (see Firestone & Rossman, 1986 for procedures). All the information on each agency was then pulled together into a case study. By examining each case and comparing pairs of cases a typology of agency approaches to their task and explanations for why one approach was selected over another were developed. This use of a variety of materials and an inductive approach in a comparative case study design is typical of a fair amount of qualitative policy research (Herriott & Firestone, 1983).

Exploration of the pairs of cases showed that environmental constraints were similar. In Pennsylvania, for instance, state law which gave school boards control of IU budgets made those agencies responsive to district concerns.[3] However, the districts suffered from severe financial constraints and saw those agencies as competitors for funds. This concern was an important barrier to efforts to increase services by seeking grants. While environmental constraints were similar, the orientations of agency leaders reflected the difference in approach. The director of the high-service entrepreneurial IU set the tone for his agency by aggressively looking for new services to offer and new sources of funds. When his board objected to this approach, he found ways to better justify new programs, but he did not give up the search. The leaders of the more laissez-faire IU were more defensive, spending relatively more time justifying their budget than seeking funds. The director of the high-service agency challenged environmental constraints, but he did not simply "cause" the high-service approach. In fact, he appeared to be chosen because he reflected high-service orientations preferred by a key constituency on the board when the IU was founded. His contribution was important but did not provide a complete explanation.

The Studies Compared

An examination of the rhetorical elements of those studies indicates that they use quite different strategies to persuade the reader of the validity of the analysis and that they project different assumptions about organizational phenomena. An important by-product of these differences is that they provide complementary information to the readers.

Persuasion

The quantitative study persuades by deemphasizing individual judgment and stressing the use of established procedures. While the language of hypothesis testing is avoided, the impression is given that the whole study is a disciplined exploration of a preexisting conceptual framework. This is done in a variety of ways. At the most obvious level, almost as much space is given to describing the study's methods (four pages) as the results (six pages, including tables). The methods section describes the study's sample in a paragraph. The rest of the section is devoted to a detailed discussion of measurement procedures. Another limitation to individual discretion is the use of a theoretical model to guide the analysis. This model is provided in a pictorial form in the introductory theory section, and criteria for determining when a hypothesized relationship is deemed to be supported are described in the results section and justified with reference to previous methodological research. Thus, the text gives the strong impression that exploratory "data dredging" has been avoided.

In this case, the form hides part of the story because there was an exploratory element to the study. The study was triggered by the finding of negative associations between centralization and student outcomes when validity analyses were done for a manual describing the survey instrument. We viewed this finding as contradictory to the effective schools research which argues that strong leadership promotes achievement. We reasoned further that if this finding could be replicated when controlling for student background, it would be an important contribution. Reporting this personal aspect would undercut the impression the paper now gives of being a detached "test" of a theory.

Less attention is given to describing procedures and how individual judgment is disciplined in the qualitative study. The study is presented as frankly exploratory. The strategy is one of comparing pairs of agencies known to be different in order to discover what might explain those differences. That search is not described as strongly controlled by preexisting theory. There is no preliminary model. Instead, reference to past research is incorporated into the presentation of findings. The methods section is only two pages long while the results take over twenty. About half the methods discussion describes the agencies selected and demonstrates that they did in fact differ in services provided since the reader must be convinced of that fact to be persuaded of the value of what follows.

While analysis procedures are not described, some controls stemming from the criteria of good qualitative analysis were used. One of these is the admonition to search for competing explanation and negative evidence (Campbell, 1979). This served well in the analysis of leader contributions. The first analysis showed a remarkable similarity between the values professed by the top leaders and the organizations' approaches. This could have led to an overestimate of leaders' influence on those approaches, especially where the entrepreneurial IU maintained its approach in spite of external opposition. However, further exploration indicated that the director there had been selected because his values fit the interests of a strong constituency. Openness to this possibility helped to avoid an overestimate of leader influence.

That search is not described in the text, in large measure because it is less relevant for persuading the reader. In fact two very different strategies are used: rich depiction and strategic comparison. The first is the hallmark of most qualitative research; the second is required by the effort to understand differences between pairs of agencies. Taken together, these approaches pile up a series of significant, concrete details to give a convincing depiction of each agency and of the differences between them. For instance, several different kinds of data were used to show that Farmland IU was more entrepreneurial than Rural-Industrial. These included telling quotes from interviews, a description of agency staffing patterns, and excerpts from agency history illustrating the entrepreneurial orientation in action. The details are convincing because they create a gestalt that makes sense to the reader. This is a process Polanyi and Prosch (1975) describe as building up a focal impression out of a series of subsidiary details. It depends upon the active effort of the reader and the reader's willingness to check these details against personal experience.

In sum, the persuasive strategies of the two kinds of research are very different. The quantitative study must convince the reader that procedures have been followed faithfully because very little concrete description of what anyone does is provided. The qualitative study provides the reader with a depiction in enough detail to show that the author's conclusion "makes sense." For that reason, discussion of procedure is not emphasized. Too much attention to procedure can get in the way of the narrative line which attempts to build a concrete impression of the phenomenon studied.

Assumptions

In addition to using different persuasive strategies, the two studies make different assumptions about the world. This distinction is highlighted when one focuses on how each handles causation.[4] It can be described through three dichotomies: variables vs. actions, hydraulic determinism vs. limits and opportunities, and randomness and error vs. choice.

The quantitative study portrays a world of variables and static states. The text refers to levels of centralization or principal support, but one can only infer from the questionnaire items what a principal does to centralize or how (s)he provides support. By contrast the qualitative study describes people acting in events. A director tells how he uses hiring interviews to encourage staff to actively sell services or an informant tells about the political battles that led to the legislation governing IUs. Even the "state" of entrepreneurialism is portrayed through a dispute between an agency's board and its top leadership over how actively outside funding should be pursued.

The quantitative study uses a hydraulic image of determinism as if pressure from one variable changes another. Regression coefficients indicate how much one might expect the dependent variable to increase for a given change in an independent variable. The effect of the tables is reinforced by language about the "per cent of variance" in one variable that is attributable to others. The implicit imagery is of a system of interconnected variables where pressure from one forces change in another. The abstraction process that directs attention from the total situation in a school to a set of variables implies an almost physical connection between those variables. The qualitative study presents a more complex view of a world in which there are limits and opportunities that individuals must take into account and use. These include the IUs' required budget approval procedure and external funding competitions. These limits and opportunities shape action, but do not determine it.

Finally, the two studies suggest different alternatives to causality. The quantitative study emphasizes randomness and error. The study design, especially the sampling procedure and instrumentation, are intended to reduce the amount of error in the study. They are described to help the reader assess how well that task was accomplished. Once as much error is eliminated as possible, two alternatives remain—randomness and the causal forces of the measured variables—and statistical tests are used to choose between them. The alternative to causality in the qualitative study is choice. Constraints and opportunities are real but ambiguous. Leaders decide how to respond to them, for instance, when they encourage or discourage fund seeking. If their choice violates those constraints, there will be a response that requires a change of strategy (as in Farmland's case) or even organizational demise (as in the New Jersey situation not discussed).

These different assumptions do not stem from the phenomenon studied. They come in large measure from the way the researchers collect and process their information. These steps shape the nature of the final text which then reinforces those assumptions stylistically.

Complementarity

The differences presented above give qualitative and quantitative studies different descriptive strengths. The quantitative study assesses the magnitude of relationships more precisely. One can say rather clearly that 61 percent of the variance in LRN is explained. The qualitative study concludes with more ambiguous statements like "strong leadership is necessary, but not sufficient for excellence." The other advantage of the quantitative study is that it shows a pattern that extends across a large number of situations. In fact, the conclusion rests on showing the joint association of variables in many settings. The use of many sites increases confidence in the generalizability of results although technically gener-

alizability depends upon the randomness and representativeness of sample selected. The trade-off of course is in abstraction. One's confidence in the conclusions depends on one's comfort with the way variables are measured and relate
to the issues of interest, the quality of the sample, and the general design of the
study.

The classical strengths of qualitative methods are concrete depiction of detail,
portrayal of process in an active mode, and attention to the perspectives of those
studied (Patton, 1980). These strengths help to overcome the abstraction inherent
in quantitative studies. These advantages appear in this qualitative study through
quotations and descriptions that illustrate the perspective of staff, leaders, and
outside clients. However, the description is thinner than in more ethnographic
studies. On the other hand, the use of four cases allows for some comparison in
order to identify patterns across situations. It also gives greater confidence that
conclusions do not depend upon the idiosyncrasies of the specific situation so it
is something of a mixed case.

Used separately, qualitative and quantitative studies provide different kinds
of information. When focused on the same issue, qualitative and quantitative
studies can triangulate—that is, use different methods to assess the robustness or
stability of findings (Jick, 1979). In this case the two studies generally corroborate
each other. The quantitative analysis shows that SES has the strongest impact on
LRN, but the leadership variables also have an undeniable effect. The qualitative
study shows a strong congruence between leader values and organizational approach. Leaders can even challenge the environment. Yet, it is also clear that
leaders are partly chosen for their values and have their greatest effect at certain
critical times so their influence is limited. In the main the two studies corroborate
each other.

Conclusion

A rhetorical analysis of these two studies of the same topic suggests that there is
an aesthetic connection between method-types and paradigms. The methods
used in each express the values of the related paradigm about what the world is
like [ontology] and how one must show the truth of an argument [epistemology].
The methods of quantitative [rationalistic] research, indirect perception controlled by study design and instrumentation, voice the concerns of the positivistic
[rationalistic] paradigm to identify objective social facts and eliminate error.
Quantitative procedures also give the impression of detachment and lack of bias
[ideology]. The whole strategy of abstraction through measurement is intended
to apprehend "the facts" without distortion by irrelevant detail. Persuasion depends upon showing the adequacy of one's methods for identifying the single,
undistorted truth.

Qualitative [naturalistic] studies devote less space to procedure and more to
description because less emphasis is placed on identifying a single truth. Through
presentation of numerous specifics, the qualitative account shows how the con-

crete facts of the situation fit the explanation proposed. The persuasive strategy has two parts. First, the reader must be convinced that the researcher has become immersed enough in the setting to know it well. Second, sufficient concrete detail must be provided to permit comparison with the reader's own experience to see if the findings "make sense." This strategy fits with a view which holds that bias can be minimized but not eliminated and that in any case there are multiple realities that are socially constructed.

Quantitative studies also project very different assumptions about the world from qualitative studies. The measurement strategies [epistemology] employed portray an image of a world of static variables, social facts that are linked through hydraulic causal connections. Human action only plays a role to the extent that it can be "measured." Qualitative studies are much more likely to describe that action and leave room for interpretation and choice. "Causation" is not so much a hydraulic or mechanical process as the constraints and opportunities that shape choice.

These rhetorical differences in method do not negate the view that there are instrumental reasons for choosing particular methods in specific situations (Patton, 1980). Each method-type does provide different kinds of information. Their strengths and weaknesses are complementary. Quantitative studies assess relationships precisely without describing how conclusions apply in any particular context. Qualitative studies show the connection between conclusion and situation very clearly and also give a strong sense of process but they lack the precision of quantitative studies. Thus, each can make a contribution to a reader who is concerned about the subject of study without being firmly committed to either paradigm.

Still, choosing methods is not just a matter of coming at a single truth from different directions. While there are a number of reasons for selecting a methodological approach, one's decision often expresses values about what the world is like, how one ought to understand it, and what the most important threats to that understanding are. The method selected encourages one to deal with research issues in a particular way and to advance certain kinds of arguments for the credibility of one's conclusions. These nonlogical methodological tendencies fit with individual stylistic predilections as well as the philosophical underpinnings of the positivistic [rationalistic] and phenomenological [naturalistic] paradigms of research.

Endnotes

1. The work upon which this publication is based was funded by the Office of Educational Research and Improvement (OERI), U.S. Department of Education. The opinions expressed in this publication do not necessarily reflect the position or policy of the OERI, and no official endorsement by the OERI should be inferred. Thanks are due to Bruce Wilson and Robert Herriott for their helpful comments.

2. Examples are taken from their analysis of elementary schools. A parallel analysis of secondary schools yields substantially similar results.

3. Examples are taken primarily from the comparison of IUs. The analysis of the EICs in New Jersey yielded very different concrete events, but the conclusions of the analysis were very similar. Agency names are pseudonyms.

4. Some indication that the differences between methods are not as sharp as the purists claim comes from the observation that qualitative methods deal with causality at all.

References

Boocock, S. S. (1972). *An introduction to the sociology of learning.* Boston: Houghton-Mifflin.

Campbell, D. T. (1979). "Degrees of freedom" and the case study. In T. D. Cook & C. S. Reichardt (Eds.), *Qualitative and quantitative methods in evaluation research.* Beverly Hills, CA: Sage.

Cohen, A. (1979). Political symbolism. *Annual Review Anthropology, 8,* 87–113.

Cronbach, L. J. (1975). Beyond the two disciplines of scientific psychology. *American Psychologist, 30,* 116–127.

Duncan, O. D. (1966). Path analysis: Sociological examples. *American Journal of Sociology, 72,* 1–6.

Durkheim, E. (1938). *The rules of sociological method.* New York: Free Press.

Edmonds, R. (1979). Effective schools for the urban poor. *Educational Leadership, 37*(1), 15–24.

Eisner, E. (1981). On the differences between scientific and artistic approaches to qualitative research. *Educational Researcher, 10*(4), 5–9.

Firestone, W. A., & Rossman, G. B. (1986). Exploring organizational approaches to dissemination and training. *Knowledge: Creation, Diffusion, Utilization, 7*(3), 303–330.

Firestone, W. A., & Wilson, B. (1986). *Management and organizational outcomes: The effects of approach and environment in schools.* Philadelphia: Research for Better Schools.

Frye, N. (1957). *Anatomy of criticism.* Princeton, NJ: Princeton University Press.

Goodenough, W. (1971). *Culture language, and society.* Reading, MA: Addison Wesley.

Guba, E. G. (1978). *Toward a methodology of naturalistic inquiry in educational evaluation.* Los Angeles, CA: Center for the Study of Evaluation.

Gusfield, J. (1976). The literary rhetoric of science: Comedy and pathos in drinking driver research. *American Sociological Review, 41*(1), 16–34.

Herritt, R. E., & Firestone, W. A. (1983). Multisite qualitative policy research: Optimizing description and generalizability. *Educational Researcher, 12*(2), 14–19.

House, E. (1979). Coherence and credibility: The aesthetics of evaluation. *Educational Evaluation and Policy Analysis, 1*(5), 5–18.

Jick, T. D. (1979). Mixing qualitative and quantitative methods: Triangulation in action. *Administrative Science Quarterly, 24*(4), 602–611.

Kuhn, T. S. (1970). *The structure of scientific revolutions* (2nd ed.). Chicago: University of Chicago Press.

Parelius, A. P., & Parelius, R. J. (1978). *The sociology of education.* Englewood Cliffs, NJ: Prentice-Hall.

Patton, M. Q. (1980). *Qualitative evaluation methods.* Beverly Hills, CA: Sage.

Polyani, M., & Prosch, H. (1975). *Meaning.* Chicago: University of Chicago Press.

Powdermaker, H. (1966). *Stranger and friend: The way of the anthropologist.* New York: W. W. Norton.

Reichardt, C. S., & Cook, T. D. (1979). Beyond qualitative versus quantitative methods. In C. S. Reichardt & T. D. Cook (Eds.), *Qualitative and quantitative methods in evaluation research.* Beverly Hills, CA: Sage.

Rossman, G. B., & Wilson, B. L. (1985). Numbers and words: Combining quantitative and qualitative methods in a single large-scale evaluation study. *Evaluation Review, 9*(5), 627–643.

Sanday, P. R. (1979). The ethnographic paradigm(s). *Administrative Science Quarterly, 24*(2), 577–638.

Shulman, L. S. (1981). Disciplines of inquiry in education: An overview. *Educational Researcher, 10*(6), 5–12.

Smith, J. K., & Heshusius, L. (1986). Closing down the conversation: The end of the quantita-tive-qualitative debate. *Educational Researcher, 15*(1), 4–13.

Taylor, S. J., & Bogdan, R. (1984). *Qualitative research methods: The search for meanings* (2nd ed.). New York: John Wiley.

Chapter 3

The Role of Theory

The role of theory is to describe, explain, or predict a phenomenon. In Chapter 1 we said research has to have some impact on theory. In this chapter we expand on the definition of theory and its crucial relationship to the research process. Descriptive and prescriptive theory types are differentiated and discussed. After reading this chapter you should also be able to recognize and locate published discussions of what might be called the schools of thought that comprise a theory base in a particular field.

If a document contains no theoretical implications, the work is not explicitly research. It may be journalism or evaluation, and other researchers may use the document when augmenting theory with their own work, but, without theory being implicated, a particular piece of writing is not research. Kerlinger's definition of theory has a lot of currency in educational research:

> [A theory is] a set of interrelated constructs, definitions, and propositions that presents a systematic view of phenomena by specifying relations among variables, with the purpose of explaining and predicting phenomenon (1973, p. 9).

Notice Kerlinger says " . . . explaining and predicting phenomena." His definition reveals a slight bias for the truth-seekers, but we accommodate both the truth-seekers and perspective-seekers by saying the role of theory is to describe, explain, *or* predict. Perspective-seekers endeavor to understand a phenomenon. Describing and explaining are challenge enough. More importantly, the concern for prediction requires that generalizations be made from one setting to another. Perspective-seekers are not concerned with setting-to-setting generalizations as are truth-seekers. The setting, that is, the context surrounding a phenomenon, is too complex, according to perspective-seekers, to permit generalizations from one setting to another.

A theory of communication, for example, would include constructs, such as the intention of the sender of the message; definitions, such as the setting or context in which the communication occurs; and propositions that suggest that relationships are found between or among the various elements of theory. A sender's intentions may be related to the choice of a communication medium. For example, a sender may use the telephone or write a letter, instead of having a face-to-face confrontation.

The social sciences have more theories, than do the natural sciences, especially theories that compete with one another. Because the natural sciences—physics, astronomy, and biology, for example—have relatively few simultaneously competing theories, disconfirming one and replacing it with another is a rather momentous event and, as we have discussed in Chapter 2, has been called a *paradigm shift* (Kuhn, 1970). In education, where other social science theories are applied and adapted, it is our belief that *schools of thought* is a more descriptive phrase than *paradigm* when one wants to allude to competing theories. We concede quickly, however, and the readings support the concession, that the word *paradigm* is used commonly to mean a view of the world or some aspect of it and is also used to mean a type of research approach (see Chapter 2). It has been alleged by some that educators who use the word *paradigm* so readily may suffer from *physics envy.*

Examples of Theories

Within the social sciences one can find a variety of efforts to describe, explain, or predict a phenomenon. Language development and children's play provide two such examples.

The attempts to explain language development can be classified into a number of schools of thought: behaviorist; nativist; psycholinguist; and cognitivist. Each of these contains theoretical descriptions and explanations of how language development occurs.

The behaviorists believe language development, like all learning, is based on the notion of conditioning. According to behaviorists, children imitate the speech they hear and learn it by having such language behavior reinforced.

Nativists believe language, like other development, is innate and cannot be affected by the environment. Maturation, genetically determined, will, in time determine when a child will develop language.

Psycholinguists assume a child builds his or her own theoretical constructs about language and tests them to develop language proficiency. Language universals are believed to be innate, but language *data* from the environment are necessary for the personal construction of language theories that guide the child's language development.

Cognitive theories are unlike behaviorist theories that explain language as imitation, nativistic theories that claim language is dependent on biological development, and psycholinguistic theories that believe in the innateness of language abilities that act on language data from the environment. Instead, cognitivists assume language development is interdisciplinary, that it depends on the interaction of psychological, biological, sociological, linguistic, logical, and epistemological elements.

Even these schools of thought, however, are not always homogeneous in all their beliefs. For example, among the cognitivists, Piaget believes language is structured by logic, but Vygotsky, another cognitivist, maintains that logic is structured by language.

Each school of thought is composed of theoretical statements that describe, explain, or predict language development. These theories, or portions thereof, have been and will continue to be tested. This theory testing is done for the purpose of refining or replacing the theory that purportedly accounts for the phenomenon being examined.

Children's play, like language development, has been described and explained by a variety of theories. Gilmore (1971) categorized the theories into classical and dynamic theories of play. The classical theories and their brief descriptions are:

1. *Surplus energy theory.* Humans accumulate energy, which must be released. Play uses up energy the body does not need.
2. *Relaxation theory.* Play, because it is a relaxing activity, allows the organism to build up energy that can be used later for work.
3. *Recapitulation theory.* Humans pass through stages that parallel phases in the development of the human race. Play helps to transcend these primitive stages of life.
4. *Pre-exercise theory.* Play prepares children for their adult roles. Children, in effect, are rehearsing the skills they will use as adults.

The dynamic theories of play emanate from psychoanalytic theory and Piagetian theory. Freud's psychoanalytic theory suggests children play out distressful situations and overcome emotional pain. Play is a kind of catharsis where fears and anxieties can be expressed without raising them to the level of consciousness.

The constructivist theory of play, based on Piaget's theory of mental development, asserts that children assimilate new information from their environment and, through play, adjust their mental schemes to accommodate that which is different. Achieving equilibrium is the overall goal, and play is the child's way to reconcile the new and different experiences into his or her scheme of understanding.

Each of the theories about play contains implications for practice and research. Observations of children playing can be recorded and analyzed to see what theories best explain the observations. The extent to which such observations can be accounted for by the theory is the extent to which the theory is credible.

Any one of the elements of Kerlinger's definition of theory can be an important part of a research project. Constructs could be studied in themselves, and it would be research. For example, the construct of locus of control (LOC) (Rotter,

1966) entails the idea that people view what happens to them somewhere on a continuum from being completely self-controlled (internal LOC) to being controlled by others or circumstances (external LOC). Locus of control was studied originally by Rotter and subsequently, as it was thought to be related to other constructs, by over 600 researchers.

A research project need not deal with an entire theory (i.e., a complete set of interrelationships) but may, and usually is, confined to certain aspects of a theory. Because of this multifaceted research approach, an overview of many research findings often is necessary before a substantive change in theory can be made. Some scholars specialize in synthesizing research and write about how their findings make an impact on the more complete theory. The presence of such synthesizers, however, does not preclude any one researcher from discussing the implications of his or her research on an entire theory.

When the concentration is on a single, relatively uncluttered construct, one can see how much more can be researched (i.e., be a legitimate topic for research) than if one were confined only to complex theories that endeavor to describe, explain, or predict a phenomenon. For example, the varied use of instructional objectives, either written in a course syllabus or communicated orally, can be studied without addressing an entire theory of instruction. Certainly, the use of objectives is part of one or more instructional theories, but a researcher need not be obligated to test any theory in its entirety. The theoretical foundation or review of literature sections of a research report (discussed in Chapter 8) ought to contain a discussion of how the specific research project emanates from or has an impact on existing theory. For example, the Sassenrath et al. reading for this chapter reviews two theoretical stances on the relative success of private versus public schools and, thus, sets out to resolve some of the confusion. The conclusions and implications sections (also discussed in Chapter 8) should and do speak to the larger theoretical concerns as well.

For truth-seekers the two ways that research can have an impact on theory are: (1) the testing of a theory, or parts thereof, which is basically a deductive process and (2) creating theory where none currently exists, which is basically an inductive process. The examples from communication and instructional theories above are deductive procedures, as is the Sassenrath et al. reading at the end of this chapter: something theoretical invites examination regarding the credibility of its generalization or its efficacy in describing, explaining, or predicting a phenomenon. The Sims reading, on the other hand, seeks out theory at the end of the article that can better inform the study's results or be better understood through the study's findings.

It is possible for truth-seekers to carry out a research project where no existing theory appears to apply. Gathering, analyzing, and synthesizing data to build generalizations represent the beginning stages of theory development. Theory-development or theory-generating studies are legitimate because their end product will have a bearing on theory. Indeed, their findings and conclusions actually initiate theory where none existed before. The theory that results may be quite tentative and incomplete, but it at least represents the beginnings of an effort to describe, explain, or predict the phenomenon that has been examined. Once theoretical beginnings occur, they can be studied deductively, wherein the theoretical constructs or relationships are tested.

Just as truth-seekers do, perspective-seekers pursue questions about phenomena, but, as mentioned in Chapter 2, they typically are not interested in generalizations that will permit predictions from one setting to another. That does not mean, however, that perspective-seekers are not interested in theory. Their interest in theory usually follows their inquiry. Perspective-seekers are much more likely to pursue questions inductively, gather and analyze their findings, and then cast about for theoretical explanations of what they have discovered. The linkages made to theory help to explain the phenomenon being studied. Typically, when theoretical links to a study are sought during or after the results are available the researcher will note several bodies of knowledge related to his or her findings. Such is the case with the Sims reading.

Types of Theory

It is useful to classify theories to better understand them. Bear in mind that the classifications are somewhat arbitrary and certainly open to debate. We offer the classification here to illustrate how differentiations can be made.

Descriptive Theories

As the name implies, *descriptive* theories seek to describe a phenomenon. They do this by being based on observations of data. Chapters 4 and 6 discuss this further, but suffice it here to say that data usually are synonymous with results of observations. We say usually because some claim data exclusively mean quantitative information, such as frequencies, measurements, or test scores. Data can be words, and perspective-seekers frequently use words and other indicators as the base for their theories. The value-base of descriptive theories is more important to discuss here, however.

Particularly within the natural sciences, descriptive theories essentially seek to describe what is. The operant word here is *is*. The absence of any apparent values, attitudes, or inclinations makes descriptive theories very objective sounding, very "scientific."

Technically, such theories do have values at their base, but the values are taken for granted, not often discussed, and perhaps not even recognized by the researcher. The very act of deciding what aspects of theories should be tested or how to go about such testing, however, is a value-driven enterprise. Descriptive theories are classified this way because they appear to be objective and traditionally have been regarded as such. (See Chapter 2 for a discussion of ideology's role in research.) Truth-seekers use descriptive theories because they are striving for objectivity. Perspective-seekers lay less claim to objectivity, but they also are concerned with description. An interest in learning can illustrate the use of descriptive theories by truth-seekers.

Psychologists are interested in human learning. They seek to build and confirm theories about learning that describe the phenomenon. Psychologists use data from which they develop their learning theories. They want to describe, explain, and predict learning. Often psychologists will use laboratory animals for their experiments to control more carefully any variables that might confound their findings.

An example of a specific research question for psychologists is: How many trials are necessary before a laboratory rat learns to run successfully through a maze under certain specified conditions? If the end of the maze contains food and the rats are at various stages of hunger, the researcher can record the number of trials before success for each stage of hunger and predict or hypothesize that hungrier rats will have fewer trials before success than less hungry rats. Such a generalization, assuming the data bear it out, can contribute to a learning theory that accounts for the role of motivation within that learning theory. The degree to which such a generalization would apply to human subjects is another question. So many factors could be involved that the generalization may not always apply to human subjects.

Truth-seekers usually start with a theory and proceed deductively to test it. Suppes' reading, at the end of this chapter, is an excellent argument for the importance of theory to research. The Sassenrath et al. reading is an example of a study that begins with a theory and proceeds to test it. Perspective-seekers often begin with a question that requires investigation before theory can be brought in for explanation or confirmation; hence, they frequently proceed inductively. The Sims reading is an example of research that proceeds inductively, arriving at theory after the data are analyzed.

Prescriptive Theories

When all of the objective sounding theories are accounted for we are left with those theories that contain words like *should* and *ought*. These theories seek to tell us how and sometimes why we should or ought to behave in certain ways. "Workers should revolt" is a prescription for taking a definite action, and a reform-oriented research project could be planned around such a prescription. A less polemic prescription, one from instructional design, may help to reveal the differences between the two types of theory.

Instructional designers are in the business of telling people how to arrange subject matter or facilities to maximize or at least ensure some level of learning. Their theories contain *should's* and *ought's*, the words used to prescribe some behaviors. For example, it is common to find exhortations from individuals writing about instruction that the objectives for a lesson or unit should be communicated to the students at or near the beginning of the lesson or unit of instruction. The prescription may be based on research findings or simply may be the logical outgrowth of a reasoned approach to good practice. A specific example of a research question related to this topic would be: Will students perform better on a final test when they are told what the objectives for the lesson are at the beginning of each lesson? One could compare several groups of students: those receiving objectives early, midway, or at the end of the lesson or not at all. Based on the theory, the hypothesis, expectation, or prediction (all of which mean about the same thing) would be that the group receiving the objectives the earliest would perform better on the final test than the other groups.

Both kinds of theories—descriptive and prescriptive—are amenable to research. They are used differently by truth- and perspective-seekers, however. Truth-seekers are interested in prediction and generalization to other settings, whereas perspective-seekers are more concerned with an in-depth description and explanation of the one setting being studied.

Both kinds of theories carry implications that logically can be reduced to propositions or questions. The propositions can take the "If . . . , then . . . " form. For example, *if* motivation is critical to learning, *then* more motivated (hungrier) rats will have fewer trials than less motivated (less hungry) rats. Or, *if* objectives "should be" provided at the beginning of a lesson, *then* groups receiving objectives early should score higher than groups receiving them later or not at all.

Perspective-seekers are less interested in confirming or disconfirming theories of either type than are truth-seekers. They are more concerned with whether a theoretical explanation serves to clarify what the researcher found in a particular setting. Sometimes studies of the perspective-seeking type do serve to build new theory, but no claim would be made by the researcher that this theory was widely generalizable.

It is important to note that nothing regarding the theories or their propositions and questions is being proved or disproved. The concern instead is that the theories are being tested or examined to see if they are more or less credible. Actually, research is a way of examining how useful a theory is in describing or explaining or, in some cases, predicting a phenomenon. From a truth-seeking standpoint, research essentially is testing the theoretical view and refining it through adjustment or replacement to achieve a more complete understanding of the world. On the other hand, to a perspective-seeker research is the process of using theory to help describe and understand various perceptions of the world.

The Issue of Abstraction

The theoretical versus real view of the world argument made by some people has misled many others for a long time. Comments demeaning theory such as, "That's fine for theory, but it won't work in the real world," have not contributed anything very positive to either point of view. The problem resides in a misunderstanding of the role of theory and, even more importantly, a naive view of the world.

All of us have to deal with reality. Defining reality is not nearly as easy as some would think at first blush. In fact, at the very point of definition, when we use words to describe or define reality, we unavoidably enter the realm of abstraction. Words and the concepts they represent are abstractions from an undifferentiated mass of reality bombarding our senses. Reality is experienced through sight, sound, smell, taste, and touch. When we try to describe reality we use symbols, that is, words and phrases, to represent the piece of reality we are trying to describe.

In an effort, for example, to describe an orange, we base our description on our experience of seeing, smelling, tasting, and holding the orange, but the descriptions will be different for different people. And if an orange can be experienced even a little bit differently by a variety of individuals, imagine what happens to more complex experiences when people endeavor to abstract them into language or theory. Whenever we use language, publicly or privately, we have abstracted from the undifferentiated mass that which we wish to name, describe, or define. What can be scary about this abstracting is that there are no rules for it. To be sure, there is a public or professional domain in which a consensus has been forged over the meanings of words. Dictionaries do that well, but even dictionaries do not always agree exactly.

The abstraction issue, simply put, is that whenever words or other symbols are used to communicate to others or oneself something about reality (i.e., the real world or someone's perception of the real world), the user is engaging in abstractions. Theories, because of their use of words, are abstract too, but they are no more abstract than any other form of language. Moreover, theories are tentative descriptions (e.g., if it is round, orange, juicy, and segmented, then it probably is an orange). The components of theories—the constructs and the relationships they claim, the stuff of theories—require investigation by all manner of means. The role of theory is really two-sided: It serves to describe, explain, or predict; and it invites examination. But, because of the abstraction issue, it will always be elusive to some extent.

Sources of Theory

The subject matter of university courses, especially at the graduate level, will include theoretical considerations if the course is more than a collection of "sea stories," "war stories," or "Here's how I did it" vignettes by the professor. Textbooks for the courses contain theory about the subject matter. Reviews of textbooks or reviews of research in any area (e.g., administration, instruction, curriculum, science education, early childhood education) contain descriptions of theories, or explications of theories, or discussions of how certain research may have made some theories more or less credible. An excellent source of theory in a variety of areas is the *Encyclopedia of Educational Research*, published by the American Educational Research Association (AERA). The *Encyclopedia* is published about once every ten years. It will be somewhat dated near the end of its decade, but any edition will reveal the concern each of the contributors has for the theory that is being developed or applied within the area. In fact, theoretical pieces such as those published in the *Encyclopedia* could, in a broad sense, be considered research documents. Unlike the stereotypical term paper that merely synthesizes existing theory in a particular field, a good theoretical essay treats already existing (published) research as data and makes new statements about a certain body of knowledge.

Research conferences, including the AERA conference which meets every spring and a host of other more specialized conferences, include presentations by researchers that focus on specific topics. The research that is presented at these conferences will add to, refute, modify, or develop theory relevant to many topics. A discussion of theoretical implications of a research presentation is a criterion that usually must be met before a paper is accepted for presentation. (There are exceptions, of course. The politics of whom to invite or accept to any gathering do not always abide by public rules.)

As with research conferences, research journals endeavor to publish research reports that have some theoretical impact. Again, the effort to minimize political considerations takes the form of blind review; that is, reviewers, also called peers, judges, or jury members, examine the anonymous research report with regard to a number of criteria, not the least of which is the theoretical impact of the research. An important task for students of any area of specialization is to become familiar with the journals within their specialization. Students can and should be aware of issues, trends, and controversies within their area of specialization by attending to the content of the research and other professional journals over the last several years.

Summary

Theory is important to truth-seekers and perspective-seekers in that it helps each to understand better the world in which we live. The predictive power of theory is especially important to truth-seekers; it is of little or no interest to perspective-seekers, who rely on theory to question or corroborate findings or to assist in generating hypotheses for further research.

Theories can describe or prescribe. The descriptive theories, most often found in the natural sciences, seek to "objectively" describe phenomena, whereas prescriptive theories contain *should's* and *ought's* and endeavor to prescribe what should be done. Most professional fields, such as education, are replete with prescriptive theories. Both types of theories can be tested or used to explain findings.

Abstracting from the undifferentiated bombardment on our senses is what we do whenever we use language and the concepts words represent to communicate meanings. Theories rely on abstractions, to be sure, but any language or symbol system relies on abstraction.

When searching for theoretical links to research projects, college and university courses can be sources of theory. The *Encyclopedia of Educational Research,*

research papers presented at research conferences, and research journals are excellent depositories of theory.

Discussion Questions and Activities

1. Select any two articles from a professional journal and decide whether they constitute research. Why or why not?

2. In a short paper trace the history of your particular field of education. Were any changes in the development of your field the result of research findings? Describe one such change and how it was or was not influenced by research.

3. Find a theoretical essay and examine the various theoretical positions for traces of ideology. Are certain values either implicitly or explicitly stated in each theoretical school of thought?

4. Find an example of a descriptive and a prescriptive theory being tested in an educational research journal.

5. Explain the paradox of language for the educational researcher—how it helps to communicate but restricts the meaning that is given to certain words or phrases. How is all of this related to theory?

6. Some researchers have found that men score higher on mathematics tests than women. What explanations account for the differences? Are these explanations at least the beginnings of theories?

7. Examine some textbooks on administration or leadership. What is Theory X? Theory Y? and Theory Z?

8. The assumptions (or generalizations) from the management theories X, Y, and Z lend themselves to testing. Find a research report that tests one or more aspects of one of these theories.

Introduction to the Readings

The first reading, Suppes' "The Place of Theory in Educational Research," was the presidential address to the American Educational Research Association conference in 1974. Suppes' discussion reflects the truth-seeking view of theory. Suppes stresses that research has little or no import unless it is connected with theory. We agree with that part. He implies, however, and here is where we part company with him, that theory precedes research, and, hence, research is a deductive, hypothesis-driven enterprise. We maintain, explicitly, that the absence of theory can invite a research project—one pursued inductively, in a theory-generating mode. (Another approach to theory is also discussed in this chapter and exemplified by the Sims reading.)

The reprint of the article "Private and Public School Students: Longitudinal Achievement Differences?" by Sassenrath et al. is an example of a theory-driven, deductive study. The theory concerns private schools effecting better academic achievement than public schools and, as Sassenrath et al. indicate, has been buttressed by findings from another study. Sassenrath et al. use the other study and a recent critique of it to launch their own, more controlled study to see if the theory about private versus public schools will hold up to their scrutiny.

The Sims article, "Strong Black Girls: A Ten Year Old Responds to Fiction about Afro-Americans," is an example of research that initially acknowledges the existence of related works but is not explicitly theoretical until the findings have been categorized and analyzed. Conceptually, however, Sims' research is influenced by reader response theory which is ideologically reform oriented. Because this view maintains that any piece of literature varies in form depending on a reader's response to it, it stands in direct contrast to the more status quo related notions that certain aspects of literature, such as plot, are always constant. Therefore, Sims' article is also an example of a research project that is toward the reform end of the ideology continuum.

The Place of Theory in Educational Research

Patrick Suppes

In every modern society, the education of its citizens, young and old, is a major concern. In some developing countries, the educational activities of the government consume as much as a third of the national budget. In the United States today, it is estimated that educational activities require at least a hundred billion dollars a year. Most educational activities in this country and elsewhere are like other forms of social and economic activity in society in that only a slight effort is made to study the character of the activities and to understand them as intellectual, economic, or social processes. It is true that there has been a longer tradition, even if a fragile one, of studying the character of education, but I think all members of this Association are very much aware that educational research is a minor activity compared with education as a whole.

All of us probably feel on occasion that there is little hope that educational research, given the small national effort devoted to it, will have any real impact on education as a whole. Such pessimistic thoughts are not historically, I think, supported by the evidence, especially when we look at the evidence outside of education as well as inside. By looking outside education I digress for a moment to examine some instances of the impact of science on society. All of the characteristic features of electronic communication and rapid transportation of our society are unique products of the long tradition of science and technology, and the case is especially strong that the changes that have taken place recently, for example, the widespread introduction of color television, have depended in a direct way on prior scientific research.

It might be useful to mention eight outstanding recent cases that have been studied for the National Science Foundation (Battelle Report, 1973), because the listing of these cases gives a better sense of the diversity of important recent contributions to society arising from specific scientific work. The eight cases all represent developments that almost certainly would never have taken place simply on the basis of either enlightened common sense or some approach of bare empiricism. The eight cases range across a variety of scientific theories and technologies and a variety of segments of society in their applications. They are the heart pacemaker; the development of hybrid grains and the green revolution;

electrophotography, which led to office copiers or, as we say in ordinary parlance, Xerox machines; input-output economic analysis developed originally in the thirties by Leontief; organophosphorus insecticides; oral contraceptives, which rest on relatively delicate matters of steroid chemistry; magnetic ferrites, which are widely used in communications equipment and computers; and videotape recorders, which depended upon a confluence of electromagnetic and communication theory and the technology of audio recording. Compared with the impact of some of these scientific and technological developments, the initial cost of research and development has been relatively minor.

As these examples illustrate, research can have an impact in our society, and it certainly does in many different ways. To a large extent, education pays more lip service to research than do other main segments of the society. Every large school system has as part of its central office staff some sort of research unit. The schools and colleges of education associated with institutions of higher education throughout the country are all charged with research responsibilities, some of which are specifically written into the legislative charter of the institution.

When the Office of Education was established by federal legislation more than a hundred years ago in 1867, the first section of the Act defined the chief purpose of the new bureau, later called the Office of Education, as one of "collecting such statistics and facts as shall show the condition and progress of education in the several states and territories, and of diffusing information respecting the organization and management of schools and school systems and methods of teaching." There is not in this charge to the Office of Education a serious thrust of theory, and it is fair to say that most of the efforts of the Office of Education have not been directed toward the nurturing of educational theory, but rather to the more mundane and empirical matters of collecting statistics and facts and of disseminating information about the nation's schools.

The point I am making in leisurely fashion is that for at least a hundred years there has been a serious respect for facts and statistical data about education and also for many empirical studies, often of excellent design and execution, to evaluate the learning of students, the effectiveness of a given method of instruction, and so forth. At least until recently, the empiricism of education has been more enlightened and sophisticated than the empiricism of medicine, which represents an investment comparable to education in our society.

The period running from the beginning of this century to the onset of World War II has sometimes been described as the golden age of empiricism in education. Certainly it was marked by a serious effort to move from a priori dogmas and principles of education to consideration of empirical results and even experimental design of inquiries to test the relative efficiency or power of different approaches to a given part of the curriculum. Detailed analysis of the nature of tests and how to interpret the results was begun, and serious attempts, especially by Edward Thorndike and his collaborators, were made to apply a broad range of results from educational psychology to actual problems of learning in the classroom.

Unfortunately, this golden age of empiricism was replaced not by a deeper theoretical viewpoint toward educational research, but by a noticeable decline of research. To some extent, the overenthusiastic empiricism of the 1920s promoted a negative reaction from teachers, administrators, and parents. Opposition to achievement tests, to standardization and to too much objectivity in education became rife. A summary of many of the disappointments in the empirical movement in education may be found in the 1938 *Yearbook of the National Society for the Study of Education.* Although in many respects John Dewey can be identified with the development of the empirical tradition, it is important to note that his work and that of his close collaborators is not notable for the sophistication of its scientific aspects; Dewey himself, it can properly be said, continually stood on shifting ground in advocating empirical and innovative attitudes toward teaching. In fact, one does not find in Dewey the emphasis on tough-minded empirical research that one would like, but rather a kind of hortatory expression of conviction in the value of methods of inquiry brought directly to the classroom, and indeed more directly to the classroom than to the scientific study of what was going on in the classroom.

Beginning in the 1950s and especially since Sputnik, we have had a new era of a return to research, and without doubt much valuable work has been done in the last two decades. It is also important to recognize, of course, that much of the thrust for curriculum reform and change in the schools has been bolstered by one form or another of new romanticism untouched by sophisticated consideration of data or facts.

This superficial sketch of the historical developments over the past hundred years leads to the conclusion that research, let alone any theoretically oriented research, has occupied almost always a precarious place in education. It might therefore be thought that the proper theme for a presidential address would be the place of *research* in education and not the more specialized and restricted topic of the place of *theory* in educational research. However, as the examples I have cited from the National Science Foundation study indicate, there is more than meets the eye on the problems of developing an adequate body of theory in educational research, and success in developing such a body of theory can impact significantly on the place of research in education. I would like to turn to this question in more detail as my first point of inquiry.

Why Theory?

There are five kinds of argument I would like to examine that can be used to make the case for the relevance of theory to educational research. The first is an argument by analogy, the second is in terms of the reorganization of experience, the third is as a device for recognizing complexity, the fourth is a comparison with Deweyean problem solving, and the fifth concerns the triviality of bare empiricism. I now turn to each of these arguments.

Argument by Analogy

The success of theory in the natural sciences is recognized by everyone. More recently, some of the social sciences, especially economics and psychology in certain parts, have begun to achieve considerable theoretical developments. It is argued that the obvious and universally recognized importance of theory in the more mature sciences is strong evidence for the universal generalization that theory is important in all sciences, and consequently, we have an argument by analogy for the importance of theory in educational research.

However, since at least the eleventh century, when Anselem tried to use an argument by analogy to prove the existence of God, there is proper skepticism that an argument by analogy carries much weight. Although the argument that the success of the natural sciences in the use of theory provides an excellent example for educational research, it does not follow that theory must be comparably useful as we move from one subject to the other.

Reorganization of Experience

A more important way to think about the role of theory is to attack directly the problem of identifying the need for theory in a subject matter. In all cases where theory has been successful in science I think we can make an excellent argument for the deeper organization of experience the theory has thereby provided. A powerful theory changes our perspective on what is important and what is superficial. Perhaps the most striking example in the history of physics is the law of inertia, which says that a body shall continue uniformly in its direction of motion until acted upon by some external force. Aristotle and other ancient natural philosophers were persuaded that the evidence of experience is clear: A body does not continue in motion unless it is acted upon by force. We can all agree that our own broad experience is exactly that of Aristotle's. It was a deep insight and represented a radical reorganization of how to think about the world to recognize that the theory of motion is correctly expressed by laws like that of inertia and seldom by our direct common sense experience.

A good example in education of the impact of theory on reorganizing our way of thinking about our discipline is the infusion of economic theory that has taken place in the last decade with such vigor and impact. (A good survey is to be found in the two-volume reader edited by Blaug, 1968, 1969.) The attempt, for instance, to develop an economic theory of productivity for our schools can be criticized in many different ways, but it still remains that we have been forced to think anew about the allocation of resources, especially of how we can develop a deeper running theory for the efficient allocation of resources to increase productivity and, at the same time, to develop a better theory for the measurements of input and output and the construction of production functions.

Let me give one example from some of my own discussions with economists, especially with Dean Jamison. Starting from the economists' way of looking at output, it is natural to ask how we can measure the output of an elementary school, for example. What I find striking is the lack of previous discussion of this problem in the literature of education. (Exceptions are Page, 1972, and Page & Breen, 1973.) Even if we restrict ourselves to measurements of academic skills, and indeed only to the academic skills assessed on standard achievement tests, we still have the problem of how to aggregate the measurement of these skills to give us an overall measure of output. If one accepts the fact, as most of us do, that academic achievement alone is not important, but that a variety of social and personal skills, as well as the development of a sense of values and of moral autonomy, are needed, one is really nonplused by even crude assessments of these individual components. There is, of course, the well-worn answer that the things that matter most are really ineffable and immeasurable, but this romantic attitude is not one for which I have much tolerance. I am simply struck in my own thinking by the difficulty of making a good assessment, and my sense of the difficulties has been put in focus by trying to deal with some of the theoretical ideas economists have brought to bear in education.

Recognition of Complexity

One of the thrusts of theory is to show that what appear on the surface to be simple matters of empirical investigation, on a deeper view, prove to be complex and subtle. The basic skills of language and mathematics at any level of instruction, but primarily at the most elementary level, provide good examples. If we are offered two methods of reading it is straightforward to design an experiment to see whether or not a difference of any significant magnitude between the two methods can be found in the achievement of students. It has been progress in education to recognize that such problems can be studied as scientific problems, and it is a mark of the work of the first half of this century, the *golden age* of empiricism as I termed it earlier, to firmly establish the use of such methods in education. It is an additional step, however, and one in which the recognition of theory is the main carrier of progress, to recognize that the empirical comparison of two methods of teaching reading or of teaching subtraction, to take an example that has been much researched, is by no means to provide anything like the theory of how the child learns to read or learns to do arithmetic.

A most elementary perusal of psychological considerations of information processing shows at once how far we are from an adequate theory of learning even the most elementary basic skills. It is a requirement of theory, but not of experimentalism, to provide analysis of the process by which the child acquires a basic skill and later uses it. It is a merit of theory to push for a deeper understanding of the acquisition and not to rest until we have a complete process analysis of what the child does and what goes on inside his head as he acquires a new skill.

The history of physics can be written around the concept of the search for mechanisms ranging from the reduction of astronomical motions to compositions of circular motions in the time of Ptolemy to the gravitational and electromagnetic mechanisms of modern physics. It has been to a partial extent, and should be to a greater extent, a primary thrust of theory in educational research to seek mechanisms or processes that answer the question of why a given aspect of education works the way it does. This should be true whether we consider the individual learning of a child beginning school or the much broader interaction between adolescents, their peer groups, and what is supposed to take place in their high school classrooms. For educational purposes we need an understanding of biosocial mechanisms of influence as much as in medicine we need an understanding of biochemical mechanisms for the control of disease in a host organism. The search beyond the facts for a conception of mechanism or of explanation forces upon us a recognition of the complexity of the phenomena and the need for a theory of this complexity.

Why Not Deweyean Problem Solving?

The instrumental view of knowledge developed by Peirce and Dewey led, especially in the hands of Dewey, to an emphasis on the importance of problem solving in inquiry. As Dewey repeatedly emphasized, inquiry is the transformation of an indeterminate situation that presents a problem into one that is determinate and unified by the solution of the initial problem. Dewey's conception of inquiry can be regarded as a proper corrective to an overly scholastic and rigid conception of scientific theory, but the weakness of replacing classical conceptions of scientific theory by inquiry as problem solving is that the articulation of the historically and intellectually important role of theory in inquiry is neglected or slighted. In any case, even if we accept some of Dewey's criticisms of classical philosophical conceptions of theory, we can argue for the importance of the development of scientific theories as potential tools for use in problem solving. It would be a naive and careless view of problem solving to think that on each occasion where we find ourselves in an indeterminate situation we can begin afresh to think about the problem and not to bring to bear a variety of sophisticated systematic tools. This sounds so obvious that it is hard to believe anyone could disagree with it. Historically, however, it is important to recognize that under the influence of Dewey educational leadership moved away from development and testing of theory, and Dewey himself did not properly recognize the importance of deep-running systematic theories.[2]

The newest version of the naive problem-solving viewpoint is to be found in the romantics running from John Holt to Charles Silberman, who seem to think that simply by using our natural intuition and by observing what goes on in classrooms we can put together all the ingredients needed to solve our educational problems. To a large extent these new romantics are the proper heirs of Dewey, and they suffer from the same intellectual weakness—the absence of the felt need for theoretically based techniques of analysis.

The continual plague of romantic problem solvers in education will only disappear, as have plagues of the past, when the proper antidotes are developed. My belief about these antidotes is that we need deep-running theories of the kind that have driven alchemists out of chemistry and astrologers out of astronomy.

Triviality of Bare Empiricism

The best general argument for theory in educational research I have left for last. This is the obvious triviality of bare empiricism as an approach to knowledge. Those parts of science that have been beset by bare empiricism have suffered accordingly. It is to be found everywhere historically, ranging from the sections on natural history in the early *Transactions of the Royal Society* of the seventeenth century to the endless lists of case histories in medicine, or as an example closer to home, to studies of methods of instruction that report only raw data. At its most extreme level, bare empiricism is simply the recording of individual facts, and with no apparatus of generalization or theory, these bare facts duly recorded lead nowhere. They do not provide even a practical guide for future experience or policy. They do not provide methods of prediction or analysis. In short, bare empiricism does not generalize.

The same triviality may be claimed for the bare intuition of the romantics. Either bare empiricism or bare intuition leads not only to triviality, but also to chaos in practice if each teacher is left only to his or her own observations and intuitions. Reliance on bare empiricism or bare intuition in educational practice is a mental form of streaking, and nudity of mind is not as appealing as nudity of body.

Examples of Theory in Educational Research

There are good examples of theory in educational research. I want to consider a few and examine their characteristic features. After surveying five main areas in which substantial theories may be found, I turn to the general question of whether we can expect developments of theory strictly within educational research, or whether we should think of educational research as applied science, drawing upon other domains for the fundamental theories considered, on the model, for example, of pharmacology in relation to biochemistry, or electrical engineering in relation to physics.

Statistical Design

The bible of much if not most educational research is a statistical bible, and there is little doubt that the best use of statistics in educational research is at a high level. It is sometimes thought by research workers in education that statistical design is simply used in experimental studies and that it does not represent a theoretical component, but I think a more accurate way of formulating the situation is this. When the substantive hypotheses being tested are essentially empirical in character and are not drawn from a broader theoretical framework, then the only theoretical component of the study is the statistical theory required to provide a proper test of the hypotheses. As a broad generalization I would claim that the best-developed theory used in educational research is the theory of statistical design of experiments. The sophisticated level that has been reached in these matters by the latter part of the twentieth century is one of the glories of science in the twentieth century, and the dedication to insisting on proper organization of evidence to make a strong inference has been one of the most creditable sides of educational research over the past fifty years.

The opprobrium heaped on matters statistical in educational circles arises, I think, from two main sources. One is that on occasion the teaching traditions have been bad and students have been taught to approach the use of statistics in rote or cookbook fashion, without reaching for any genuine understanding of the inference procedures and their intellectual justification. The second is that the mere use of statistics is not a substitute for good theoretical analysis about the substantive questions at hand. There is no doubt that excellent statistical methods have been used more than once to test utterly trivial hypotheses that could scarcely be of interest to anyone. Neither of these defects, however, makes a serious case for the unimportance of statistical theory.

Test Theory

My second example is closely related to the first, but is more specific to educational matters. The educational practice of basing decisions on tests has a long and venerable history, the longest and most continuous history being the examinations for mandarins in China, running from the twelfth century to the downfall of the empire at the end of the nineteenth century. The great traditions of testing in Oxford and Cambridge are famous and in previous years notorious. As tradition has it, students preparing for the Mathematical Tripos at Cambridge worked so intensely and so feverishly that many of them went from the examination room directly to the hospital for a period of recuperation. The position that a man achieved in the Mathematical Tripos at Cambridge in the nineteenth century was one of the most important facts about his entire career.

The competitive spirit about examinations for admittance to college or graduate school in this country is not at all a new phenomenon, but rather it represents an old and established cultural tradition. What is new in this century is the *theory of tests*. In all of that long history of 700 years of Chinese examinations there seems to have been no serious thought about the theory of such tests or even a systematic attempt to collect data of empirical significance. It is an insight that belongs to this century, and historically will be recorded as an important achievement of this century, to recognize that a theory of tests is possible and has to a considerable extent been developed. By these remarks I do not mean to suggest that the theory of tests has reached a state of perfection, but rather that definite and clear accomplishments have taken place. It is in fact a credit to the theory that many of the more important weaknesses of current tests are explicitly recognized. Certainly the concepts of validity and reliability of tests, and the more specific axioms of classical test theory, represent a permanent contribution to the literature of educational theory. (Lord & Novick's systematic treatise, 1968, provides a superb analysis of the foundations of the classical theory.)

Learning Theory

In the March 1974 issue of the *Educational Researcher,* W. J. McKeachie has an article entitled "The Decline and Fall of the Laws of Learning." He examines what has happened to Thorndike's Law of Effect and Law of Exercise, especially in the more recent versions of reinforcement theory advocated by Skinner.

McKeachie is right in his analysis of the decline and fall of classical laws of learning, but I think that over the past two decades the specific and more technical development of mathematical models of learning that have not made sweeping claims as being the only laws of learning or as being adequate to all kinds of learning have accomplished a great deal and represent a permanent scientific advance. Moreover, the development of mathematical models of learning has not been restricted to simple laboratory situations, but has encompassed results directly relevant to subject-matter learning ranging from elementary mathematics to acquisition at the college level of a second language.

It is not to the point in this general lecture to enter into details, but because a good deal of my own research is in this area, I cannot forbear a few more remarks about what has been accomplished. In the case of mathematics, we can give a detailed mathematical theory of the learning of elementary mathematical concepts and skills by students. The details of the theory are a far cry from the early pioneering work of Thorndike. In fact, the mathematical tools for the formulation of detailed theory were simply not available during the time of Thorndike. I would not want to claim that the theories we can currently construct and test are the last word on these matters. The analysis of specific mathematical skills and concepts has been achieved by moving away from the simple-minded conception of stimulus and response found in Skinner's writings. In a previous paper given to this Association, I criticized in detail some of the things Skinner has had to say about the learning of mathematics (Suppes, 1972). I shall not repeat those criticisms, but rather in the present context, I shall emphasize the positive and try to sketch the kind of theoretical apparatus that has been added to classical stimulus-response theories of learning in order to have a theory of adequate structural depth to handle specific mathematical concepts and skills.

As many of you would expect, the basic step is to postulate a hierarchy of internal processing on the part of the student—processing that must include the handling at least in schematic form of the perceptual format in which problems are presented, whether they are arithmetic algorithms or simple problems of a geometric character. An internal processing language is postulated and the basic mechanism of learning is that of constructing subroutines or programs for the handling of particular concepts and skills (Suppes, 1969b; Suppes & Morningstar, 1972, Ch. 4; Suppes, 1972).

There is one important theoretical point about such work that I would like to make, because I think that ignoring this theoretical point represents a major error on the part of some learning psychologists and also of physiological psychologists. The point is that it is a mistake to think of precisely one internal processing language and one particular subroutine for a given skill or concept being learned in the same form by each student. What we can expect in an area like mathematics is behavioral isomorphism, but not internal isomorphism, of subroutines. It is important to think about the theory in this way and not to expect a point-for-point confirmation of the internal programs constructed by the student as he acquires new skills and concepts. To assume that the physiology of human beings is so constructed that we can infer from the physiology how particular tasks are learned and organized internally is as mistaken as to think that from the specification of the physical hardware of a computer we can infer the structure of programs that are written for that computer. It is one reason for thinking that the contributions of physiological psychologists to educational psychology are necessarily limited in principle and not simply in practice. This seems to me worth mentioning because currently physiological psychology is the fashion, and if we are not careful we will begin to hear that the next great hope in educational psychology will be the contributions we can expect from physiological psychology. I am making the strong claim that in principle this may not be possible, and that we can proceed independently within educational research to develop powerful theories of learning without dependence on the latest news from neurophysiology.

The kind of examples I have sketched for elementary mathematics can also be extended to language skills and to the important problem of reading. Much of my own recent work has been concerned with first- and second-language acquisition, but I shall not try to expand upon these matters except again to say that what is important about current work in these areas is that specific theories of considerable structural depth, using tools developed in logic for semantics and in linguistics for syntax, have been constructed to provide a richness of theory and a potential for subsequent development that has not existed until the past decade or so (Smith, 1972; Suppes, 1970, 1971, 1974; Suppes, Smith, & Leveille, 1972). I am sanguine about the possibilities for the future and believe that substantive contributions of importance to education may be expected from learning theory throughout the rest of this century.

Theories of Instruction

One of the most interesting and direct applications of modern work in mathematical models of learning has been to the burgeoning subject of theories of instruction. A theory of instruction differs from a theory of learning in the following respect. We assume that a mathematical model of learning will provide an approximate description of the student's learning, and the task for a theory of instruction is then to settle the question of how the instructional sequence of concepts, skills, and facts should be organized to optimize for a given student his rate of learning. My colleague, Richard Atkinson, has been successfully applying such methods for the past several years, and some of the results he has achieved in beginning reading skills are especially striking (Atkinson, 1972, 1974; Atkinson & Paulson, 1972). The mathematical techniques of optimization used in theories of instruction draw upon a wealth of results from other areas of science, especially from tools developed in mathematical economics and operations research over the past two decades, and it would be my prediction that we will see increasingly sophisticated theories of instruction in the near future.

Continuing development of computer-assisted instruction makes possible detailed implementation of specific theories in ways that would hardly be possible in ordinary classrooms. The application by Atkinson and his collaborators that I mentioned earlier has this character, and some of my own work in elementary mathematics is of the same sort. In the case of the elementary-school mathematics programs, what we have been able to do is to derive from plausible qualitative assumptions a stochastic differential equation describing the trajectory of students through the curriculum, with the constants of the solution of the differential equation corresponding to unique parameters of each individual student (Suppes, Fletcher, & Zanotti, 1973). The fits to data we have achieved in this effort are about as good as any I have ever achieved, and I think we can now speak with confidence in this area of student trajectories in the same spirit that we speak of trajectories of bodies in the solar system. But again, I emphasize that this is only the beginning, and the promise of future developments seems much more substantial.

Economic Models

As I have already remarked, economists' vigorous interest in education over the past decade has been one of the most salient features of new theoretical work in educational research. Some of us may not like thinking about education as primarily an investment in human capital, and no doubt the concepts of economics introduced into discussions of educational policy in the past few years are alien to many people in education, including a goodly number of educational researchers. Measurements of productivity, for example, that depend mainly on a measurement of output that counts only the number of bodies that pass through a given door to receive accreditation rightly raise questions in the minds of many of us, as do other measures the economists use, sometimes with apparently too much abandon. Moreover, the theoretical tools from economics that have been brought to bear in the economics of education are as yet not thoroughly developed. It is too often the case that an economic model for a particular educational process actually consists of nothing more than an empirical linear-regression equation that has little, if any, theoretical justification back of it. (See, for example, the otherwise excellent articles of Chiswick & Mincer, 1972, and Griliches & Mason, 1972.)

All the same, it is my feeling that the dialogue that has begun and that is continuing at an accelerated pace between economists and the broad community of educational researchers is an important one for our discipline. The broad global concepts that economists are used to dealing with provide in many respects a good intellectual antidote to the overly microscopic concerns of educational psychology that have dominated much of the research in education in past decades. I do not mean to suggest by this remark that we should eliminate the microscopic research—I have been too dedicated to it myself to recommend anything of the sort—but rather to say that it is good to have both kinds of work underway, and to have serious intellectual concentration on the broad picture of what is happening in our educational system. The sometimes mindless suggestions of outsiders about how priorities in education should be reallocated or how particular functions should be reduced are best met not by cries of outrage, but by sober-minded and careful intellectual analysis of our priorities in allocation of resources. Economic theory, above all, provides the appropriate tools for such an analysis, and I am pleased to see that a growing circle of educational researchers are becoming familiar with the use of these tools and are spending a good deal of time thinking about their applications in education.

Sources of Theory

I promised earlier to examine the more general question of whether theory in educational research is chiefly a matter of applying theories developed in economics, psychology, sociology, anthropology, and other sciences close in spirit to the central problems of education. I firmly believe that such applications will continue to play a major role in educational research as they have in the past, but I also resist the notion that theoretically based work in educational research must wait for the latest developments in various other scientific disciplines before it can move forward. Other areas of applied science show a much more complicated and tangled history of interaction between the basically applied discipline and the fundamental discipline nearest to it. Physics is not just applied mathematics, nor is electrical engineering just applied physics. These disciplines interact and mutually enrich each other. The same can be said for education.

In the earlier history of this century it was difficult to disentangle progress in educational psychology from progress in more general experimental psychology, and recently some of the best young economists have claimed the economics of education as the primary area of economics in which they will develop their fundamental contributions. The role of educational researchers should be not merely to test theories made by others, but, when the occasion demands and the opportunity is there, to create new theories as well. Some areas, like the theory of instruction, seem ripe for this sort of development. Another area that I like to call the theory of talking and listening, or what we might call in more standard terms, the theory of verbal communication, seems ripe also for developments special to education, and I do not propose that we wait for linguists and logicians to set us on the right theoretical tracks. What is important is not the decision as to whether the theories should be made at home or abroad, but the positive decision to increase significantly the theory-laden character of our research.

Another point needs to be made about these matters of the source of theory. One of the favorite economic generalizations of our time is that this is the age of specialization. Not every man can do everything equally well, as most of us know when faced with the breakdown of a television set or a washing machine or some other modern device of convenience. This same attitude of specialization should be our attitude toward theory. Not everyone should have the same grasp of theory nor the same involvement in its development. Physics has long recognized such a division of labor between experimental and theoretical physics, and I have come to believe that we need to encourage a similar division in educational research. Ultimately, the most important work may be empirical, but we need both kinds of workers in the vineyard and we need variety of training for these various workers, not only in terms of different areas of education, but also in terms of whether their approach is primarily theoretical or experimental. It is a mark of the undeveloped character of current educational research that we do not have as much division of labor and specialization of research technique as seems desirable.

According to one apocryphal story about the late John von Neumann, he was asked in the early fifties to put together a master list of unsolved problems in mathematics comparable to the famous list given by Hilbert at the beginning of the century. Von Neumann answered that he did not know enough about the various branches of mathematics as they had then developed to provide such a list. I shall be happy when the same kind of developments are found in educational research, and when not only inquiring reporters but also colleagues across the hall recognize that the theoretical work in learning theory, or theories of instruction, or the economics of education, or what have you, is now too richly developed and too intricate to have more than amateur opinions about it.

It is often thought and said that what we most need in education is wisdom and broad understanding of the issues that confront us. Not at all, I say. What we need are deeply structured theories in education that drastically reduce, if not eliminate, the need for wisdom. I do not want wise men to design or build the airplane I fly in, but rather technical men who understand the theory of aerodynamics and the structural properties of metal. I do not want a banker acting like a sage to recommend the measures to control inflation, but rather an economist who can articulate a theory that will be shown to work and who can make explicit the reason why it works (or fails). And so it is with education. Wisdom we need, I will admit, but good theories we need even more. I want to see a new generation of trained theorists and an equally competent band of experimentalists to surround them, and I look for the day when they will show that the theories I now cherish were merely humble way stations on the road to the theoretical palaces they have constructed.

Notes

1. Presidential address to the American Educational Research Association. Chicago, April 17, 1974. Some of the research reported in this article has been supported by National Science Foundation Grant NSFGJ-443X.

2. The most detailed expression of Dewey's (1938) view of scientific inquiry as problem solving is to be found in his *Logic*. A critical, but I think not unsympathetic, analysis of this work is to be found in my account of Nagel's lectures on Dewey's logic (Suppes, 1969a).

References

Atkinson, R. C. (1972). Ingredients for a theory of instruction. *American Psychologist, 27,* 921–931. Republished in M. C. Wittrock (Ed.), *Changing education: Alternatives from educational research.* Englewood Cliffs, N.J.: Prentice-Hall, 1973.

Atkinson, R. C. (1974). Teaching children to read using a computer. *American Psychologist, 29,* 169–178.

Atkinson, R. C., & Paulson, J. A. (1972). An approach to the psychology of instruction. *Psychological Bulletin, 78,* 49–61.

Blaug, M. (Ed.) (1968). *Economics.* Vol. 1. Harmondsworth, Middlesex, England: Penguin Books.

Blaug, M. (Ed.) (1969). *Economics.* Vol. 2. Harmondsworth, Middlesex, England: Penguin Books.

Chiswick, B. R., & Mincer, J. (1972). Time-series changes in personal income inequality in the United States from 1939, with projections to 1985. *Journal of Political Economy, 80,* 534–566.

Dewey, J. (1938). *Logic, the theory of inquiry.* New York: Holt.

Griliches, Z., & Mason, W. M. (1972). Education, income, and ability. *Journal of Political Economy, 80,* 74–103.

Lord, F. M., & Novick, M. R. (1968). *Statistical theories of mental test scores.* New York: Addison-Wesley.

McKeachie, W. J. (1974). The decline and fall of the laws of learning. *Educational Researcher, 3,* 7–11.

National Science Foundation, Science, Technology, and Innovation. (1973). *The place of theory in educational research.* Columbus, Ohio: Battelle, Columbus Laboratories.

Page, E. B. (1972). Seeking a measure of general educational advancement: The Bentee. *Journal of Educational Measurement, 9,* 33–43.

Page, E. B., & Breen, T. F., III. (1973). Educational values for measurement technology: Some theory and data. In W. E. Coffman (Ed.), *Frontiers of educational measurement and information systems.* Boston: Houghton Mifflin.

Smith, R. L. (1972). *The syntax and semantics of ERICA.* (Tech. Rept. No. 185) Stanford, Calif.: Institute for Mathematical Studies in the Social Sciences, Stanford University.

Suppes, P. (1969a). Nageljs lectures on Dewey's logic. In S. Morgenbesser, P. Suppes, & M. White (Eds.), *Philosophy, science, and method.* New York: St. Martin's Press. (a)

Suppes, P. (1969b). Stimulus-response theory of finite automata. *Journal of Mathematical Psychology, 6,* 327–355. (b)

Suppes, P. (1970). Probabilistic grammars for natural languages. *Synthese, 22,* 95–116. Republished in D. Davidson & G. Harman (Eds.), *Semantics of natural language.* Dordrecht, Holland: Reidel, 1972.

Suppes, P. (1971). *Semantics of context-free fragments of natural languages.* (Tech. Rept. No. 171) Stanford, Calif.: Institute for Mathematical Studies in the Social Sciences, Stanford University. Republished in K. J. J. Hintikka, J. M. E. Moravcsik, & P. Suppes (Eds.), *Approaches to natural language.* (1973). Dordrecht, Holland: Reidel.

Suppes, P. (1972). Facts and fantasies of education. *Phi Delta Kappa Monograph.* Republished in M. C. Wittrock (Ed.), *Changing education: Alternatives from educational research.* Englewood Cliffs, N.J.: Prentice-Hall, 1973.

Suppes, P. (1974). The semantics of children's language. *American Psychologist, 29,* 103–114.

Suppes, P., Fletcher, J. D., & Zanotti, M. (1973) *Models of individual trajectories in computer-assisted instruction for deaf students.* (Tech. Rept. No. 214) Stanford, Calif.: Institute for Mathematical Studies in the Social Sciences, Stanford University.

Suppes, P., & Morningstar, M. (1972). *Computer-assisted instruction at Stanford. 1966–68: Data, models, and evaluation of the arithmetic programs.* New York: Academic Press.

Suppes, P., Smith, R., & Leveille, M. (1972). *The French syntax and semantics of PHILIPPE, Part 1, Noun phrases.* (Tech. Rept. No. 195) Stanford, Calif.: Institute for Mathematical Studies in the Social Sciences, Stanford University.

Private and Public School Students:
Longitudinal Achievement Differences?

Julius Sassenrath

Michelle Croce

Manuel Penaloza

Abstract

Two groups of 49 students were matched on age, ethnicity, gender, socioeconomic status, and IQ on data obtained 10 years earlier when they were in public elementary schools. One of the groups switched from public to private schools with an average amount of time in the private schools being about 5.5 years. The other group remained in public schools. Ten years later when they were seniors in high school, both groups were given the same reading and mathematics tests. The results of this longitudinal study do not show any mean differences in achievement test scores between the private and public sectors. The results are discussed largely in the context of two recent and well-known studies on the same topic by Coleman, Hoffer, and Kilgore (1981) and Page and Keith (1981).

In a report to the National Center for Education Statistics (of the U.S. Department of Education) by the National Opinion Research Center (NORC), Coleman, Hoffer, and Kilgore (1981) concluded that private schools effected better cognitive (achievement) outcomes than did public schools. Even when family background factors were presumably controlled statistically, achievement for students in Catholic and other private schools appeared to be higher than for students in public schools.

In a critique and reanalysis of the data used by Coleman et al., Page and Keith (1981) stated that they believed that the conclusion favoring student achievement in private schools depended on a faulty definition of "family background." Coleman et al., employing socioeconomic status (SES), race, and parent expectation as a measure of family background, found that this composite measure correlated .55 with achievement. Page and Keith then suggested that in addition to family background, a measure of general ability should be used to control for student intelligence, because it is well known that intelligence and academic achievement are moderately correlated. In their reanalysis of the data, Page and Keith reported that far and away, general ability has the largest influence on achievement ($r = .72$), both directly and as a transmitter of parent and race influences. Thus, race and family background exert most of their influence via ability. Finally, Page and Keith reported that after controlling for intelligence in the Coleman et al. study, only a small correlation of attendance at private schools with achievement ($r = .18$) was obtained. This correlation was far less than claimed in the NORC report. In studying academic achievement, one needs to control for general ability as well as family background. Students' intelligence or general ability cannot be ignored as an explanation of academic achievement. On this basis, Page and Keith suggested that the conclusions by Coleman et al. regarding higher academic achievement for private than for public school students were false.

In a rejoinder to Page and Keith, Coleman (1981) pointed out, among other things, that the general ability control factor employed by Page and Keith was heavily weighted with a vocabulary measure. Coleman went on to say that scores on the vocabulary tests were higher for private than public school students. He also said that, to a lesser extent, this was also true for the nonverbal or perform-ance measures (mosaics, picture-number, spatial-visualization) used in the analy-sis by Page and Keith. Thus, Coleman suggested that Page and Keith threw the baby (academic achievement differences) out with the bath water (controlling for general ability). Coleman indicated that because vocabulary is more like reading and mathematics achievement (it is taught in school), use of performance tests as ability controls for vocabulary, reading comprehension, and mathematics achievement would still result in a positive effect for private schools.

What seems strange is Coleman's acknowledged need to use truly family background measures as controls or covariates while omitting students' general ability or intelligence as a covariate in analyzing for achievement differences between the private and public sectors. Yet we know that direct measures of students' individual ability (intelligence or aptitude) correlate higher with sub-sequent academic achievement than do indirect measures of family background, which by definition deal primarily with parental influences. It is common knowl-edge that students with higher general ability or intelligence will achieve more, on the average, than students with lower general ability in similar instructional programs.

To meet Coleman's criticism of Page and Keith for controlling for verbal and performance abilities statistically (after the fact), we have attempted to control for these abilities before the fact (i.e., the fact of attendance at different types of schools). We matched students in private schools with students in public schools on verbal and performance abilities (total IQ), as well as on other relevant char-acteristics. Thus, in an effort to throw more light on this controversial issue of great importance, we employed a technique of matching pairs early rather than late in the academic careers of private and public school students. In effect, we have a quasi-experimental design with half of the students receiving largely a private school and half a public school education. Also, because the students were matched on intelligence (general ability), SES, age, ethnicity, and gender about 10 years before they were tested for academic achievement, we have a longitudinal or long-term study dealing with the effects of private and public schools on academic achievement.

Method

Subjects

The students consisted of two groups of 49 each who were participating in a much larger study dealing with the validation of the System of Multicultural Pluralistic Assessment (SOMPA). The original SOMPA study was initiated in 1972 in most of the public school districts of California in an effort to standardize the SOMPA test battery on a large sample (Mercer & Lewis, 1978). Recently, when these children were retested for the validation study of the SOMPA, it was discovered that 49 of the students had switched from public to private schools. These 49 students were enrolled in 47 different private high schools, most of them Catholic. As a result, some students had spent as many as 10 years and some as few as 2 years in private schools, with the remaining years spent in public schools. More specifically, 15% of the students attended private school for 10 years, 30% attended for 6–8 years, 37% attended for 3–5 years, and only 18% attended for only 2 years, with an average stay in the private sector of about 5.5 years. Thus if private schools were going to have an effect it should have appeared over an average attendance of about 5.5 years. Nevertheless, these self-selected students in private schools (experimental group) were then matched on gender, ethnicity, age, Wechsler Intelligence Scale for Children–Revised (WISC-R) (Wechsler, 1974), Full Scale IQ, and SES to 49 students who had remained in public schools (control group). These 49 students were enrolled in 47 different public high schools. The two matched groups each consisted of 24 females and 25 males, with 30 Anglos, 10 Hispanics, and 9 blacks in each group.

Measures

Near graduation from high school, the 98 students took special achievement tests consisting of reading and mathematics sections of the Stanford Test of Academic Skills (TASK). The WISC-R was administered to students in 1972 by school psychologists (Dr. Jane Mercer had permission from the publishers of the WISC-R to use it in her study before it was available to the public). The SES measure used was developed by Duncan (Reiss, 1961), and classifies occupations on a scale from chronically unemployed (0) to high level professional (9) on the basis of education, skill, and responsibility.

Results

Table 1 presents the means and standard deviations on the SES, age, and IQ measures for private and public school students when they were matched on data obtained in 1972.

It can be seen that the mean difference in SES was slightly in favor of the children attending private schools. However, the difference was not statistically significant ($t = .69$, $df = 48$, $p > .05$). Also, the mean difference in age between the two groups was not significant ($t = .12$, $df = 48$, $p > .05$). Finally, and most important, the mean difference in IQ for the private and public school pupils was so close that there was no statistically significant difference ($t = .39$, $df = 48$, $p > .05$). Thus our matching of the two groups was quite close, necessitating the use of t tests for matched groups.

Table 2 presents the means and standard deviations on the reading and mathematics tests administered in 1982 to the private and public school groups. It can be seen that the mean reading score for the students from the private and from the public schools could not have been closer. Thus, a t test on the mean differences was obviously unnecessary. The mean score on the mathematics test was slightly higher in this instance for the private sector. However, the mean difference was far from being statistically significant ($t = .07$, $df = 48$, $p > .05$).

Discussion

In this study the variables SES, gender, age, ethnicity, and general ability (total IQ) were carefully controlled in an effort to determine the "pure" effects of private versus public schooling on academic achievement. By matching pairs of students in the two groups early in their school careers on all of those variables, we tried to eliminate as much as possible the influences discussed by Page and Keith (1981): general ability and family background. As a result, the achievement test data collected about 10 years later led us to the conclusion that private and public schooling has (on the average) about the same influence on academic achievement (reading and mathematics). Remember that originally Page and Keith, and recently Wallberg and Shanahan (1983), argued against the conclusion of Cole-

TABLE 1 Means and Standard Deviations for SES, Age, and IQ for Private and Public School Students

Measures	Private		Public	
	M	SD	M	SD
SES	5.80	2.29	5.55	3.10
Age	8.10	5.23	8.02	4.79
IQ	101.00	15.49	101.26	14.53

TABLE 2 Means and Standard Deviations for Reading and Mathematics Raw Scores for Private and Public School Students

Test	*Private*		*Public*	
	M	SD	M	SD
Reading	33.10	9.80	33.10	10.45
Math	30.12	10.68	30.00	10.88

man et al. (1981) that student achievement was higher in private than in public schools. However, for the record, Coleman (1981) did admit that "one should not make a mistake: our estimates for the size of the private-sector effects show them not to be large" (p. 19), even when not controlling for ability level between the two sectors. Furthermore, Coleman et al. (1981) also admitted that "despite extensive statistical controls on parental background, there may very well be other unmeasured factors in the self-selection into the private sector that are associated with high achievement," possibly general ability or total IQ. Nevertheless, Coleman et al. (1981) and Page and Keith (1981) indicated that private schools have more homework and better classroom discipline. Because homework and discipline relate to the amount of time on academic tasks, and time on task relates to achievement, we certainly could expect that students in the private sector would do better in achievement than students in the public sector. Because they did not, it seems that the public schools are doing something right (e.g., good teaching, better teaching materials, etc.). Also, it is well recognized that parents who send their children to private schools not only can afford it financially, but obviously value education highly and prepare their children well for school. The resulting motivation and preparation should bring about higher academic achievement scores for private than for public school children even if the quality of instruction for the two sectors was equal. Because private school children did not have higher achievement scores in this study, it appears again that the public schools are able to hold their own, despite having to enroll any student (good or bad) in their residential area and having to offer a wider range of courses (i.e., in various vocations). However, in the final analysis this whole argument boils down to which public or private school you are talking about and at what time. As Cronbach (1981) pointed out, the question is similar to whether one gets better food at home or at a restaurant: It depends on the home and the restaurant. Because a large number of private and public schools were involved in this study, our result should be fairly representative of a large number of private and public schools, at least in California.

What implications, if any, can be inferred from our study? If parents want a certain kind of environment, or even a certain kind of education (e.g., one less secular), private schools may be worth the cost. Speaking of costs, if the taxpayers wish to contribute to this cost by either tuition tax credits or educational vouchers (because of the savings in public school funds when children attend private schools), is a matter for debate by lawmakers and the public. But the results of this study indicate that this decision should revolve around financial reasons, and should *not* rest on the claim that private schools necessarily effect higher achievement. What little higher achievement private schools may bring about appears to be the result of self-selection on SES and ability, not of truly important, large differences in academic achievement.

We wish to thank Jane Mercer and Richard Figueroa for making possible the use of data collected for the SOMPA project, and Donald Arnstine, Carl Spring, and Dona Brandon for reviewing our manuscript.

References

Coleman, J. (1981). Response to Page and Keith, *Educational Researcher, 10,* 18–20.

Coleman, J., Hoffer, T., & Kilgore, S. (1981, March). *Public and private schools: A report to the National Center for Education Statistics by the National Opinion Research Center.* Chicago: University of Chicago.

Cronbach, L. J. (1981, April). *Comments on the NORC study.* Paper presented at the annual meeting of the American Educational Research Association, Los Angeles.

Mercer, J. R., & Lewis, J. F. (1978). *System of multicultural pluralistic assessment.* New York: Psychological Corporation.

Page, E., & Keith, T. (1981). Effects of U.S. private schools: A technical analysis of two recent claims. *Educational Researcher, 10,* 7–17.

Reiss, A. J., Jr. (1961). *Occupations and social status.* New York: Free Press.

Walberg, H. J., & Shanahan, T. (1983). High school effects on individual students. *Educational Researcher, 12,* 4–9.

Wechsler, D. (1974). *Wechsler Intelligence Scale for Children* (Revised). New York: Psychological Corporation.

Strong Black Girls:
A Ten Year Old Responds to Fiction about Afro-Americans

Rudine Sims

My friend Osula, at almost 11, was an avid reader. While a few months earlier she had been "into science fiction, and read a lot of science fiction about time lines and stuff like that," her interests had changed: "I like fiction, but I read a lot of books about Black girls: that's my first choice."

Our interests coincided. Having just completed a study of children's literature about Afro-Americans (Sims, 1982) which contends that such literature is essential to the educational and psychological well-being of both Black and White children in this nation, I saw an opportunity for Osula to help me begin to understand whether such literature is as important to Black children, in their own view, as I think it is. Further, it was an opportunity to try to discern what elements or factors in literature about Afro-Americans might be appealing to children, as well as those that might turn them away from such literature.

Accordingly, this paper reports on an interview with Osula in which she discusses her reactions and responses to books about Afro-Americans. The interview is placed in the context of the research on response as it relates to such books, and of an analysis of the content of 150 books of contemporary realistic fiction about Afro-Americans. While the interview itself constitutes only a tentative preliminary to a study of response, it does raise some issues and does give rise to questions which might be explored in further research.

Research Evidence on Response

In general, two arguments are given in support of demands for the inclusion of authentic Afro-American experience in children's literature. The first is that the exclusion of Afro-Americans from literature, or the inclusion of negative stereotypes and subtle racism is harmful to Black and White children alike. Black children are denied their basic humanity and human dignity, and White children are fed the poison of racism and presented a false picture of the world and their place in it. The second argument, the positive side of the coin, is that books have the power to promote favorable attitudes and foster positive behaviors on the part of their readers.

Sims, Rudine. (1983). Strong black girls: A ten year old responds to fiction about Afro-Americans. *Journal of Research and Development in Education, 16*(3), 21–28.

Providing empirical support for these arguments has proved to be a difficult and complex task. Surveys and content analyses such as those by Larrick (1965) and Broderick (1973) have documented both the historical near-exclusion of Black characters, and the negative images and stereotypes presented when Black characters did appear. Other studies (see below) have examined the effectiveness of books or stories about Blacks in changing attitudes or self-concepts. This latter set of studies provides support for the argument that books can have a positive effect on readers' attitudes towards themselves and others.

As early as 40 years ago, Jackson (1944) exposed White adolescents to a set of books which portrayed Blacks in a favorable light. She found that, following experience with the books, the experimental group showed more positive attitudes towards Blacks than a control group. Reviews of more recent research also indicate, though not unquestioningly, that literature has an effect on its readers' attitudes. Campbell and Wirtenberg (1980) state unequivocally that books can make a difference, and cite 12 studies in which exposure to "multicultural" materials, i.e., books which portrayed Blacks and other people of color in a positive manner, had a positive effect on children's self-concepts, academic achievement, or attitudes toward so-called minorities.

Monson and Peltola (1976) cite several dissertation studies which examined the effects of books about Blacks on the attitudes and responses of children. The results are mixed. For example, Frankel (1972), Woodyard (1970), and Hayes (1969) all report positive results, i.e., enhanced feelings of self worth or more positive attitudes towards another race. Lancaster (1971), Brewbaker (1972) and Walker (1972), on the other hand, obtained results that were generally inconclusive, or indicated no significant effects from exposure to materials about Blacks.

In a very comprehensive and analytical review of research in response to literature, Purves and Beach (1972) give cautious credence to the contention that reading can change attitudes. While they cite evidence that attitudes can change as a result of reading, they also cite evidence that such changes may be relatively short-lived. In the section of their review which focuses on studies of "preconceptions and their effects on response," Purves and Beach draw three conclusions which are relevant to the present discussion: (a) Readers find interesting that which is related to their personal experience; (b) readers seek characters and works with which they can identify and become more involved with that which is related to them: and (c) readers tend to judge most favorably characters who most resemble them.

Response to What?

Given those conclusions, then, Osula's preference for books about Black girls is not at all surprising. However, only in the past decade and a half has there been available a relatively large body of realistic fiction about contemporary Afro-American children and adolescents. As recently as 1965, Larrick noted that the world of children's books was "all-White," with only 6.7% of books in her survey including even one Black character. Furthermore, only four fifths of 1% of the books in Larrick's survey dealt with contemporary children.

Fortunately, by 1980 the situation had improved sufficiently that it was possible to examine a sample of 150 books of contemporary realistic fiction about Afro-Americans published since 1965 (Sims, 1982). The analysis focused on discerning themes, patterns, values and images found in such books written for children from pre-school to about eighth grade. The analysis was guided by three questions which relate to three debatable issues concerning Afro-American children's literature: (a) Who is the primary projected audience for books about Afro-American children? (b) How is the concept of a unique Afro-American experience defined and dealt with? (c) From what socio-cultural perspective have the books been written?

On the basis of those three questions, the books could be divided into three categories. In the first, the "social conscience" books, the primary audience appears to be White children. These books almost always involve Black-White conflict, often over desegregation of schools or neighborhoods. In the social conscience books, Afro-American experience is frequently viewed from a paternalistic height, and is seen as slightly exotic, "different," or humorous. The authors, none of whom were Afro-American, all wrote from an ethnocentric "outsider's" perspective. Many of these books seem to be a juvenile treatment of "The Black Problem."

The second group, the "melting pot" books were written for an integrated audience. Their distinguishing characteristic is that they ignore the existence of any uniqueness in the Afro-American experience, and present all characters as culturally homogeneous. Only illustrations indicate ethnicity; skin color is treated as a superficial difference: people are people are people. Many melting pot books involve the initiation or development of an interracial friendship. The perspective of the authors, most but not all of whom are White, is a kind of assimilationist middle-class one.

The third group, the "culturally conscious" books, deliberately set about to recreate a uniquely Afro-American experience, primarily for a Black audience. This is the largest subgroup, and includes a range of themes—from celebrating an African heritage, to common everyday experiences, to urban living, to the typical adolescent growing up story. Some of the culturally conscious books are more successful in reflecting Afro-American experience than others, since some are written from a much stronger base of knowledge and understanding of Afro-American culture than others; i.e., the authors' perspectives range from "ethnocentric outsider" to self-consciously Afro-American.

Since each subgroup displayed a characteristic set of recurring features which distinguished it from the other two, they could possibly provide a framework for analyzing readers' responses. In a formal study, one could try to ascertain, on the basis of readers' responses to those elements common to each category, whether any subset has greater or lesser appeal to child readers than any other. However, since the books Osula read were not pre-selected to permit such an analysis, it is possible only to speculate about whether her preferences were influenced by features identified in the Sims analysis.

Osula and the Books

Osula arrived for our interview with her unsolicited but welcome list of the books with Black characters she remembered reading in recent months. Her list included 30 books. In terms of the Sims analysis, 8 were melting pot books, 11 were culturally conscious books. Of the 11 others, 5 were realistic fiction not included in the Sims sample, and 6 were classified as other than realistic fiction, e.g., folk tales, fantasy, biography. The social conscience category was not represented on Osula's list.

The books on her list were written by 23 different authors. It was not possible to identify the ethnicity of all of them, but so far as is known, about half are Black. One author, Ezra Jack Keats, accounts for half the melting pot books on Osula's list. In light of the fact that most authors of melting pot books are White, it is interesting that two of her melting pot books were written by Black authors. The authors of the culturally conscious books on Osula's list were distributed ethnically in a manner similar to those in the Sims sample—two Black authors, Lucille Clifton and Mildred Taylor, account for approximately one third of the books, and about one fourth were written by White authors.

In addition to the books on Osula's list, we included in our discussion some books which had been pulled from the interviewer's library and displayed on the table at which we worked. This group did include a few social conscience books, although they were not discussed in any great depth. Mainly, the list and the table top library served to remind Osula of the books she had read and wanted to discuss.

The interview was conducted in my home over juice and cookies. Osula was at the time 10 years, 10 months old, and in fifth grade. She lives in a small New England college town where she attends one of the local public schools. She is precocious, verbal, a self-described "very good reader." She numbers several adults among her friends, and is generally relaxed, comfortable and outgoing in her conversations with them. After some initial anxiety about the tape recorder, she became quite relaxed, articulate and talkative. What follows is culled from an analysis of the typescript of that interview.

Bases for Selection

One of the most obvious and yet possibly overlooked factors in determining Osula's and other Black children's choice of reading matter about Afro-Americans may be the availability of such books. She relies on her school library, her local public library, and family and friends as sources of books to read. Clearly the extensiveness of Osula's reading list is due in part to her family's conscientious effort to provide suitable reading matter for her. It was her mother's requests for recommendations that drew my attention to Osula's strong interest in books about Black girls. She is apparently also influenced by her peer group: she exchanges books with friends and, at the time of the interview, shared her preference with one of her friends. (The friend was unavailable for interviewing.) Both were seeking books about Black girls.

As it is, Osula's list is largely composed of books written between 1970 and 1980, though at least seven (23%) were published before 1970. Since no effort was made to pinpoint the source of each book on the list, it is not possible to know to what to attribute the relative paucity of newer books. However, there are indications that fewer books about Blacks are being published today than in the 1970's.

Osula's responses to my questions about her preferences conform to the expectations generated by Purves and Beach that she would seek books related to her personal experiences, and characters with whom she could identify. Her prime criterion, as has been pointed out, was "books about Black girls." Thus she affirmed a desire to see and read about people like herself. Not only was this evident in the fact that she chose so many female characters, e.g., Beth Lambert (*Philip Hall Likes Me. I Reckon Maybe*, Greene, 1974), Louretta Hawkins (*The Soul Brothers and Sister Lou*, Hunter, 1968), Ludell (*Ludell*, Wilkinson, 1975), Justice (*Justice and Her Brothers*, Hamilton, 1978), but also in one of her comments about Virginia Hamilton's character Zeely:

> I like that a lot. I've been reading it over and over again.
> I like the way they describe her. She must have been so pretty.

Zeely, who helps her father raise pigs, is described this way by Hamilton (*Zeely*, 1967):

> *Zeely Tabor was more than six and a half feet tall, thin and deeply dark as a pole of Ceylon ebony. She wore a long smock that reached to her ankles. Her arms, hands and feet were bare, and her thin oblong head didn't seem to fit quite right on her shoulders. She had very high cheekbones and her eyes seemed turned inward on themselves. Geeder couldn't say what expression she saw on Zeely's face. She knew only that it was calm, that it had pride in it, and that the face was the most beautiful she had ever seen.* (p. 37)

Her strong favorable response to this decidedly African standard of beauty is an affirmation of Osula's identification with her own cultural heritage.

Osula also expressed a preference for reading about experiences which were similar to her own. She comments about *Daddy* (Caines, 1977):

> *Well, it was kind of like my own experience. Because when I still lived in Boston, I used to visit my father every weekend. Her father comes to pick her up just like my dad used to come and pick me up. So it was fun to remember that, because I can't see him every weekend now.*

And about *Cornrows* (Yarbrough, 1979):

> *. . . the thing that really got to me in that book was that I used to wear my hair like that. Like in a basket cornrow. When I went to my uncle's wedding I wore my hair like that.*

On the other hand, Osula welcomes the opportunity to stretch a bit, to live through in books experiences different from her own. At the end of a discussion of *The Soul Brothers and Sister Lou*, which is set in an inner city, Osula states:

> *I like reading stories about [Black] kids whose lives are different from mine. I like . . . to learn about their lives. That's why I like stories about when people were in the South and stuff.*

Her reference to the South relates to an earlier discussion of *Ludell*, and should be taken to mean "Black people living in the South." Thus Osula reaffirms her identification with Black characters, while at the same time expresses a recognition that the Black experience in the U.S. is a varied, rich source of stories.

Not only does Osula express a strong preference for characters who are Black and female, but she also likes her girls strong and active. Her clearest expression of this preference is in relation to Beth Lambert of *Philip Hall Likes Me. I Reckon Maybe*:

> *I like all the things she does. Like all the things she beats him [Philip Hall] in, and she rescues him when he's on the mountain and stuff like that.*

And a bit later:

> *I look for people like Ludell and Beth Lambert. I like girls who are strong. They know what they're doing.*

Osula's second stated criterion for book selection is humor: "I like to read books about Black people that are funny." (It is clear from her intonation that it is the books that are to be funny, not the people.) Her examples of books and elements that she found funny indicate that she responds to the humor in situations. She mentioned as funny *Mojo and the Russians* (Myers, 1977), in which a group of teenagers try to "un-mojo" Dean, who they believe has been "fixed" by a woman with whom he'd collided while riding his bicycle: "I gonna make his tongue split like a lizard's and his eyes to cross . . . I'm gonna fix him for good. Make his monkey ears fall off!" (p. 9). Another example was *The Twins Strike Back* (Flournoy, 1980), in which twin girls devise a way to exact revenge on the people who are continually confusing one with the other.

From her more mature vantage point, Osula also found amusing the behavior of fictional characters younger than herself, such as Peter's attempt to preserve a snowball in his pocket in *The Snowy Day* (Keats, 1962), or Desire Tate's exasperation with her family's apparent failure to remember their promises in *Don't You Remember?* (Clifton, 1973).

Osula also identified language and illustrations as elements to which she sometimes responds favorably. She mentioned liking the pictures in *The Snowy Day*, apparently a purely aesthetic response: "I like the pictures because I like the way he goes out in the snow. He has a snowsuit and everything. I like those pictures." Her mention of the snow and snowsuit, which is bright red, may be an indication that Osula responds favorably to Keats' use of contrasting colors and collage. The other illustrations Osula mentioned were the drawings in *Cornrows* of recognizable Black heroes, e.g., Malcolm X and Lena Horne. My sense was that in *Cornrows*, it was the recognizable images to which she responded, rather than the purely aesthetic properties of the drawings themselves.

Osula mentioned language once spontaneously and once in a response to a specific question. In speaking of *Cornrows*, Osula said, "I like the way the Grandmother speaks in poems. I like the way they sing to them, and tell in their songs and poems about cornrows." Thus it appears that the lyrical, rhythmical, poetic use of language that is a major feature of the book was an important factor in Osula's response.

The question was my attempt to discover how she dealt with language clearly different from her own. In books with Black characters, authors frequently use phonetic spellings, "eye dialect," to indicate how the language of the characters would sound to the ear. This is the case in *Ludell* (Wilkinson, 1975), which represents the speech of Black people in Waycross, Georgia. The following is a sample of Ludell's grandmother's speech:

> *Naw, mostly I got Mr. Henley's white shirts to do . . . Rich as they is, you'd thank he'd send them thangs to the cleaners! You gone play—but don't git carried away and let the street lights catch you out there again. If you aine here 'fore dark, I'm gone come beat you rat there in front of everybody—you hear? (p. 13)*

"What do you think of the language in *Ludell*?" I asked Osula.

> *Well, sometimes I had to since I don't speak that way, I had to say it. So, I'd be saying it, reading out loud and people would say, "Can't you read to yourself?" But I can't because I couldn't understand it written down. Some of the words I couldn't understand. I had to ask my mother what they meant.*

The dialect spelling apparently caused some problem, but some other factor, perhaps the story line or the character of Ludell, inspired Osula to use the best available strategies for handling the unfamiliar language—reading it aloud, and asking someone who knew.

While Osula focused our conversation on books she had liked, with some probing she was also willing to discuss some things she disliked. In response to the question of whether she had read any books about Blacks which she had not liked, she named *The Legend of Africania* (Robinson, 1974). While she stated that she did not know why she did not like it, she proceeded to describe the plot ("I can tell you what it's about"). Her description of "what it's about" indicates that the story is an allegorical tale of Africans being forcibly taken to the New World, enslaved, denied a socio-cultural heritage, and recreated in the images of their captors. It is not clear whether Osula's negative response is to the allegorical nature of the story, or is related to the plot line; i.e., she dislikes the idea of the negation of Africania's self image.

> *She has to straighten her hair and make her skin white. I just didn't like it. And she couldn't laugh and dance and play. She just had to be straight like he did, and do everything he did. I didn't like it.*

The possibility that Osula's response is to the story line rather than the style or form is supported by her earlier unsolicited comment about being offended (her word) by the killing of the innocent young man in *The Soul Brothers and Sister Lou*. It is apparently a response to the event as the author describes it rather than to the story as a literary creation.

Osula's other negative response was to *Nobody's Family Is Going To Change* (Fitzhugh, 1974). Her first characterization of the book was. "[I like it] sort of. But it was kind of strange to me." My attempt to clarify "strange" led to her characterization of the book as "not interesting."

> *It's not a book that you pick up and you can't put down, like* Mojo and the Russians. . . . *When she's [Emma] talking and she's imagining she's a lawyer, it was boring. . . . But to me, she [Louise Fitzhugh] writes boring books. I didn't like* Harriet the Spy, *either.*

Further probing led to the idea that the book fails the "reality test"—"It's not like anybody's family is like that."

In summary, it appears that, in her reading of literature about Afro-Americans, Osula responded positively to: (a) experiences which related to her own, (b) distinctly Afro-American cultural experiences, (c) Black female characters with whom she could identify, (d) characters who were strong, active, clever, (e) humorous situations, (f) lyrical language, (g) aesthetically pleasing illustrations. She responded unfavorably to books she considered boring, with easily predictable plots or unrealistic characters; and to events in which Black characters are denied human dignity or treated unjustly.

Discussion and Implications

This conversation with one loquacious 10-year old raises some interesting issues for discussion, and points to some possible areas needing future research. One of the issues it raises is whether or not, when Black children seek characters with whom they can identify—people like themselves—such characters can be found.

While Chall, Radwin, French and Hall (1979) declared that by 1975 the percentages of books including Black characters had doubled, there are reports that fewer such books are being published currently than in the 70's (Myers, 1979; Walter & Volc, 1980). Thus Black children may be denied access to just those books that could provide important self-affirmation and possibly create lifetime reading habits.

Whether or not such books are being published in adequate numbers, there is an apparent problem, demonstrated by Osula's mother's search for appropriate books, in finding books about Blacks in bookstores. Two assumptions seem to operate. One is that the market for books about Blacks is exclusively a Black market (no pun intended). Therefore bookstores in small New England college towns with small Black populations need not stock such books. One counter to this assumption is, of course, that while Black characters are essential for Black children, they should not be limited solely to Black readers. Black children are not likely to read such books exclusively, partly because of the lack of availability; partly because, as the breadth of their reading expands, they will want to read genres in which few Black children appear, e.g., fantasy and science fiction; and partly because such books will become a base on which they will build their experiences of reading about people who both share their human characteristics and who are unlike them in many ways. So, too, non-Black children, who find ample self-affirmation in children's literature, need in their fiction to see the world reflected in all its diversity, as well as to confirm the universality of human experience.

A second assumption appears to be that, even where a large Black population exists, books about Blacks are not likely to sell. On a visit to a downtown New Orleans bookstore in 1981, Lucille Clifton and I were not only unable to locate any of her books, but found *Little Black Sambo* to be almost the only book by or about Blacks available in the large children's section. (We later discovered a display advertising Bill Cosby's "Fat Albert" books.) This situation may be related to the traditional tendency of publishers of children's books to rely on institutional markets rather than bookstores, but that situation is changing. Nevertheless, in the case of books about Blacks, a cycle is created. Unsuccessful searches lead to abandoning the quest, which in turn leads to low sales and a subsequent lack of availability.

Osula's preference for Black characters was complicated by her preference for female characters as well. In the Sims survey of realistic fiction about Blacks, only 37% of the books featured a girl as the major character. Fortunately, although there is variation in their characterizations and not all are positive, generally the females are portrayed as active, resourceful, intelligent, capable of solving problems, resolving conflicts, or acquiring important insights about life and living. In any case, Osula's expressed preferences point to a need for the continued publication of authentic books about Afro-American children. Apparently they meet a need that goes unanswered when the world of children's books is all White.

A second issue is the extent to which a reader's preferences and responses to books relate to needs that arise from the developmental stage in which a reader finds herself. "Developmental stage" is probably too rigid a concept to apply accurately to any individual child at any given moment. However, one can reasonably expect that a child in the "middle childhood" years (7 to 12) will display psychological characteristics common to children of approximately the same age. These characteristics might then partly explain or predict the preferences and responses that "middle age" children might express in relation to the books they read. In Osula's case, the influence of her developmental phase is probably most apparent in her preference for female rather than male characters, as well as in her preference for characters who are "strong" and "know what they're doing."

Schlager (1978) used a developmental approach in an attempt to explain why children appeared, based on circulation figures, to enjoy certain Newbery Award winners, and to reject others. She found that the popular books presented an identifiable stage of development in which the main characters (a) coped successfully with difficult "reality situations" without adult assistance, (b) demonstrated the skills and ability to successfully carry out tasks and create items they had envisioned in their planning, (c) differentiated between that which could and could not be controlled in their environment and exercised control when necessary, and (d) made moral decisions to which the readers could relate. Schlager's description provides a ready explanation for Osula's preference for Ludell, Louretta, Beth, and even Mayer's (1976) Liza Lou. It may also help explain her dislike for The *Legend of Africania,* since Africania apparently displays none of those characteristics.

In the case of Black children responding to books about Black children, there is a related developmental question. Osula's expressed preference for such books was prefaced by her statement that she had recently been "into science fiction." That raises the issue of whether there is a particular time in the lives of young Black readers when their developing sense of cultural group identity points to a strong need for books about people in their own cultural group. Osula's reading of such books had clearly not been limited to the period just before our interview, but her conscious seeking of them, and her expressed preference for them may well have been a function of her psychological stage of development. It is not clear, however, whether, had she not been exposed to such books all her reading life, she would even have been aware of the possible choices available to her at 10.

Galda (1982) suggests that development will also have an influence on the relative maturity of the response itself. She asserts, after Britton, that a mature reader must assume a "spectator stance," i.e., to delay judgment until the completion of the work, and at that point to evaluate the text in relation to the artistic universe the author has created. However, this "spectator stance" may be particularly difficult to achieve when reading "Afro-American" literature in which the artistic universe which is supposedly a reflection of Afro-American reality is distorted. Thus, it becomes important in assessing and describing children's response to Afro-American literature to examine the content of the literature. There is a possibility that to achieve a "spectator stance" in responding to literature which violates not merely one's sense of whether the events portrayed could really happen, but one's very perspective on the world, requires more maturity than even most adults can muster.

A third and related issue is the extent to which the unique characteristics of Afro-American children's literature appeal to young readers, especially young Black readers. Adults who write, elect and buy such literature frequently seek to inculcate particular values and attitudes, or to provide self-affirmation. To the extent that Afro-American culture and experience are unique, books that reflect that culture and experience may focus on elements and factors not emphasized in books about other life experiences. According to the Sims analysis, Black authors tend to focus on the following: Afro-American heritage and history; pride in one's blackness; a strong sense of community; warm human relationships, especially within the family; a sense of continuity; and the will and strength to survive oppression and other hardship. Within these themes, the authors tend to emphasize or include authentic Black language, both in terms of syntax and vocabulary, and in terms of communication style.

A recounting of the factors Osula professed to like about her books suggests that the elements that Black authors tend to stress can coincide with children's preferences. Most obviously, Osula's desire to read about people like herself, and about experiences like hers can probably only be met by such books. Surely her desire to read about Black experiences which are unlike her own can be met only if there is available a variety of books which present the full range of Afro-American experience with all its commonality as well as its diversity. Books which focus on survival will by their very nature, feature strong characters, though they may not necessarily be female. And books which feature Black communication styles will also include humor, since linguistic humor has long been one of the survival strategies of Afro-Americans.

The final issue raised by the conversation with Osula is the limited quantity and applicability of available research on response, particularly the response of elementary school children. A review of the literature reveals that, historically, studies of response to literature have centered on adolescents or college students; only recently has attention turned to elementary school-age students. This focus on older students may have been an artifact of the frequent use of such measuring instruments as questionnaires, scales, or written responses, which require a certain maturity or skill in writing. There has also been a tendency, in studies of expressed response, for researchers to focus their analyses on developing schemes for classifying and categorizing responses. Such schemes may be useful descriptors, but do not necessarily help us understand either the content of the responses or the factors which led to them.

Hickman (1981) has pointed out the shortcomings of this research as it applies to elementary school-age children: its failure to take account of responses beyond the initial or immediate ones, its reliance on verbal responses and consequent ignoring of important and relevant non-verbal responses, and the effect of the research procedure itself on children's responses; that is, the failure to study spontaneous, unsolicited responses. Hickman points to ethnographic [perspective-seeking, qualitative] research techniques as one means to discover and class-ify children's responses to literature.

With the increasing use and sophisticated application of naturalistic research in studying child language development, future researchers may find children's responses to Afro-American literature a fertile area for study. The following are a few of the possible questions that could be explored:

1. Assuming that the categories of books about Blacks—social conscience, melting pot, culturally conscious—are themselves tenable, do children's responses vary according to those categories?

2. Is there an optimum age at which it is especially important for Black children to have Black literature available to them?

3. Does exposure over time make a difference, i.e., when children have been exposed to Black literature as an integral part of their reading experience, do they respond differently from those with limited and experimental exposure?

4. Do Black and non-Black children respond to the same elements in Black fiction?

5. To what extent are children's responses affected by those themes, values, and images which are unique to or especially emphasized in Afro-American literature?

Fifteen years ago there probably was not a sufficient body of Afro-American children's literature to attempt to answer these questions. Perhaps now we can begin to wonder what might be the effects of having produced a body of literature in which Osula can find her strong Black girls, literature in which the Osula's of this country can, in the words of the untitled David McCord (1961) limerick (from the front of *Take Sky*) "be enchanted, enthralled; be the caller, the called; the singer, the song, and the sung."

References

Brewbaker, J. M. (1972). *The relationship between the race of characters in a literary selection and the literary responses of Negro and white adolescent readers.* Unpublished doctoral dissertation, University of Virginia.

Broderick, D. M. (1973). *The image of the Black in children's fiction.* New York: R. R. Bowker.

Caines, J. (1977). *Daddy.* New York: Harper and Row.

Campbell, P. B., & Wirtenberg, J. (1980). How books influence children: What the research shows. *Bulletin on Interracial Books for Children, 2*(6), 3–6.

Chall, J., Radwin, E., French, V., & Hall, C. (1979). Blacks in the world of children's books. *The Reading Teacher, 32,* 527–33.

Clifton, L. (1973). *Don't you remember?* New York: E. P. Dutton.

Fitzhugh, L. (1974). *Nobody's family is going to change.* New York: Farrar, Strauss and Giroux.

Flournoy, V. (1980). *The twins strike back.* New York: Dial Press.

Frankel, H. L. (1972). *The effects of reading The Adventures of Huckleberry Finn on the racial attitudes of selected ninth grade boys.* Unpublished doctoral dissertation, Temple University.

Galda, L. (1982). Assuming the spectator stance: An examination of the responses of three young readers. *Research in the Teaching of English, 16*(1), 1–20.

Greene, B. (1974). *Philip Hall likes me. I reckon maybe.* New York: Dial Press.

Hamilton, V. (1967). *Zeely.* New York: Macmillan.

Hamilton, V. (1978). *Justice and her brothers.* New York: Greenwillow Books.

Hayes, M. T. (1969). *An investigation of the impact of reading on attitudes of racial prejudice.* Unpublished doctoral dissertation, Boston University.

Hickman, J. (1981). A new perspective on response to literature: Research in an elementary school setting. *Research in the Teaching of English, 15*(4), 343–354.

Hunter, K. (1968). *The soul brothers and sister Lou.* New York: Charles Scribner's Sons.

Jackson, E. (1944). Effects of reading upon attitudes toward the Negro race. *Library Quarterly, 14*, 52–53.

Keats, E. J. (1962). *The snowy day.* New York: Viking Press.

Lancaster, J. W. (1971). *An investigation of the effect of books with Black characters on the racial preferences of white children.* Unpublished doctoral dissertation, Boston University.

Larrick, N. (1965). The all-white world of children's books. Saturday Review, II, 63–65; 84–85.

Mayer, M. (1976). *Lisa Lou and the yeller belly swamp.* New York: Parents' Magazine Press.

McCord, D. (1961). *Take sky.* Boston: Little, Brown and Company.

Monson, D., & Peltola, D. (1976). *Research in children's literature: An annotated bibliography.* Newark, Del.: International Reading Association.

Myers, W. D. (1977). *Mojo and the Russians.* New York: Viking Press.

Myers, W. D. (1979). The Black experience in children's books: One step forward, two steps back. *Bulletin on Interracial Books for Children, 10*, 14–15.

Purves, A., & Beach, R. (1972). *Literature and the reader: Research in response to literature, reading interests, and the teaching of literature.* Urbana, Ill.: National Council of Teachers of English.

Robinson, D. (1974). *The legend of Africania.* Chicago: Johnson Publications.

Schlager, N. (1978). Predicting children's choices in literature: A developmental approach. *Children's Literature in Education, 9*(3), 136–142.

Sims, R. (1982). *Shadow and substance: Afro-American experience in contemporary children's fiction.* Urbana, Ill.: National Council of Teachers of English.

Walker, P. (1972). *The effects of hearing selected children's stories that portray Blacks in a favorable manner on the racial attitudes of groups of Black and white kindergarten children.* Unpublished doctoral dissertation, University of Kentucky.

Walter, M. P., & Volc, J. (1980). What's ahead for the Black writer? *Publisher's Weekly, 25*, 90–92.

Wilkinson, B. (1975). *Ludell.* New York: Harper and Row.

Woodyward, M. A. (1970). *The effects of teaching Black literature to a ninth grade class in a Negro high school in Picayune, Mississippi.* Unpublished doctoral dissertation, University of Tennessee.

Yarbrough, C. (1979). *Cornrows.* New York: Coward, McCann and Geohegan.

Chapter 4

Research Designs

Truth-seeking research and its frequent use of statistical methodology is a tradition in education. Thus, the concept of design in research books is often associated with gathering and analyzing data. In this chapter we have broadened the discussion by outlining the steps you might go through that precede and therefore guide your study: the selection of a topic; rationale and background for the study; formulation of question(s) or hypothesis(es); and identification of subjects or participants and other sources of data (Chapter 5); and analysis of data (Chapter 6). Because sources of data are discussed in Chapter 5, here we will only touch on the topic. This chapter also introduces, compares, and contrasts variations of design as they relate to the different philosophical combinations of studies. A conceptual explanation of data analysis appears in Chapter 6.

Your design can be chosen by considering several options, but the most important determinant is your goal: Do you want to make generalizations (truth-seeking) about persons or events not in the study or do you wish to make statements about one person or group in the particular context being studied (perspective-seeking)?

Sometimes, research investigations are related specifically to a topic or academic field and are better suited to the perspective- or truth-seeking views of the world. For example, anthropological research often deals with data other than numbers, which can only be understood and interpreted within their context. Thus, the perspective-seeking approach would be warranted. Conversely, an inquiry in educational psychology to determine the effects of a certain lesson on students' attitudes most probably would be cast in a truth-seeking mold (see Chapter 1). Research with different views of the world can be conducted within the same academic field, however. (See the Firestone reading in Chapter 2 for a discussion of a truth-seeking quantitative and a perspective-seeking qualitative study, both of which focus on the same topic and seek to answer similar questions.)

Selection of a Topic

At first, selecting a topic may seem overwhelming. Where do you begin? Although, eventually, your research must transcend your own personal and professional interests (as we will explain later in more detail), initially the idea for most research projects derives from an individual's personal and professional experiences. For example, Bar-On (1991), an Israeli psychologist who worked with survivors of German Nazi death camps was intrigued with the survivors' efforts to "normalize" their traumatic experiences, especially with regard to how they related the experiences, if at all, to their children. What intrigued him more, however, was how the children of the German perpetrators viewed their parents' pasts. His research asks the question: How do adult children of the perpetrators deal with the reality of what their parents did to Jews and other "enemies" of the Third Reich? It would seem that through his research he is looking for ways to bridge the gap between enemies from another era, and, perhaps, he is also looking for peace within himself.

Rationale and Background

Irrespective of your personal interests, eventually your research project should begin with a conceptual perspective. For example, do not begin your rationale by saying, "As an administrator I have had problems controlling tenured teachers, therefore I wish to investigate the efficacy of tenure." Rather, begin with a discussion of the concept of tenure throughout the United States. Perhaps you might want to trace its historical origins and then find scholars whose research has both criticized and applauded the practice. Your discussion should then indicate the need for further research either to augment existing theory (truth-seeking) or to generate new theory (perspective-seeking). You will probably find it easier to defend the need for a study when you can locate a readily identifiable theory base in need of augmentation. For example, the Sassenrath et al. reading in Chapter 3 begins with reference to theory about positive effects on academic achievement associated with attendance at private schools.

The conceptualization of the Vaughn and Liles reading at the end of this chapter provides another example. Liles has been a history teacher all of his adult life. He has chosen this field despite the fact that many friends have derided his small salary and relative lack of professional prestige. As a historian, Liles, therefore, was drawn to study turn-of-the-twentieth century male teachers, because at that time a smaller percentage of males to the total number of teachers were in classrooms than at any other time in the history of American education. After selecting the topic, Liles and Vaughn shifted their focus from Liles's personal and professional orientation to other scholars' work on the topic. They found little research that specifically focused on male teachers, and most historians' statements about men's motivations to teach were speculative. Thus, the authors designed a study with a somewhat perspective-seeking view of the world. Although the work does subject the historical assumptions to scrutiny, it does not emanate from a theory base established by research studies focused on the topic of male teachers. It therefore generates many more questions than it answers.

The Aagaard reading illustrates how, in the absence of an established theory, you might construct a rationale. The author does not include a review of literature (theory from which a hypothesis is created). Rather, a simple question is posed: Why did the Bagby Human Resources Center fail to fulfill its intended purpose? However, the study is couched within a conceptual framework that explains how it "may retroactively explicate the failure of similar community projects attempted in the past, and thus, as a bad example help provide a better foundation for future community education projects of this sort." Aagaard goes on to note that the research will examine the Bagby facility from sociological and psychological perspectives, tracking the concept and growth of an institution and the motivations of Byers, its founder. Near the end of the prospectus Aagaard offers three theory bases to which her findings may contribute or that may help her interpret the data she collects and thereby help to answer the research question.

Formulation of Question(s) or Hypothesis(es)

The development of the rationale will argue for and lead into a statement of questions or hypotheses. Unlike a question, which could have any number of answers, the hypothesis is a statement that the research project will or will not verify. At this point you should be aware that a truth- or perspective-seeking approach should frame your study. Because theory-driven studies rely on already established facts in a given field, this type of research usually contains a hypothesis or expectation for which existing theory suggests a tentative answer. For example, when selecting a topic of interest and reading works related to it, you may encounter concerns that inherent ideological biases are present in much of the literature or that major portions of a field concerning individual perceptions has been generated from instruments that are questionable. Then it would seem logical to conduct perspective-seeking research that begins anew to look at an issue. For instance, Gilligan (1982) criticized Kohlberg's typology of moral development because it was created solely from male subjects. Therefore, Gilligan developed her own typology by generating perceptions of morality by women. Her work was then criticized for using white (Euro-American) women and making broad statements about the differences between male and female definitions of morality (Kerber et al., 1986). Because of the polemical nature of the theory on moral development, you might design a perspective-seeking study that begins anew with a distinct, selective population of individuals and asks: What are the participants' perceptions of morality in given situations?

Other, less controversial knowledge bases may have been so exhaustively researched from any number of perspectives that there are only fine details to clarify. The choice to accept the truth of this knowledge and then to proceed deductively might seem warranted. For example, the conservation tasks on which much of Piaget's theory of mental development is based, have, with few exceptions, withstood many tests. The tasks (conservation of length, mass, and quantity) have been used extensively to confirm not only various aspects of Piaget's theory, but also as possible indicators of such phenomena as reading readiness and problem-solving abilities (Piaget, 1969).

Identifying Subjects, Participants, and Other Sources of Data

The next consideration in the research process is how you decide what information is necessary to answer a particular research question. Each inquiry will lead to a number of archival collections or samples of people from whom you obtain data. (See Chapter 5 for more information about sources of data.) For example, in addition to retrieving numerous documents chronicling the history of the Bagby center, Aagaard noted that she would interview the founder and other people involved in conceiving of and chartering the facility. Also Aagaard proposed to interview some of the people for whom the center was intended and to observe at the building to determine its accessibility and utility to its clients. In short, Aagaard stated that she would gather data from a number of sources, all of which would provide her with the information needed to help answer the research question.

Vaughn and Liles went to the United States Census and other federal government reports to collect quantitative information that could help them evaluate the merit of the historical assumptions mentioned in their study. They obtained data on teachers in the forty-eight contiguous states and the District of Columbia so that they could then compute relative differences in the work patterns of men and conditions for teaching in the ten states that provided the nexus for their research.

Two other readings for this chapter, one by Palmieri and another by Franklin et al., exemplify how truth-seeking researchers create samples. Although the types of data and methods of analysis are different in each of these articles, in each case, a sample of people is used to answer the study's research question(s). Because Palmieri's study relies on qualitative data and methods, she presents and analyzes her sample of Wellesley College's female professors in historical context. The fourth graders who filled out the Piers-Harris Children's Self Concept Scale in the Franklin et al. piece provide the sample of subjects crucial to answering these authors' questions concerning the validity of the instrument.

Truth-Seeking Quantitative Designs

The primary purpose of employing a truth-seeking quantitative research design (involving participants in a series of measurement and potential intervention experiences) is to study the influential relationships between and among variables and to control for the influence of variables other than those of interest. Thus, the way participants are selected, assigned to groups (if it is a group

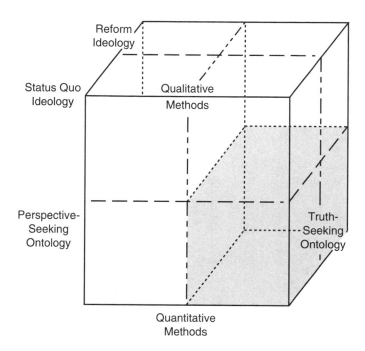

FIGURE 4.1 Truth-Seeking, Quantitative, Any Ideology

comparison study), assessed/measured, and exposed to interventions is very important and has a particular logic to it. The typical truth-seeking quantitative study is plotted on the cube in Figure 4.1. The Franklin et al. reading provides a specific example of truth-seeking quantitative research. It conducts a construct validity test of the Piers-Harris Children's Self Concept Scale and therefore reflects status quo elements. However, it also discusses an experiment done with the children to test the instrument and suggests a slightly reform stance when concluding that the scale is probably not appropriate for detecting changes in self-concept. The Franklin reading is plotted in Figure 4.2 on page 84.

True Experimental Designs

The classic truth-seeking quantitative design is that of the true experiment. Campbell and Stanley (1966) first articulated the true experimental design, as well as others, in their chapter in Gage's *Handbook of Research on Teaching* (1963). One of the true experimental designs is called the pretest-posttest control group design.

$$R\ O_1\ X\ O_2$$
$$R\ O_3\ \ \ O_4$$

This design requires random assignment (R) of subjects to experimental (X) and control groups. After assignment, both groups are pretested (O_1 and O_3) for the

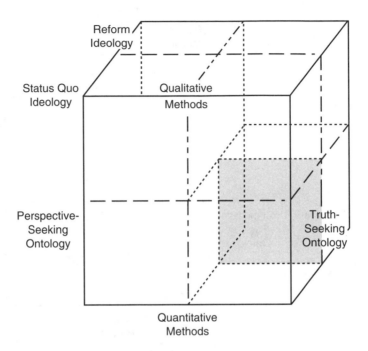

FIGURE 4.2   Franklin et al. (Truth-Seeking, Quantitative, Moderate)

variable being tested. The treatment (X) is applied to the experimental group and a posttest is given (O_2 and O_4). If the gain in scores ($O_2 - O_1$) and ($O_4 - O_3$), determined by a statistical test, is greater for the experimental group, the researcher has reason to believe that the treatment is at least associated with improved performance on the posttest.

An example illustrates this design in use. A music teacher is interested in the beneficial effects of children participating in dramatic activities. To test his hunch that positive effects will accrue to children who do participate in such activities— a hunch based on personal experience, research reports, and theoretical literature—he designs a study. He randomly assigns children from several classrooms to an experimental or a control group. After assignment, both groups are measured (pretest) for the variable being studied, for example, creativity. Then the treatment is applied to the experimental group, for example, participating in dramatic activities for six weeks. The control group does not participate in such activities, but, instead, reads about and discusses great composers. A final measurement is made after the treatment (posttest), and the scores of the two groups are compared. If the increase in scores (gain scores) of the experimental group is higher—determined by a statistical test—the experimenter has reason to believe that participation in dramatic activities benefits subjects' creativity.

Although the results in the above example may please the researcher—a subjective effect in the aftermath—every effort is made in the design and conduct of the study to be objective. As a truth-seeker, this researcher makes every effort to discover the objective truth. The use of test scores, in this case the scores on a test of creativity, is consistent with the effort to objectively test the hypothesis or expectation that participation in dramatic activities will positively affect children's creativity (as measured, at least, by the test). The ideology of this example is slightly reform oriented, assuming the researcher's initial interest was in challenging the status quo of no such dramatic activities. But, he was not, from this description, trying to dismantle the school curriculum or even necessarily wanting to argue for more time allocation to such activities. Therefore, the location on the ideology continuum would be only slightly toward reform and still within the status quo half.

Variations on the pretest-posttest control group design include the Solomon Four Group and the posttest-only control group design. The Solomon Four Group is symbolically represented as:

$$R \quad O_1 \quad X \quad O_2$$
$$R \quad O_3 \qquad O_4$$
$$R \qquad \quad X \quad O_5$$
$$R \qquad \qquad O_6$$

wherein there is random assignment (R) to groups; pretests (O_1 and O_3) for one experimental group and one control group; and no pretests for the other experimental and control groups. All of the groups receive a posttest (O_2, O_4, O_5 and O_6). The Solomon design is appropriate for instances when the pretests might sensitize subjects to the effects of the treatment (X). For example, a pretest on prejudicial feelings could sensitize members of the experimental group regarding such feelings and make the treatment appear "more effective" simply because of the sensitizing effect of the pretest and not necessarily because the treatment was more or less effective than some other treatment or control.

The posttest-only control group design is represented as:

$$R \quad X \quad O_1$$
$$R \qquad O_2$$

wherein random assignment to groups occurs but no pretest is given.

Single subject research, a design that is used often in special education settings, involves a single subject; observations for establishing a baseline of data; an intervention with continued observation; and then no intervention with continued observation. Symbolically, the single subject design can be portrayed as:

$$O \, O \, O \, O \, O \, X \, O \, O \, O \, O \, O$$

or as

$$A \, B \, A$$

wherein initial observations (O) establish a baseline (A), an intervention or treatment (X)(B) is introduced, and observations continue to see if subsequent behavior (A) is changed from the baseline. A variation of this A B A design is:

A B A B *or*

O O O O X O O O O X O O O O

wherein baseline data are recorded, a treatment occurs, observations continue and the treatment is reintroduced, followed by additional observation—all in an effort to determine if the intervention or treatment, and not some uncontrolled-for variable, can be legitimately linked to the changes in the subjects' behavior (see Tawney & Gast, 1984).

Truth-seeking quantitative designs represent attempts to control for variables that might account for observed differences in groups or individuals that are outside the realm of what the experimenter is studying. Uncontrolled-for variables (extraneous variables) erode the validity of research. Campbell and Stanley discuss eight threats to internal validity, that is, that the experiment is indeed testing what it intends to test and is not being affected by extraneous variables:

1. History—the occurrence of an event in the environment that is not part of the experiment. For example, in a study of several small high schools regarding student morale, one high school unexpectedly participates in the state basketball tournament. The results of the study would be confounded by the one school's experience.

2. Maturation—factors that occur naturally with the passage of time, such as growing older, becoming hungrier, and getting tired. If a physical education teacher were testing a new exercise program and did not use a control group, the changes in physical strength might be attributable to the students' maturation only and not the exercise program.

3. Testing—taking a pretest will often enhance subjects' performance on a post-test.

4. Instrumentation—changes in the procedures for collecting data. For example, in a comparison of different methods of classroom discipline the observer becomes ill and a new observer finishes the job.

5. Statistical regression—subjects who score low on a pretest tend to score higher on a retest, and those who score high on a pretest tend to score lower on a retest. (In both cases their scores regress toward the mean.)

6. Biases due to differential selection—subjects are selected to participate in a treatment group because of variables unrelated to those being studied. For example, in an experiment to study the effects of having every school child drink a pint of milk a day, teachers chose for treatment those children who appeared underfed. A greater proportion of the underfed group received the treatment, thus confounding the results of the study.

7. Experimental mortality—a loss of subjects from the groups being studied. For example, if a new approach to teaching algebra were tested with two classrooms

(one receiving the treatment and one as the control group) and the new approach proved so difficult that poorer students dropped out, leaving only the better students in the experimental group, the results could not be attributed to the new approach.

    8. Interaction of selection with other factors—when groups are used without random assignment, other variables may affect the outcome. For example, a foreign language teacher wants to compare two different approaches to teaching Spanish. Although the language classes are not consciously grouped by ability, the English classes are and, because of scheduling conflicts, one Spanish class has a higher proportion of high-ability English students.

    Three factors discussed by Campbell and Stanley that affect external validity, that is, the combination of characteristics that allows generalization from a specific experimental situation to other settings, are:

1. Reactive or interactive effect of testing—the pretest itself sensitizes the subjects to the ensuing treatment. For example, in a study of prejudice, a pretest could sensitize the subjects to make them more likely to respond to the experimental treatment in ways that would not have occurred had they not taken the pretest.
2. Reactive effects of experimental arrangements—the experimental setting may be so artificial that generalizations to others in natural settings may be precluded. For example, behaviors that occur in an antiseptic laboratory may be less likely to occur in a classroom filled with distracting stimuli.
3. Multiple treatment interference—as with reactive effects of testing, initial treatments may sensitize subjects to subsequent treatments and thus reduce the likelihood that the subsequent treatments alone were responsible for the changes in behavior.

    The true experimental designs are intended to control for many of the above threats to validity, but none does it perfectly. Actually, randomization is the key ingredient in the control group designs because it enhances the probability of internal validity by randomly assigning subjects to the treatment and control groups. This increases the likelihood that the groups are equal to begin with, and it enhances the probability of external validity if the subjects are randomly selected from the larger population to which we wish to generalize.

    The greatest difficulty for educational researchers in maintaining the integrity of the true experimental designs is random selection and assignment to experimental and control groups. Virtually all educational institutions have intact groups—classrooms—and are unlikely to permit random selection and assignment procedures. The use of a laboratory-type setting could solve the problems of random selection and assignment, by carefully controlling for extraneous variables, but introduces the problem of generalizing back to natural settings.

    Educational researchers inevitably make compromises regarding how much control they have when planning research that uses true experimental designs as models. Campbell and Stanley coined the term "quasi-experimental" to describe the designs that come close but do not exactly fit the model. Researchers typically list a series of limitations to their study whenever they are unable to meet all of the possible threats to the validity of their study, that is, when they cannot make use of the true experimental designs. Other examples of threats to validity are contained in the *Handbook* (Gage, 1963) and in the subsequent publication of a separate book by Campbell and Stanley (1966).

Correlational Studies

Another truth-seeking quantitative type of study is the correlational study. A correlation coefficient is a measure of the extent to which variables are related in some way. Coefficients can range from –1.0 to +1.0, with 0 meaning no relationship between the variables. A correlation of 1.0 means a perfect relationship between the variables. A positive correlation exists when an increase in one variable is associated with an increase in another. A negative correlation is when one variable increases and the other decreases.

Correlational studies, that is, searches for variables that are related, are good examples of quantitative exploratory studies. Effective schools research, for example, began with examinations of school variables that were related to higher achievement scores. Often the results of correlational studies help to launch studies that use experimental or quasi-experimental designs. It is important to remember that relationships detected through the calculation of correlation coefficients do not imply cause-effect relationships. Two variables may be related, but each could be affected by a third, unexamined variable.

Truth-Seeking Qualitative Traditions

The ideal design for truth-seeking qualitative researchers is not as easily defined as are the true experimental designs. Generally, truth-seeking qualitative researchers hope that their work will have meaning and applicability beyond the specific setting for a given research project. This goal—to find some ontological truth—encourages the truth-seeking qualitative researcher to transpose some quantitative epistemological procedures to qualitative data and means of analysis. For example, Guba (1981) introduces and discusses four terms that seem to parallel internal validity, external validity, reliability, and objectivity as they are used by truth-seeking quantitative researchers. *Credibility* (internal validity) asks, "Do the data stand for what we think they stand for?" or, "Are the data true?" *Transferability* (external validity) can be achieved if enough thick description is available to permit some transferability of results to other like settings. *Dependability* (reliability), sometimes referred to as *consistency*, answers the questions, "Are the results stable? Are we fairly certain that the same general results would occur time and time again?" And *confirmability* (objectivity) establishes certainty of findings and conclusions by establishing the trustworthiness of the data and of the entire study. Several techniques, such as triangulation (finding three sources that say the same thing), help confirm a study's findings. (See Chapter 6 for more details.)

The Smith reading for this chapter outlines two categories of truth-seeking qualitative designs: "theory-driven" and "systematic" approaches. For a better visual understanding of these two approaches, we have plotted each one separately on our cube (Figures 4.3, below, and 4.4 on page 90). (Notice that, depending on the ideological assumptions or assertions of a specific study, research couched within either of these designs could lie anywhere along the ideological continuum within the prescribed ontological and methodological boundaries.)

Of the two, the theory-driven approach lies more near the truth-seeking end of the ontological continuum, because a study couched from this perspective contains a very structured question (possibly a hypothesis). At least in the manner that the article is written, the Palmieri reading appears to be an example of theory-driven qualitative research. (Palmieri did use quantitative methods when generating her sample.) Early in her written paper, Palmieri cites other historians' scholarship that concludes that turn-of-the-century Wellesley College professors were demure and passive. We have plotted the reading on our cube. In so doing we shaded the area near "reform" to represent the work's ideology because, contrary to accepted standards for white female acquiescence during the early

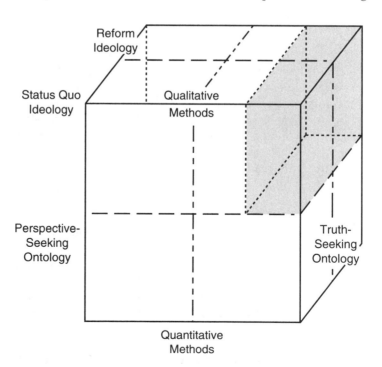

FIGURE 4.3   Theory-Driven Approach

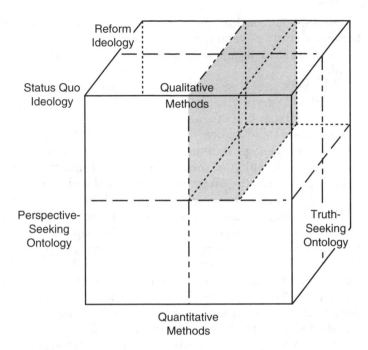

Reform / Ideology

Status Quo Ideology

Qualitative Methods

Perspective-Seeking Ontology

Truth-Seeking Ontology

Quantitative Methods

FIGURE 4.4   Systematic Approach

twentieth century, the female professors exercised a good deal of control over their own lives (Figure 4.5). Essentially, historical research in general (the telling of a story within the context of a given time period) can fall anywhere within the cube. Also, most historical theory is ideological, suggesting that such scholarship usually involves a good deal of interpretation from the authors who produce it (see Chapter 1).

The Smith reading cites certain ethnologists or ethnographers, such as Willis (1981) or Wolcott (1982), who also employ truth-seeking qualitative designs. Essentially, ethnography, and particularly educational ethnography, examines an educational culture in context, employing observation, interviews, and examination of documents (Spindler, 1982). (See Chapters 5 and 6 for more details on sources of data and methods of analysis.) Ethnologists conduct culturally comparative studies. Both traditions derive from the academic field of anthropology (see Chapter 1). The ethnologists' goal is to study various cultures' values, beliefs, and practices, ultimately to make cultural comparisons and generalizations about their universality (Trigger, 1982). The interest in generalizations is what binds them to the truth-seeking category. Spindler (1982), for example, states that ethnographic research can be generalized as adequately as quantitative research because, unlike experimental designs, ethnographic ones analyze data by taking context and meaning into consideration.

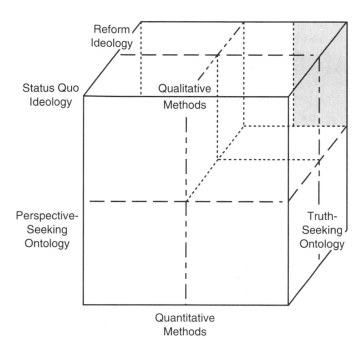

FIGURE 4.5   Palmieri (Truth-Seeking, Qualitative, Reform)

According to Smith's discussion, systematic approaches also lie within the truth-seeking qualitative region of the cube but more near the perspective-seeking area than does theory-driven qualitative work. Here, Smith raises an interesting issue that illustrates the inevitable relationship between ontology and methods as part of design structuring. For example, LeCompte and Goetz (1982) exemplify the systematic approach. In their ethnographic methods book, Goetz and LeCompte (1984) discuss how ethnographers can strive for both external and internal validity. As noted in Chapter 2, reliability is particularly crucial for truth-seeking researchers, who maintain that to be good research a project must have replicability. Therefore, Goetz and LeCompte are truth-seekers because they employ procedural rules from that point of view and from quantitative methodology.

The ethnoscience research design is yet another example of the systematic approach. A branch of ethnography, ethnoscience is the systematic mapping of a culture's language. Thus, an ethnoscientific researcher enters a setting with one expressed purpose: to categorize words with a common semantic linking pattern. Ethnoscientists contend that the more exploratory type of ethnography (discussed later) can follow ethnoscientific investigations, but the researcher must first be equipped with a culture's dictionary of verbal and written meanings. Therefore, the production of ethnoscientific investigations is groundbreaking.

Our language-arts students have found ethnoscience particularly intriguing. Such students' research questions often involved understanding ways children or adults speak and write and the meaning attached to such communications (Werner & Schoepfle, 1987).

Perspective-Seeking Qualitative Traditions

Tesch, in her reading at the end of this chapter, and Smith divide perspective-seeking qualitative designs into two categories of research and discuss their basic differences and similarities. Tesch discusses ethnography and phenomenology while Smith outlines the interpretive and artistic approaches. Ethnography and the interpretive design are not necessarily synonymous and phenomenology and the artistic tradition not exactly the same. But, these two sets roughly represent two halves of the perspective-seeking qualitative quarter of our cube.

Generally, perspective-seeking qualitative researchers are interested in an extensive understanding of their participants' or informants' world, and the results of such studies apply only to the setting and/or people from which data are obtained. Moreover, they are both exploratory and therefore may have emergent designs. In other words, the entire focus of the study can change during the research process; even the research question(s) can be renegotiated if more intriguing ones arise. The Tesch reading includes an excellent appendix that compares the two types of studies for twelve different criteria, including the elements of design listed in the first paragraph of this chapter. Tesch defines each type of study and explains what researchers from each do. She indicates from whom they collect data, how many persons are involved, and how data are categorized and understood. She also discusses how the validity or trustworthiness (accuracy of facts or correct interpretation of an informant's or a participant's thoughts) of data is determined and what the results mean. (See also Tesch, 1990.)

Interpretivism/Ethnography

Interpretivism, or *ethnography,* as defined by Tesch, are plotted on the cube (Figure 4.6; again note that depending on the ideological implications of any particular study the work could be placed at any point on the ideology continuum). The tendency to use different terminology is common among those who conduct or write about perspective-seeking qualitative research and is part of the reason we included two general introductions to the topic in the readings. When referring to one of the two major divisions of perspective-seeking, qualitative research we prefer *interpretivism* to ethnography largely because, as discussed previously, various designs that could be called *ethnography* or that are related to ethnography can presume a truth-seeking viewpoint, and, at times, employ some quantitative methodology.

Interpretivistic research intends to explain the perspectives of each group whose values and behavior comprise a given educational culture. It is therefore

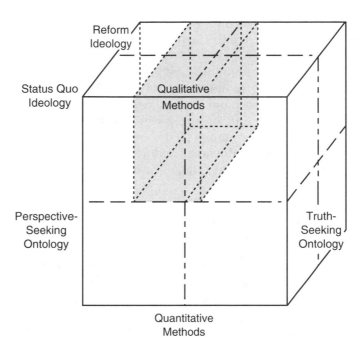

Reform/
Ideology

Status Quo
Ideology

Qualitative
Methods

Perspective-
Seeking
Ontology

Truth-
Seeking
Ontology

Quantitative
Methods

FIGURE 4.6   Interpretive Approach/Ethnography

likely that the same behavior will be interpreted differently from one culture to another (Feinberg & Soltis, 1985). Interpretivism's parent research design, symbolic interactionism, is one of the oldest perspective-seeking traditions. It originated early in the twentieth century at the University of Chicago under the leadership of Mead (Bogdan & Biklen, 1992). This research design never achieved hegemony among sociological researchers, who, as the decades wore on, were drawn instead to truth-seeking designs that incorporated newly invented statistical techniques (Bannister, 1987). Symbolic interactionists persisted, however, claiming that human beings' own experiences provide the filter through which all that happens to and around them is interpreted. True to the perspective-seeking tradition, symbolic interactionists accept only a participant's perceptions of the phenomenon being examined.

Perspective-seeking ethnography and other research traditions related to it derive from anthropology (see Chapter 1). Sometimes you will hear ethnography referred to as *educational anthropology*. Like interpretivists, perspective-seeking ethnographers maintain that generalizations should be left "in the public domain, open to the reactions of other persons, scholars and laymen alike, who can affirm or deny by virtue of their own data and experience" (Peshkin, 1982, p. 63).

Smith lists several other "related approaches" that fall under the general category of ethnographic or interpretivist research: ethnomethodology, constitutive ethnography, ethnosemantics, and cognitive anthropology. These all share "an emphasis on the contents of the mind, how they are organized, and how they interact with features of the cultural and social situation" under investigation.

Also under the umbrella of ethnography/interpretivism is *grounded theory*, which has its origins in the work of Mead. This particular research tradition was developed by Glaser and Strauss (1967). Grounded theory is used to build theory in an area where little or none exists. The primary instrument of data collection and analysis in a grounded theory study is the investigator. The mode of investigation is inductive rather than deductive (see Chapters 2 and 3). Final results from a grounded theory study should be hypothetical speculations based on the data collected.

The steps normally taken in grounded theory research include identifying a practical problem and posing a question to answer it; collecting data through observations and interviews; coding and analyzing data; categorizing data; developing substantive theory (related to the study at hand); and developing formal theory (relating findings to those of other studies and in tangential theory bases). Characteristic of the *emergent design* in perspective-seeking research, except for the last phase, these steps may occur simultaneously.

Ethnohistory represents a combination of historical and ethnographic approaches. It examines a culture or people within historical context. Ethnohistorians are dedicated to investigating various underclasses and their cultures throughout the world. The ethnohistorian intends primarily to unearth the traditional elements of a culture and to pinpoint where and how it has been contaminated by Euro-American chauvinism. Of particular interest to the educational ethnohistorian is the study of American Indian education in cultural and historical perspective, particularly in light of the recent tribal consciousness expressed by various Native American groups (Olson & Wilson, 1984).

Case study, like historical research, could be placed anywhere within the cube, depending on the manner in which an individual study is conducted. A case study is the in-depth study of one thing, an institution, a person, or any defined cultural group. Aagaard's reading is an example of a case study. We have plotted this particular one within the perspective-seeking, qualitative region and near the status quo end of the ideological continuum (Figure 4.7). We regard this work as status quo because the author accepts the reality with which she is dealing (that the Bagby center essentially failed its original mission) and merely asks "why?" Various educational researchers have adopted the case study strategy and produced books on how to set one up and carry it out (see, for example, Merriam, 1988).

Similar to case study are various designs in what has been discussed in Chapter 1 as *applied research*. Conceivably, existing examples of applied research could be plotted anywhere within our cube. (Action science and participant action research are unique among these, however, because their social intervention bent would place them toward the reform end of the ideology continuum.) Much of the applied research would be perspective-seeking, because, like grounded theory, action research, action science, policy studies, participant action

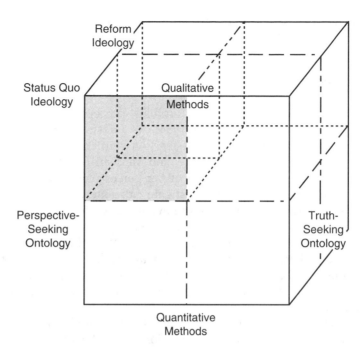

FIGURE 4.7   Aagaard (Perspective-Seeking, Qualitative,
Status Quo)

research and evaluation studies address and attempt to find a solution for a particular educational problem. In so doing the researcher must recognize the varieties of perceptions that participants may have. Probably, talking to and observing the people involved in the study and assessing what they say (qualitative data and analysis) would be the most accurate way to find out what is on the minds of a certain group of people (Guba, 1981; Argyris et al., 1987; Tesch, 1990).

A master's project of one of our students provides an example of applied research (Schornick, 1992). As a kindergarten teacher interested in developmentally appropriate early childhood settings, Schornick briefly reviewed the literature and related research to provide the foundation for the study of her own classroom. Her research question was, "What evidence is there that children utilize those aspects of a developmentally appropriate classroom (e.g., block, sand and water activities) in manners consistent with and supportive of the traditional interests of schooling (i.e., language development, social studies, math, and science)?

She acted as an observer/participant, recording the times and behaviors of randomly selected children from her kindergarten over a nine-day period. The data from her observations, after coding and analyzing, were sufficient to conclude that developmentally appropriate materials and activities aided children in their progress within the traditional areas of language development, social studies, math, and science.

Phenomenology/Artistic Approach

Phenomenology seeks the individuals' perceptions and meaning of a phenomenon or an experience (Tesch, 1984). As a design tradition, phenomenology's historical roots go back to the early twentieth century, beginning within the philosophies of Husserl, Sartre, and Merleau-Ponty. They maintain that a person cannot be separated from his or her perceptions of the environment, and, therefore, phenomenologists investigate not external truths but their participants' interpretations of emotions and events. In so doing, phenomenologists help educators to be aware of the multifaceted and holographic educational world (Bogdan & Biklen, 1992; Lincoln & Guba, 1985). Educational phenomenology has addressed children's impressions of and reflections on a new school, a classroom, being afraid of the dark, or feeling understood, to name a few (van Manen, 1990; Van Kaam, 1959). The phenomenological or artistic approaches are plotted on Figure 4.8.

The Sims reading in Chapter 3 is an example of a phenomenological study. Sims offers a good conceptual rationale for the study, but her work is not theory driven. Sims's introduction cites several sources calling for the need to know about children's responses to literature about African-Americans. Sims chooses to focus on the reactions of one black child, allowing her to select the books and to create her own categories of responses to those works. Near the article's end, Sims links her findings to various educational theories. It is noteworthy that her review of literature comes near the end of her report, unlike truth-seeking reports, which typically review the literature near the beginning.

As Tesch and Smith suggest, much diversity exists among phenomenological and artistic researchers. Dealing with participants' perceptions can lead a researcher far away from his or her original questions. As is sometimes the case in ethnographic or interpretivist work, the researcher might even abandon the question and come up with another, more intriguing one. This shift in procedure is part of what qualitative perspective-seekers refer to as the *emergent design*, referred to earlier in conjunction with grounded theory.

Phenomenologists and those researchers whose work takes an artistic course seem to disagree on two fundamental points: interpretation of findings and the role of ideology. Many phenomenologists take participants' words literally and return to the people to make sure that what was heard and recorded is what the participant meant. Yet, other phenomenologists point out that many people are not totally aware of their subconscious feelings, compelling the researcher to speculate about them. Moreover, a participant may suffer from *false consciousness*, identifying with, not rebelling from, their oppressors or failing to associate with other people whose socioeconomic station is the same as their own. Such participants resemble the female educator mentioned in Chapter 2 who told a

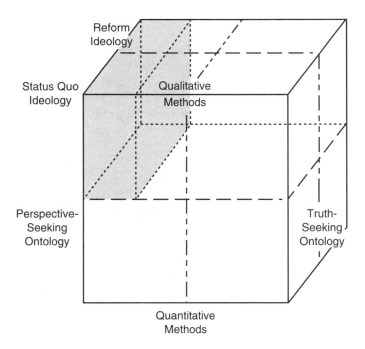

FIGURE 4.8   Artistic Approach/Phenomenology

researcher that what was wrong with the world was working women, although she had worked outside the home her entire life and found nothing wrong with that. In cases such as these some phenomenologists feel compelled to interpret what their participants say, which may result in meanings of which the participant may not be aware.

Thus, a researcher's ideology can play a part in how he or she may interpret participants' words. Some researchers are so ideologically driven that they may prefer to conduct participant action research (noted earlier as an example of practical research), a tradition that openly intends to liberate or empower participants and actually turns the study over to them early in the research process. Whatever the participants want from the study drives how it is designed and carried out (Maguire, 1987).

Heuristic research can be seen as another extreme form of the artistic or phenomenological approach (Moustakas, 1990). It encourages an individual to discover more about himself or herself, even including the researcher as a participant. Because typical topics investigated by the heuristic researcher are loneliness or suicide, he or she must be constantly aware of his or her own personal involvement in the data generated in a particular study. When gathering and analyzing findings, the researcher actually moves in and out of a hermeneutic circle, being both totally in harmony with a participant's mind and then extracting himself or herself so as to conduct a meaningful assessment of what is found (Feinberg & Soltis, 1985; Packer, 1985).

One of our students conducted a heuristic dissertation. After extensive reading and documentation, he concluded that the existing models to explain cognitively the writing process were inadequate. He therefore launched an inductive exploratory investigation using himself as the only participant. He kept a journal as he wrote an adolescent novel and examined records of his thought processes to create his own model (Wyatt, 1990).

Perspective-Seeking Quantitative Designs

Rarely will you find an explicitly perspective-seeking quantitative study. Many interpretivists and phenomenologists believe that using numbers to represent human perceptions and then analyzing those numbers through quantitative means oversimplifies the human motivations under scrutiny. Yet, because one of the goals of a perspective-seeking researcher is to generate questions for further study, perspective-seeking quantitative studies have been done. Such works would lie on or within the shaded area of the cube in Figure 4.9. They, too, must be concerned with the validity or trustworthiness of the data used to

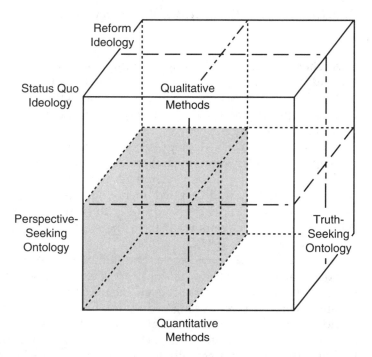

FIGURE 4.9   Perspective-Seeking, Quantitative, Any Ideology

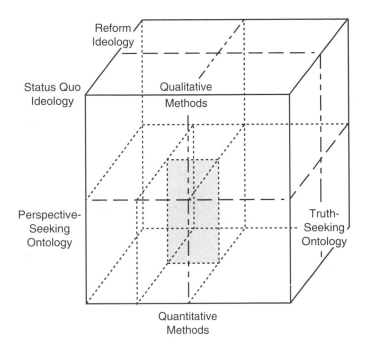

FIGURE 4.10   Vaughn and Liles (Perspective-Seeking, Quantitaive, Moderate Ideology)

answer research questions. But because they are exploratory and may take a different path if conducted by another researcher, they need not be concerned with reliability.

The Vaughn and Liles reading is an example of a perspective-seeking quantitative study. We have plotted it on the cube (Figure 4.10). As noted earlier, its view of the world is more perspective-seeking than are many others that employ quantitative analysis; hence, we place it in the perspective-seeking realm. Methodologically it is quantitative. It is noteworthy that reform-oriented feminist researchers would probably consider the piece status quo because it focuses on male teachers and concludes that some of them may have had reasons to teach other than the largely pejorative ones that historians have mentioned. However, the research conclusions do challenge current stereotypes about why men may have taught, suggesting that they may be more nurturing than we might expect. Therefore, the study has reform elements, as well, and is plotted near the center of the ideological continuum.

Some forms of applied research, such as policy studies, could be perspective-seeking and quantitative. For example, a school superintendent might want to know if the needs of her or his educational community are being met. Because it would be too time-consuming to talk to hundreds or thousands of people, the superintendent might have the district's office of research send out a questionnaire that includes queries about the satisfaction with the schools, various problems that the subjects perceive, and possible solutions to those problems.

Summary

In this chapter you have been introduced to research at its beginning stages. At this point you are learning how to generate ideas for research projects; how to defend to the scholarly community the need for such a study; and how you might go about identifying data to answer those questions. From the many designs or traditions discussed here (and there are more), it should be clear that there are many ways to proceed. All kinds of research is done in education that is designed from these approaches. As a means of bringing much of the material on design together, near the end of Chapter 6 we include two descriptions of our students' work, beginning with how they got the idea for their project and ending with their studies' conclusions. After you read Chapters 5 (data sources) and 6 (data analysis) you might want to review this chapter before reading the descriptions at the end of Chapter 6.

Discussion Questions and Activities

1. Generate some research topics that you might pursue.

2. Transcending your own personal interests, explain why it is necessary to conduct research on a given topic.

3. Look up five or six research reports referred to in the textbooks you have read for other college courses. Identify the design that was used to conduct each of these studies.

4. At this point can you tell the difference between an opinion piece, a discussion of theory, and an actual research study (Chapter 1)? Find examples of each; bring them to class and explain why they are so labeled.

5. Using one research report as an example, indicate where on the conceptual cube it would be located. (Review Chapter 2 if necessary.)

6. Examine the research reports that appear in the journal that is in or closest to your area of interest. Consider the past year as an example. Are certain research designs used more often than others? What are they? Can you speculate as to why some are more prevalent than others?

7. What design(s) comes closest to your own personal manner of determining the truth of a situation? Explain your answer.

8. Identify a specific educational problem and design an action research study to solve it.

Introduction to the Readings

The first three readings elucidate major conceptual differences and similarities between truth-seeking and perspective-seeking research. Van Dalen's reading, taken from his book *Understanding Educational Research,* provides a good example of the assumptions made by truth-seekers regarding their view of reality, the influences of the natural sciences on the social sciences, and the goals of truth-seekers (largely quantitative truth-seekers): explanation, prediction, and control.

Van Dalen's sensitivity to the nature of perceptions (how our perceptions can trick us) is noteworthy, but is offered as a challenge to researchers to work harder to objectify their observations, that is, to overcome the multiple realities to get at the one true reality. He eloquently states the case for truth-seekers. Van Dalen is also eloquent in describing the function of conceptualization and theory. His discussion of facts, theories, and models applies equally well to perspective- and truth-seekers.

Smith's reading, "Publishing Qualitative Research," bridges the gap between truth-seeking qualitative and perspective-seeking qualitative research. Through her discussion of two categories ("theory driven" and "systematic") of truth-seeking qualitative research, she illustrates how differently qualitative studies might be designed even when they are couched within one ontology or general view of the world.

Although some types of ethnography constitute truth-seeking qualitative work, Tesch's work, "The Contribution of a Qualitative Method: Phenomenological Research," focuses on the major differences between two types of perspective-seeking qualitative designs, ethnography and phenomenology. These two roughly parallel Smith's "interpretive" and "artistic" approaches. Together, Smith and Tesch's articles outline two sets of very different rules, more loosely constructed for phenomenology and the artistic approach than for ethnography and the interpretive tradition. But adherence to some set of rules occurs in perspective-seeking studies.

Each of the next four readings exemplifies one quadrant of our cube (presented in Chapter 2). The first by Franklin et al., "Construct Validation of the Piers-Harris Children's Self Concept Scale," is truth-seeking and quantitative. It is theory-driven, adding to a piece of the puzzle that comprises theory on the validity of the Piers-Harris Children's Self Concept Scale. While the instrument was found to be valid, the authors note that it may not be useful when determining self-concept changes in children due to some treatment. Thus, the piece is somewhere between status quo and moderately reform. Although it verifies the construct validity of an established instrument, it notes its limitation, as well.

The Palmieri reading, "Here Was Fellowship: A Social Portrait of Academic Women at Wellesley College, 1895–1920," is an example of a truth-seeking qualitative study. Driven by existing theory about Wellesley College professors, it notes those sources and questions their credibility, suggesting that the plausibility of the current puzzle (theory base) must be tested further. Palmieri's work therefore begins the construction of a competing school of thought, illustrating what Kuhn

(1970) calls a *paradigm shift* (see Chapters 2 and 3). The Palmieri article is reform because it represents a radical departure from current literature in the related field.

The Aagaard reading, "The Bagby Human Resources Center: A Case Study of Unrealized Potential," proposed a perspective-seeking qualitative study that is somewhat status quo on the ideology continuum. Aagaard begins with the assumption that the Bagby community center has failed to fulfill its original mission (reform) but depending on how the researcher answered the research question, reform or status quo elements could be added to the study.

The Vaughn and Liles reading, "Identifying Patterns, Speculating on Motivations for American Men's Persistence in Teaching, 1880–1920," is an example of perspective-seeking quantitative research, the ideology of which is closer to reform than status quo. It is exploratory in nature, inspired by the dearth of theory in the study of turn-of-the-twentieth century male teachers, and focuses specifically on outliers rather than the average male who might substantiate what little theory exists. The conclusions suggest more reasons why men may have taught, especially in certain states, so Vaughn and Liles conducted a follow-up perspective-seeking qualitative study focusing on the diaries, letters, and oral histories of male teachers in one state (Farr & Liles, 1991).

Concepts Concerning the Scientific Method

Deobold Van Dalen

The scientific method has evolved down through the years out of the various methods scientists have devised for solving problems. Particularly since the beginning of this century, scholars have critically examined the scientific method, and the steps listed in the last chapter summarize one well-known analysis that materialized. This simplified account provides a thumbnail sketch of the activities involved in scientific investigations. But to comprehend the conceptual framework upon which the scientific method is founded, one must also examine the goals that scientists hope to achieve and the assumptions they make about the universe that enable them to hope for success in their ventures.

Assumptions Underlying the Scientific Method

The scientific method rests upon certain fundamental assumptions about nature and the psychological processes. These assumptions directly influence all research activity: they form the basis for the research procedures, influence the methods of executing them, and affect the interpretation of the findings. Probing the validity of these assumptions falls within the domain of the philosophy of science. The researcher merely accepts them on a common sense basis because one cannot proceed in a quest for scientific knowledge without assuming that they are valid.

Assumption of the Nature of Reality [Ontology]

Scientists [truth-seekers] assume that we live in a knowable, real world. They do not necessarily agree on the nature of the reality that exists "out there" awaiting discovery, but they assume there is an objective reality which is not the creation of the individual human mind. If the real world exists only in the human mind, if it consists only of orderly mental constructs without objective referents, scientists could present no empirical evidence to support their facts and theories. Logical consistency would be the only possible test of the truth value of scientific statements. Scientists justify their assumption that there is an objective reality on

Van Dalen, D. B. (1979) *Understanding educational research: An introduction* (4th ed.), pp. 17–32, 39–59. New York: McGraw-Hill. Reprinted with permission of McGraw-Hill.

the pragmatic grounds that this assumption is more fruitful for inquiry than any alternative explanation of reality [e.g., perspective-seekers' explanation].

Assumption of the Uniformity of Nature

The principle of the uniformity of nature means that "there are such things in nature as parallel cases; that what happens once, will, under sufficient degree of similarity of circumstances, happen again, and not only again, but always" (73:184). The scientist must accept the assumption that nature is so constituted that whatever is true with any one case is probably true in all cases of a similar description, that what has been found to be true [valid] in many instances in the past will probably continue to hold true in the future [reliable]. In other words, nature is orderly; events in nature are not purely random or unrelated occurrences. Assuming that nature is absolutely uniform in all respects is not necessary; but science is only possible to the extent that nature is reasonably uniform.

If the assumption of the uniformity of nature is divided into individual postulates, each can be examined in greater detail. Thus, the following paragraphs discuss the postulates of (1) natural kinds, (2) constancy, and (3) determinism.

Postulate of Natural Kinds

When people observe natural phenomena, they notice that some objects and events possess a number of striking likenesses. Consequently, they examine phenomena to determine their essential properties, functions, or structures. After finding several objects or events that have common characteristics, they place them in a group; give them a class name; divide the class into categories, each characterized by object resemblances and distinguishable from other categories; and, if possible, order the categories according to quantity or amount. The resemblances they note may be of color, size, shape, function, structures, occurrences, or varied combinations of relationships between these resemblances. Thus, investigators may group people by color of hair; or they may observe structural resemblances, such as a relationship between blond hair and delicate skin, or functional relationships, such as poor muscular coordination and poor mechanical skills; or they may correlate structural and functional resemblances, such as cleft palate and difficulty in pronunciation.

People have always turned to pigeonholing like events and objects when trying to understand phenomena and to solve problems. In the interest of survival, members of cultures in early times classified berries as edible or poisonous, animals as dangerous or harmless, neighbors as friendly or unfriendly. Classification is also characteristic of the early developmental stage of any science. Researchers must have some knowledge of the resemblances and regularities in nature before they can discover and formulate scientific laws.

By classifying phenomena in accordance with their resemblances, scientists organize masses of information into a coherent and unified structure that is useful. The organization of plant and animal life into species, genus, and order and the periodic table of chemical elements worked out by Mendeleev have proved invaluable to investigators in those fields. Classification schemes help workers in a discipline to (1) identify and deal with individual cases, (2) communicate with colleagues more efficiently and accurately about phenomena in their fields, (3) search for additional resemblances that members of categories may have in common, and (4) formulate hypotheses that suggest why differences between categories exist.

By looking for resemblance between things, classifying the things into groups, and summarizing information about the entities in categories, scientists gain a better understanding of phenomena, but they also lose some information—some of the richness and variety of individual differences. Any classification scheme magnifies some differences and ignores others. Observations must be placed on one side or the other of the classification line. Classification has drawbacks as a scientific tool, but to avoid any classification or generalization makes science impossible. Scientists, therefore, assume that although no two things or people are exactly alike, they may be similar enough to make classification fruitful for their purpose.

If importance is attributed to resemblances that are of no significance, a classification scheme is of little value. If several girls flunk chemistry in a given class, the professor may observe that they all wear the same shade of lipstick, but this resemblance is not the key factor causing their failure. If an alcoholic notes that he always adds soda to his bourbon, gin, or scotch, he has recognized a resemblance among his drinks, but giving up soda will not cure his drunkenness. Classification schemes that prove most useful penetrate to the underlying key characteristics of phenomena. These characteristics are not usually the most obvious ones; they are discovered through intensive and devious examination rather than casual and superficial observation.

Postulate of Constancy

The postulate of constancy assumes that relatively constant conditions exist in nature; that is, some phenomena do not appreciably change their basic characteristics over time. The postulate of constancy does not demand absolute conditions of fixity, persistency, or permanency, nor does the postulate deny that rates of change vary for different phenomena. Some phenomena remain substantially unchanged over the years; other phenomena exhibit relatively marked rates of change. The sun, planets, and diamonds display exceptionally enduring qualities down through the millennia; fruit flies, blooming flowers, and chicken eggs do not. In some respects, John and Mary remain more or less the same throughout grade school; in other respects, they change rapidly. Their peripheral personality traits may change considerably as they react to certain kinds of experiences, but their central core of personality traits will not vary appreciably.

The postulate of constancy is a prerequisite for scientific advancement. Absolute constancy is not required, but changes must take place slowly enough for scientists to draw valid generalizations concerning phenomena that will hold true for a given period of time. The period must be long enough for other men to confirm the findings and for society to apply the knowledge before subsequent events render it useless. If phenomena were capricious, all inquiries into the innermost secrets of nature would be fleeting, fruitless historical accounts. The knowledge gained in one study could never be applied when dealing with the same phenomena in the future. Without some permanence of phenomena, science cannot carry out its primary function, the accumulation of verified and predictable knowledge. If science denies the postulate of constancy, its predictions possess little value, for they merely rest on blind speculations and chance occurrences.

Postulate of Determinism

The postulate of determinism denies that the occurrence of an event is the result of chance or an accidental situation, or that it is purely a spontaneous incident. Rather, the postulate affirms that natural phenomena are determined by antecedent events. If water is to boil, a definite set of conditions must exist before the event will take place. If an explosion occurs, one is certain that sufficient and necessary circumstances existed before this event happened, and whenever these conditions occur one can be certain that an explosion will follow. The postulate of determinism assumes that the occurrence of a given phenomenon is invariably preceded by the occurrence of other events or conditions.

Human beings have been aware of orderliness in nature since earliest times. They noticed regularities in nature: day followed night and seasons came in a regular order. To understand nature, they also searched for antecedent conditions that appeared to be related to events, but they often concluded that supernatural forces or whatever immediately preceded an event was the cause of it. Hence, they reasoned that the floods were caused by the thunder of angered gods and that a good day of hunting was the result of finding a rare flower at dawn. By attacking problems more systematically and searching more deeply to find functional relationships, modern research workers have been able to discover regularities in nature that are not detected through casual observation.

Determinism is a necessary and fundamental concept that underlies all scientific enterprises. Yet, rigidly interpreted determinism, belief in eternal natural stability and absolute certainty of uniformity, is questioned as a result of modern developments in physics. Scientists no longer assume that they deal with absolute certainty, but only with levels of probability. This revised version of determinism continues to play a role in research, for the scientist requires lawfulness in the events of nature. If any phenomena fall outside the postulate of determination, they are also outside the realm of scientific investigation.

If scientists must consider each phenomenon as a capricious rather than a determined event, they are deprived of a means of attacking problems that enables them to formulate laws capable of explaining large bodies of phenomena. No pattern or scheme for setting up and controlling an experiment can be established and no predictions about what will happen in the future can be made if the assumption that what has happened in the past will happen again is false. The best that scientists can do in an undetermined situation is to describe the character of an isolated incident.

Assumptions Concerning the Psychological Process

Research workers accept the assumption that they can gain knowledge of the world through the psychological processes of perceiving, remembering, and reasoning. The scientific method cannot operate without utilizing these processes. Perceiving, remembering, and reasoning, however, are subject to error. If inaccurate processes are at work, they subsequently reflect their unreliability in the results of the investigation and invalidate it. Research workers, therefore, must acquaint themselves with the nature of these psychological processes and must take the necessary steps to obtain the highest possible degree of accuracy when employing them.

Postulate of the Reliability of Perceiving

In their laboratories, investigators routinely record information they have experienced through their senses. Yet they know that the human sense organs are limited in range and in fineness in discrimination. A dog can hear the high tones of a whistle that are inaudible to them. Their colleagues may be able to hear a greater range of sounds than they can. Their sense perceptions may differ not only from those of their friends but also in successive observations they make themselves. Because their senses are subject to fatigue and adaptation, they may experience varied perceptions when exposed repeatedly to the same sound, taste, or order.

Errors in visual perception are as commonplace as errors in auditory perception. Through illusions and shifts of attention, a chic dress designer, a deft magician, a war camouflage expert, a football strategist, or a clever advertiser can lead people to make false judgments and inferences. For example, twenty subjects in a psychological experiment were shown a line drawing of a man's expressionless face on a screen. After seeing the word "happy" intermittently flashed beneath the picture, they thought the face gradually became happier even though it had not changed.

Everyone experiences visual deceptions. On her annual August vacation, an elementary school teacher may encounter several perceptual puzzles. At the railroad station, she may have the illusion that her train is pulling out, when it actually is standing still but the train on the next track is beginning to move in the opposite direction. At the beach, she may notice that her vertically striped swimming suit makes her appear thinner than the one with horizontal stripes. When she looks down the road, her eyes will tell her that it converges at a point in the distance.

Scientists have no more natural immunity to faulty perception than the elementary school teacher. When working on a problem, they may make inaccurate observations because of momentary distractions, strong intellectual biases, personal prejudices, emotional sets, and inaccurate discriminations. Sometimes they may see what they expect to see whether it is there or not, or they may fail to perceive relevant factors. History is studded with stories of scientists who failed to track the trail of truth because they were guilty of making perceptual blunders.

Despite the untrustworthiness of the perceptual processes, scientists assume that they can obtain reliable knowledge through their sense organs. But they familiarize themselves with the common errors made in observation and take the necessary precautions to prevent such errors from creeping into their work.

Postulate of the Reliability of Remembering

Remembering, like the activity of perceiving, is subject to error. Everyday experiences indicate the frailties of our mental processes. A teacher may be unable to recall where she parked her car or the name of a former student. We often recall only those things we want to recall: A boy may remember that his mother promised to take him to the circus but forget that she asked him to mow the lawn. Scientists may remember things that support their beliefs rather than those that do not.

Despite the weaknesses of the human memory, the research worker accepts the assumption that one can obtain fundamentally reliable knowledge from this source. An investigator must accept this assumption, for progress would terminate if one questioned the accuracy of every single fact. But since forgetting information or recalling it inaccurately is easy, a scientist develops systematic methods of recording information; periodically reviews these data; and sometimes takes photographs, movies, recordings, or x-rays of conditions or events for future reference. Adopting such practices enables one to improve the range, accuracy, and completeness of one's memory.

Postulate of the Reliability of Reasoning

Reasoning, even by exceptionally intelligent individuals, is beset by many potential pitfalls. Mistakes in reasoning occur because of use of false premises, violation of the rules of logic, presence of intellectual biases, failure to grasp the exact meanings of words, and the making of faulty judgments regarding the suitability and use of statistical and experimental techniques.

Despite the limitations of the reasoning process, scientists recognize its value as an implement of research. Any attempt to order a mass of data into a coherent and intelligible narrative, with accompanying interpretation, calls for the constant exercise of reasoning powers. More specifically, researchers resort to reasoning when selecting and defining their problems, when framing solutions, when deciding what observations to make, when devising techniques for obtaining data, when interpreting their data, and when determining whether to accept, modify, or reject their hypotheses. Without mentally manipulating ideas, scientists cannot make much progress in any investigation. Therefore, they accept reasoning as a generally reliable tool of research. They take many precautions, however, to detect and to check errors in their thought processes. They examine the premises on which their reasoning is based to determine whether these premises are true, and they subject their arguments to the rules of logic that govern correct reasoning. Since confused reasoning can stem from the slovenly use of language, they endeavor to assign clear, correct, consistent, and specific meanings to words, phrases, and terms. Because personal prejudices and wishes may cause them to ignore facts and to reason illogically, they deliberately search for and give fair consideration to evidence that does not conform to their hypotheses.

Goals of Scientists

The goals of scientists are not unlike those of other human beings as evidenced down through the ages. Centuries ago people were led by a craving for knowledge of the world about them to construct crude explanations for phenomena. A deep desire was to acquire knowledge that would enable them to control floods, famine, diseases, and other forces impinging upon their lives. With more refined methods, modern scientists also seek to understand the phenomena they observe. Discovering order in the universe, comprehending the laws of nature, and learning how to harness the forces of nature are their objectives. The goal of scientists [rationalists] is to improve their ability and success in explaining, predicting, and controlling conditions and events.

Explanation as a Goal of Scientists

The essential purpose of research is to go beyond mere description of phenomena and provide an explanation for them. Scientists are not completely satisfied with naming, classifying, or describing phenomena. Rather than terminating their investigations with simple observations, such as that apples fall down, balloons rise, some children stutter, or certain diseases kill, they probe more deeply to find reasons for the occurrence of these events. Going behind casually observed factors to search for some underlying pattern that explains them is their objective. After discovering a possible relationship between antecedent factors and the particular event or condition, they frame a verifiable generalization that explains how the variables involved in the situation behave. Explanation—not mere description—is the product of their effort.

Scientists do not want to know only what phenomena are, but also how phenomena act as they do. A person may notice, for example, that on a hot summer day a steel cable expands, as do metal beams. From one's observation of these particular incidents, one may propose the generalization that heat expands metal. This low-level explanation is useful information for it describes what happens to heated metals, but it does not reveal how metals expand when heated.

When scientists tried to find some underlying principle to account for the fact that heat expands metal, they framed the following explanation: all heat is caused by the motion of molecules of matter: the greater the motion of the molecules, the greater is the heat of a body. The agitation of the molecules makes them jostle one another apart; hence, they take up more space. Thus, an increase in temperature results in expansion. This generalization gave scientists a better understanding of the phenomena observed, for it revealed the causes of the expansion of metal.

Once investigators understood and confirmed this scientific principle, they were able to apply it to other facts. Thereafter, upon encountering any phenomena involving expansion, they looked for heat as a possible cause; whenever heat was present, they considered expansion as a possible effect. Thus, the principle not only helped them to understand a particular phenomenon, but it also enlarged their capacity to explain a large range of natural events. Basically, scientific knowledge explains phenomena by locating their place in a larger body of systematic coherent relations.

Formulating generalizations—conceptual schemes—that explain phenomena is a major goal of scientists. A generalization which explains a limited body of phenomena is useful, but scientists aim to develop ever more far-reaching conceptual schemes. Their ultimate goal is to seek laws of the highest generality—laws of the utmost comprehensiveness. Newton's theory of gravitation is an example of a comprehensive explanation. Before Newton was born, Galileo formulated his law of falling bodies, which explained the motion of bodies on the surface of the earth. About the same time that Galileo proposed his explanation for terrestrial motion, Kepler formulated the laws of celestial motion. When Newton came upon the scene, he devised a more comprehensive generalization that applied to all massive bodies, whether terrestrial or celestial. His new theory performed the work of the two generalizations it replaced. Thus, Newton helped scientific knowledge take a giant stride forward. Since his time, a procession of creative geniuses has been endlessly "lifting science from problem to problem and adequate theory to more adequate theory with greater and greater generality" (77:29). Their successively more comprehensive theoretical explanations have given humankind important keys to understand the universe.

Prediction as a Goal of Scientists

An explanation that does not increase our power over natural events may be useful, but it is not as valuable as one that enables us to predict events. Scientists [rationalists], therefore, are not satisfied merely with formulating generalizations that explain phenomena; they also want to make predictions concerning the way a generalization will operate in new situations. Their objective is to take known data and accepted generalizations and from them to predict some future event or hitherto unobserved phenomenon. By noting gaps in the periodic table that classified the known chemical elements, Mendeleev was able to predict in 1871 the existence of a new element, germanium, fifteen years before it was discovered. By studying the data, theories, and laws available in their fields, modern research workers also make rather accurate forecasts concerning the coming of an eclipse, future weather conditions, or the probable scholastic success individual members of the freshman class will attain in college.

The natural scientist has been able to make predictions in many fields, and some of these predictions possess such a high degree of probability that they are almost absolutely certain. Making predictions has been much more difficult for social scientists, and the predictions they have proposed are of an approximate character or are confined to relatively simple problems. Because of the difficulty of the feat, making an accurate prediction is a satisfying and spectacular achievement.

Control As a Goal of Scientists [Rationalists]

Scientists dig deeply into the nature of phenomena to discover the specific factors and relationships that cause a particular condition to exist. They strive to attain such a thorough understanding of the laws of nature that they are able not only to predict but also to control an increasing range of events. "Control" refers to the process of manipulating certain of the essential conditions that determine an event so as to make the event happen or prevent it from occurring. Doctors, for example, know that if the pancreas fails to secrete insulin, the body is unable to utilize properly the carbohydrates in the body. Doctors can predict what will happen to patients when this condition, diabetes, exists, and they can control diabetes by giving the patients injections of insulin. When doctors predict and control a diabetic condition, they are actually demonstrating their understanding of the nature of the disease.

Psychologists and educators have long been investigating the skills and aptitudes that lead to success in particular vocations. They hope that sufficient understanding of the conditions necessary to become a superior dentist, teacher, doctor, or electrician will enable them to construct aptitude tests that will predict the caliber of work an individual will do in a given field. If such knowledge is obtained and predictions are made with a sufficiently high degree of accuracy, these vocational guidance instruments will prevent square pegs from trying to force themselves into round holes. If the selection of students trained in each field is controlled through an aptitude testing program, the nation will be assured of a more effective utilization of the human potentialities in our society.

One of the goals of scientists is to control natural events, but this objective is difficult to achieve. Scientists can predict but cannot control many events. Qualified individuals are able to predict, with varying degrees of success, the weather, the coming of a comet, or the course of cancer, but they are unable to control the conditions causing these phenomena. Scientists can neither predict nor control some events. They cannot yet predict precisely, for example, when and where earthquakes will take place, nor can they control them. In general, scientists have made greater progress in learning to control natural than social phenomena. One of the desperate demands of society today is to discover means of controlling phenomena such as destructive wars, juvenile delinquency, human oppression, and intergroup tensions that weaken our social structure.

Differences between the Social Sciences and the Natural Sciences

As we have noted, the natural scientists have made considerable progress in achieving some of their aims. Progress in the social sciences, such as history, economics, and education, has lagged far behind. A few leaders believe that our approach to the social sciences never can become "scientific." Some authorities contend that progress will gradually be made, but our knowledge of the social sciences will not reach the high level of that of the natural sciences. Other authorities admit that our understanding of the social sciences is on an immature level, but they claim that research in these areas eventually will become as "scientific" as in the natural sciences. A number of obstacles, however, will prevent the ready realization of this objective. In the endeavor to obtain a better understanding of the fundamental factors underlying human behavior so that they can explain, predict, and control social phenomena, the social scientists encounter many difficulties. The following paragraphs discuss some of their problems.

Complexity of Subject Matter

Natural scientists are concerned with phenomena on the gross physical level. Their studies involve a comparatively small number of variables (the set of conditions required for an event) that can be measured quite precisely. Because social scientists are concerned with people as individuals and as members of groups, they must disentangle much more complex systems of interaction. Social problems may involve such a large number of variables that they overwhelm investigators with the possibilities to consider.

When a natural scientist investigates a chemical explosion, relatively few physical factors will account for the event. When a social scientist investigates a social explosion—a riot or a crime—innumerable factors, some of them not physical, may be involved: a switchblade knife, the force and direction of the blow, blood vessels severed, the intoxicated condition of the murderer, the strength of the adversary, biological heredity, gang social pressures, the lack of police protection, the hot and humid evening, rejection by parents, poverty, and strained race relations.

A number of physical explanations may be given for a crime or any other social phenomenon. Moreover, social phenomena may be observed not only on the physical level but also from the sociological or psychological point of view, or from any combination of these. They can be explained in patterns of—just to mention a few—growth, time, type, place, activities, motivation, or trends. This state of affairs creates many difficulties. One is always plagued with the problem of what points of view and what variables to select to explain phenomena satisfactorily.

Observability of Subject Matter

Direct observation of phenomena is more difficult in some respects for the social scientist than for the physical scientist. A social scientist cannot see, hear, touch, smell, or taste phenomena that existed in the past. An educator studying colonial schools cannot personally view the children, teachers, and instructional procedures of that early era in American history. A chemist or physicist can set up the same desired conditions again and again and directly observe what takes place, but a psychologist cannot put ingredients into a test tube and conjure up the exact events of an adult's childhood. The nature of past social phenomena precludes direct and repeated observation.

Social scientists can observe some present social phenomena directly, but they cannot bring others into the open for scrutiny. In a child study laboratory, investigators may observe whether Johnny Jurk slaps his companions, how many words he reads in a minute, and what range of sounds he can hear. But some social factors, such as his preferences, motives, and dreams, are matters of inner consciousness and are not accessible to direct public examination. Investigators must either (1) interpret that "inner state" themselves, which they can do only in light of their own life experience, a process that leaves room for error, or (2) accept their subject's description of his inner state, which may be inaccurate.

Social facts are more variable than physical facts. For most purposes in chemistry, an observation of any cubic centimeter of sulfuric acid will be as good as another. But observations of 30 seventh-grade pupils in one city will not necessarily coincide with the observations of a like number and age of pupils in another city. The height, weight, size of vocabulary, play participation, and arithmetic achievement of one ten-year-old may vary widely from those of his age-mates. In some situations, a social scientist may treat all individuals alike, such as in the tabulation of births. But because of the wide range of differences in humans, attributing to a whole class what is true of selected samples is dangerous.

Non-Repeatability of Subject Matter

Social phenomena are less repeatable than natural phenomena. Many phenomena of the natural sciences are highly uniform and recurrent; they lend themselves to abstraction and the precise, quantitative formulation of generalizations. Social problems usually deal with specific historical happenings; they are concerned with singularities, with events that occur but never recur in exactly the same way. Some generalizations may be made about social life and human behavior. Generalizations may be formulated, for example, about certain features that wars, raids, and revolutions or adults, adolescents, and infants have in common. Yet a social phenomenon has its unique and non-repeatable character that needs to be comprehended in its entirety if it is to be understood. Thus, abstracting factors that are common to several social events so as to formulate a generalization cannot be carried too far without falsifying the material. Because social phenomena are less uniform and recurrent than natural phenomena, it is more difficult to establish and verify social laws.

Relationship of Scientists to Their Subject Matter

Physical phenomena such as chemical elements are impersonal. Natural scientists do not have to consider the purposes or motives of planets or oceans. But social science phenomena are concerned with human beings, who are purposeful creatures. People seek certain desirable ends and possess the capacity to make choices, which enables them to modify their conduct. Human free will is the "incalculable element" in social phenomena. Because people are subject to certain geographical, historical, physiological, and social-economic forces, they may ordinarily operate in a rather uniform way in a given space and time context. But such uniformity is relative, for human free will enables people to make themselves exceptions to laws in some instances. Since social science subject matter is strongly influenced by human decisions, social phenomena are constantly changing as a result of action taken by human beings.

Natural scientists inquire into nature's processes and formulate general laws governing these processes. They do not expect to alter nature or to approve or disapprove of its processes. They merely hope their knowledge of physical phenomena will enable them to make better use of nature's processes. When natural scientists construct a hypothesis to explain a physical phenomenon, they know that their generalizations will not cause the phenomenon to modify its character. If an astronomer formulates a generalization to explain the orbits of planets, he does not expect the planets to react to his theory in any way. The celestial bodies will remain unchanged by his pronouncements. They will not call a celestial congress to campaign for the adoption of new patterns of movement.

Because the social sciences are integrally interwoven with the social fabric, they present a different situation. Generalizations made to explain social phenomena may affect social events and conditions. If people accept an explanation of social phenomena, they may decide to readjust social patterns in view of this knowledge and thereby create conditions which make the generalization invalid. Consequently, accurate prediction is more difficult in economics and education than in astronomy or physics.

Predictions about population growth and the accompanying problems may cause young people to limit the size of their families. A prediction that a school board candidate will lose an election may cause his partisans to rise to the emergency and help him win. A prediction about the number of people who will be killed in highway accidents over the Memorial Day weekend may alarm citizens and cause them to conduct nationwide safety campaigns that reduce the anticipated highway slaughter. The findings in natural science lose their strength only when they are replaced by better insight into the phenomena. But findings in the social sciences may lose their value if the knowledge they provide causes humans to change the social conditions.

Social scientists are not impartial observers who stand outside society to watch its processes. They are an integral part of the subject matter they observe. People may impartially observe physical phenomena such as the structure of protoplasm, but their own interests, values, preferences, and purposes [axiology] influence their judgments when they observe social phenomena. People are much less capable of remaining objective about human reactions in school segregation incidents than about chemical reactions in test tubes, about social stress in slum areas than about physical stress in physics, about a communist system of government than about the solar system in nature. Emotional attachments to particular systems of values tend to make social scientists approve or disapprove of particular social processes. Eliminating personal biases when observing social science phenomena is difficult.

Natural scientists are concerned with problems of fact; they confine their investigations to the conditions that exist in nature. Social scientists are also interested in problems of fact. To ascertain what conditions exist in society, they study the characteristics and causes of poverty, juvenile delinquency, reading failure, or a similar problem. But social scientists are interested not only in understanding society as it is but also in developing theories to designate what ought to be—what is socially desirable. Some social scientists contend they are not concerned with social ends, but they may unconsciously accept the prevailing order as the ideal [status quo on the cube]. Some researchers may ignore social ends, but the findings of their studies may cause others to seek the development of an ideal social order. Because social science subject matter is intimately related to human beings, who are purposeful, value-seeking creatures, it presents types of problems that the natural sciences do not present.

Nature of Observation

Observation is fundamental in research, for it produces one of the basic elements of science: facts. Observing is an activity research workers engage in throughout the several stages of their investigations. By utilizing their senses of hearing, sight, touch, and taste, they gather facts—empirical data—that help them locate a problem, construct theoretical solutions for it, and determine whether there is evidence that will support their solution. From the inception of an inquiry to the final confirmation or rejection of their proposed problem solution, research workers rely on observation to keep them on the trail to truth.

Because observation, facts, and theories are closely related factors that play a significant role in scientific investigations, understanding their nature, function, and relationship is important. The layman is familiar with these terms, but his concept of their meaning is usually quite different from the definition a scientist would give. This chapter, therefore, will explore the following questions: What is the nature of scientific observation? What is the nature of a fact? What is the nature of theories? What is the relationship between theory and fact in research?

Conditions Necessary for Observation

Since observation is essential in scientific inquiry, neophytes should learn how to establish the conditions within themselves and their working environment that will enable them to obtain reliable facts with maximum efficiency. Involved in observation are four psychological factors to which they must give due consideration: attention, sensation, perception, and conception.

Attention

Attention is a necessary condition for successful observation. This condition is characterized by a mental set or a state of alertness which an individual assumes so as to sense or perceive selected events, conditions, or things. Being bombarded constantly by a multiplicity of stimuli, the nervous network of the human organism cannot simultaneously channel all of them to the cortex for interpretation. Hence, an observer sifts out the specific ones from which he wants to receive messages. This process of selection is attention. Adequate attention is imperative if one is to acquire clear, concise and detailed information about phenomena. If thoughts about the attractive young woman or man across the aisle are flashing through your mind at the moment, you are probably receiving blurred messages from this printed page. Indeed, you may "read" the whole page without acquiring any knowledge of its contents, for your attention is elsewhere: you are not ready to receive the stimuli of the printed word.

Learning to "pay attention" is an important part of observational training. By cultivating a deep interest in a particular point of view when engaged in research you can motivate yourself to observe a specific segment of phenomena with an active, inquiring mind. By incorporating control procedures in your research design, you can fix your attention on the phenomenon you want to observe and can screen out competing stimuli. By exercising a high degree of self-control, you can keep strong and interesting extraneous stimuli from capturing your attention and can curb any natural restlessness that might permit your attention to wander.

Human beings cannot successfully fix their attention upon objects or events that are exceptionally unstable or elusive. Thus, phenomena too big, too small, too fleeting, or too chaotic to be perceived with the senses and special instruments are not suitable subjects for an investigation [by rationalists]. When engaged in [rationalistic] research, you will want to direct your attention toward phenomena that are small enough to be encompassed and are sufficiently stable, constant, and manageable that others can view them at the same time or check them at a later date.

Sensation

You become aware of the world about you through your senses or their extension by appropriate "sensing" apparatus. When changes occur in your internal or external environment, they stimulate your sense organs, which in turn excite your sensory nerves. When these sensory impulses reach your brain, you experience a sensation: a smell, a taste, a shape, or a sound.

Your sense organs can detect thousands of qualities, yet they have definite limitations. They are not reliable tools for making exact measurements of distance, speed, size, or intensity, and they are poor instruments for making comparisons. The observations you make can be distorted for a variety of reasons. Your sense organs may be too limited in scope to detect certain differences, or may be defective because of a congenital imperfection, such as color blindness, or may be temporarily impaired by fatigue, drugs, or emotional status, or may be deteriorating because of age or illness. Strong competing stimuli or a confusion of extraneous ones makes it difficult for your senses to isolate the significant stimuli. A foreign or distracting medium that comes between you and your subject matter can create many problems. A dirty test tube, for example, or undetected biases of subjects in an experiment may cause you to make startling but faulty observations. The mere presence of you and your research equipment and recording devices may affect the phenomena you wish to study and change the signals you receive from them. Social scientists, for example, have found that responses to interviews vary with the differences between the interviewer's and the respondent's sex, age, color, religion, and other background factors. If a sixty-year-old man is asked his opinions on some educational issue, he may respond quite differently if the interviewer is a barefoot, long-haired male than if it is an attractive young woman or a conservatively dressed middle-aged woman.

To obtain clear, undistorted, normal signals from phenomena, you can take the following precautions: Remove any cues that might cause subjects to alter their behavior, eliminate competing sensory stimuli, place yourself in the most favorable vantage point for observations, and employ specially devised instruments to extend the range and clarity of your observations.

Perception

Observation is more than experiencing sensations. Observation is sensation plus perception. Sensation is the immediate result of a stimulus to the sense organs: a sound, a smell, or a visual experience. This information is not useful unless it is interpreted. One can hear a sound, but it remains a mere noise until one learns to identify it as the ringing of the telephone, rumbling of thunder, or mewing of the cat. Perception is the art of linking what is sensed with some past experience to give the sensation meaning. When the Hontoon family is at the park, tiny baby Tim notices a moving object; his four-year-old brother Dale recognizes that it is a bird, for he has seen them in his storybooks; his mother explains that a recent magazine called these small yellow birds warblers; and his father, an ornithologist, identifies the bird as a Nashville warbler. Aside from the baby, each member of the family linked up what he had seen with his past experience; each engaged in perception.

Meanings are in people's minds rather than in the objects themselves. Hence, when looking at the same object, everyone does not "see" the same thing. A layman may view chairs as solid objects; a physicist may view them as unstable, moving clusters of atoms. One person, moreover, may see the same object in different ways at different times. One may look at a line drawing of a cube, for example, and see it as an open box at one moment, a solid cube of ice at another time, and a square wire frame at a later date. The drawing does not change, but the observer's organization of what he sees does.

Perceptions may be relatively simple or highly complex. They may involve a single sense organ, as when one identifies the color of an object. On the other hand, several senses, a wide background of experience, and prolonged training may be required for a person to give a detailed interpretation of the sensations contributing to a given experience. The perceptions of a novice in any field—science, education, music—are apt to be vague, meager, and uncritical. Those of an expert are more definite, detailed, and discriminate.

Conception

An investigator cannot rely exclusively on attention, sensation, and perception to observe and gain reliable knowledge about phenomena. On some occasions one encounters similarities in diverse phenomena for which one's current perceptions—storehouse of past experience—do not provide adequate meaning. If these similarities appear to give a meaningful insight into some differentiating characteristic of reality, a researcher may construct and define an imaginative concept—brain waves, genes, self-concept, attitude, social distance—to identify and explain this phenomenon that has not previously been stored in scientists' perceptual memory banks.

A concept is a symbol or term—a class name—that is invented to communicate with others about the similarities or relationships that one has noted. In a nonresearch environment, one can talk loosely about motivation, social cohesiveness, morale, or any other concept; but in a research situation, one defines concepts clearly and devises indexes that will enable another observer to identify the value of the concept in any particular occurrence. The definition states explicitly not only what to observe—what to include and exclude—but also how to observe and measure it.

Concepts are products of both abstracting and generalizing; they contain both more and less meaning than the empirical data from which they are derived. The concept of "liquidity," for example, can be derived from experiences with honey, water, milk, brandy, syrup, and oil. This concept makes one see what is common in objects that are quite different and enables one to identify and group similar entities under this unifying concept. The concept of liquidity is more meaningful than the observation of honey alone, since it summarizes a number of observations, yet it loses some of the uniqueness and concreteness of honey, such as its color and sweetness.

Concepts can range from simple similarities which are directly observable, such as liquidity, to complex relationships which are hidden from view but presumably exist. Through logical arguments one ties concepts to empirical referents—observable evidence. Knowledge, for example, is not an observed entity; it is merely inferred from using instruments which sample subject behavior. Motivation is inferred on the basis of observed relationships between entities and events. Reading readiness, cooperative attitudes, and conditioned reflexes cannot be observed directly; they are observable only indirectly as they manifest themselves in behavior.

After constructing a concept or conceptual scheme, one reobserves phenomena to see whether one can find facts—observable evidence—that fit into this framework. If support is available, the newfound concept feeds back into perception, giving scientists cores of knowledge that they can use and need not learn again. What one observes depends, in part, on one's conceptual equipment, one's ability to conceive of logical constructs that are meaningfully related to education but are not obvious to everyone.

Conditions That Impede or Improve Observation

Observations can be made by anyone, but accurate and fruitful observations are usually the product of considerable practice and training. The following discussion gives a brief survey of some of the conditions that impede or improve observation.

Obstacles to Accurate Observation

People in all walks of life use their sensory capacities to become aware of phenomena in their environment and interpret these sensations in terms of their past experiences. All too frequently, they quickly associate a sensory signal with some previously acquired knowledge and jump to the conclusion that they have seen or heard something they really have not. When a small, dark object travels across a picnic table, you may immediately associate this occurrence with your storehouse of picnic information and conclude that the object is an ant when it actually is a crumb that has rolled off the chocolate cake. Anticipation of an event can also cause people to make a faulty inference. Newspaper stories concerning flying saucers usually bring a rash of reports from readers who have seen a moving object and have concluded that it is a spaceship. The possibility of perceptual error is always present when the observer makes inferences on the basis of scanty sensory cues.

Strong personal interests tend to make research workers see only those things they want to see. After having reviewed many scientific studies made of animal learning, Bertrand Russell noted that

> . . . *all animals have behaved so as to confirm the philosophy in which the observer believed before his observations began. Nay, more, they have all displayed the national characteristics of the observer. Animals studied by Americans rush about frantically, with an incredible display of hustle and pep, and at last achieve the desired result by chance. Animals observed by Germans sit still and think, and at last evolve the solution out of their inner consciousness (87:32–33).*

Because human beings can choose to interpret or ignore stimuli impinging upon them, their private passions and preconceptions can often serve as stumbling blocks to impartial observation.

Perceptions are subject to distortions because of the observer's emotions, motivations, prejudices, mental sets, sense of values, physical condition, and errors of inference. Psychology professors often demonstrate the unreliability of human observation by staging a well-rehearsed mock shooting and asking students to write a description of what they have seen. The results are amazing! Not uncommonly students fail to agree on the size, age, dress, and number of participants in the incident, as well as the order of events and the type and number of weapons used. They not only miss seeing some important things but also report details that are pure fabrications.

A person tends to see what he knows. If a teacher, doctor, and architect inspect a school building, each will see the things that are of special interest to him or her and will tend to overlook other matters. The teacher will notice the instructional situations, the doctor the health conditions, and the architect the structure and design of the building. If one knows little about a particular subject, one usually does not "see too much" when observing it.

Efforts to Objectify Observations

Everyone observes, but usually casually rather than systematically. To increase the range, richness, and accuracy of scientific observations, a researcher acquires a broad background of knowledge in the field wherein a problem lies. This knowledge helps one to determine what facts to look for and when and where one may find them and to perceive them when they are present. A scientist also studies the special observational instruments and procedures designed to gather facts, learns about their limitations, and becomes proficient in employing them and checking their operational performance for precision and accuracy. Movie cameras, mechanical counters, tape recorders, and similar devices are not subject to selective memory decay and may provide an investigator with firsthand knowledge that is more richly detailed and more reliable than a human observer can record. The evidence, moreover, can be studied immediately or as often as necessary in the future.

Because workers in a research project may fail to record significant data or may interpret what they observe in light of their own cultural experiences and biases, a scientist gives explicit directions for making measurements and observations and works out special devices and procedures to reduce the amount of variation that will occur in viewing phenomenon or reporting data. Like a proofreader, piano tuner, teataster, or airplane spotter, a researcher trains the people who work with him to discriminate between similar stimuli that are encountered in the field. Alfred Kinsey required that his interviewers have a full year of training before he would accept their data.

To guard against becoming so obsessed with a hypothesis—so set on finding facts that support a proposed solution to a problem—that they fail to detect or ignore facts that do not conform to it, researchers make a serious study of competing hypotheses, that is, of proposed explanations differing from their own. When making observations, they strive to notice all significant aspects of the situation—unanticipated as well as anticipated events and conditions—and deliberately search for unsuspected facts that disprove their hypothesis. Researchers always invite colleagues to check their findings. Whenever possible, they repeat experiments to see whether the results will be the same on each occasion.

To avoid errors in perception that arise because of faulty recall, researchers record their data in an exact system of notation as soon after making an observation as possible. Delaying the compilation of their notes may cause them to forget relevant data or to have blurred, distorted, or incorrect impressions of what happened. When recording data, they include every significant detail about the phenomena, equipment, procedures, and difficulties encountered. To avoid overlooking important facts, they may construct a list of items to be noted during each observation. A novice observer may err in keeping too few and too scanty notes. Experience teaches trained scientists to record comprehensive, complete notes and to make detailed drawings of all pertinent incidents that transpire during the investigation, for these items prove to be invaluable possessions when the time comes to analyze and interpret the data or to explain and defend their findings.

A researcher worker soon learns that words that seem to be specific may carry more than one meaning. As one man suggests, "age" of the subject may refer to present age, age at last birthday, or age at next birthday. Consequently, in scientific work investigators define their terms and check to make certain that each sentence describes exactly what they observe and that no other interpretation can be placed upon their words.

Whenever possible, [truth-seeking, quantitative] investigators describe their data quantitatively: in terms of height, distance, duration, speed, or number of units. Rather than describing pupils as large boys, they give anthropometric measurements. Rather than recording that pupils look at television programs frequently, they record the number of minutes per day which the pupils spend viewing television. Rather than describing their subjects as "a group of students," they state the exact number of pupils of each sex in the group and the range of their ages. Numerical measures are more precise than word descriptions and may make possible further analysis of the problem by statistical procedures. Whenever scientists use questionnaires, ratings, or lists to gather data, they try to put them in a form that requires quantitative answers.

Nature of Facts

Scientists make observations to get at facts. But what are facts? Facts are different things to different people. When laymen speak of wanting the facts, they may have a rather narrow concept of the nature of facts. They may believe that facts are precise, permanent, and self-evident in meaning. To scientists, facts are not things that are evident but, rather, data one discovers through purposeful probing.

Scientists are not dogmatic about the certainty of facts. They emphasize the usefulness of facts but are constantly critical of them. They do not expect all facts to be equally stable, precise, and accessible. Their prolonged pursuit of facts has taught them that some can be expressed quantitatively, others can be expressed only in words, and some do not readily lend themselves to either mathematical or verbal descriptions. To scientists, facts are events that occur and leave records. They may occur naturally or researchers may make them occur. Since facts are records of occurrences, scientists devote considerable effort to developing techniques or devices for making records of events. Ultimately, facts are also statements in words or mathematical symbols that are based on records of events. To scientists, a fact is any experience, change, occurrence, or event that is sufficiently stable and supported by enough evidence to be counted on in an investigation.

Accessibility of Facts

Not all facts are equally accessible to the observer. Personal or private facts, such as dreams, fears, preferences, feelings, and revelations, lie hidden deep within the individual. They may be very real to the person concerned and pass that individual's personal tests of reliability, but they are not accessible for examination by others. Pink elephants are real to the alcoholic and horrible dreams are real to a child, but these specific facts cannot be verified empirically by someone else. One cannot observe these inner, personal phenomena directly to see whether one draws the same conclusions about them as other observers or the individual having the experience. If one relies on the individual's description of a personal experience, the observer may obtain inaccurate information. Tommy may tell the doctor that his stomach hurts when the pain is actually located in his chest or when he feels good but has an intense longing to stay home from school.

Research workers may infer that the private experience of an individual is like one they themselves had under similar circumstances, but this may not be true. In daily life people often make such errors. Joe Adams assumes that his wife gets as much pleasure out of witnessing a football game as he does. Investigators studying people of a culture, social status, or era different from their own may fall into error if they conclude that their subjects experience the same reaction to given stimuli as they do. Raw fish eyes served at a puberty rite feast may be a nauseous form of nourishment to an American anthropologist, but a delightful delicacy to the natives. Watching a child being flogged will not arouse the same response in a modern educator as it did in a teacher of ancient Sparta. When seeking reliable information, it is always dangerous for a scientist to equate another person's inner experiences with his own.

Because of the hidden nature of personal facts, social scientists often have difficulty in interpreting a commonplace event. If a student takes the smallest piece of cake at a tea, for example, different observers may conclude that he is trying to be polite, doesn't like chocolate cake, or thinks the hostess is a poor cook. The student may report that his doctor has placed him on a diet to conceal the fact that he has just eaten two candy bars and is not hungry. Personal, inner facts are one person's knowledge, and that person may not be willing or able to analyze his experience accurately.

Public facts—those which can be observed and tested by everyone—constitute relatively impersonal knowledge. They do not depend on the peculiarities of a single individual for verification. Because they are open to inspection by everyone and are agreed upon by a number of independent observers, public facts are much more reliable than inner, personal facts. If one observer asserts that an object weighs ten pounds, for example, it is not necessary to take his word for it. Any normal person can test the validity of that statement by reference to evidence which is independent of the observers. If many people use their senses and special instruments to test the weight of the object and they all reach approximately the same conclusion, findings can be accepted as being quite reliable. In time, public facts win common acceptance as the most trustworthy knowledge available.

Natural scientists deal primarily with public facts, but some of the most pressing problems demanding solution in the social sciences involve personal, inner facts or a mixture of public and personal facts. Natural scientists have devised a number of reliable instruments that enable workers to weigh, measure, and time phenomena in their field. When social scientists attempt to create similar instruments, they are confounded by the concealed, elusive nature of private facts.

Level of Facts

Some facts are derived directly from the impact of stimuli upon the senses; others are reached by conceptual manipulations. For purposes of summarization, the following paragraphs discuss three levels of facts that range from (1) those that one becomes aware of through immediate sense experiences to (2) those that one identifies by describing or interpreting immediate personal experiences to (3) those one identifies by engaging in a highly abstract reasoning process.

Facts of immediate experience are pure sensations without any names or labels. They represent raw experiences because no attempt is made to identify, interpret, or assign meaning to them. These facts are known by immediate apprehension alone. It is doubtful that people other than babies can have such raw experiences, for human beings early in life begin to name or assign meaning to experiences [abstract]. Even the most primitive type of "knowing" involves a slight degree of conceptualization [abtraction].

The second level of facts, those describing or interpreting immediate experience, comprises not just raw experience. When you describe or interpret a sensation as a sound of a jet engine, you engage in perception or a low level of conceptualization. Through an intellectual process, you associate the raw sensation with your past experiences and identify it with that class of things you call "sounds from jet aircraft." Facts describing immediate experiences are relatively close to sensory experiences. They are not highly conceptualized. Some, however, are more conceptual than others. Facts which are primarily sensory in nature, such as sound or smell, are less conceptual than those derived from thought or reasoning experiences, such as memories or ideas.

The third level of facts includes those which are highly abstract and conceptual in nature. These facts are remote from sensory experiences. They are derived primarily from human reasoning processes and cannot be observed directly by the senses. Although they are highly conceptual in nature, they are supported by enough empirical evidence to prove they exist and, therefore, are acceptable as facts. Through an involved reasoning process, for example, you construct the proposition: The world is "round."[1] You cannot see that it is round with your naked eye, but you can provide sufficient evidence traceable to various forms of sensory experience to confirm this proposition. You may point out that a ship disappears over the horizon progressively—hull, cabins, and finally smokestack. Another example of a fact derived from abstract reasoning is one that shows the relationship between two concepts. That reading ability is closely related to arithmetic ability is accepted as a fact. This relationship cannot be observed directly by an individual; it can be only experienced on the conceptual level. Since this concept can be traced to empirical referents, it receives indirect substantiation as a fact. Most people do not realize how little of what they accept as facts is given by raw experience alone. Conceptualizing plays a major role in obtaining facts.

Life of Facts

Scientists do not claim that facts possess everlasting validity; they believe that facts are subject to reinterpretation or revision whenever researchers gain a better insight into phenomena. Facts, especially those that are highly conceptual in nature, can have careers. They are born to satisfy a need; they survive and are used elsewhere. Some facts experience a long life—what may appear to be an everlasting life. But, as the years pass, other facts may gain new meanings—meanings that may broaden, narrow, negate, or contradict the original functions of the concepts. The term "good health" once conveyed the meaning of physical well-being, but later was broadened to include mental and emotional well-being. The meaning of "democracy" was once confined to political aspects of life, but later broadened to include economic and social aspects of life. Words have meanings that people give them. Believing that concepts bearing the same label are the same functionally may lead a researcher into serious trouble. A fact may have validity in one context, at one point of time, when measured by one type of technology, but be invalid if any of these factors change. Researchers are always wary of facts; they want to know how the observed facts were defined and what techniques were employed to measure them.

Functions of Facts

Human beings are forever searching for a better understanding of the world in which they live. Finding answers to their questions entails a persistent search for facts. The marriage of facts and theories produces many advances in science. The following paragraphs examine some of the functions facts play in this marriage.

Stimulation of Theorization by Facts

The scientist does not theorize in a vacuum. The history of science is replete with instances of simple observation of facts that have led to the formulation of important theories. When Archimedes observed water overflowing while he was taking a bath, he grasped the principle of displacement. When Newton saw an apple fall, he developed the principle of gravitation. When Watt watched steam escape from a teakettle, he envisioned the principle of steam power. Facts are provided that stimulate the theorizing process.

Of course, not everyone is capable of leaping from a fact to a theory; many people made the same observations as Newton, Watt, and Archimedes without being intellectually stimulated. Several scientists noticed the inhibition of bacterial growth by molds before Fleming saw the significance in this fact that led to the discovery of penicillin. As Pasteur pointed out, when people make observations, "chance favors the prepared mind." One must have a broad background of knowledge if one is to recognize an unusual fact and utilize this sudden insight to structure an explanation for the nature of the phenomenon. Facts cannot initiate theorization unless an alert, disciplined, and imaginative mind observes them and mentally constructs a possible explanation for them.

Confirmation of Theories by Facts

Facts are essential for the establishment of a scientific theory: they determine whether a theory can be confirmed or should be rejected or reformulated. Facts may not be available immediately for the confirmation or rejection of a theory, but they are necessary for the eventual acceptance or abandonment of it. The discovery of pertinent facts that support a theory strengthen it. But, if facts are found that do not substantiate the theory, one must reject or reformulate the theory to fit the new evidence. Theories must be tailored to fit the facts and remolded whenever new facts reveal the need for such action.

Clarification of Theories by Facts

Theories are refined and clarified as knowledge accumulates. New theories in the social sciences are apt to be elusive and ill-defined; they often give a rather crude, general explanation of phenomena. Further observation and experimentation may reveal, however, facts that not only agree with the theory but also specify in detail and with precision what the theory states in a general way. For instance, modern psychologists have developed the so-called "field theories of learning" which contribute to our general understanding of the learning process. Yet, investigations conducted by Tolman, Lewin, Anderson, Murphy, and many others have added considerable substance and depth to these general theories of learning. Their work illustrates how additional facts can give greater specificity and breadth to a theory.

Nature of Theories

What are theories? They are statements that explain a particular segment of phenomena. These statements, which may be called "guesses," "hunches," "principles," "empirical generalizations," "models," "hypotheses," "theories," or "laws," differ in explicitness, scope, depth, and fertility of explanation. They range along a continuum from nonscientific to scientific, from the very crude to the quite refined. Some theories, for example, deal with practical classroom problems, such as methods of teaching addition. More sophisticated theories may seek to explain learning, retention, or transfer, which apply to all school subjects and to all ages of humans.

The average person thinks that the philosopher is concerned with theories and the scientist with facts. A scientist is envisaged as a disciplined, dedicated investigator who searches for the "true" facts, rather than as an unconventional intellectual adventurer who creates imaginative structures. Many people dismiss theories as mere speculations or daydreams, but they respect facts. They believe that facts are definite, real, and concrete, and that their meaning is self-evident.

Many educators also scoff at theories and demand that researchers provide them with "practical facts" that will help them in the classroom. But a mass of isolated concepts—some that have been verified as facts through observation and others that are suspected but as yet unverified facts—are not adequate tools for solving problems. To push back the frontiers of knowledge, concepts must be bound together into a testable theory. Consequently, researchers move back and forth between the operational, inductive activities of observing, defining, and accumulating facts and the conceptual, deductive activities of theorizing about facts and their relations to one another.

Construction of Theories

A scientific theory consists of statements which connect concepts in a logically unified way to provide an interpretation of a particular segment of phenomena. The theorist formulates and uses concepts that have a particular relevance for the phenomena under study. And, in addition to checking the substance and clarity of the concepts, he or she states explicitly the functional relationship between or among them. By the means of logical inference, the theorist ties the concepts together into an internally coherent framework that provides an explanation of events.

A scientific theory consists of concepts and their relations to one another. A theory is, ideally, a universal empirical statement which asserts a causal connection between two or more types of events. At its simplest, a theory states that whenever X occurs, then Y occurs. A scientific theory is universal because it states something about the conditions under which one class of phenomena will be connected with another class of phenomena so that an event occurs. Theories have universal applicability, assert general rules, and make statements about whole categories of events rather than particular events; but they are empirical in that consequences can be deduced from them which can be checked by observations of particular events.

Little scientific progress would be made if researchers rejected reasoning and accepted only those facts that the senses could immediately apprehend. Conceptual fertility—the capacity to structure bold and radical guesses about how facts are ordered—is the greatest gift a scientist can possess. Although science stresses objectivity, it is to a large degree concerned with the subjective art of theorizing. Theorizing is not an esoteric exercise that researchers practice in their "ivory towers," but rather a practical form of mental gymnastics that enables them to explore the underlying mechanisms of their phenomena. Theorizing provides the road maps for research; without it new knowledge cannot be discovered.

Types of Theories

The entities, events, or relationships that researchers choose to observe are dictated by some theory. They cannot proceed without a theory, but they may proceed without clearly identifying their theory. Their theory may be a vague hunch, an informed guess, a set of inconsistent assumptions, or a logically structural explanation. When structuring theories, not all scientists give equal emphasis to the fact-gathering inductive procedures and the theory-formulating deductive procedures, nor do they move from one procedure to the other in the same order (71:4–46).

Hypothetical-Deductive Theory

Deductive theories emphasize logical coherence. The knowledge systems developed by logicians and mathematicians, which may state nothing about the real world, are by their very nature deductive. That is, they consist of sets of axiomatic statements which are true by definition, and then by logical argument other statements are derived. All well-developed scientific theories have this form of logical-deductive character, but scientific theories cannot rest solely on logic. The logical claims must be verified by actual observation of what happens in the real world of experience.

Some researchers emphasize the explicit and logical formulation of explanatory propositions even when the observational evidence is known to be inadequate. Their motto is: Theorize first and then make empirical checks to correct the theory. The hypothetical-deductive theory consists of (1) a set of definitions of the critical terms, (2) a set of hypothetical statements concerning the presumptive relationships among the phenomena represented by the critical terms, and (3) a series of deduced consequences that are logically derived from the hypothetical statements.[2] These elements are tied together in the form of a conditional "if-then" statement which stipulates: If such and such antecedent condition exists, then such and such consequences will be observable. The validity of a hypothetical-deductive theory is dependent upon the extent of the agreement between the deduced consequences, on the one hand, and the observation of phenomena to which it refers, on the other.

Functional Theory

Some theories are evolved in a less formal manner. Many investigators believe that an undue, premature concern with ordering facts and structuring highly formalized theories may cause them to terminate their exploratory activities too soon and may blind them to other facts and ordering possibilities. To them, a theory is a provisional tool. They place less emphasis on elegant conceptualizations and logical-deductive procedures and more explicit emphasis upon observation and data-oriented explanations. They believe that the interaction of observational and conceptual processes is necessary for scientific progress and that, therefore, the two processes should proceed simultaneously and should be given more or less equal emphasis.

Inductive Theory

The inductive theory emphasizes after-the-fact explanation. Facts are established first, and theory emerges from a careful consideration of these facts. Factual acquisition is maximized and the hypothetical-deductive process is minimized. The theory is no more than a summarizing statement about specific, concrete observations. Some highly imaginative and productive researchers claim that this is the procedure that they follow. But their claims are exaggerated, for they do not merely make chance observations. Their minds are not virgin receptacles and their observations are not completely unbiased. They start out with some expectations; some informal theory governs the choices they make. They cannot keep these hunches private forever; eventually, they must communicate them effectively. Critics of the radical empiricists also believe that a reluctance to utilize deductive procedures makes it more difficult to deal with the intricacies of complex phenomena.

Model

The term *model* (paradigm) has become quite fashionable in the literature, and a bewildering array of models have been developed. Essentially, models are simplified or familiar structures which are used to gain insights into phenomena that scientists want to explain.

Models may be drawings or physical replicas that represent the real thing, or they may be more abstract. Mathematical equations, verbal statements, symbolic descriptions, graphic presentations, or electromechanical devices may be used to represent objects and relationships that are being modeled. Some investigators locate a structure about which much is known and use it to gain insight into a field about which little is known. A researcher who wishes to study how rumors spread, for example, may wonder whether they spread in the same way as diseases. In other words, the researcher may utilize the laws of epidemiology, about which much is known, as a model for a theory about rumor transmission.

Some scholars contend that models and theories are one and the same thing, but other scholars make the following distinction (71:104–129): Both theories and models are conceptual schemes that explain the relationships of the variables under consideration. But models are analogies (this thing is like that thing) and therefore can tolerate some facts that are not in accord with the real phenomena. A theory, on the other hand, is supposed to describe the facts and relationships that exist, and any facts that are not compatible with the theory invalidate the theory. In summary, some scholars argue that models are judged by their usefulness and theories by their truthfulness; models are not theories but tools that are used as a basis for formal and rigorous theory construction.

Functions of Theories

Theories serve as tools and goals, as means and ends. As goals, they provide explanations for specific phenomena with maximal probability and exactitude. As tools, they provide a guiding framework for observation and discovery. The following paragraphs explain how theories help researchers examine and explain phenomena and thereby contribute to the advancement of knowledge.

Identification of Relevant Facts

Theories govern the kind of phenomena that investigators study. Theories provide frameworks within which and against which investigators observe, test, and interpret their observations. Scientists cannot collect facts about everything. They must narrow the area of their interest to limited segments of phenomena and give these segments their undivided attention. Investigators, for example, may study the game of baseball in the sociological framework of play, in the physical framework of stress and velocity, in the economic framework of supply and demand, or in many other ways. But a multiplicity of facts are associated with any of these problem areas. Not until researchers construct theoretical solutions for their problems do they know precisely what facts to observe. After theorizing that there is a relationship between A and B, they know which specific facts to locate: those that will provide the empirical evidence necessary to confirm or disconfirm their theory. The theory determines the number and kinds of facts that are relevant to a study. Facts do not identify themselves as relevant; only a theory can tell an investigator what to observe and what to ignore.

Formulation of Logical Constructs

Reliable knowledge can be acquired through direct observation and measurement, but many factors that contribute to the educational phenomena are not observable directly. Consequently, investigators often create imaginative concepts, such as anxiety, dogmatism, or motor set, to account for behavior or effects that they observe. These concepts may be called logical constructs, theoretical constructs, or just constructs. A concept is a product of observing diverse entities, abstracting similarities from them, and making a generalization about them. Observation precedes the theoretical operation, but the intellectual process of abstracting and generalizing are necessary to produce a new core of meaning about some aspect of reality. Concept development and the precise description of the referent behavior are of utmost importance in research, for these shorthand symbols are the major elements of theories; they guide theoretical and experimental thinking. Concepts convey considerable compact information to scientists and make it easier for scientists to manipulate facts and to communicate findings.

Classification of Phenomena

Scientists cannot work efficiently and effectively with masses of assorted facts; they need some scheme for ordering the data in their fields. Therefore, the first stage in any science consists in constructing theoretical frameworks for classifying facts. Classifying involves formulating hypotheses as to the nature of subject matter in a field. In the beginning, any arbitrary scheme of grouping phenomena may be temporarily adopted in the interest of mastering the subject matter. Phenomena in any field have many similarities that may be employed as a basis for classification. Using the more obvious ones is often the initial step taken in deriving a classification system. With more experience, scientists usually detect less obvious but more relevant and significant concepts or principles for grouping, dividing, and analyzing subject matter. Classifying substances in accordance with their color, for example, gives us some knowledge about them, but classifying them in accordance with their chemical composition gives us knowledge about all the known reactions that depend on that composition. Classification systems differ widely in their fruitfulness as principles for yielding and organizing knowledge. Some classification schemes serve very limited purposes; they are derived from concepts that do not provide a framework for systematizing all that is known or can be found out about phenomena. The objective in any science is to develop classification systems that will provide the most significant clues to the nature of phenomena in the field and that will allow the discovery of many more resemblances among like phenomena and many more hypotheses about the subject matter than were originally recognized.

The older sciences have been quite successful in devising such systematic conceptual schemes. Geologists have developed systems for classifying rocks, and botanists have developed systems for classifying plants. Educators have devised some classification schemes for phenomena in their field, but many of these schemes have been rather crude and of limited usefulness. But as more and more investigators describe the complex and diverse facts relating to their subject matter, note the similarities, differences, and relationships among them, and structure frameworks to categorize them, they should gain a deeper and clearer insight into teaching, learning, and the development of children.

Summarization of Facts

Theorization is used to summarize knowledge with varying degrees of comprehensiveness and precision. These summaries may range from relatively simple generalizations to exceedingly complex theoretical relationships. A summarization may describe a limited range of events, such as when an educator makes a generalization about the practice of granting varsity letters to high school athletes. This low level of summarizing is not usually referred to as a "theory." But one might later note a relationship between varsity letters, honor societies, and certificates of achievement and construct the broader generalization that public recognition rewards are a means of motivating pupils. Summarization on a high scientific level, of course, involves integrating the major empirical generalizations into a more comprehensive theoretical framework.

Prediction of Facts

A generalization about data—a theory—enables one to predict the existence of unobserved instances conforming to it. For instance, if the generalization that a high rate of truancy is associated with slum areas has been confirmed, one can look for and expect to find this pattern in slum areas where no truancy statistics have been compiled. Theory enables one to predict what should be observable where data are not available. Theory serves as a powerful beacon that directs investigators in their search for facts.

Revelation of Needed Research

Because theories may lack some supporting evidence that is necessary to provide the maturity and vitality essential for their proper functioning, they are an excellent source to turn to when in search of research problems. Even a rather low level of theorization can point out the need for further research. Suppose, for example, that an investigator finds evidence supporting the following generalization: A rather high correlation exists between the physical endowments and proficiencies of students in a suburban junior high school and the frequency, duration, and nature of their play activities. This generalization suggests problems that other workers might explore: Does the general relationship above hold true for elementary and high school students? Does this pattern hold true for rural groups or youths in other countries? Does it hold equally true for both sexes? Does grouping the students in accordance with their body builds (ectomorphy, mesomorphy, and endomorphy) or their intelligence influence the general relationship in any way? Theorization on any level tends to open up new avenues of inquiry even as it did in this instance.

Notes

1. Studies of the orbital flight of Vanguard I show the earth to be slightly pear-shaped rather than a bulging sphere.

2. Hypothetical statements may be referred to as "postulates" or "axioms," and deduced consequences may be called "theorems."

References

Marx, M. H. (1963). *Theories in Contemporary Psychology.* New York: Macmillan.

Mill, J. S. (1846). *A System of Logic.* New York: Harper.

Northrop, F. S. C. (1949). *The Logic of the Social Sciences and the Humanities.* New York: Macmillan.

Russell, B. (1927). *An Outline of Philosophy.* London: G. Allen.

Publishing Qualitative Research

Mary Lee Smith

This paper constitutes a slight departure from editorial policy for AERJ. Far from contributing to general knowledge through empirical analysis, the paper is meant to serve a self-referent and practical purpose. It is meant to signify to the discipline that manuscripts based on qualitative research are being welcomed by AERJ editors. It is also meant to assist the editors in recognizing instances of qualitative research and choosing those manuscripts with the greatest relevance and scholarly merit. The author was asked to define qualitative research in education, describe what form an AERJ article based on qualitative research might take, and state some criteria that can be used by the editors and referees to judge the merit of such studies.

Seemingly straightforward, the task could hardly be more daunting. The body of work labeled qualitative is richly variegated and its theories of method diverse to the point of disorderliness. Qualitative research is vexed by the problem of different labels. One sees terms such as naturalistic research, participant observation, case study, and ethnography, as well as qualitative research, used interchangeably. If the terms and the work described can be distinguished, it would be a task that requires a separate paper, and, for the present purposes, I will treat them as a package. In addition to the diversity of labels, the field has grown out of diverse disciplines (anthropology, sociology, psychology). Qualitative research is further divided by differing views of the nature of reality (whether there is a world of social objects and forces separate from the observer's perception of them) [ontology], of object fields judged to be appropriate for study (from whole institutions or communities to brief encounters), of beliefs about the merits of different research methods and ways of representing findings, and of criteria for judging studies. These divisions have created socially bounded territories, acrimonious exchanges among adherents, and institutionalized schools of thought. How then should the editors judge and select manuscripts when such different ways of thinking about and doing qualitative research exist? It is my contention that AERJ must welcome all approaches, recognize the purpose and background of the particular study, find appropriate referees, and employ criteria relevant to the particular approach to qualitative research used.

Qualitative research defies simple description. Those who have attempted to simplify have done so by exclusion. For example, it has been argued that only real anthropological ethnography counts and other forms of qualitative research are inconsequential, or that structural functionalism is "positivist" and therefore outside the category. Such definition by exclusion not only rules out informative research (e.g., Willis, 1981) but also creates theoretical confusion. Smith (1983), for example, equated qualitative with interpretive, then argued that procedures used to verify conclusions were incompatible with the epistemology of interpretive or hermeneutic research. Despite Phillip's (1983) helpful analysis of the concept of positivism, authors continue to label anyone who is not phenomenological with the epithet of positivist. As Stryker (1980), Kirk and Miller (1986), and Campbell and his colleagues (e.g., Brewer & Collins, 1981) have noted, many intermediate philosophical positions are possible. Moreover, many extant qualitative studies seem to be at least implicitly grounded in them. The editors of AERJ ought to give in to the assertion that qualitative research is equivalent to any single approach within it.

This paper has two parts. In the first, I attempt to describe the common features of what is called qualitative research. It is not my intent, in so doing, to suggest a rapprochement among approaches or encourage an unlikely consensus, but to show that the category is more than an empty label. The second section describes four different approaches to qualitative research.

What Is Qualitative Research in Education?

First, qualitative research is empirical. The researcher collects sense data about the phenomenon under study and works on them in some way—organizes them, and holds them up against ideas, hypotheses, and categorical definitions as a way of testing them. In some approaches, one says that abstractions emerge from the data; in others, that a language is chosen and imposed on the data. In some approaches, the primary data are emic (i.e., expressed in the categories and meanings of the subject or "native"). Other approaches involve etic data (i.e., data expressed in the researcher's language or the categories of some theory).

Qualitative researchers study qualities or entities and seek to understand them in a particular context. As Dabbs (1982) wrote, "Quality is the essential character or nature of something; quantity is the amount. Quality is the what; quantity is the how much. Qualitative refers to the meaning . . . while quantitative assumes the meaning and refers to a measure of it" (p. 32). Though it focuses on definitions, meanings, and descriptions, refining and placing them in context, and frequently portraying them in words rather than numbers, qualitative is not antiquantitative.

Qualitative research is based on the notion of context sensitivity. What sets qualitative research apart most clearly from other forms of research is the belief that the particular physical, historical, material, and social environment in which people find themselves has a great bearing on what they think and how they act. Acts must be interpreted by drawing on those larger contexts. Qualitative researchers reject the notion of universal, context-free generalization. Learning to solve word problems in arithmetic, for example, is not something that occurs in isolated, antiseptic, laboratory-like settings; rather, it takes place in contexts of human and institutional purposes, prior learning and teaching, and the presence of others; it is facilitated or inhibited by material and physical resources; it involves personal and interpersonal histories, and the like.

Other characteristics of qualitative research follow from the conviction that human acts are context-sensitive. Most importantly, the researcher must personally become situated in the subject's natural setting and study, firsthand and over a prolonged time, the object of interest and the various contextual features that influence it. This introduces notions about the "personhood" of the qualitative researcher and what roles and relationships are formed between researcher and subject. Unlike the model experimenter, the qualitative researcher is not a faceless replicate. Objectivity in the conventional sense is an illusion; the subject's intentions, beliefs, views of the researcher, and interests must be considered. A further implication of the belief in context sensitivity is a deemphasis of standardized or general research methods. The social scene is thought to be so complex that one cannot anticipate it sufficiently to select a priori a single or even a few meanings for a construct (as one does in operationalization) and adopt a uniform way of measuring it. Standardized methods have little utility, and because preordinant procedures are not used, establishing such things as interobserver agreement and representative sampling become problematic and, in some approaches, irrelevant. Methods are not viewed as guarantors of truth, as they seem to be in the orthodox, textbook model of experimentation. Rather, methods are used inventively and tailored to the situation. In many cases, multiple methods are employed, and the findings of alternative methods are played off against each other. In addition, descriptions of methods used are frequently accompanied by justification of the methods chosen, their underlying assumptions, and their limitations. Because there is no catalog of qualitative designs or certified methods, thoughtful researchers describe what they did in detail. Qualitative research is marked by self-examination and criticism of the roles established, of the methods used, and of mistakes made.

Here the resemblance among schools of qualitative research ends. The following section describes several approaches or divisions within the field. This subdivision is meant to be not an exact taxonomy but a heuristic device to inform AERJ editors of the range of possibilities they are likely to encounter.

Interpretive [Perspective-Seeking, Qualitative] Approach

Erickson's (1986) chapter in the *Handbook of Research on Teaching* illustrates well the interpretive approach to qualitative research. Indeed, Erickson equates qualitative with interpretive, thereby excluding by implication approaches that use interpretations as points of departure for explanations of the social world based on conflict or structural-functional theories, for example. For interpretive approaches, the object field to be studied is the acts and meanings ascribed to events by actors in a particular social context. Acts are distinguished from behaviors in that, while behaviors are overt and may be objectively observed and counted, acts imply purposeful constructions on the part of an actor that can be understood only from the actor's point of view. Acts are social in that the events of classroom life acquire significance in the immediate and particular setting and are "worked out" together by the teacher, pupils, and others. In other words, the causal dynamics of social life are the reciprocal actions taken by others within the immediate social environment. As described by Erickson (1986), fieldwork based on the interpretive approach "involves being unusually thorough and reflective in noticing and describing everyday events in the field setting, and in attempting to identify the significance of actions in the events from the various points of view of the actors themselves" (p. 121). The qualitative researcher attempts to understand the question

> *How are the happenings organized in patterns of social organization and learned*
> *principles for the conduct of everyday life—how, in other words, are people in the*
> *immediate setting consistently present to each other as environments for one*
> *another's meaningful actions? (p. 121)*

Having understood these local rules for relating and symbolizing, the researcher interprets them in light of what is happening in wider social contexts and comparative settings.

The interpretive approach embraces a type of philosophical idealism in believing that the mind creates reality and that an objective world separate from the perceptions of the person cannot be known. Social knowledge is gained by *Verstehen,* or subjective, participative understanding and cannot be verified by appeal to external criteria. There are no universal laws to search for; instead, the goal is to understand particular actions and meanings in particular contexts. Data are primarily emic.

Erickson (1986) described what a report based on qualitative research would contain: empirical assertions; narrative vignettes; quotations from observational field notes and interviews, maps, tables, or figures; interpretive commentary; theoretical discussion; and a description of the research process itself. Empirical assertions are statements of findings derived inductively from a review of field notes and a systematic search for confirming and disconfirming evidence on the assertions ("establishing the evidentiary warrant," p. 146). Vignettes and quotes provide vivid "documentary evidence that what the assertion claimed to have happened did occur at least once. General description . . . provides evidence for the relative frequency of occurrence of a given phenomenon . . . [and] display[s] the breadth of evidence" (p. 149). Interpretive commentary tells what the portrayals and general descriptions mean from the author's perspective. These elements of the report

> *allow the reader to experience vicariously the setting that is described, and to confront instances of key assertions and analytic constructs . . . to survey the full range of evidence on which the author's interpretive analysis is based . . . and to consider the theoretical and personal grounds of the author's perspective as it changed during the course of the study. (p. 145)*

Erickson also identified some problems of fieldwork that journal editors might use as indicators of the scholarly merit of qualitative research based on the interpretive approach. These include inadequate negotiation of entry into the field setting, limiting the researcher's access to relevant data (p. 141), inadequate amount of data, inadequate variety of data sources, faulty interpretive status of evidence, inadequate disconfirming evidence, and inadequate discrepant case analysis (p. 140).

For examples of the interpretive approach, see Hood, McDermott, and Cole (1980) and Erickson (1975).

Related Approaches

Work falling under a variety of labels (e.g., ethnomethodology, constitutive ethnography, ethnosemantics, cognitive anthropology) shares with the interpretive approach an emphasis on the contents of the mind, how they are organized, and how they interact with features of the cultural and social situation. Most notable for education is the research on "working intelligence" or "everyday cognition" (Rogoff & Lave, 1984). Researchers study cognitive activities such as remembering, categorizing, and solving problems. They observe such activities in different contexts, for example, in formal learning situations versus in shopping or in the pursuit of a hobby. Besides observation, the researchers rely on formal elicitation procedures to reveal systematically the meaning of mental concepts and how they are organized and used. They also conduct formal tests of hypotheses about the influence of context (the purpose and nature of the activity, the intellectual requirements of performing the task, the guidance provided by experienced adults, peer interaction, and the like) on language and conceptual performance. Research by Scribner (1984) and Newman, Griffin, and Cole (1984) is illustrative.

Artistic [Perspective-Seeking, Qualitative] Approaches

The artistic approach departs most obviously from familiar formats in scholarly journals. Rather than empirical assertions supported by description, the report is an artistic rendering, usually a narrative account, of what the researcher has discovered in the case studied. In research, the investigator seeks to experience directly the qualities inherent in the setting, appreciate the meanings held by the people there, and then represent these discoveries so that the reader can have a vicarious experience of the case. Nisbet (1976) recalled "Weber's insistence upon the primacy of . . . Verstehen, of understanding that penetrated to the realm of feeling, motivation, and spirit" (p. 12), understanding that is rooted in intuition and based on experience and observation.

There is little to distinguish the data collection or field relations of the artistic from other qualitative researchers, except that one assumes a person with acute sensitivities who can appreciate and convey the unique qualities of the case. The object fields are more likely to be "the experience the individuals are having and the meaning their actions have for others" (Eisner, 1981, p. 6) than they are observable behaviors or social facts. The sequence of activities followed is usually inductive. Systematic forms of data analysis or verification are not prominent. Instead, the researcher intuitively seeks out themes that will depict experience and meaning in a vivid and significant way.

There is no standard form for presenting results. According to Eisner (1981), "What one seeks is not the creation of a code that abides to publicly codified rules, but the creation of an evocative form whose meaning is embedded in the shape of what is expressed" (p. 6). The researcher preserves, in a coherent account, the concrete details of everyday life. He or she uses elements of storytelling, such as dramatic structure, interpretive ordering of events, narrative voice, and generative metaphors. According to House (1980), these elements "are distinguished from logical entities in that aesthetic elements are apprehended immediately without recourse to formal arguments" (p. 105) and assimilated into the reader's system of tacit meanings. The storytelling form is best illustrated by Brauner (1974) and in the works of Rob Walker and students of Eisner and Stake.

How can editorial decisions be made about reports such as these? Rein (1978, p. 77) suggested these criteria. First, the story should be true. Second, the story should be the simplest internally consistent account that can be offered. It should emphasize those qualities of the situation that can be translated to broader contexts. Finally, there should be minimal distortion by the ideology of the storyteller, who should have subjected his or her values and work to scrutiny. Donmoyer (1985) wrote that, because the primary aim of artistic researchers is to explicate meaning rather than to establish truth, their work should be afforded considerably more latitude than that of other researchers. According to Eisner (1981):

> *Validity in the arts is the product of the persuasiveness of a personal vision; its utility is determined by the extent to which it informs. . . . What one seeks is illumination and penetration. The proof of the pudding is the way in which it shapes our conception of the world or some aspect of it. (p. 6)*

Without standardized criteria, in other words, the editors must rely on the completeness, coherence, and internal consistency of the account; whether it penetrated and illuminated the subject; its plausibility; and the credibility of the author.

Systematic [Truth-Seeking/Qualitative] Approaches

In sharp contrast to the approaches so far described, some qualitative research might best be described as systematic (although the label might not be accepted). Those who practice and advocate this approach seem to base their arguments on a need for greater credibility and accessibility of their findings. They assume that more systematic and better described methods of data collection and analysis will achieve this end and in addition will improve the teaching of methods (Miles & Huberman, 1984b). Methodologists like LeCompte and Goetz (1982) recommend that qualitative researchers adopt criteria such as reliability and validity to judge their work, thereby enhancing its contribution to the general scientific enterprise. Likewise, Kirk and Miller (1986) identify qualitative research with scientific purposes [truth-seeking] and name objectivity as a canon of all forms of research.

Analysis of the arguments of these and others reveals a purpose different from, say, the interpretive approach. They propose not only to discover but also to verify. LeCompte and Goetz's remarks are illustrative: "Although ethnographers customarily depend on generative and inductive strategies in the early phases of a research study, they direct later stages of the interactive collection-analysis process to deductive verification of findings" (1982, p. 34). A realist or critical-realist epistemology is revealed in statements such as this by Kirk and Miller: "There is a world of reality out there. The way we perceive it is largely up to us, but the world does not tolerate all understandings of it equally" (1986, p. 11). However, they deny the "positivist" [rationalistic] view that "the external world itself determines absolutely the one and only correct view that can be taken of it, independent of the process or circumstances of viewing" (p. 14). In this, as well as their call for triangulation and replication, their view of knowledge is revealed, although none of the authors mentioned here believe that finding an absolute or universal truth is the goal of research. All acknowledge the complexity of contexts and the limitations of research methods to deal with them.

If one were to shadow an interpretivist and a systematic qualitative researcher in their interactions with the field setting and collection of data, one would not necessarily observe a difference. Nothing in principle would prevent a systematic researcher from focusing on emic data; therefore, their respective object fields are not necessarily different. One sees the distinctions most clearly in their purposes, assumptions about the nature of reality, and the manner in which they analyze data and represent their evidence and methods.

The form of the report of a systematic qualitative study is likely to be discursive, that is, with conclusions logically argued from empirical evidence. Descriptive data from field notes and interviews will be liberally used but will have been systematically selected to illustrate the process the researcher used to move from evidence to conclusion. This is in contrast to the way the artistic researcher selects data, that is, intuitively or rhetorically to influence the imagery of the reader. The report is structured so that one can judge its scientific credibility. That is, the researcher will attempt to show how the study is objective, reliable, and valid. According to LeCompte and Goetz (1982), the external reliability, or replicability, of a study can be affected by the role taken and relationships formed by the researcher (consequently the data to which the researcher has access), informant choices, social situations and conditions (what informants are willing to reveal in the presence of others or in alternative social contexts), the major analytic constructs employed by the researcher, and the methods used to collect data. Variation in any of these areas will reduce the chance that one ethnographer will reach the same conclusions as another. The correction for this consists not of an operational technique (e.g., high interobserver reliability) but of the researcher's "recognizing and handling" these five problems. By this is meant that the researcher fully discloses his or her role, methods, and constructs. Although there is no complete cure for problems of internal reliability—"whether, within a single study, multiple observers will agree" (LeCompte & Goetz, 1982, p. 41)—LeCompte and Goetz recommend certain procedures to enhance it, such as using low-inference descriptors, multiple researchers, local informants who may examine and verify the researcher's account, or mechanically recorded data. Kirk and Miller (1986) echo these notions about reliability, calling for the researcher to detail the "relevant context of observation" (p. 52), including a thorough description and criticism of the author's personal traits, interests, theories, and methods. They advocate in addition routinized, legible, public field notes so that subsequent analysts may follow the researcher's logic and procedures.

A correspondence theory of validity seems to be held by systematic qualitative researchers, as they not only call for checks on internal coherence and consistency (e.g., searching the data record for discrepant cases or disconfirming evidence) but also appeal to external verification. According to LeCompte and Goetz, "validity necessitates demonstration that the propositions generated, refined, or tested match the causal conditions which obtain in real life" (1982, p. 43). They name threats to internal and external validity of qualitative research that are analogous to those for experimental research. Unlike in the latter, however, threats to the validity of qualitative research are addressed by descriptions and logical analyses rather than by techniques like random assignment.

In addition to their offering a set of routinized procedures for analyzing qualitative data, Miles and Huberman (1984a, 1984b) suggested some techniques a researcher could use to verify propositions and enhance validity. These include

> *checking for representativeness . . . checking for researcher effects . . . triangulating across data sources and methods . . . weighting the evidence or deciding which kinds of data are most trustworthy . . . making contrasts/comparisons, checking the meaning of outliers, and using extreme cases . . . ruling out spurious relationships; replicating a finding in another part of the data, or a new data source or set; checking out rival explanations . . . getting feedback from informants . . . using an audit trail. (1984a, p. 28)*

The analysis and report of the systematic qualitative research will highlight these features. The researcher would probably wish his or her manuscript to be assessed according to how well it demonstrated them.

Theory-Driven [Truth-Seeking/Qualitative] Approaches

Although their adherents would be uncomfortable lumped in the same category, conflict theories and structural-functional theories are two of several social theories used by qualitative researchers to explain social life. Researchers in this category establish field relations, collect data, respect the context as an influence on human behavior, and strive to understand the meanings of the people they encounter. Unlike the interpretivists, however, they use the meanings of actors as a point of departure. They explain meanings and acts from a deterministic framework of more basic and supraindividual social structures and forces. Thus, a conflict theorist sees schools as both representing and reproducing the existing class and economic divisions in the society as a whole. The researcher operating from this framework will choose topics for study and focus the analysis of data around these themes, showing how the underlying social forces are worked out in the particular contexts studied. Structural functionalism, in contrast, views schools as one component in a cohesive system of interlocking parts. The researcher identifies how the schools function with respect to the larger system and identifies dysfunctional aspects. In addition, researchers may view schools as smaller social systems that themselves have connecting substructures, each functioning to maintain the integrity of the school and contributing to the achievement of common goals. Because these approaches are deterministic, standards of reliability and validity, outlined above, may be applied. Illustrative works are Willis (1981) and Wolcott (1977).

Conclusion

The policy of the AERJ editors to encourage the submission of qualitative research will be welcomed by qualitative researchers of all types. Such a policy can only mean that editors will use different criteria to judge and select such studies from those they use for experiments and surveys. Editors should also understand that different ideologies exist within the discipline of qualitative research. To send a manuscript submitted by an interpretivist to a systematist (or vice versa) is more likely to provoke unresolvable methodological debate than meaningful criticism or fair editorial recommendations. The editors must become ethnographers of the culture of qualitative research. Then reviews can be fairly solicited and properly understood.

References

Brauner, C. J. (1974). The first probe. In D. Sjogren (Ed.), *Four evaluation examples* (pp. 77–98). Chicago: Rand McNally.

Brewer, M. B. & Collins, B. E. (1981). *Scientific inquiry and the social sciences.* San Francisco: Jossey-Bass.

Dabbs, J. M., Jr. (1982). Making things visible. In J. Van Maanen, J. M. Dabbs, Jr., & R. F. Faulkner (Eds.), *Varieties of qualitative research* (pp. 31–66). Beverly Hills, CA: Sage.

Donmoyer, R. (1985). The rescue from relativism: Two failed attempts and an alternative strategy. *Educational Researcher, 14*(10), 13–20.

Eisner, E. (1981). On the differences between scientific and artistic approaches to qualitative research. *Educational Researcher, 10*(4), 5–9.

Erickson, F. (1975). Gatekeeping and the melting pot: Interaction in counseling encounters. *Harvard Educational Review, 45*, 44–70.

Erickson, F. (1986). Qualitative methods in research on teaching. In M. Wittrock (Ed.), *Handbook of research on teaching* (3rd ed., pp. 119–161). New York: Macmillan.

Hood, L., McDermott, R. P., & Cole, M. (1980). "Let's try to make it a good day": Some not so simple ways. *Discourse Processes, 3*, 155–168.

House, E. R. (1980). *Evaluating with validity.* Beverly Hills, CA: Sage.

Kirk, J. & Miller, M. L. (1986). *Reliability and validity in qualitative research.* Beverly Hills, CA: Sage.

LeCompte, M. D. & Goetz, J. P. (1982). Problems of reliability and validity in ethnographic research. *Review of Educational Research, 52*, 31–60.

Miles, M. B. & Huberman, A. M. (1984a). Drawing valid meaning from qualitative data: Towards a shared craft. *Educational Researcher, 13*(5), 20–30.

Miles, M. B. & Huberman, A. M. (1984b). *Qualitative data analysis: A sourcebook of new methods.* Beverly Hills, CA: Sage.

Newman, D., Griffin, P., & Cole, M. (1984). Social constraints in laboratory and classroom tasks. In B. Rogoff & J. Lave (Eds.), *Everyday cognition* (pp. 172–193). Cambridge, MA: Harvard University Press.

Nisbet, R. (1976). *Sociology as an art form.* New York: Oxford University Press.

Phillips, D. C. (1983). After the wake: Postpositivistic educational thought. *Educational Researcher, 12*(5), 4–12.

Rein, M. (1978). *Social science and public policy.* New York: Penguin Books.

Rogoff, B. & Lave, J. (1984). *Everyday cognition.* Cambridge, MA: Harvard University Press.

Scribner, S. (1984). Studying working intelligence. In B. Rogoff & J. Lave (Eds.), *Everyday cognition* (pp. 9–40). Cambridge, MA: Harvard University Press.

Smith, J. K. (1983). Quantitative versus qualitative research: An attempt to clarify the issue. *Educational Researcher, 12*(3), 6–13.

Stryker, S. (1980). *Symbolic interactionism.* Menlo Park, CA: Benjamin-Cummings.

Willis, P. (1981). *Learning to labor: How working class kids get working class jobs.* New York: Columbia University Press.

Wolcott, H. F. (1977). *Teachers versus technocrats.* Eugene, OR: Center for Educational Policy and Management, University of Oregon.

The Contribution of a Qualitative Method:
Phenomenological Research

Renata Tesch, Ph. D.

Introduction

We have recently been reminded that qualitative research encompasses many different approaches. Although I find it difficult to believe that educational researchers ever considered qualitative methods "monolithic" (Fetterman, 1987, p. 1), and that they ever were "confused," because they used the "one-approach treatment" (Jacob, 1988, p. 23), it is true that in education we have paid attention mostly to one qualitative method: ethnography. Any educator interested in research, however, will also be acquainted with, or at least have heard of, naturalistic research (Guba, 1978; Lincoln & Guba, 1985), artistic approaches (Eisner, 1981), and the qualitative evaluation strategies Michael Quinn Patton has described (Patton, 1980). It seems odd that Jacob felt she must look at non-educational disciplines to enlighten us about the diversity of qualitative methods, since "qualitative approaches [with]in the field of educational research represent a wealth of useful, practical alternatives" (Fetterman, 1987, p. 1). I especially regret the omission of a method that has a long history of contributions to education: phenomenological research.[1] Curiously, it showed up in the AERA convention subject index for the first time as early as 1979, just one year after ethnography was introduced as a subject. Unlike ethnography, however, phenomenological research has made only sporadic appearances since then in the convention index, in spite of the fact that the contingent of phenomenological researchers has grown, that a journal specifically for phenomenological research in education has been published for six years, and that phenomenological researchers have presented their work regularly at AERA conventions since 1982, regardless of whether the subject index actually included the term or not.

I am not sure why phenomenological research has remained relatively obscure in AERA circles. Perhaps the very term "phenomenological" has contributed to this state of affairs, since it is not one we encounter frequently in the regular course of events. "Phenomenological" sounds somewhat esoteric and mystifying. Accordingly, the phenomenological method might be presumed to be too philosophical or too intuitive; at any rate: not very concrete or systematic.

Tesch, R. *The contribution of a qualitative method: Phenomenological research.* Paper presented at AERA, 1988. Available from Qualitative Research Management, 73425 Hilltop Road, Desert Hot Springs, CA 92240. Reprinted with permission.

Whether or not such prejudices exist, the contribution of phenomenological research has been too substantial to be disregarded. The purpose of this paper is to rectify the omission of phenomenological research from the recent attention to alternate perspectives within qualitative research methodologies, and perhaps to correct some misperceptions.

What is phenomenological research, where did it come from, how does one conduct it, what did it contribute to the discipline, and what are its shortcomings and merits as seen by its critics and its advocates? These are the questions that will be briefly addressed in this paper.

What Is Phenomenological Research?

Unlike ethnography, phenomenological research did not grow out of a specific social science discipline. Instead, it is based on a set of philosophical notions, entertained originally by Edmund Husserl, a German of Bohemian extraction, during the early part of this century. "Phenomenology is the study of the structure, and the variations of structure, of the consciousness to which any thing, event, or person appears. It is interested in elucidating both that which appears and the manner in which it appears, as well as in the overall structure that relates the 'that which' with its mode or manner." (Giorgi, 1975, p. 83). This is the definition provided by A. Giorgi, the psychologist who probably has written more about phenomenological research than any other American scholar. It is hardly surprising that phrases like these do not immediately inspire the ordinary researcher. Less dramatically, one could say that "phenomenology is the systematic investigation of subjectivity" (Bullington & Karlson, 1984, p. 51). Its aim is "to study the world as it appears to us in and through consciousness" (ibid., p. 51). Since it is only "in the description of experiences that human consciousness can be revealed" (Barritt et al., 1985, p. 29), "phenomenology asks: What is the participant's experience like?" (Barritt et al., 1983, p. 140). These latter are quotes from Loren Barritt, a prominent phenomenological researcher, whom I regard highly for daring to use simple language in his scholarly writings. He summarizes: "We mean by it the understanding of an event from the point of view of the participant" (Barritt, ibid., p. 140).

Expressed this way, the entire matter now appears so simple that one might wonder: What is scientific about exploring experience; isn't experience common knowledge? "Not quite" would be the phenomenologist's response. In the case of ourselves, our awareness might need to be heightened, and in the case of others, our perception may be distorted by various cultural habits of thinking, or by theoretical constructs that we habitually draw upon to explain the world to ourselves. That is why one of Husserl's main tenets was: Go to the things themselves, i.e. "examine experience critically by bracketing out preconceived ideas." (Barritt et al., 1985, p. 20) We must make an effort to rid ourselves of our preconceptions; we must suspend them, or lay them aside. Only then can we transcend the taken-for-granted aspects of everyday experiences, only then can we see them in a new way and "explore the tacit understanding from which the social and educational world is constructed" (Shapiro, 1983, p. 131).

Granted, you might say, that this kind of reflection would produce greater insight into our experiences; but what good would it do us? What would we gain? The phenomenologist's answer is: a better understanding of the meaning an experience has for others (and also for ourselves). To quote Barritt again: "From phenomenological study one hopes to achieve an awareness of different ways of thinking and acting" (Barritt et al., 1985, p. 32). Rather than asking what the underlying causes are, i.e., what relationship one variable has to other variables, "the researcher's aim . . . is to uncover the inherent logic of the experience or phenomenon, the way it makes sense to its subjects" (Dukes, 1984, p. 199).

Let me exemplify the phenomenological approach on a concrete topic. If a phenomenological researcher were asked to consider the problem of discipline in the classroom, s/he would not try to measure anything or even operationally define discipline. Instead, the question would immediately translate into: What does "discipline" mean to the two parties involved? First, what does discipline mean to the student? Since discipline problems occur when rules are broken, perhaps the following would be the specific question the researcher would ask: What is the experience of breaking rules like? S/he would proceed to find out from the students directly. Before she begins, she would question her own assumptions. For instance, one of her assumptions might be that breaking rules in the classroom is a form of insubordination, i.e., a challenge to authority. Once aware of such presupposition, she is prepared to set this notion aside and be open to quite different perspectives. In fact, students might provide information that leads her/him to conclude that breaking rules is an antidote for boredom, or that it has the attraction of adventure because of the risk involved of getting caught, or that it improves one's standing in the eyes of the classmates, or that it means still something else, or all of this. Likewise, the researcher would explore what "discipline" means to the teacher, i.e., how student rule-breaking affects her, what it feels like to stand in front of a hard-to-control class, what the notion of "being in control" signifies to the teacher, etc.

Once the phenomenon is more deeply understood on this subjective level, educators could ask questions like: In what situations do discipline problems arise most easily, and what would we want to do about them? If the researcher had found out, for instance, that for most students rule-breaking means relief from boredom, the teacher's intervention would be quite different from the one she would have undertaken had she acted on her assumption of insubordination.

Of course, ethnography and other qualitative research methods pay attention to subjective aspects in their explorations as well. The feature that distinguishes phenomenology from other qualitative research approaches is that the subjective experience is at the center of the inquiry. Whether or not a certain teacher is lenient or tough in matters of discipline, for instance, is not important when the student's experience is investigated; what matters is that the student experiences the teacher as tough or lenient. That is how the student's own behavior makes sense to her or him. "Phenomenology . . . makes no judgment with respect to the reality status of experiences. It merely wants to understand how, through experience, all the events and objects of the world appear to the consciousness" (Giorgi, 1988, p. 12).

Studying human experience can be done from a psychological, educational, sociological, and still other perspectives. Phenomenological research, therefore, is inter-disciplinary. Furthermore, it is by no means a unified approach. As a philosophy phenomenology has developed many different strands.[2] The research approaches that evolved from or were influenced by phenomenological thought are even more numerous (Chris Aanstoos identifies 11 of them in psychology alone) (Aanstoos, 1987). Naturalistic inquiry and grounded theory incorporate phenomenological assumptions, and Magoon's "constructivist perspective" is based on premises that sound very similar to phenomenological ones (Magoon, 1977). The most important new development for educational researchers is likely to be phenomenography, a type of research growing out of the work of the Swedish educator Ference Marton.

The group of researchers around Marton at the University of Goeteborg is concentrating on the study of learning and thinking, focussing on people's common sense conceptions with which they explain the world around them. Marton contends that just as, over the course of history, the understanding changes that science provides us about phenomena such as velocity, proportions (in mathematics), pricing (in economics), etc. so individual understandings change among and within learners. Rather than studying the process of thinking and learning on some abstract structural level, he proposes to study the content of thinking, i.e., the explanations people carry around in their heads for the various aspects of reality they encounter. There exists, he suggests, only "a relatively limited number of qualitatively different ways" in which any given phenomenon is conceptualized (Marton, 1981, p. 181). Therefore, it is possible to describe and categorize these conceptions, although, of course, a complete and "ultimate" description of the substance of human thinking can never be achieved (ibid., p. 197), especially since new forms of explanations and conceptions are continually introduced by science.

Phenomenography is not, like phenomenology, the application of a philosophical method to research; the name was chosen in 1979 after the approach had been developed, since it has in common with it as an aim the "description, analysis, and understanding of experiences" (ibid., p. 180). While it has similarities to phenomenological research, it cannot be considered typical of this method. Actually, the "typical" phenomenological researcher does not exist, since "phenomenology encompasses a loose confederation of people who share some important beliefs about the content of a human science" (Barritt et al., 1985, p. 30). However, these shared beliefs have resulted in some commonly accepted practices among phenomenologists. In order to clarify further the unique features of phenomenological research, I will compare some of its major characteristics to our familiar ethnography.

Some Distinctions between Phenomenological Research and Ethnography

Both phenomenological research and ethnography are descriptive/interpretive forms of research. At the center of ethnographic research, however, is the concept of culture; at the center of phenomenological research is the human experience of the "life-world." "Ethnography is concerned with discovering the relationship between culture and behavior" says George Spindler, for instance (Spindler & Spindler, 1988, p. 1). A major part of the ethnographic task is to elicit " . . . sociocultural knowledge in as systematic a fashion as possible" (ibid). If one would claim that phenomenological research is interested in any relationship at all, it would be the relationship between "consciousness" or "awareness" and the personal construction of one's world, i.e., the sense-making. Therefore, in principle, phenomenological research can be (and occasionally has been) done with a single case, or even just the researcher's personal experience. There is, however, a requirement in phenomenology to explore what is invariable across all the manifestations of the phenomenon. Although some researchers use imaginative variation to ascertain the invariable, most prefer the concrete variations among different people, and therefore, phenomenological researchers have traditionally worked with at least five to ten people. The limits on the number of participants are imposed by the researcher's available resources in conducting intensive, multiple, in-depth explorations with each of her study participants.

Ethnographers call the people from whom they collect information "informants," rather than participants. They usually study "sites" not individuals. Typically, the ethnographer's primary form of data collection is observation, either as a participant or as a designated observer, with occasional interviewing for clarification and detail. Phenomenological researchers rely almost exclusively on interviews, using observation only where verbalization is insufficient, as for instance with children or mentally handicapped people. The phenomenological interview is very different from the ethnographic one. Whereas the ethnographer pays a lot of attention to language, and especially to the use of terms that are used in unique ways in a certain culture, language for the phenomenological researcher is a mere means of expressing awareness, and an inadequate one at that. Therefore, phenomenological researchers encourage their participants to reiterate, to express things in different ways, even just to "carry on." It is the researcher who later puts all these statements together and reads between the lines, then transforms the participant's language into a more professional one, according to the scholarly discipline in which s/he is working.

The phenomenological interview is not a series of questions and answers. It could be more aptly described as dialogical reflection. Together, the researcher and the participant, who is invited to act as co-researcher, attempt to arrive at the heart of the matter, trying out different paths. The researcher is at her best when she gets answers of importance to questions she has not specifically asked. The interview is "a social encounter which will go its own way if done well" (Barritt et al., 1985, p. 204), and the interviewer's toughest task is "learning to be silent so the participant can speak" (ibid., p. 54).

The phenomenological analysis of the transcribed interview data has much in common with other qualitative analysis procedures (Tesch, 1987), but is more open at the beginning, more tentative, and more intuitive. This does not mean that it is done haphazardly or impressionistically. Quite to the contrary, phenomenologists expect data analysis to be thorough and systematic; "its rigor consists in the insistence that its analyses account for *every* encountered instance of the phenomenon" (Fischer, 1975, p. 150). Rather than partitioning the transcripts according to events, phenomenological researchers identify and examine "meaning units," the smallest segments of text that are understandable by themselves. They do not establish categories, but aim at discovering the "themes" in the data, or, as phenomenologists sometimes say, the "constituents of the phenomenon." The final result is not a set of relational assertions about the culture (or phenomenon) studied (Erickson, 1986, p. 146), but a narrative that delineates a pattern, or, expressed phenomenologically, a description of "the structural invariants of a particular type of experience" (Dukes, 1984, p. 201).

Whether or not a result is plausible depends, of course, on some of the same criteria that any descriptive/interpretive research employs: provision of evidence, consistency, and freedom from obvious bias. While ethnographers, however, make use of triangulation to strengthen the trustworthiness of their results, phenomenologists hardly ever have that option: What is going on inside a person is usually not accessible other than through reflective dialogue. On the other hand, the participants themselves provide a panel for judgment: if they do not recognize their own case in the researcher's analysis results, the results are obviously unacceptable. Consequently, phenomenological researchers usually return to their participants for confirmation and correction. Sometimes, of course, the topic is too delicate to make such action advisable, for instance, where the participants would find themselves depicted in a way that is not flattering. In addition to the participants themselves, the reader of the phenomenological description is called upon to ascertain whether the description rings true, provided, of course, that the phenomenon under study is a general experience, or one the particular reader is familiar with. In the case of education the value of a phenomenological study is measured in terms of its power to let us come to an understanding of ourselves, and "an understanding of the lives of those for whom we bear pedagogic responsibility" (Langeveld, 1983, p. 7).

Phenomenological Research in Education

History and Current Status

The last quote was from the Dutch educator Martinus Langeveld. I remember hearing of him first during my own time of teacher training in the 1950s in Germany. He differed from other researchers by his method of observing and talking with children in everyday situations, rather than talking about them in generalizations. Langeveld maintained that "pedagogical theory must first of all be helpful, and the only way it can be helpful is not to concentrate on generality, but insist on relevance to life" (in Bleeker et al., 1986, p. 4). It was Langeveld's student Ton Beekman who probably was most influential in bringing phenomenological research to educators in the USA. He is the author of the first workbook for doing phenomenological research. Through his connection with Loren Barritt, who had studied phenomenology in the Netherlands and translated the workbook and collaborated on it (Barritt et al., 1985), Ton Beekman was invited for lectures at the University of Michigan in Ann Arbor in 1976, where he taught and inspired young researchers, and was re-invited several times. During the past decade, the researchers he and Barritt trained have, in turn, taught others, thus creating a network of capable phenomenological researchers in pockets all over the United States. In addition, phenomenological work had been promoted since the early 1970s at the Center for Teaching and Learning of the University of North Dakota in Grand Forks (Carini, 1975), and David Denton from the University of Kentucky was probably the first educator to acquaint AERA researchers with phenomenology in 1979 (Denton, 1979).

While the University of Michigan still seems to have the most active research center for phenomenological research in education, groups of phenomenological scholars in education and developmental psychology or educational sociology have begun to be established at other universities, including the University of Florida, Syracuse University, and the University of California at Davis. At many other places individual researchers use phenomenological methods in their research, often at the expense of not being acknowledged as serious scholars by their more traditional colleagues.

Compared with selected other countries, the American community of phenomenological researchers in education is still relatively small. In Canada, four major centers exist: at the University of Alberta in Edmonton, at York University in Ontario, at Laval University, and at the Ontario Institute for Studies in Education in Toronto. In the Netherlands, of course, the tradition of phenomenological research is being upheld, especially in Utrecht, where Langeveld is professor emeritus. Germany also has a long history of phenomenological thought in education, and current contributions are made by a number of first-class researchers from at least four different universities. In Sweden, Ference Marton is doing "phenomenography," as described earlier in this paper. He introduced this concept with a group of his colleagues from the University of Goeteborg in 1980 to the AERA audience in Boston. Smaller groups of phenomenological researchers work in Denmark, Belgium, England, Brazil, Australia, South Africa, and Japan.

Many of these researchers have been getting together annually since 1982 at an international and interdisciplinary meeting called the "Human Science Research Conference." In 1983 a journal specifically devoted to phenomenological studies in education began to appear in Canada under the editorship of another Dutch-educated scholar, Max van Manen. It is called "Phenomenology + Pedagogy." 1986 saw the beginning of a journal devoted to the process and principles of Human Science work, called *methods,* which is connected with the Saybrook Institute in San Francisco.

The translation of Ton Beekman's book in 1983 and publication in 1985 made available the first methodological text in the U.S. An earlier attempt (in 1977) to describe practical steps in the conduct of phenomenological research, undertaken by Rolf von Eckartsberg at Duquesne University, had remained unpublished. To assist beginning researchers, Phenomenology + Pedagogy devoted its fourth issue (Polakow-Suransky, 1984) to teaching and doing phenomenology. In addition, many papers on methodological issues have been presented at the Human Science Research conferences over the years. Thus the phenomenological researcher is no longer a pioneer, although this work still requires flexibility and inventiveness. One of the main characteristics of the phenomenological method is its openness and creativeness, which resists codification. There will never be a canon of fixed phenomenological procedures that a researcher can follow rather mindlessly. In essence, so agree phenomenologists, phenomenology "is not a methodology at all, but a perspective on what constitutes knowledge in the human sciences" (Dukes, 1984, p. 202).

The Contributions of American Educational Phenomenologists

The list of important phenomenological studies in education begins with Langeveld's work and has grown impressively during the past decade. A selected list of studies is appended to this paper. Let me give you a brief and incomplete overview.

Loren Barritt and Valerie Polakow-Suransky are the most prominent educational researchers from the Ann Arbor circle. Both have concentrated on issues in early childhood. Barritt's studies of the meaning of the environment to young children and their world of play reveal the impact of our modern city designs on their life-world. Polakow-Suransky's provocative book on modern child care institutions was followed by research on such fundamental early childhood events as learning to read and telling stories. Other American educators have explored a myriad of topics, in particularly those phenomena of childhood to which adults rarely give a second thought because they are so ordinary that it is difficult to realize how differently the child experiences them. Much attention has been paid to children in difficult circumstances, as well as to mundane educational processes like classroom life and homework that educators in the past have neglected to view through the child's eye. What it is like to be an educator, such as a student teacher, a teacher of the disabled, a school principal, etc. are also questions that have not traditionally been asked by researchers, but can be of great significance for educational decision-making.

In addition to these practical topics, various issues in the philosophy of education have received phenomenological consideration by authors that include Maxine Greene (1983, 1985) and Henry Giroux (1985). Furthermore, the discipline of psychology has contributed a number of important studies to education, notably the illumination of the process of learning through the work of two prominent psychologists from Duquesne University (Giorgi and Colaizzi). Graduate programs in phenomenological psychology had been established at Duquesne (MA 1958, doctoral 1962) through Adrian van Kaam, another Dutchman. Some of the faculty and students have subsequently dealt with educationally relevant topics like intelligence (Fischer, 1975), motivation (von Eckartsberg, 1975), remembering (Lyons, 1983), and thinking (Aanstoos, 1983).

Critique of Phenomenological Research

Phenomenological research is, naturally, not without opponents. There are two main directions from which criticism has been leveled against phenomenological research. One comes from more traditional researchers and attacks mainly the methods used. The other originated from proponents of a critical social science and concerns the results.

The traditional accusation that the method is not "scientific" since it is not "rigorous" and has no "external validity" to speak of, is one that phenomenological research shares with other descriptive/interpretive methodologies. The arguments are familiar to all qualitative researchers, and, therefore, no longer worth repeating. Most of us have become tired of the debate, which has by now shifted from questioning the legitimacy of the method to a discussion about the complementarity of the two approaches as opposed to their philosophical incompatibility. Suffice it to say that the person who made phenomenology a vital force in the field of psychology in the U.S., Amedeo Giorgi, came to phenomenology through his search for an alternative to experimental research that, specifically, would be "rigorous, [but] did not involve transformation into numbers" (Giorgi, 1975, p. 72). He did not look for a soft science or even anti-science.

The criticism by scientists who base their work on the philosophical thoughts of Horkheimer, Adorno, Marcuse (Carr & Kemmis, 1986, p. 131), but particularly Juergen Habermas (ibid., p. 133), and therefore believe that science must "serve the emancipatory interest in freedom and rational autonomy," is more intriguing. These scientists see the shortcomings of phenomenology (and other description/interpretive methods) in the neglect to question "the relationship between the individual's interpretations and actions and external factors and circumstances." "While it may be true that social reality is constructed and maintained through the interactions of individuals, it is also the case that the range of possible interpretations of reality that are open to individuals is constrained by the particular society in which we live" (ibid., p. 95). By merely exploring how persons experience their life-world, "all those situations in which people's self-understanding of what they are doing is illusory or deceptive will be left unexplained" (ibid., p. 96). Phenomenologists, it is claimed, do not take into account the possibility of a "false consciousness," created by "social mechanism [that] operate to bind people to irrational and distorted ideas about their social reality" (ibid., p.

96). Therefore, research must go beyond the "subjectivist" stance of the interpretive researcher (ibid., p. 183) and "problematize" its accounts (ibid., p. 215).

As far as I know, phenomenological researchers have not yet responded directly to these fairly recent criticisms (Carr & Kemmis, 1986). However, there is an element within phenomenological research that has always taken a critical stance rather than merely a descriptive one. Its most outspoken representative is Valerie Polakow-Suransky, who considers phenomenology explicitly a "force for social change" (Polakow-Suransky, 1980). She points to the notion of the dialectic that is inherent in phenomenology, which "forces us continually to view the world in flux, in terms of a conflict mode of existence" (ibid., p. 171). As an example she cites Paulo Freire, who has shown that "it is only through this dialectical reflection upon the given social reality that a new social consciousness will emerge which paves the way for praxis" (ibid., p. 172). Polakow-Suransky concludes that "conscientization espouses a dialectical orientation toward the educational process and engenders liberating education" (ibid., p. 175).

The critics of phenomenology might counter that awareness and action are not as easily linked as this phenomenologist seems to imply. Nevertheless, most mainstream phenomenologists would tell you that they think of their efforts as directed towards more than mere description. If people understand themselves better, if we understand each other better, if teachers understand children better, these awarenesses are bound to make a difference. "By heightening awareness and creating dialogue, it is hoped research can lead to a better understanding of the way things appear to someone else, and through that insight lead to improvements in practice" (Barritt, 1986, p. 21). Whether or not it is sufficient to "hope" for an improvement in practice is disputed, but it is doubtlessly true that awareness is a precondition for change. Without the kind of understanding, to the systematic study of which phenomenologists are devoted, transformation in educational practice in terms of human, rather than mere technical improvement cannot possibly occur.

Notes

1. Fetterman does mention phenomenography, a method that is based on some of the same principles as phenomenological research.

2. The main "branches" of phenomenology are transcendental, existential, and hermeneutic. (Barritt et al., 1985, p. 23)

References

Aanstoos, C. M. (1983). A phenomenological study of thinking. In Giorgi, A., Barton, A., & Maes, C. (Eds.), *Duquesne studies in phenomenological psychology*. Vol. IV. (pp. 244–256). Pittsburgh: Duquesne University Press.

Aanstoos, C. M. (1987). A comparative survey of human science psychologies. *Methods, 1*(2), 1–36.

Barritt, L. (1986). Human science and the human image. *Phenomenology + Pedagogy, 4*(3), 14–22.

Barritt, L., Beekman, A. J., Bleeker, H., & Mulderij, K. (1983). The world through children's eyes: Hide and seek & peekaboo. *Phenomenology + Pedagogy, 1*(2), 140–161.

Barritt, L., Beekman, A. J., Bleeker, H., & Mulderij, K. (1984). Analyzing phenomenological descriptions. *Phenomenology + Pedagogy, 2*(1), 1–17.

Barritt, L., Beekman, A. J., Bleeker, H., & Mulderij, K. (1985). *Researching education practice.* Grand Forks, ND: University of North Dakota, Center for Teaching and Learning.

Beekman, A. J. & Mulderij, K. J. (1977) *Believing in ervaring: Werkboek fenomenologie voor de sociale wetenschappen.* Meppel, Germany: Boom.

Bleeker, H., Levering, B., & Mulderij, K. (1986). On the beginning of qualitative research in pedagogy in the Netherlands. *Phenomenology + Pedagogy, 4*(3), 3–13.

Bullington, J. & Karlson, G. (1984). Introduction to phenomenological psychological research. *Scandinavian Journal of Psychology, 25,* 51–63.

Carini, P. F. (1975). *Observation and description: An alternative methodology for the investigation of human phenomena.* Grand Forks, ND: University of North Dakota, Center for Teaching and Learning.

Carr, W. & Kemmis, S. (1986). *Becoming critical: Education, knowledge, and action research.* Philadelphia: The Falmer Press.

Coalizzi, P. F. (1971). Analysis of the learner's perception of learning material at various phases of a learning process. In Giorgi, A., Fischer, W. F., & von Eckartsberg, R. (Eds.), *Duquesne studies in phenomenological psychology.* Vol. I. (pp. 101–111). Pittsburgh: Duquesne University Press.

Curtis, B. & Mays, W. (1978). *Phenomenology and education.* London: Methuen & Co. Ltd.

Denton, D. E. (1979). *Concepts and strategies of phenomenological research.* Paper presented at the annual convention of the American Educational Research Association, San Francisco.

Dukes, S. (1984). Phenomenological methodology in the human sciences. *Journal of Religion and Health, 23*(3), 197–203.

von Eckartsberg, R. (1975). The eco-psychology of motivational theory and research. In Giorgi, A., Fischer, C., & Murray, E. (Eds.), *Duquesne studies in phenomenological psychology.* Vol. II. (pp. 155–181). Pittsburgh: Duquesne University Press.

Eisner, E. W. (1981). On the differences between scientific and artistic approaches to qualitative research. *Educational Researcher, 10*(2), 5–9, (April).

Erickson, F. (1986). Qualitative methods in research on teaching. In Wittrock, M. C. (Ed.) *Handbook of research on teaching.* New York: Macmillan Publishing Company.

Fetterman, D. M. (1987). *Qualitative approaches to evaluation research.* Paper presented at the American Educational Research Association annual convention, Washington D. C.

Fischer, C. T. (1975). Intelligence contra IQ: A human science critique and alternative to the natural science approach to man. In Giorgi, A., Fischer, C., & Murray, E. (Eds.), *Duquesne studies in phenomenological psychology.* Vol. II. (pp. 143–154). Pittsburgh: Duquesne University Press.

Giorgi, A. (1975). A phenomenological approach to the problem of meaning and serial learning. In Giorgi, A., Fischer, W. F., & von Eckartsberg, R. (Eds.), *Duquesne studies in phenomenological psychology.* Vol. I. (pp. 88–100). Pittsburgh: Duquesne University Press.

Giorgi, A. (1975). An application of phenomenological method in Psychology. In Giorgi, A., Fischer, W. F., & von Eckartsberg, R. (Eds.) (1975) *Duquesne studies in phenomenological psychology.* Vol. II. (pp. 82–103) Pittsburgh: Duquesne University Press.

Giorgi, A. (1985). The phenomenological psychology of learning. In Giorgi, A. *Phenomenology and psychological research.* Pittsburgh: Duquesne University Press.

Giorgi, A. (1988). Saybrook at a glance. *Saybrook Perspective,* Winter, (12).

Giroux, H. A. (1985). Intellectual labor and pedagogical work: Rethinking the role of teacher as intellectual. *Phenomenology + Pedagogy, 3*(1), 20–31.

Greene, M. (1983). How I came to phenomenology. *Phenomenology + Pedagogy, 1*(1), 3–4.

Greene, M. (1985). Consciousness and the public space: Discovering a pedagogy. *Phenomenology + Pedagogy, 3*(2), 69–83.

Guba, E. G. (1978). *Toward a methodology of naturalistic inquiry in educational evaluation.* Los Angeles: Center for the Study of Evaluation, University of California.

Jacob, E. (1987). Qualitative research traditions: A review. *Review of Educational Research, 57*(1), 1–50.

Jacob, E. (1988). Clarifying qualitative research: A focus on traditions. *Educational Researcher, 17*(1), 16–24.

Langeveld, M. (1983). Reflections on phenomenology and pedagogy. *Phenomenology + Pedagogy, 1*(1), 5–7.

Lincoln, Y. S. & Guba, E. G. (1985). *Naturalistic inquiry.* Beverly Hills: Sage Publications.

Lyons, J. (1983). Remembering and psychotherapy. In Giorgi, A., Barton, A., & Maes, C. (Eds.), *Duquesne studies in phenomenological psychology.* Vol. IV. (pp. 47–70). Pittsburgh: Duquesne University Press.

Magoon, A. J. (1977). Constructivist approaches in educational research. *Review of Educational Research, 47*(4), 651–693.

Marton, F. (1981). Phenomenography—Describing conceptions of the world around us. *Instructional Science, 10*, 177–200.

Patton, M. Q. (1980). *Qualitative evaluation methods.* Beverly Hills: Sage Publications.

Polakow-Suranski, V. (1980). Phenomenology: An alternative research paradigm and a force for social change. *Journal of the British Society for Phenomenology, 11*(2), 163–179.

Polakow-Suransky, V. (1982). *The erosion of childhood.* Chicago: University of Chicago Press.

Polakow-Suransky, V. (1984). Reflections on pedagogy, research, and praxis. *Phenomenology + Pedagogy, 2*(1), 29–35.

Polakow-Suransky, V. (1984). On meaningmaking and stories: Young children's experiences with texts. *Phenomenology + Pedagogy, 4*(3), 37–47.

Shapiro, H. S. (1983). Educational research, social change and the challenge to methodology: A study in the sociology of knowledge. *Phenomenology + Pedagogy, 1*(2), 127–139.

Spindler, G. & Spindler, L. (1988). *Outline of the substance of ethnographic research.* Workshop handout, Qualitative Research Workshop, Athens, Georgia.

Tesch, R. (1987). *Comparing the most widely used methods of qualitative analysis: What do they have in common?* Paper presented at the annual convention of the American Educational Research Association, Washington, D. C.

van Manen, M. (1986). We need to show our human science practice is a relation of pedagogy. *Phenomenology + Pedagogy, 4*(3), 78–93.

Appendix A: Some Distinctions between Phenomenological Research and Ethnography

Ethnographic Research	*Phenomenological Research*
study of culture	study of the human experience of the "life-world"
discovering the relationship between culture and behavior	exploring the relationship between "consciousness" or "awareness" and the personal construction of one's world, i.e, sense-making
studying "sites"	studying individuals
as many "informants" as possible	between 5 and 15 "participants"

Ethnographic Research	*Phenomenological Research*
primarily observation, some interviewing	primarily in-depth, unstructured interviews
linguistically oriented	"meaning"-oriented
analysis structured	analysis open, tentative, intuitive
item of analysis: event	item of analysis: meaning unit
ordering according to categories	ordering according to "themes"
result: set of relational assertions about the culture	result: narrative that delineates a pattern
validity criteria: provision of evidence, consistency, and freedom from avoidable bias	validity criteria: provision of evidence, consistency, and freedom from avoidable bias
use of triangulation	confirmation by participants and reader

Appendix B: Education Topics Studied by American Phenomenological Researchers (A Selection)

Play (Valerie Polakow-Suransky, paper presented at the AERA convention 1984 in New Orleans.)

Hide-and-seek (Barritt, Beekman, Bleeker, and Mulderij, (1983). *Phenomenology + Pedagogy, 1*(2), 140–161.

Toys (Jay Mullin, 1984, *Phenomenology + Pedagogy, 1*(3), 268–284.)

Children's sense of time (Marc Briod, 1986, *Phenomenology + Pedagogy, 4*(1), 9–19.)

Children's space (Ellen Benswanger, *Duqesne Studies Vol. III*, 1979, 97–110.)

Children's jokes (Stephen Karatheodoris, 1984, *Phenomenology + Pedagogy, 1*(3), 285–295.)

Learning (Amedeo Giorgi, *Duqesne Studies Vol. I*, 1971, 88–100; Paul Coalizzi, ibid. 101–111; Amedeo Giorgi, 1985, Phenomenology and psychological research, p. 23–85.)

Thinking (Chris Aanstoos, *Duqesne Studies Vol. IV*, 1983, 244–256.)

Philosophical thinking in children (Gareth Matthews, 1983, *Phenomenology + Pedagogy, 1*(1), 18–28.)

Intelligence and IQ (Constance Fischer, *Duqesne Studies Vol. II*, 1975, 143–154.)

Cognitive structure and development (Marton, Erickson, White, Hewson, McDermott, papers presented at the AERA convention 1984 in New Orleans.)

Reading (Margaret Hunsberger, paper presented at the AERA convention 1982 in New York.)

Stories (Valerie Polakow-Suransky, 1986, *Phenomenology + Pedagogy*, 4(3), 29–47.)

Children's concerns in middle childhood (Beverly Hardcastle, paper presented at the Human Science Research conference 1985.)

Children whose parents are unemployed (E. Keairns, paper presented at the Human Science Research conference 1984.)

Children whose mothers are in prison (Christina Jose, paper presented at the Human Science Research conference 1985.)

Suffering in children (Kathleen Lentz, paper presented at the Human Science Research conference 1985.)

Coping styles of children (Marilyn Maxson, paper presented at the Human Science Research conference 1985.)

Father-daughter incest (Rebecca Reviere, paper presented at the Human Science Research conference 1984.)

Autism (Kathleen Haney, paper presented at the Human Science Research conference 1984.)

The uncooperative, "difficult" child (Jane Adan, 1987, *Phenomenology + Pedagogy*, 5(1), 22–34.)

Being labeled "learning disabled" (John Murphy, paper presented at the Human Science Research conference 1987.)

Teaching neglected and abused children (Ann Wood, paper presented at the Human Science Research conference 1985.)

The schooling experience (Marion Evashevski, paper presented at the Human Science Research conference 1985.)

The urban classroom (Forrest Parkey, paper presented at the Human Science Research conference 1985.)

The meaning of curriculum (Francine Hultgren, 1982, doctoral dissertation, Pennsylvania State University, and Terrance Carson, 1984, doctoral dissertation, University of Alberta at Edmonton.)

Teaching loyalty (Mary Moore, 1984, *Phenomenology + Pedagogy*, 1(3), 312–318.)

Art classes in grade one (Catherine Wynnyk, paper presented at the Human Science Research conference 1986.)

Computer-mediated education (John Murphy, 1985, *Phenomenology + Pedagogy*, 3(3), 167–176, and Walter Parker, 1986, *Phenomenology + Pedagogy*, 4(1), 20–31.)

Learning computer skills (Chris Mruk, paper presented at the Human Science Research conference 1984.)

The anxious math student (Michael Smith, paper presented at the Human Science Research conference 1984.)

The role of homework in the lives of children (Jeanne Sullivan, paper presented at the Human Science Research conference 1986.)

The student athlete (Harry McLaughlin, paper presented at the Human Science Research conference 1987.)

Physical education games (Nancy Wessinger, paper presented at the Human Science Research conference 1987.)

Classroom management (J'Anne Ellsworth and Alicia Monahan, paper presented at the Human Science Research conference 1987.)

Teacher-student relationships (Carol Becker, paper presented at the Human Science Research conference 1985.)

The student teacher (Francine Hultgren, 1987, *Phenomenology + Pedagogy*, 5(1), 35–50.)

Novice teachers (Sharon Santilli, Earl Seidman, paper presented at the 1988 AERA convention in New Orleans.)

Being an English teacher (Chett Breed, paper presented at the Human Science Research conference 1984; Loren Barritt, paper presented at the AERA convention 1984 in New Orleans.)

The meaning of children in the lives of adults (David Smith, 1983, doctoral dissertation, University of Alberta at Edmonton.)

The racial integration of an elementary school (Virginia Bartel, paper presented at the Human Science Research conference 1985.)

Home schooling (Claudia Beaven, paper presented at the Human Science Research conference 1985.)

Adolescent drug abuse (Barry Wolf, 1979, doctoral dissertation, University of Michigan at Ann Arbor, and Marita Delaney, paper presented at the Human Science Research conference 1986.)

Marginal college students (Jack Ling, paper presented at the Human Science Research conference 1986.)

Adult education and learning (John Dewitt, paper presented at the Human Science Research conference 1987, and Elissa Isaacson, paper presented at the Human Science Research conference 1987.)

Adult doctoral students (Ann Clark, 1980, doctoral dissertation, The Humanistic Psychology Institute, San Francisco, and Renata Tesch, 1983, paper presented at the CERA meeting 1983 in Los Angeles.)

Construct Validation of the Piers-Harris Children's Self Concept Scale

Melvin R. Franklin, Jr.

Stephen M. Duley

Elaine W. Rousseau

Darrell L. Sabers

Abstract

An investigation was conducted to determine the construct validity of the Piers-Harris Children's Self-Concept Scale (P-H). Evidence for the validity of the instrument was analyzed according to the model for construct validation proposed by Sabers and Whitney. The main parameters of the model include the convergent validity, discriminant validity, internal consistency, and stability of the measure. Results indicated that the P-H demonstrates both convergent and discriminant validity in an assessment of a relatively stable and internally consistent construct.

Educational goal-makers have tended to vacillate between an emphasis that is based solely upon cognitive outcomes and an emphasis that is concerned with non-cognitive social and affective outcomes. As there has been a noted re-emphasis on the non-cognitive outcomes of education, objectives and corresponding measures representing these outcomes have been incorporated into several educational programs. Torshen, Kroeker, and Peterson (1977) reported that twelve states have included self-concept measures as part of their statewide educational assessment programs. It is incumbent upon educators to demonstrate construct validation of self-concept prior to any formulation of educational goals and policies.

Wylie (1974) discussed the unresolved need for maximizing the construct validity of self-concept measures. Cowan, Altmann, and Pysh (1978), who used a form of both the multitrait-multimethod approach and factor analysis to investigate the construct validity of self-concept measures, suggested the existence of discriminant validity of the self-report self-concept instruments. Shavelson, Hubner, and Stanton (1976) concluded from a review of literature that scores on the Piers-Harris Children's Self Concept Scale (P-H) (Piers, 1969) warranted self-concept interpretations based on convergent validity coefficients. Watkins and Astilla (1980) found modest evidence of stability, discriminant validity, and convergent

Franklin, M. R., Duley, S. M., Rousseau, E. W., & Sabers, D. L. (1983). Construct validation of the Piers-Harris Children's Self Concept Scale. *Educational and Psychological Measurement, 41*(2), 439–443. Reprinted with permission.

validity for the Coppersmith (1967) Self-Esteem Inventory (SEI) but did not report an internal consistency coefficient. The Sabers and Whitney (1976) procedure provides a model for an extensive empirical construct validation of an instrument by examining four basic categories of evidence: convergent validity, discriminant validity, internal consistency, and the sensitivity of the measure to change.

Procedures

The methodology for establishing the construct validity of the P-H followed the model developed by Sabers and Whitney (1976). Efforts were directed toward answering the four questions considered basic to construct validation.

1. Does the P-H measure what it should (convergent validity)? This information was obtained through computation of the Pearson product-moment correlation of scores on the P-H and the SEI.
2. Does the P-H measure what it should not (discriminant validity)? Evidence for this category was secured by examining the Pearson product-moment correlation between the scores on the P-H and academic achievement—composite grade equivalent scores obtained from the Iowa Tests of Basic Skills (ITBS) (Lindquist and Hieronymous, 1955–1980), socioeconomic status (derived from eligibility figures for free and reduced breakfast and lunch programs), special education placement (based on entry on state special education rosters), ethnicity (designated according to United States Department of Health, Education, and Welfare guidelines), grade placement, gender, and age.
3. What conditions produce change in the scores (sensitivity to change)? An experimental (pretest-posttest control group) study was conducted in which the treatment was designed to improve the self-concept of fourth-grade children.
4. Does the P-H measure more than one thing (internal consistency)? Kuder-Richardson formula 20 reliability coefficients were obtained for the P-H for each group of students involved in the study.

Results

Convergent Validity

The P-H and the SEI were administered to all fourth-grade pupils (N = 248) from five elementary schools and to all seventh-grade students (N = 321) from a junior high school located within a metropolitan school district of approximately 9500 students in the southwestern United States. The composition of the sample was approximately 21% Hispanic, 75% Anglo, and 4% other ethnic classification. Both measures were administered in a group setting following standardization procedures.

A correlation coefficient of .78 ($p < .001$) was found between scores obtained on the P-H and the SEI for the combined sample of 569 children. The coefficients computed for the sample of fourth-grade pupils ($r = .75$; $p < .001$) and for the sample of seventh-grade students ($r = .81$; $p < .001$) separately provided additional evidence that the two instruments measured the same construct.

Discriminant Validity

Correlation coefficients of .18 for fourth-grade pupils and .22 for seventh-grade students between the P-H and academic achievement were significant at the .01 level. However, this degree of relationship accounted for less than 5% of the variance in the P-H scores. The P-H was not correlated significantly with socio-economic status, special education placement, ethnicity, grade placement, gender, or age for the 569 children in the previously described sample. Because the multiple correlation between the P-H and all other variables did not exceed .25 for either grade, it was concluded that the P-H has discriminant validity with respect to all the variables included in this analysis.

Sensitivity to Change

For this experiment, permission was obtained from Ellen Piers (1978) to divide the P-H into two 40-item forms for administering one as a pretest and the other as a posttest. The content of the two forms was made similar by content division. The data from the 569 children tested earlier were used to equate means and internal consistency coefficients.

Pupils participating in this aspect of the study came from five elementary schools located within a school district of over 11,000 students in the southwestern United States. The sample was approximately 60% Hispanic, 22% Anglo, and 17% Native American. After the administration of a pretest, fourth-grade classes were randomly assigned to a control group ($N = 90$) or to an experimental group ($N = 90$) receiving cross-age tutoring from high school students. The instruction, which lasted from four to six months, focused on each child's autobiography to emphasize the unique place of the child in his/her family. A posttest was given to all pupils six months after the pretest. With the exception that the tests had only 40 items, the administration of both pretests and posttests followed all standardization procedures.

A two-way repeated measures analysis of variance (ANOVA) was used for the analysis, with the interaction term intended to measure significance of the change that was associated with the treatment. The lack of significance of both the interaction ($F [1,178] = .56$) and of the main effect for tests ($F [1,178] = .93$) attested to the stability of the measure. Additional evidence of the stability of the P-H was given by the correlations between pretests and posttests. The coefficients, .48 ($p < .001$) for the experimental and .48 for the control group could be interpreted as measuring equivalence plus stability as they represent between-forms over-time correlations.

Internal Consistency

An internal consistency coefficient was equal to .92 ($p < .001$) for the total P-H scale relative to the combined samples of fourth- and seventh-grade students and exceeded .92 ($p < .001$) for the two grades separately. In addition, coefficients for the two 40-item forms previously described were .74 ($p < .001$) for the pretest relative to the combined treatment and control groups and .77 ($p < .001$) for the posttest also relative to the combined experimental and control groups. These findings, which represented a relatively high degree of internal consistency, suggested that the P-H measures essentially one trait.

Summary

The P-H was shown to have the convergent validity with respect to the SEI, discriminant validity relative to the other variables included in this study, and a comparatively high degree of internal consistency. The experiment conducted to change children's self-concept was not successful, in that the P-H scores appeared to be moderately stable over six months. In view of the failure of other efforts to demonstrate a change in self-concept (Peterson, 1977; Runion, 1976), it appears that, as Wylie (1974) has cautioned, measurement of change in self-concept may be better effected in some format other than that provided by self report. Further research into the issue of sensitivity of the measure to change is needed before the construct of self-reported self-concept is understood.

References

Coopersmith, S. (1967). *The antecedents of self-esteem.* San Francisco: W. H. Freeman and Co.

Cowan, R., Altmann, H., & Pysh, F. (1978). A validity study of selected self-concept instruments. *Measurement and Evaluation in Guidance, 10,* 211–221.

Lindquist, E. F. & Hieronymous, A. N. (1955–1980). *Iowa Tests of Basic Skills.* Houghton Mifflin.

Peterson, G. G. (1977). Developmental guidance activity and discussion groups' effect on first graders' self-concepts and behaviors. (Doctoral dissertation, University of Arizona, 1977). *Dissertation Abstracts International, 38,* 117A. (University Microfilms No. 77-15, 342).

Piers, E. V. (1969). *Manual for the Piers-Harris Children's Self Concept Scale.* Nashville, Tenn.: Counselor Recordings and Tests.

Piers, E. V. (1978). Personal communication, August 10.

Runion, K. B. (1976). The effects of activity group guidance on children's self-concept and social power. (Doctoral dissertation, University of Arizona, 1975). *Dissertation Abstracts International, 36,* 5057A. (University Microfilms No. 76-2539).

Sabers, D. L. & Whitney, D. R. (1976). *Suggestions for validating scales and attitude inventories* (Technical Bulletin No. 19). Iowa City: University of Iowa, Evaluation and Examination Service (mimeographed).

Shavelson, R. J., Hubner, J. J., & Stanton, G. C. (1976). Self-concept: Validation of construct interpretation. *Review of Educational Research, 46,* 407–441.

Torshen, K. P., Kroeker, L. P., & Peterson, R. A. (1977). Self-concept assessment for young children: Development of a self report, peer comparison measure. *Contemporary Educational Psychology, 2,* 325–331.

Watkins, D. & Astilla, E. (1980). The reliability and validity of the Coopersmith Self-Esteem Inventory for a sample of Filipino high school girls. *Educational and Psychology Measurement, 40,* 251–254.

Wylie, R. C. (1974). *The self-concept* (Vol. 1). Lincoln, Nebraska: University of Nebraska Press.

Here Was Fellowship:
A Social Portrait of Academic Women at Wellesley College, 1895–1920

Patricia A. Palmieri

In 1929, Historian Willystine Goodsell noted the meager professional opportunities available to academic women. Only in the women's colleges did women professors of all ranks considerably outnumber the men. Goodsell concluded, "In the realm of higher education this is their one happy hunting ground and they make good use of it."[1] One such golden arena was the academic community of Wellesley College 1895–1920. Wellesley was the only women's college which, from its founding in 1875, was committed to women presidents and a totally female professoriate. In the Progressive era this professoriate was a stellar cast: it included Katharine Coman, historian; Mary Calkins, philosopher; Vida Dutton Scudder, literary critic and social radical; Margaret Ferguson, botanist; Sarah Frances Whiting, physicist; Emily Greene Balch, economist; and Katharine Lee Bates, author of *America the Beautiful*. To outside observers this group had created a female Harvard, a "bubbling cauldron that seethed," a "hotbed of radicalism."[2] To their students the noble faculty provided a rich world which stirred them. To the next generation of faculty women the "old crowd" were completely dedicated "war horses."[3] To each other, they were kindred spirits, diverse, but united in the "bonds of Wellesley."[4]

Today such outstanding academic women are relatively unknown. It is not solely the passage of time, however, that has distanced these women from us; historians have not considered them worthy of study. Traditional scholarship in the history of academe has tended to focus on presidents, not academic faculty. Moreover, there has been an implicit presumption that only one model of the academic exists—that of the male professional. Even in the recent renaissance in women's educational history, historians have tended to dismiss women scholars *a priori*. Thus Sheila Rothman in *Women's Proper Sphere* concludes that women's colleges were dens of domesticity where female virtue and morality "intruded" on women's intellectual life. According to Rothman, the women's colleges did not hire women renowned for their intellectual achievement, but rather ones representative of "female grace and virtue." She asserts that "they rarely employed teachers of scholarly stature." In her ground-breaking *Collegiate Women*, Roberta Frankfort, depicts the culture of Wellesley (1885–1910) as one of "subdued famil-

Palmieri, P. A. (1983). Here was fellowship: A social portrait of academic women at Wellesley College, 1895–1920. *History of Education Quarterly, 23*(2), 195–214. Reprinted with permission.

ial grace," epitomized by Alice Freeman (Wellesley's president from 1881 to 1887). For Frankfort, the faculty of Wellesley play almost no role at all in creating the culture of the college.[5] But to so dismiss the faculty is to misread fundamentally the history of the Wellesley College community in the Progressive era. Indeed, the academic women of Wellesley shaped this major liberal arts college and were responsible for its "golden age."[6] In this essay, using both qualitative and quantitative techniques [data and analyses] I will sketch a social portrait of the fifty-three women who attained the rank of senior or associate professor at Wellesley College by 1910.[7]

This collective portrait highlights the fact that the women attracted to academe shared a core set of experiences and attributes derived from their sex, class, family relationships, geographic origins, education and social ideals. Such women were comfortable in what they termed their "Wellesley world"; they fashioned their professional and private lives around the college and each other.[8] They form not merely a collection of disparate individuals, but a discernible social group, who created at Wellesley a cohesive intellectual and social community. That community is as central to my portrait as any of the individual faculty members: it illuminates the history of academe as it was writ by women scholars, outside the research universities so commonly thought to be the only citadels of genuine intellectual creativity.

In this essay I am not particularly concerned with Wellesley's institutional history. However, it is useful to know something of that history for it provides the backdrop to the emergence of the faculty community under consideration. Wellesley's founders Henry and Pauline Durant were bent on establishing more than a women's college. Typical late-nineteenth century evangelical communitarians, they wanted Wellesley to be a model community which would serve as an exemplar to the nation of the possibilities of individual and societal transformation through the regeneration of women. Wellesley served the alienated Durants as a sanctuary and a home; it became, for them as well as for early faculty and students, a romantic refuge, a "little world under one roof."[9]

Wellesley's most radical feature was its dedication to the principle of education of women by women scholars. Wellesley was to be a "woman's university," equivalent to Harvard, presided over and staffed entirely by women. This bold experiment captured the imagination of the public. One newspaper noted:

> *The President, professors and students are all women; only two men belong to the establishment: the chief cook and the chief baker.*

Another hailed Wellesley as an institution which "confirmed the century's progress."[10]

While Henry Durant lived, however, his patriarchal style and evangelical zeal prevented the attainment of his radical ideal of an academic community controlled by women. For example, several of the first group of women faculty appointed by Durant voiced their dissatisfaction with his strict behavioral code, which they saw as a vestige of the seminary model. Durant forced the resignations of five faculty women in 1876 but replaced them with other college-educated women. With Durant's death in 1881 and the elevation of Alice Freeman to the presidency, the gap between the real and the ideal narrowed. Her appointment created the basis for a genuine female intellectual community.

To students and faculty, the twenty-nine-year-old Freeman epitomized the "new" college woman. Freeman's charismatic personality and exceptional organizational talents allowed her to rally the Wellesley community from within and to elevate Wellesley to a respected place within the ranks of liberal arts colleges. Freeman resigned to marry Harvard philosopher George Herbert Palmer in 1887, but until her death in 1902, she remained Wellesley's most powerful trustee, controlling the college from behind the scenes. She personally selected as Wellesley's next three presidents women who could be trusted to execute her master-plan for the college. By 1899, Freeman had orchestrated a purge against several old-line faculty women, hiring in their stead junior scholars who could teach a new elective curriculum. Further, she wooed and won a hesitant Caroline Hazard as Wellesley's fifth president. Wellesley sorely needed the wealth and social connections that Hazard brought to the presidency. Her gentility and concern for social reform harmonized well with the spirit of social service which characterized the newly hired faculty. Ill-at-ease with the role of president, Hazard left much of the internal administration to the women professors. Using as their power base the Academic Council formed by Alice Freeman, these strong-minded women "reared the college from its struggling babyhood to glorious womanhood."[11]

By 1910, fifty-three women had been on the faculty for more than five years and had reached the rank of senior or associate professor. They constitute the faculty group under consideration. Table 1 lists them with their principal academic department.

What characteristics distinguish this group of academic women? They are strikingly homogeneous in terms of social and geographic origins, upbringing, and socio-cultural worldview. Nearly 50 percent were born in New England, with 22 percent from the Midwest and another 20 percent from the Mid-Atlantic region. Four women were born in Europe; there was only one Southerner. Over half (52 percent) of the group was born in the decade 1855 to 1865, with another 30 percent born 1865 to 1875. One hundred percent were single.[12]

Almost all of these women were children of professional, middle-class families. Their fathers were cultivated men—ministers, lawyers, doctors, college presidents and teachers. These men were also committed to abolitionism, temperance and prison reform. They passed on to their daughters their respect for learning, their zeal for social reform, and their preference for service over financial success. Several of the fathers abandoned careers in business or law for more fulfilling service oriented vocations.[13] They were, to use William James's term, "tender-minded" in their cultural sensitivity and in their ability to form close bonds with their daughters. Almost all took an avid interest in their daughters' education. For example, when Katharine Coman's father saw that she was making little progress in her seminary, he directed her to tell the principal to give her more work. The

TABLE 1

Edith Rose Abbot	Art
Emily Greene Balch	Economics
Katharine Lee Bates	English
Malvina Bennett	Elocution
Charlotte Almira Bragg	Chemistry
Caroline Breyfogal	Latin
Alice Van Vechten Brown	Art History
Ellen Burrell	Mathematics
Mary Whiton Calkins	Psychology/Philosophy
Ellor Carlisle	Pedagogy
Mary Alice Case	Philosophy
Eva Chandler	Mathematics
Angie Chapin	Greek
Katharine Coman	History; Economics
Grace Cooley	Botany
Clara Eaton Cummings	Botany
Grace Davis	Physics
Katharine May Edwards	Latin
Margaret Ferguson	Botany
Elizabeth Fisher	Geology
Caroline Rebecca Fletcher	Latin
Eleanor Gamble	Psychology
Susan Maria Hallowell	Botany
Sophie Hart	English
Adeline Hawes	Latin
Ellen Hayes	Mathematics
Marion Hubbard	Zoology
Margaret Hastings Jackson	Italian
Sophie Jewett	English
Elizabeth Kendall	History
Eliza Kendrick	Biblical History
Adelaide Locke	Biblical History
Laura Emma Lockwood	English
Anna McKeag	Pedagogy
Hellen Abbott Merrill	Mathematics
Edna Virginia Moffett	History
Annie Sybil Montague	Greek
Margarethe Muller	German
Julia Orvia	History
Ellen Fitz Pendleton	Mathematics
Frances Perry	English
Ethel Puffer	Philosophy
Charlotte Fitch Roberts	Chemistry
Vida Dutton Scudder	English
Martha Hale Shackford	English
Margaret Pollock Sherwood	English
Caroline Rebecca Thompson	Zoology
Roxanne Vivian	Mathematics
Alice Waite	English
Alice Walton	Greek; Archaeology
Sarah Frances Whiting	Physics
Mary Alice Wilcox	Zoology
Natalie Wipplinger	German

principal refused because he thought the female mind incapable of comprehending more difficult material. Mr. Coman thereupon transferred Katharine to a public high school, scorning the dire predictions of what would happen to his daughter's manners and morals in a co-educational environment.[14]

To a remarkable degree, the academic women of Wellesley grew up with such special sponsorship and familial support. Lida Kendrick, who became a professor of Biblical History, complained in 1881 as a Wellesley freshman of her ill-preparation for college. Her father responded that he regarded her depression as "nothing more than a temporary blue spell." He reminded her that she was eminently qualified to distinguish herself and that she should dismiss all doubts from her mind and think of her family who "hoped that she would dream good things and awake with new vigor for the battle."[15]

Similarly, Emily Greene Balch's father counseled her against joining him in his law practice because to do so would not provide sufficient opportunity for her talents. He encouraged her instead to be a pioneer and to continue her social science research and her reform activity.[16]

Such fathers often acted not as marriage brokers but as career brokers for their daughters, arranging for them to take special graduate programs and even securing their daughters' professional placement. While Mary Calkins was traveling in Europe after her Smith graduation, her father Wolcott Calkins arranged for Mary to have an interview with Wellesley's president, Alice Freeman. Mary Calkins subsequently joined the faculty. Later, when Mary sought a Ph. D. in psychology from Harvard, which did not admit women, Wolcott petitioned the Harvard Corporation to admit his daughter as a special visitor. Mary Calkins went on to study with William James and Josiah Royce.[17]

Mothers also were ambitious for their daughters. A considerable number of the faculty recalled that their mothers sponsored or even arranged for their higher educations. The mothers of faculty women, many of whom had themselves attended seminaries, "bewailed the fact that they couldn't go to college" and thus were eager that their daughters embrace the new opportunity.[18] Mothers endorsed as well as their daughters' spirited activism. Repeatedly, in reminiscences and autobiographies, the academic women of Wellesley proudly proclaimed that their mothers had not expected them to be passive, submissive, dutiful daughters. Rather, as Ellen Hayes, professor of mathematics, noted: "Mother never rebuked me for spatterings or stains . . . she let me live." Economics professors Emily Greene Balch echoed this sentiment: "My mother did not spoil us with tonic. A tumble was not met with sympathy, but with Jump and take another dear."[19]

Often described as remarkable by their daughters, several mothers had achieved distinction in their own lives and communities. Many mothers had been teachers in seminaries. Often mothers collaborated with their daughters on books or in reform activity. Mother-daughter relationships in this group are characterized by their close, often lifelong companionship. Indeed, one of the distinctive features of the Wellesley academic community was its mother-daughter colony. Seven faculty women lived with their mothers. Partially these living accommodations were the result of a demographic pattern in which wives survived their husbands and were then cared for by their daughters. But mothers could substantially further their daughters' careers by providing social and psychological support.[20]

Entire families took pride in and sacrificed for high-achieving daughters. Katharine Lee Bates, the "gifted and youngest daughter," was encouraged to go to Wellesley despite familial financial reverses which forced her brother Arthur to find work. Bates's sister Jennie subordinated her own life, caring for their mother and serving as Katharine's secretary and typist. Likewise, when as a senior at Bryn Mawr Emily Balch felt guilty about accepting a fellowship for graduate study in Europe, her sister Annie scoffed at her "bad New England conscience." She reassured Emily that she and another sister, Betsy, would manage the Balch home. She rejoiced in Emily's success and suggested that "bells should be rung" to extol Emily's honor.[21]

Wellesley had a colony of such supportive sisters. About one-quarter of the academic women in this study had sisters who lived at Wellesley or worked nearby. Some faculty women had their sisters appointed to the faculty. More commonly, sisters administered faculty homes and served as social companions. Thus, the academic women of Wellesley routinely escaped the demands of domesticity; such duties fell to their sisters.

In short, the Wellesley faculty were exempted from what Jane Addams called the "family claim."[22] Nor were they expected to be emblems of conspicuous consumption. Rather, they were emblems of another kind—of their middle-class families' desire to purge superfluity, sponsor reform and enhance their status through their daughters' higher education and careers. These women illustrate that what Burton Bledstein calls the "culture of professionalism" of post-Civil War America was not limited to men; it affected as well the life cycles and careers of women.[23]

Notwithstanding their relative freedom from the social norms of "true womanhood," almost all the faculty expressed frustration with the limitations placed on their energies by those social expectations.[24] Repeatedly the academic women reveal that they had been mischievous, even rebellious children. Many felt keenly the contradiction between their privileged family positions and society's demands for their submissiveness. In a sense, many experienced a revolution of rising expectations; their desire to do everything that boys did often tried the patience of even their liberal parents. Quite a few emulated independent, spinster aunts who provided models for—and encouraged—their rebelliousness.[25]

This rebelliousness took many forms. It can be seen, for example, in their attitudes towards religion. Several of the women abandoned the stern, Calvinistic religions of their families, choosing instead more liberal faiths, tolerant of their equal participation and intellectual contribution. Women became Quakers, joined the Companions of the Holy Cross, practiced private faiths, and even became atheists. But it should also be stressed that a late-nineteenth-century evangelical, religious impulse underlay the philosophical idealism and civic humanism which characterized the faculty. Many were active proponents of the social gospel.[26]

This cohort of women, reared in rural environs, venerated nature. Their private letters, autobiographies and reminiscences are filled with fond memories of having grown up in close harmony with nature. The faculty found the unspoiled physical environment of Wellesley College, with its 300 acres of fields and lake, perfectly in tune with their sentiments. The beauty of the Wellesley campus brought them not only aesthetic pleasure, but symbolized as well the struggle of romantic idealism against commercialism and urbanization. Thus, in 1899, a plan to crowd buildings around College Hall, the center of academic life at Wellesley, provoked the faculty's vehement objection. As Ellen Burrell noted, the "natural loveliness of Wellesley should not be sacrificed" for it was a "part of the hither values for which the college exists." Conscious of living in a beautiful environment, the Wellesley faculty reveled in their secular retreat.[27]

Nature as therapeutic was another common theme which resounded in the group's world-view. The entire group moved between their Wellesley world (already a splendid setting) to other escapes in Maine, Massachusetts, and New Hampshire, where they built and gathered in summer compounds.[28]

These women's fondness for nature also appears to have been part of their rebellion against the prevailing societal norms which prescribed domesticity and passivity for women. Every woman on whom information is available passionately loved being physically out-of-doors. They were never so happy as when they were mountain climbing, hiking and bicycling. Sometimes such passion led to humorous extremes, as when English professor Sophie Jewett "took her typewriter up into a tree, having had a loft, complete with table and chairs built into a huge maple"![29]

These apostles of the strenuous life denounced the excessive confinement to which women were subject and lamented its cost in loss of vigor. In their lives, as well as in their educational philosophy, they upheld the image of the pioneer, the New Woman. Individually and collectively, the academic women of Wellesley fashioned a modern identity for women, though one based paradoxically on premodern virtues and values. Their ideology emphasized equally women's physical and intellectual capabilities—strengths which had been sapped by second-class citizenship and especially by the denial of access to higher education.

Extensive education was, of course, another common characteristic of this group. Ninety percent had Bachelors degrees, 35 percent Masters degrees, and 40 percent held Ph.D.s. In addition to formal degrees, over 80 percent studied summers or during leaves both in this country and in Europe; many did so repeatedly. Education was lifelong. Mary Case, for example, wrote an essay on Hegel that earned her a Masters degree in philosophy at the age of 86. Many of the faculty were highly talented in areas outside of their academic specialty; quite a few painted, wrote poetry, or were inventors. Some took up second and even third careers over the course of their lifetimes.[30]

The foregoing are some of the shared characteristics of the women who made up the senior faculty at Wellesley College 1895–1920. They give us some clues as to what motivated these women to enter academe. For some, the choice of the profession was inherent in family culture: the intellectual life was sanctioned and indeed sanctified. Women like Margaret Sherwood, Mary Calkins, Mary Alice Willcox, and Alice Van Vechten Brown, came from scholastic families where brothers and sisters became college professors. For others, an offer to teach at Wellesley came at a propitious moment, rescuing them from their post-graduate drift. After her graduation from Smith, Vida Scudder felt like a "lady in waiting," waiting not for her destined mate but for her "destined cause." Upon being hired at Wellesley, Carla Wenckebach similarly informed her family that she had made a "superb catch: not a widower, nor a bachelor, but something infinitely superior"—useful, intellectual work.[31]

Another motivation was disillusionment with secondary school teaching. These women were dominant, assertive and highly achievement-oriented. Yet, since secondary school teaching had been the most common vocation for women in New England since the 1830s, many of the women had originally chosen or had been channeled into such teaching. But with the opening of the women's colleges, new and more challenging posts became available. Thus Ellen Burrell, after teaching for five years in a seminary, resolved to be a "big frog in a big puddle," and joined the Wellesley faculty.[32]

The opportunity for distinction and innovation attracted many of the faculty women to academe. Women who had been the natural leaders of their siblings and their peers sought an adult role where they could again be in the lead. Ellen Hayes captured this motivation when she spoke of college teachers as "trailblazers."[33] Those faculty women who found it difficult to justify personal ambition, did feel justified in leading the movement for women's higher education. To these women, the reform of women's higher education was a revolution which signalled the millennium; one termed the movement the "Second Reformation."[34] To be a part of the academic profession when the women's colleges first opened was romantic, and women college teachers, conscious that they were the vanguard, felt "flushed with the feeling of power and privilege."[35]

Recruitment by friends, former mentors and family members also brought many women into the Wellesley community. For example, professor of psychology Mary Calkins was instrumental in having her childhood chum Sophie Jewett appointed in English. In addition, by 1910 there were thirteen Wellesley alumnae on the faculty (30 percent). Several of these formed mentor-disciple relationships termed "Wellesley marriages," in which pairs of women lived together and entwined their lives around the college.[36]

Given these motivations and recruitment patterns, Wellesley was very much like an extended family. Its members, with shared backgrounds and tastes, shared visions of life and work, and often shared bonds of family or prior friendship, could hardly but produce an extraordinary community. In this milieu, no one was isolated, no one forgotten. In contrast to today, when occupational and private selves rarely meet, the academic women of Wellesley conjoined public and private spheres. Individual patterns of association overlapped: one's friends were also friends and colleagues to each other. Networks which provided both social camaraderie and intellectual stimulation were characteristic of Wellesley community. It is difficult, if not impossible, to dissect this community, for any attempt to do so is in some ways artificial. In this short article, it is not possible to convey the full range and depth of this community, but I will sketch some of its contours, quality and flavor.

The Wellesley faculty were not merely professional associates, but astoundingly good friends. They formed a world whose symbols were respect for learning, love of nature, devotion to social activism, a fondness for wit and humor, frequent emotional exchanges, and loyalty to Wellesley and to each other. In 1890, when one can discern the beginnings of this group, they were young and at the height of their energies. For example, members of the English department ranged in age from 26 to 31. They had a vivacity and energy that made them "brimful of life."[37] Their students remembered confusing them with brilliant seniors and that they were "more like playmates than professors."[38] They perceived themselves to be a colony. When someone entered, there was joyful exhilaration; whenever someone died the group mourned together and consoled themselves that their departed friend had "joined their advance guard on the other side."[39] With a mean tenure of thirty-two years and with fifteen academic women staying at Wellesley over forty years, theirs was a rich river of memories and shared experiences.

Faculty homes, where women lived together, were centers for social and academic occasions. It was common for women who saw each other during the day—between teaching assignments, at departmental meetings and in the faculty parlor for tea—to drift together in the evenings for fun and conversation. One young instructor recounted her reactions to these nightly roundtables at the home of Katharine Lee Bates, where she lodged for a year:

> *Miss Jewett lived with us and Miss Balch who lived down the street had dinner with us every night. And if you ever sat at a table night after night with Miss Jewett who was a poet, Miss Bates, who was a poet and a joker, and Miss Balch . . . well, . . . that was a wonderful year.*[40]

Professionally, collaboration was standard: books were co-authored; lectures and courses conceived in concert; social and political causes sponsored jointly. For example, when Katharine Lee Bates took a young Vida Scudder under her wing in 1887, she introduced her not only to the ways of the English department but also to economics professor, Katharine Coman, who shared Scudder's concern for social reform. Coman and Scudder together formed Denison House, a social settlement in Boston. They were joined in this endeavor by Emily Greene Balch whom Coman had recruited.[41]

The social concerns of the faculty sometimes found expression in literary endeavors. Margaret Sherwood fictionalized in 1899, the group's debate over whether to accept tainted money from John D. Rockefeller in a novel, *Henry Worthington, Idealist*. The Rockefeller monies issue, which divided the community, illustrates not only the idealism of the faculty but also its tolerance for divergent opinion. Conflict was contained by the crosscutting ties of friendship and by loyalty to the group life.[42]

Such loyalty spilled over into concern for the health and welfare of comrades. Thus, when Katharine Lee Bates and Katharine Coman were in Spain on a research trip, Emily Greene Balch wrote them frequently. The correspondence is revealing, for it depicts not only Balch's shared interest in her friends' professional work, but her sisterly and motherly attention. In answer to one of Balch's solicitous notes and gifts, Coman wrote:

> *Dear Emily: Heartfelt thanks are due for the hot water bottle which arrived in good condition and is being cherished for the exigencies of the journey we are about to undertake.*[43]

Similarly, the entire community expressed concern for Elizabeth Kendall, who took frequent research trips to China and other remote parts. A slew of letters, birthday greetings and Christmas cards followed Kendall wherever she journeyed; the chain of friendship ceased only with her death in 1952.

Networks at Wellesley reveal not only shared professional and social lives; they were built as well from deeply emotional bonds. Single academic women expected and derived all the psycho-social satisfaction of a family from their female friendships. How to treat such relationships is currently at issue among historians of women. Lilliam Faderman, in her recent *Surpassing the Love of Men*, has demonstrated that romantic love between women was common in the nineteenth century. Faderman concludes that such relationships were often not primarily defined by genital contact but were nonetheless sensual, serious engagements, not to be dismissed as sentimental nonsense. Blanche Cook believes that historically "women who love women, who choose women to nurture and support and to create a living environment in which to work creatively and independently" should be acknowledged as lesbians. Faderman contends that the contemporary term lesbian cannot appropriately be applied to the experience of women in the late nineteenth century. Her discussion of "Boston Marriages"— friendships between independent career women who were involved in social and cultural betterment—provides an excellent context within which to understand "Wellesley marriages." At Wellesley, the academic women spent the main part of their lives with other women. We cannot say with certainty what sexual connotations these relationships conveyed. We do know that these relationships were deeply intellectual; they fostered verbal and physical expressions of love. Many women who had complained of being shy, isolated individuals before coming to Wellesley became more self-assured and less withdrawn. Frivolity, intimacy and emotional interdependency often developed between senior and associate professors. Lifelong relationships of deep significance to women's careers and personal identities were common at Wellesley.[44]

A few examples should suffice to convey the quality of these relationships. Vida Scudder and Florence Converse were a couple devoted to each other but not to the exclusion of a wider network of friends. They met as teacher and student at Wellesley and became lifelong companions. Besides teaching together, they were also both socialists who labored in the Denison House Settlement. Each wrote books dedicated to the other, and often their fiction draws on their relationship. An aged Scudder wrote that despite being increasingly feeble, she was "content to stay in my prison of time and space on Florence's account." When Scudder died, she left their home and the bulk of her money to Converse.[45]

Similarly, Katharine Lee Bates and Katharine Coman lived, traveled, and collaborated together. In letters to mutual friends, they fondly detailed their numerous walks and conversations and praised each other's accomplishments. Bates nursed Coman throughout her terminal illness. Coman's will left all of her personal possessions to Bates. Bates then moved into Coman's room and thereafter did all her writing there, including *Yellow Clover,* a volume of poetry dedicated to the memory of her lifelong intimate. Publication of these poems inspired the entire Wellesley friendship network (and even Jane Addams) to send Bates notes of appreciation for having captured "a woman's love for a woman," and the "new type of friendship between women."[46]

Bates' intimacy with Coman did not prevent her from having other deep relationships. The most notable of these was with President Caroline Hazard. The Bates-Hazard friendship is typical of female friendships at Wellesley; it endured for over twenty-five years, fusing private and public roles and giving each mutual support from youth to old age.[47]

As pioneers in their fields at a time when college educated women felt special and united, these women were anxious to encourage, to assist and to learn from one another. Academic women looked to each other for the definition of the professional woman, and for the skills necessary for conducting a professional life. They exchanged bibliographies and syllabi freely. More importantly, women served as mentors and role models to each other. A young, shy, and insecure Vida Scudder reported that she had gained confidence from her association with her senior colleagues. Such associations casually mixed shop talk with gossip sessions, walks, teas and luncheons.[48]

Florence Converse wrote in her 1939 history of Wellesley College that the "intellectual fellowship among the older women in the community is of a peculiarly stimulating quality."[49] And indeed, Wellesley fostered many distinguished achievers. The science departments had sixteen members; fourteen are listed in James M. Cattell's *American Men of Science.* A review of five compendia (*American Men of Science, Notable American Women, Dictionary of American Biography, Who Was Who In America* and *Woman in the 20th Century*) found that 50 percent of the 53 women in this essay were cited at least once. More than 20 percent were cited two or more times. It is worth noting that no faculty member had achieved prominence prior to Wellesley, and most who achieved distinction in their scholarly fields also were carrying heavy teaching loads. Far from embracing an ethos of domesticity, Wellesley professors pioneered in laboratory and seminar methods, field research, and courses in the new social sciences. Faculty noted with pride their innovations, citing their advocacy of methods and courses current at such places as Harvard or the University of Michigan, or only later adopted by such universities.[50]

The community at Wellesley was also a hothouse of reform. Social activism was pervasive among the faculty. Of the 53 women in this study, 39 (74 percent) were active in at least one of the following broad areas of reform: women's education and health reform; suffrage; social reform (temperance, consumer leagues, settlements, socialism, pacifism and opposition to tainted monies); and religious activism. Twenty-three women (44 percent) were active in two or more reform categories. Given these figures it is not surprising that Wellesley was one of the colleges branded by Vice-President Calvin Coolidge in 1921 as a "hotbed of radicalism."[51] This contravenes the prevailing scholarly consensus that the Wellesley faculty were proponents of "subdued familial grace."[52]

Of course, there were costs associated with the creation and maintenance of such a community. Women so deeply involved in so many social reform movements did not always form a united front. Again and again, a recurring question strained friendship ties: when should commitment to social activism yield to institutional loyalty? For example, Katharine Lee Bates, Vida Scudder's mentor, close friend and department head, was appalled when Scudder gave a speech endorsing the Lawrence Strike of 1912. She asked for Scudder's resignation, then quickly rescinded the request. Yet Bates worried lest socialist propaganda intrude upon Scudder's classes and forbade her to teach her famous course on Social Ideals in English Literature that year. Many years later, Bates did not recommend Scudder to succeed her as head of the English Department.[53]

The case of Emily Greene Balch, who was terminated by the college for her pacifism in World War I, caused the most serious division within this community. Many colleagues disagreed with Balch's politics yet rallied to defend her right to espouse an unpopular cause. They addressed repeated petitions to the Trustees to keep Balch at Wellesley. Partially because Balch herself was reluctant to make an issue of her firing, these protests were unavailing. Balch's dismissal severely strained friendships within the community, but not irrevocably. After her activism for international peace drew to a close, Balch chose to retire at Wellesley.[54]

Other tensions beset this faculty community. Wellesley's finances were often precarious, teaching loads were heavy. Women in science often complained that they could only conduct original research at odd moments between teaching and committee work. They envied the "prima donnas" in belles letters, but the professors in the humanities also felt constrained by too many students and too heavy a teaching load. In 1919, Vida Scudder rejoiced that retiring Katharine Lee Bates could now listen to her own music, which had been somewhat smothered by the "drone of student recitations."[55]

The pressure of teaching caused many women to shelve pet projects, putting them off until retirement. German professor Margarethe Muller decided to retire in 1908, before she became eligible for a Carnegie Foundation pension, in order to "do a piece of creative work which I have wanted to do for more than fifteen years." She forfeited the pension, yet never completed her manuscript.[56]

Commitment to Wellesley and the desire to remain within the community also at times conflicted with the opportunity for other kinds of professional advancement. An offer of employment from a publishing house attracted poet

Katharine Lee Bates. The Wellesley community pressured her not to defect. Personal ties, especially with her companion Katharine Coman, were "love anchors" keeping Bates at Wellesley. She rejected the offer, but confided to her diary that she was a "reluctant captive."[57]

To be fair to those who turned down invitations to teach at other institutions, however, it must be said that Wellesley often did offer the better professional opportunity. Mary Calkins, a senior philosopher who was elected president of the American Psychological Association and the American Philosophy Society, rejected an offer from Columbia University because she wanted to remain close to her family and friends at Wellesley and because she feared that she would be trapped teaching elementary laboratory psychology at male-dominated Columbia.[58]

These potent, strong-minded women, who ran their departments in dictatorial fashion, affected not only the style of the college's administration, but the career ambitions of junior faculty in the 1920s. In self-conscious recognition of their enormous power, they jokingly referred to each other as "benevolent despots" and "little Bismarcks."[59] The situation of younger instructors, locked out of power by these "absolutely dedicated war horses," was "pretty grim."[60] They were too intimidated to speak at Academic Council and had no vote. A revolt by junior faculty in 1920 was crushed by their senior counterparts. It was not until the late 1940s, when most in the charmed circle had either retired or died, that young faculty found a voice. Even then these junior women stood in awe of their "exceptional" elders. They envied their dedication and admired their intellectual vitality. The younger generation also admitted that although the old guard kept them impotent in departmental affairs and Council, they did allow them full freedom in their classrooms.

Perhaps the most remarkable quality of the Wellesley community was its endurance. Despite the inevitable clash of temperaments, such factors as career commitment, respect for each other, and tender memories bound these women to each other and to Wellesley. When in 1927 professor emeritus Vida Scudder spoke on teaching at Wellesley, she noted that "cooperation in group life was its highest privilege." Notwithstanding obstacles and "weary moments" when they questioned whether their fellowship was a sham, Scudder emphasized that

> *At our best we know that it is a triumphant reality. We meet the challenge of our privilege with gaiety and courage, and with a sense of the dramatic fascination there is in our task of living together. And through accelerations and retards, through concessions and slow innovations, we do move on.*[61]

Indeed until the end of their lives, this extraordinary group remained loyal and committed to each other. The constant stream of life which flowed among them removed in their old age any final sense of isolation, despair or remorse. They looked back on lives which had been fun and which were blessed with the quest for truth, adventure, and friendships. The group, whose mean age at death was 76 years, remained quite healthy, active in social causes, and involved in their work and the College. At the age of eighty-one, Margaret Sherwood wrote a novel; at eighty-six, Mary Case wrote a scholarly article on Hegel; Emily Greene Balch wrote essays well into her eighties.

Together the academic women of Wellesley had spent their youths and adulthoods, together they embraced old age and even death. As Margaret Sherwood wrote to her friend Elizabeth Kendall:

> *The road seems long as one draws nearer to the end, long and a bit lonely. It is good to have footsteps climbing with one's own, and to know that a friend in whom one has a deep and abiding trust is on the same track, moving toward the same goal.*[62]

And echoing these sentiments an aged Vida Scudder wrote to an old student:

> *I am sorry for your long winter of illness. It is hard for me to think of you and Florence and my other "girls" as elderly women, but time marches on. Miss Balch told me last evening that she woke up a night or two ago, laughing incredulously, because she was an old woman! We agreed that age was really just a joke.*[63]

Of course these women were not spared the toll of time. They grew infirm. Rebels till the end, they yearned to be the vanguard still. Emily Balch epitomized this striving when she lamented that at times "old age was duller than ditchwater."[64] Yet old age never diminished the spirit of this community. In 1953, over sixty years after the formation of this group, Martha Hale Shackford wrote to a former student:

> *Just a word of greeting and good wishes from us (Margaret Sherwood), and, on my part, to tell you that a few weeks ago Miss Sherwood was able to make a call upon Miss Scudder who you know is exceedingly lame and also deaf. Florence Converse was there too. I wish you could have seen the meeting—with our friends sitting on the sofa very much themselves in spite of time.*[65]

These women share one final quality. As old women, they were prone to embellish the memory of their role as pioneers. Faculty autobiographies and reminiscences contain a near-mythic account of their struggles, one which understates the enormous sponsorship and ease with which this select elite navigated the uncharted waters of women's roles in academe. Once again they sought to distinguish themselves, this time from younger generations of college educated women; they thus upheld their collective identity.

Here indeed was fellowship! Women born and reared in a similar tradition, who wove their lives around a similar set of educational and socio-cultural ideals and who remained at the same institution for a lifetime found the meaning of life not simply in professional experiences or achievements, but as well in the inexhaustible human treasury of which they were a part. These academic women did not shift their life-courses away from the communal mentality, as did many male professionals; nor did they singlemindedly adhere to scientific rationalism, specialization, social science objectivity, or hierarchical associations in which vertical mobility took precedence over sisterhood.[66] Of course this constancy was not the product of choice alone. Many of these academic women were the "uninvited"—locked out of the research universities, excluded from the professional patronage system of male academics. For example, Harvard refused to grant Mary Calkins a Ph. D., although the entire Harvard philosophy department petitioned that she be awarded the degree. The Museum of Comparative Zoology at Harvard denied Mary Alice Willcox a place because "we have one room with three windows and a man for each window." Women chafed in private against this discrimination, but most did not publicly protest, especially as they grew older.[67]

Despite having accomplished so much, many of these women could have done more. Partially this is the result of their relative insulation from the larger academic community. Historian of science Margaret Rossiter has observed that these women, unlike men, were not going to be invited to the major research universities. For them, Wellesley was the pinnacle of their careers.[68] Lacking mobility, many remained satisfied with a few stellar articles or just one good discovery. Many compensated for stalled careers with trips or homes. Despite their class, family backgrounds and a supportive community, as women these academics were susceptible to breakdowns and conflicts over achievement. Several took pains to dismiss or minimize their accomplishments. Vida Scudder, for example, was a prolific writer, ardent social radical and charismatic teacher, who berated herself for "scattering her energies."[69] She judged herself a failure by the male norm of achieving professional eminence in a single narrow field. Praise for her individual achievement made Scudder uncomfortable; instead she drew attention to her work in groups. Many others shied away from public recognition, and even refused to list their publications for college and national biographies.[70]

It should be clear that the Wellesley faculty do not fit what Robert McCaughey terms the "Harvard model" of the modern academic professional—the cosmopolitan who felt no personal attachment to his institution, valuing academic mobility over loyalty. Neither did they tread the predominant path of late nineteenth century academics outlined by Mary Furner in *Advocacy and Objectivity:* the Wellesley academic women never abdicated advocacy nor relinquished reform as a crucial component of the scholar's role. The Wellesley group of academics defined themselves intellectually and socially in a local, particularistic, face-to-face community rather than a bureaucratic, professional society. In short, their achievements and their legacy defy the prevailing paradigms [theory bases] used to explain the late nineteenth century culture of academe. Their experience demands that we seek new ways of seeing the richly pluralistic history of the academic profession in the United States and that we devote more scholarship to academic subcultures.[71]

And what of the unique community they created? Hugh Hawkins has highlighted the tragedy of academic life at Johns Hopkins where an unbreachable gulf existed between isolated, specialized researchers. Men there found it extremely difficult to get to know fellow faculty members. A senior professor lamented:

We only get glimpses of what is going forward in the minds and hearts of our colleagues. We are like trains moving on parallel tracks. We catch sight of some face, some form that appeals to us, and it is gone.[72]

How different from Wellesley where the academic women wrought a world which touched every woman in every aspect of her life, and gave each a sense of belonging to an all-purposive, all-embracing whole. Virtually without exception, historians have seen the research university as an advance over the sterile, old-time, liberal arts college.[73] This view understates the costs of the research university, while at the same time it belittles the benefits of at least some liberal arts colleges. To assess accurately the relative benefits and costs of each educational institution, we need to accord more value to community. For women, the liberal arts college provided a rich and professionally pivotal milieu at a time when the research university denied them careers. At Wellesley, the faculty flourished in what they called their "Adamless Eden."[74] Their community cannot be recreated, nor, perhaps, should it. However, like all Edens, it compels us still.

I wish to thank the following people for helping me to refine the ideas presented in this article: George H. Ropes; Barbara Sicherman; Joseph Featherstone; Charles Strickland and an anonymous reviewer from the *Quarterly*.

Notes

1. Goodsell, Willystine. (May, 1929). "The Educational Opportunity of American Women—Theoretical and Actual," *The American Academy of Political and Social Science*, 143:12.

2. Diary of Horace Scudder, February 23, 1891, Box 6, Horace Scudder Papers, Houghton Library, Harvard University, Cambridge, Mass. Calvin Coolidge, "Enemies of the Republic: Are the Reds Stalking Our College Women?," *The Delineator* (June, 1921):67.

3. Transcribed oral interview with Lucy Wilson, p. 15. 1H/1975. Centennial Historian. Wellesley College Archives (hereinafter cited as WCA).

4. Ellen Burrell to Mildred H. McAffee, November 16, 1938. 3L. Math Department Folder, WCA.

5. Rothman, Sheila. (1978). *Woman's Proper Place: A History of Changing Ideals and Practices,* *1870 to the Present* (New York), p. 39; Frankfort, Roberta. (1977). *Collegiate Women, Domesticity and Career in Turn-of-the-Century America* (New York), p. 64.

6. Marks, Jeannette. (1955). *Life and Letters of Mary Emma Woolley* (Washington, D. C.), p. 47.

7. This social portrait studied every woman faculty member at Wellesley who satisfied two criteria: tenure of at least five years on the Wellesley faculty between 1900 and 1910 and attainment of the rank of associate professor. I imposed these conditions because I was interested primarily in the senior faculty and because records are fuller for them. Selection by these criteria yielded a total of fifty-three women; the two men who met the criteria were excluded. The ten-year duration (1900–1910) seemed to satisfy the need both for a manageable study and for one which would produce a valid picture of a faculty

group over time. However, it should be noted that the group mean for service to the college is thirty-two years and this many women were still teaching at Wellesley in the 1920s and 1930s. The quantitative study was processed with the Statistical Package for the Social Sciences (SPSS). I am indebted to George H. Ropes for his assistance in quantifying data.

8. Caroline Hazard speaks of a "Wellesley world" in "Tribute to Katharine Lee Bates," *Wellesley Alumnae Magazine, 12,* no. 3 (June, 1929): 15 (hereinafter cited as *WAM*).

9. Burke, Mary Barnett. (February, 1959). "The Growth of the College," *WAM*:179.

10. "A Woman's College," *Boston Daily Advertiser* (October 28, 1875); Tilley, Henry A. "Wellesley College for Women," *Washington Chronicle* (November 14, 1875). 1H Histories, WCA.

11. Bates, Katharine Lee. (May 16, 1925). "The Purposeful Women Who Have Reared the College From Struggling Babyhood to Glorious Womanhood, and the Men Who Have Aided Them," *Boston Evening Transcript.* For a more detailed discussion of the Alice Freeman presidency and the years of transition which followed, see: Palmieri, Patricia A. "In Adamless Eden: A Social Portrait of the Academic Community at Wellesley College, 1875–1920" (Diss. Harvard University Graduate School of Education, June 1981), esp. chapters 2 and 3.

12. Statistics computed from data taken from Faculty Biographical Files, WCA; also: U.S. Federal Census of 1880.

13. Examples of such fathers include: Walter Willcox; Thomas Sherwood; Levi Coman.

14. Coman, Katharine, ed. (1913). *Memories of Martha Seymour Coman* (Boston, n.p.), p. 46.

15. Dr. Kendrick to Lida Kendrick, September 15, 1881. Elizabeth Kendrick Unprocessed Papers, WCA.

16. Francis V. Balch to Emily Greene Balch, March 8, 1896. Folder 89, Box 52, Emily Greene Balch Papers, Swarthmore College Peace Collection (hereinafter SCPC).

17. Furumoto, Laurel. (1979). "Mary Whiton Calkins (1863–1930): Fourteenth President of the American Psychological Association," *Journal of the History of Behavioral Sciences*, 15:346–356.

18. Dietz, Jean. (June 17, 1962). "Wellesley's Miss Mary Linked Dreams to Real Life," *Boston Sunday Globe*.

19. Ellen Hayes as quoted in Louise Brown, *Ellen Hayes: Trail Blazer* (n.p., 1932), p. 20. Emily Greene Balch as quoted in Mercedes Randall, *Improper Bostonian* (New York, 1964), p. 44.

20. The seven faculty women who lived with their mothers are: Vida Dutton Scudder; Elizabeth Kendall; Katharine Lee Bates; Katharine Coman; Adelaide Locke; Mary Calkins; Margaret Jackson.

21. Burgess, Dorothy. (1952). *Dream and Deed, The Story of Katharine Lee Bates* (Norman, Oklahoma), pp. 30–35. Anne Balch to Emily Balch [n.d., probably 1899], Folder 505, Box 63, Balch Papers, SCPC.

22. Addams, Jane. (1965). "The Subjective Necessity of Social Settlements," in Christopher Lasch (ed.), *The Social Thought of Jane Addams* (New York), pp. 151–174.

23. Bledstein, Burton J. (1976). *The Culture of Professionalism* (New York).

24. According to historian Barbara Welter, the mid-Victorian "true woman" was supposed to cultivate piety, purity, domesticity and submissiveness. Welter, "The Cult of True Womanhood," *American Quarterly, 18* (1966): 151–174.

25. Women who were influenced by independent aunts include: Emily Greene Balch, Vida Dutton Scudder, Ellen Burrell.

26. Examples of faculty religious attitudes are contained in: Margaret Sherwood to Marion Westcott, April 17, 1937. Sherwood Faculty Biographical File, WCA; also see: "Gracious Ladies (newspaper clipping) n.p., n.d., Sherwood Faculty Biographical File, WCA; Vida Dutton Scudder, *On Journey*, pp. 43; 37–390; 416.

27. ALS. Ellen Burrell to Louise McCoy North, June 4, 1899. WCA.

28. For information on one such compound, see: Anna Jane McKeag, "Mary Frazier Smith," *Wellesley Magazine, 18*, no. 1 (October, 1933): 6–9.

29. Bates, Katharine Lee. (N. D.). "Sophie Jewett: The Passing of a Real Poet," [untitled newspaper clipping], Jewett Faculty Biographical File, WCA.

30. Emily Green Balch wrote essays, painted and wrote poetry well into her late 80s; at the age

of 50 Professor of Latin Katharine May Edwards began another career dating Corinthian coins.

31. Scudder, Vida Dutton. (1908). *On Journey*, p. 94. Carla Wenckebach as quoted in Margarethe Muller, *Carla Wenchebach, Pioneer* (Boston), p. 213.

32. Ellen Burrell as quoted in Helen Merrill, "The History of the Department of Mathematics," p. 51. 3L. Mathematics Department Folder, WCA.

33. Hayes, Ellen. (1929). *The Sycamore Trail* (Wellesley Mass.).

34. Hodkins, Louise Manning. (November 1892). "Wellesley College," *New England Magazine*, 380.

35. Florence Converse as quoted in Jessie Bernard, *Academic Women* (New York, 1964), p. 31.

36. Dorothy Weeks, a student of this faculty group who returned to live at Wellesley, noted that pairs of faculty women were termed "Wellesley marriages." Personal interview with Dorothy Weeks, February 5, 1978.

37. Haskell, Mary. (February, 1903). "Professor Wenckebach's Relation to Her Students," *Wellesley Magazine*, 160.

38. "Tribute to Miss Kendall," [Typescript], p. 4. Kendall Faculty Biographical File, WCA.

39. Marion Pelton Guild to Birdie Ball Morrison, December 6, 1930. 6C. Box 2, Class of 1880, WCA.

40. Transcribed oral interview with Geraldine Gordon, p. 25. WCA.

41. Scudder, Vida. *On Journey*, pp. 109–110.

42. Margaret Sherwood. (1899). *Henry Worthington, Idealist* (New York); a fuller discussion of the Rockefeller "tainted monies" issue is given in "In Adamless Eden," chapter 6.

43. Katharine Coman to Emily Greene Balch, February 28, 1914. Coman Unprocessed Papers, WCA.

44. Faderman, Lillian. (1981). *Surpassing the Love of Men: Romantic Friendship and Love Between Women from the Renaissance to the Present* (New York), Introduction; pp. 190–230; Cook, Blanche Wiesen. (1977). "Female Support Networks and Political Activism: Lillian Wald, Crystal Eastman, Emma Goldman," *Chrysalis*, 3, 43–61. Also see: Smith-Rosenberg, Carroll. (Autumn, 1975). "The Female World of Love and Ritual," *Signs, 1*, no. 1:1–29.

45. ALS. Vida Scudder to Louise Manning Hodgkins, May 29, 1928, WCA.

46. Caroline Hazard praised Bates' *Yellow Clover* in a letter to Bates, April 25, 1922. WCA; Vida Scudder to Bates, April 1922; WCA. Jane Addams to Bates, May 9, 1922. Jane Addams Unprocessed Letters, WCA.

47. There is extensive correspondence between Caroline Hazard and Katharine Lee Bates in both the Bates and Hazard Papers, WCA.

48. Scudder, Vida Dutton. *On Journey*, pp. 107–109.

49. Converse, Florence. (1939). *Wellesley College. A Chronicle of the Years 1875–1938* (Cambridge, Mass.), p. 98.

50. The fourteen women scientists listed in Cattell's *American Men of Science* (the first five editions: 1906; 1910; 1921; 1927; 1933) are:

Calkins, Psychology and Philosophy	Hayes, Astronomy
Case, Philosophy	Hubbard, Zoology
Cummings, Botany	Puffer, Philosophy
Ferguson, Botany	Roberts, Chemistry
Fisher, Geology	Thompson, Zoology
Gamble, Psychology	Whiting, Physics
Hallowell, Botany	Willcox, Zoology

These dictionaries of notable Americans are among the best reference guides to the biographies of academic women. They are by no means exhaustive. Each employs subjective criteria to determine what constitutes achievement. For a discussion of the kinds of women scientists included in James M. Cattell (ed.), *American Men of Science*, see: Rossiter, Margaret. (May/June, 1974). "Women Scientists in America Before 1920," *American Scientist*, 312–333.

51. Coolidge, Calvin. "Enemies of the Republic."

52. Frankfort, Roberta. *Collegiate Women*, p. 64.

53. Scudder, Vida. *On Journey*, pp. 189–190.

54. A full discussion of the Balch case is contained in the epilogue, "Eden's End," in "In Adamless Eden." See also the extensive correspondence in the Emily Greene Balch papers, SCPC.

55. ALS. Vida Scudder to Katharine Lee Bates, August 6, 1919. WCA.

56. ALS. Margarethe Muller to Caroline Hazard, Autumn 1908. WCA.

57. Katharine Lee Bates to Katharine Coman, February 28, 1891. 3). Katharine Lee Bates Papers, WCA. Diary of Katharine Lee Bates, March 5, 1896. Box 3, Katharine Lee Bates Papers, WCA.

58. Furumoto, Laurel. "Are There Sex Differences In Qualities of Mind? Mary Whiton Calkins Versus Harvard University. A 37-year Debate," pp. 42–43. WCA.

59. Vida Scudder discusses Katharine Lee Bates' despotism in *On Journey*, p. 123 and Scudder, "Katharine Lee Bates, Professor of English Literature," *WAM*, Supplement, 13, 5 (June, 1929):5.

60. Transcribed oral interview with Luch Wilson, p. 15. WCA.

61. Scudder, Vida Dutton. (August 1929). "The Privileges of a College Teacher" *WAM*, 327.

62. Margaret Sherwood to Elizabeth Kendall, December 2, 1945. Kendall Unprocessed Papers, WCA.

63. Vida Dutton Scudder to Jeannette Marks, July 9, 1939. Scudder Papers, WCA.

64. Emily Greene Balch as quoted in Mercedes Randall, *Improper Bostonian*, p. 443.

65. Martha Hale Shackford to Jeannette Marks, May 27, 1953. Shackford Papers, WCA.

66. For a general discussion of the increasing bureaucratization characteristic of American culture 1870–1920, see: Wiebe, Robert. (1967). *The Search for Order: 1877–1920* (New York); in the various professions this shift manifests itself as a loss of respect for the amateur and the glorification of the highly credentialed professional. See: Bledstein, *The Culture of Professionalism*; Furner, Mary J. (1975). *Advocacy and Objectivity. A Crisis in the Professionalization of American Social Science 1865–1905* (Lexington, Kentucky).

67. Mary Alice Willcox to Marian Hubbard, December 2, 1927. Willcox Faculty Biographical File, WCA.

68. Rossiter, Margaret. "Women's Education: The Entering Wedge." Chapter from a forthcoming book on women scientists at the women's colleges 1865–1940. I am grateful to Prof. Rossiter for sharing this work with me.

69. Scudder, Vida Dutton. *On Journey*, p. 175.

70. See, for example: Mary Alice Willcox to Miss Whiting, March 27, 1948. Willcox Faculty Biographical File, WCA; ALS. Louise Manning Hodgkins to Martha Hale Shackford, November 12, 1924, WCA; Emily Greene Balch ["I am no princess . . .]. Folder 604, Box 66, Bach Papers, SCPC.

71. McCaughey, Robert A. (1974). "The Transformation of American Academic Life: Harvard University 1821–1892," *Perspectives in American History*, 8, 239–232; Mary J. Furner, *Advocacy and Objectivity.*

72. Hawkins, Hugh. (1960). *Pioneer: A History of the Johns Hopkins University, 1874–1889* (New York), p. 237.

73. James McLachlan reviews and criticizes standard historical accounts of the "old-time" liberal arts college in "The American College in the Nineteenth Century: Toward a Reappraisal," *Teachers College Record, 80* (December, 1978): 287–306.

74. When President Caroline Hazard retired in 1910, rumors spread that she was to be replaced by a man. Alumnae and faculty cried out, "What and spoil our 'Adamless Eden'?" "Man to Rule Wellesley? No! Say Graduates," *Evening Newspaper*, Minneapolis, Minnesota, [n.d., probably 1910]. Hazard Scrapbook, 1909–1910, WCA.

The Bagby[1] Human Resources Center: A Case Study of Unrealized Potential

A Dissertation Prospectus

Lola J. Aagaard

Background of the Study

Prologue

There will not be any other name on the building except what you see on the architect's drawing: Bagby Human Resources Center. And I think it is significant that we don't put any other name on it. I hope that's the way it goes because that's what it is! A Human Resources Center. It's not a school or a library. It is a new kind of facility that houses several agencies. . . . Now certainly there's a—to be realistic everybody knows that from dream to reality is a long time, a long gap and there's many a pitfall in between. And certainly, we don't conceive of this facility from the first day it's opened serving all the needs of the community or doing all the things or being involved in all the kinds of programs that we would hope that it would develop into but these are things that are going to take us at least five years to develop. (M. T. Byers, 1977.)[2]

Excerpt from field notes, March, 1987—downtown Bagby:

LA: Excuse me, could you give me directions to the Human Resources Center?

Woman behind counter in bakery: The Human Resources Center? Ummm, I don't know, I think it's—just a minute. (She leans back and shouts to someone in the back room.) Honey, where's the Human Resources Center? Isn't it out by the library? (Receiving an affirmative answer from the invisible personage in back, she leans across the counter again.) Yes, it's out by the library, do you know where that is? Out by the schools?

LA: Yes, but is it in the same building as the library?

Woman: Ummm, I think it's in front of the library.

Aagaard, L. J. (1987). The Bagby Human Resources Center: A case study of unrealized potential. A dissertation prospectus. Reprinted with permission.

Actually, the woman in the above transcription was exceptional; other people of whom I inquired had either never heard of the Human Resources Center, or they directed me to the Community Center (at the opposite end of town) which is the site of the community gymnasium, swimming pool, and tennis courts. Truly, for the Bagby Human Resources Center (HRC), the reality has not matched the dream, and in fact the dream may have been forgotten by all except M. T. Byers.

The Setting

The HRC in Bagby is a 52,000 square foot facility which houses the middle school (complete with gymnasium and auditorium), the public library and school library combined, a community meeting room (with kitchen), the county Public Health Department, and the Board of Education. It is a long, low building, set back off the road on a piece of gently sloping land in what is mainly a residential area of town. The elementary school is right next door. In the middle of the circular drive in front of the HRC is a grassy soccer field, and the drive also continues around the back of the facility to where the track and other playing fields are located. The front face of the building evidences only one floor, but if you follow the drive around to the back you will see that the building is actually two stories, set into the hill, and the middle school occupies the bottom floor.

The library and the community meeting room occupy 9,400 square feet, while the other agency offices encompass only 2,100 square feet; the rest is primarily the middle school. Looking in from the front doors, the upper floor is laid out roughly like an inverted T, with agency offices forming the cross bar and the library being the stem. The community room can be accessed either from the front hall or from inside the library.

The town of Bagby seems incongruous with this facility. Bagby is the kind of small (population 5000) town where the main street is really named Main Street, and in addition, is made of brick, and cars park down the middle as well as along the edges. The business section of town is located on both sides of Main Street, and extends all of three blocks. A lot of town business is conducted in the downtown cafe, and if you know the newspaper editor then you never have to worry about any bad news concerning you getting published in Bagby.

Brief History of the HRC

The history of this unique facility is tied to that of the former high school principal turned assistant superintendent of the Bagby school district, M. T. Byers—the man with the dream. Actually, the original impetus for what turned into the HRC project was prosaic in the extreme: in 1976 the school district needed a new middle school and did not have the money to pay for one, nor the hope of getting a bond issue passed. Consequently the superintendent, Patrick Knegh, and his assistant, Byers, decided to look for some alternative methods of funding schools. Byers had become intrigued with the community school concept and the possibility of joint occupancy of public buildings. He had also become aware that the federal government was establishing Public Works grants in the spirit of the old WPA. Byers and the superintendent presented all of this to the Board of Education and asked for permission to pursue the grant idea, which would include the community school and joint occupancy facets. Joint occupancy of the facility by several community service agencies was presented as a savings to the taxpayer, while the community school was tied into both fiscal accountability (the school would not stand vacant outside of regular school hours) and community mindedness (the HRC would be a life-long learning center and a referral service and source of empowerment for the unemployed). Permission was granted.

Visits with other local agencies were fruitful as well. Byers spoke to the Bagby Chamber of Commerce, the City Council and numerous citizens of Bagby, outlining the philosophy behind the project and his vision of what it could be, and all were excited about and supportive of the HRC idea.

In the end, the public library, Health Department, Board of Education, a community action agency, and the County Youth Services agreed to be included in the project. The agreement was that the school would own the facility, and the agencies would hold annually renewable leases for their space. Payments would be pro-rated on the basis of floor space and time usage to provide for differences in maintenance and utilities costs.[3]

The grant application was filed October 25, 1976. On December 22, Byers received a call from his senator in Washington D. C. informing him that not only was Bagby going to get the grant, but that it was the largest one awarded in the state. There were 37 projects funded in the state (from over 400 applications submitted), and Bagby got 10% of the total amount of money granted statewide.

Groundbreaking was held March 13, 1977 with visiting state dignitaries, two ministers, and the Bagby High School Choraliers. M. T. Byers was on the program to explain the goals and objectives of the Human Resources Center.[4] The actual occupation of the building took place in April of 1978, and roughly a year later M. T. Byers took a position as superintendent of a neighboring school district.

The Problem

The Dream

Byers' vision was clearly articulated during the initial development of the HRC, and was published in several publications as well as presented to various community groups. His dream for the Bagby HRC included all of the following aspects:

- community use of the 400 seat school auditorium for concerts, plays and other cultural productions;
- community fitness classes in the school gymnasium both before and after regular school hours;

- community education in the school facilities after school hours, to include adult basic education as well as arts and crafts;
- senior citizens would be able to eat a hot lunch in the cafeteria with the students at noon, and would be employed as arts and crafts instructors for the community;
- the community meeting room would be used for a meeting place for local clubs, as well as a space for art exhibits and community education;
- the combination public/school library would provide a variety of referral services for community needs, as well as being a place where children and adults could interact and benefit from one another.[5]

The Reality

It is now nearly ten years since the Bagby Human Resources Center opened its doors, well past the five years which Byers expected it to take to realize its potential in the community. As described in the prologue, few people in the community know it by the name Byers wished it to be called, although that is the only name which appears on the front of the building.

The HRC does house the library, middle school, community meeting room, Board of Education, and the Public Health Department, but that is about the extent to which the initial vision has been fulfilled. The reality, taken point by point as was the dream, is described below:

- the "400 seat auditorium" looks like a gym with a concrete floor. There is no seating except for some bleachers at one end. It is primarily used as a school cafeteria, as evidenced the day I was there by folding cafeteria tables lining the walls, and an empty salad bar being swabbed down by a kitchen worker at the far end of the room. The school secretary says that although the school is "real community minded," nothing has ever been held in the auditorium for the community's benefit or enjoyment;
- the gymnasium is never used before school, and the school secretary confided that it was used after school only once when one of the teachers offered an aerobics class there for the other school teachers. The secretary also told me that the community had its own gym at the other end of town;
- no community education of any kind is conducted at the HRC. There are no adult basic education classes, no arts and crafts, no classes whatsoever;
- the senior citizens do not eat lunch in the school cafeteria, and since there are no arts and crafts classes, the seniors obviously do not teach anything either. The same school secretary met these questions with great candor: "Why, the senior citizens have their own building downtown. Why would they want to come all the way out here?" As it turns out, the senior citizens are now housed in what used to be the old library building;
- the community meeting room is scheduled by the librarians. Priority in the use of the room is given to the agencies which occupy the HRC, and other groups may not hold meetings there on a regular basis, nor may they sched-

ule more than one meeting at a time. The library uses the room to show pre-school films, have story hour, and other things of a similar nature. The Board of Education holds its meetings there. Other groups who have scheduled the room include the Highway Patrol (for driving classes), Girl Scouts, and the Bagby China Painting Club among others. There have been art exhibits, and in fact the room is equipped with special hardware and lighting especially for such a purpose;

- the library has no referral services of any kind. Nor do the children have unlimited opportunities to mix with adults, for the school library is relegated to the back of the building, and during school hours the children are not normally allowed up front. The library opens at 9 a.m. and closes at 6 p.m. (5 p.m. on Fridays) and is closed on Sunday. During my days of observation in the library, it seemed that more people came there to make photocopies than to check out books, although there was a fairly high-volume paperback trade. I observed very little interaction among patrons or between patrons and librarians.[6]

There seems to be little inter-agency cooperation also. I questioned the head librarian, Sandy Parents, about whether the library trade had increased due to the Public Health Department being there. I thought perhaps that patrons of the health department might stop in the library as they were waiting for vaccinations on clinic day or something. However this does not seem to be the case and Parents partially attributes it to the kind of people who frequent the health department ("They don't read books.") and partially to the attitude of the health department. An illustration she gave was enlightening. One clinic day she noticed a very long line of mothers and whiny children in the outer hall, waiting for vaccinations. Sandy Parents decided to set up a pre-school film in the community meeting room and invite all the children in to watch it while they waited. When she went out into the hall and made her announcement, no one moved. If they went in to watch the film they would lose their place in line and the wait would be even longer. I mentioned that the health department could give them all numbers and come call out the ones which were up next, and Parents agreed that this was a possibility, but that she felt she had done her part, and that it (the health department) was not interested in cooperating.[7]

Problem Statement

What happened at the Bagby Human Resources Center, or in Bagby more generally, that resulted in such a disparity between the dream and reality? The proposed study will attempt to answer that question.

Initially it will be necessary to clearly and completely describe both the dream and the reality, which will entail compiling a history of the development of the HRC. The problems in the school system leading up to the need for the middle school, Byers' ideas and suggestions for the HRC, finding cooperative agencies to occupy the proposed building, the process of writing the grant proposal, the occupation of the facility, the 18 months prior to Byers' departure, the successive administrators of the HRC, current community attitude concerning the HRC—all these stages of the HRC's history have their own key players, who in turn had (and have) their own motivations and goals, implicit as well as explicit. Because M. T. Byers was the first director of community education in Bagby, it will also be helpful to trace the coincident development of the community education program as part of the reality which did not match the dream.

Additionally, Byers' life history is an essential piece to the puzzle. Has he been caught up in other "dreams" before or since? Was he a newcomer to Bagby or a "good old boy"? Is he, in a way, a true believer? In what else has he believed? These are simply initial guiding questions intended to help unravel the obscurity of the problem.

Significance of the Study

Smith and Keith, in their *case study* of an innovative school, said, "We thought as hard and as well as we were able to understand Kensington as an individual case study and as an illustration of broad and significant issues in social science and education."[8] I hope to do the same with the Bagby Human Resource Center. Aside from its inherent interest, the case study of Bagby has aspects of significance for disciplines as disparate as community education, sociology, organizational theory and psychology.

On the surface, the Bagby case study may retroactively explicate the failure of similar community projects attempted in the past, and thus, as a bad example, help provide a better foundation for future community education projects of this sort. At a slightly wider level of analysis, the Bagby attempt to integrate several community agencies which were accustomed to operate independently is of interest from the standpoint of organizational theory.

There also exists a still broader sociological view of the community's role in the emasculation of the Bagby HRC, the converse effect of the weakened HRC on the community, and the community's response to this attempt at innovation. Finally there is a much narrower aspect, of interest to psychology, in the focus on Dr. Byers. His life history, motivations, and modi operandi, while central to the Bagby case, are also an important psychological study of a true believer.

Methodology

Data Collection

The data will be collected through:

1. semi-structured and unstructured interviews with key informants (tape-recorded for transcription);

2. perusal of pertinent documents such as the original grant, newspapers, and minutes of the various community meetings dealing with the HRC;
3. limited direct observation in the HRC.

The various sources of data allow triangulation—data collected from one source are compared to data collected from another source to cross-check the accuracy of the information.[9]

Analysis

Analysis of the data will follow the constant comparative (or grounded theory) method of Glaser and Strauss.[10] The data collected from different sources will be used for description and for generation of concepts and hypotheses about the problem. The document information, information from present and former HRC personnel, perceptions of the HRC from others, and my own perceptions of the HRC from observation and conversation will be compared, contrasted and finally converged in an attempt to find explanatory patterns. These patterns will then be examined in the light of relevant literature for similarities to other published cases and possible theoretical explanations. Further data collection will be guided by emerging themes resulting from analysis of initial data. Verbatim excerpts from transcriptions will be used to lend credibility to the final report.[11]

Preliminary Analysis and Related Literature

Organizational Theory

There are some concepts in organizational theory which may possibly be of use in understanding what happened in Bagby.

First, there is the idea of Byers as a charismatic leader or evangelist. The evangelist term is borrowed from K. E. Weick: "Because managers traffic so often in images, the appropriate role for the manager may be evangelist rather than accountant."[12] The image of the evangelist is particularly apt though, because evangelists come into towns, fire up the citizenry with propaganda, baptize them into the faith, and then depart, leaving in their wake a stream of converts who are unable to live up to the vows of their new-found faith without aid. It may be that Byers can be viewed in this way. He was the one selling the idea to the community, he was primarily responsible for writing the grant, he was the one who explained the goals of the facility at its groundbreaking. Perhaps when he left after the Center had only been open for 18 months the remaining people could not keep up the faith. Byers himself said: "The kinds of things that can be done with this organization structure and this facility will only be limited by the limitations of vision of the people involved in administering this."[13] Perhaps no one else had enough unrestricted vision.

Alternatively, it may not have been that Byers was the only one with vision, but that the vision was so different from the current reality that it was difficult for the rest of the community to really become accustomed to it. The idea of a community school is radically different from the traditional view of schooling, and the traditional view is so ingrained in our "dark ages" (to use Schumacher's term[14]) that the proposed change may well have been difficult at best, and impossible at worst. R. H. Brown and A. Sheldon discuss this in terms of paradigm shifts, borrowing the paradigm idea from Kuhn.

> *Brown (1978) maintained that the development of shared paradigms is what occurs in formal organizations. Standard operating procedures, shared definitions of the environment, and agreed-upon system of authority and power represent the organization's worldview and paradigm. . . . Sheldon (1980) used the idea of paradigm as a diagnostic to help forecast when change would be relatively easy (when fundamental parts of the paradigm were not at issue) and when change would be more difficult and would need to be more comprehensive (when the basic paradigm was the object of change).[15]*

A third possibility is that the community never bought into the whole scheme to begin with, but were simply serving their own interests in playing along. The head librarian alluded to this in my interview with her—she came along with it because there was a desperate need for a new library and the city council was not about to finance it, and she suspects that the other agencies involved felt much the same way. There's ample evidence that this was the case with the middle school, because that's what started the ball rolling in the first place. *The Handbook of Social Psychology* puts it this way:

> *Why should the various managers in the organization be expected to act in the organization's as contrasted with their own, more parochial interests? The answer to this question is proposed in various perspectives on organizational control. There are, essentially, two perspectives on achieving control. A period of socialization in which the organization's culture, values, and preferences become internalized by the various participants . . . or the use of compensation schemes that attempt to develop a high correlation between the interests of the organization and the interests of its employees and the managers. This is presumably accomplished by having compensation based importantly on overall organizational performance so that by acting in one's individual self-interest, one is automatically led to take actions that are rational from the perspective of the total organization.[16]*

These three theoretical explanations overlap a great deal. Perhaps because Byers left when he did, the period of socialization discussed above was interrupted, and therefore subverted. Or perhaps no compensation or period of socialization would have been enough to get people to accept the new paradigm of community school because it was just too different from the old tradition. The possibilities are legion.

Community Education

There have been other community facilities, much like the one in Bagby, both in the United States and in Britain. Early in the 20th Century there were "Village Colleges" established in England by Morris which included many of the same aspects as the Bagby HRC: school for children as well as adults, adult leisure center, rooms for use by local organizations, and the public library adjacent for use by both the school and the adult community.[17] Within the U.S., Flint and Pontiac, Michigan, and Philadelphia, PA currently have (or formerly had) similar facilities. The histories of these other similar facilities may provide a comparison which would be helpful in understanding this case.

Other Literature

I expect to be led into other literature as patterns appear in the data. It is possible that some of the studies of latent and manifest purposes (Merton), or instrumental and symbolic motives (or actions or goals) may be useful. Hoffer's concept of true believers is especially apt. In talking with M. T. Byers it is easy to get caught up in the dream that was, and he seems not to even be aware that it remains simply that—a dream that never attained reality.

Notes

1. All proper names have been changed to help assure anonymity to the town and its people.

2. Pp. 6, 7, "Development of Bagby Human Resources Center as told by M. T. Byers."

3. *Community Education Update*, Vol. IV (3), Jan-March, 1978.

4. Program from the groundbreaking ceremony.

5. "Local Public Works Capital Development and Investment Program Application—Project Narrative" and "Development of Bagby HRC."

6. From field notes 3 April, 1987; Contract to Lease Space in the Bagby Human Resources Center to the Bagby Public Library—Rules for the Use of the Community Room in the Bagby Human Resources Center.

7. Interview with Sandy Parents, head librarian, 3 April, 1987.

8. Smith, Louis M. & Keith, Pat. (1976). *Social Psychological Aspects of School Building Design*, p. 15.

9. Glaser, Barney G. & Strauss, Anselm L. (1967). *The Discovery of Grounded Theory: Strategies for Qualitative Research*, Chicago: Aldine. Goetz, Judith Preissle & LeCompte, Margaret Diane. (1984). *Ethnography and Qualitative Design in Educational Research*, Academic Press: New York.

10. Glaser and Strauss. (1967).

11. Pohland, Paul A. (1969). Dissertation proposal, Washington University. Bogdan, Robert C. & Biklen, Sari Knopp. (1982). *Qualitative Research for Education: An Introduction to Theory and Methods*, Allyn and Bacon: Boston.

12. Weick, K. E. (1977). "Cognitive processes in organizations." In Staw, B. M. (Ed.) *Research in Organizational Behavior*, Vol. I. Greenwich, Conn.: JAI Press, pp. 41–74. Quoted in Lindzey, Gardner and Aronson, Elliot (eds.) (1985). *Handbook of Social Psychology*, Vol. II, p. 423.

13. Pp. 15, "Development of Bagby HRC."

14. Schumacher, E. F. (1973). *Small Is Beautiful*, Harper & Row, p. 75.

15. Brown, R. H. (1978). "Bureaucracy as praxis: toward a political phenomenology of formal organizations." *Admin. Sci. Quart.*, *23*, 365–382. Sheldon, A. (1980). "Organizational paradigms: a theory of organizational change." *Organizational Dynamics*, *8*, 61–80. Kuhn, T. S. (1970). *The structure of scientific revolutions*. (2nd edition). Chicago: University of Chicago Press.

All of these are cited in Vol. I of the *Handbook of Social Psych.*, p. 424.

16. Lindzey, Gardner and Aronson, Elliot (Eds.), *Handbook of Social Psychology*, Vol. I, p. 403.

17. Brookfield, S. (1984). *Adult Learners, Adult Education, and the Community*, New York: Teallus College, Columbia University.

Identifying Patterns, Speculating on Motivations for American Men's Persistence in Teaching, 1880–1920

Courtney Vaughn

Jeffrey A. Liles

A major focus for social historians has been the feminization of teaching beginning during the nineteenth century and ending in 1920 when 84.5 percent of the nation's teachers were female. Usually, these scholars only speculate why men remained in the field and focus instead on why men left teaching. Various studies maintain that from the late nineteenth century until 1920 males persisted in teaching within regions that provided few professional options for men; enforced low educational standards (thereby making it easy for men to become and remain teachers); recorded small salary differentials between male and female educators and low average teachers' salaries, making it economical for male-dominated school boards (preferentially) to hire men rather than women; and provided many more opportunities for male than for female teachers to move into administration (Elsbree, 1939; Kennedy, 1940; Hofstadter, 1963; Mattingly, 1975; Tyack & Strober, 1981; Morain, 1980; Richardson & Hatcher, 1983; Rury, 1986).

Data from the U.S. Bureau of the Census (1923) indicate that by 1920, Arkansas, Indiana, New Mexico, Oklahoma, Utah, and West Virginia were the only states reporting over 20 percent of their total teaching forces to be male (Hansot & Tyack, 1988). Significantly, these nationally comparative percentages produced z scores of 1 or more, meaning that they were at least one standard deviation above the national mean of all forty-eight states and the District of Columbia. Iowa, Nebraska, Nevada, and Vermont were the only states whose percentages of male teachers produced z scores of -1 or less, indicating that comparative percentages of male teachers in those states were at least one standard deviation below the national mean. Therefore, these ten states represent the two extremes—the best states from which to begin an examination of historians' assumptions about men in teaching.

Vaughn, C., & Liles, J. A. (1992). Identifying patterns, speculating on motivations for American men's persistence in teaching, 1880–1920. *The Tower Review, 9*(1), pp. 14–21. Reprinted with permission.

The First Generalization: Professional Options

Also computed from Census data recorded for 1920 were percentages and z scores for the total number of male professional service employees categories. Those for Arkansas (–1.14), New Mexico (–.97), Utah (–.15), and West Virginia (–.64). These figures confirmed the belief that men remained in teaching because they had few other professional options. The above states were largely rural and had not yet produced the many other professional opportunities that were becoming available to males in more industrial areas. Also, the positive z scores for this measure in Iowa (.34) and Nebraska (.01) show that professional alternatives were relatively abundant for males, possibly accounting for their low percentages in teaching (U.S. Census, 1923). Percentages and z scores were also figured for the number of male teachers to male professional service employees reported by the Census in 1920. The negative z scores in Iowa (–.30), Nebraska (–.20), Nevada (–2.46) and Vermont (–.51) indicated that men were taking advantage of these other options (U.S. Census, 1904, 1914, & 1923). A look at aggregate numbers of male teachers in the ten states suggest that from 1900 to 1920 younger male teachers were non-existent, as in Nevada, or lost some ground, as in Vermont, for which 57 men out of 380 were reported in 1900, and 55 out of 211 in 1920.

However, data from eight states cannot be used to make assumptions why men may have taught in all states. For example, in 1920, the relative number of professional opportunities produced positive z scores in Indiana (.51) and Oklahoma (.34), suggesting that factors other than limited options attracted men to teaching. Moveover, from 1900 to 1920, male teachers who were 45 years of age or older increased in Arkansas, Indiana, New Mexico, Oklahoma, Utah, West Virginia, and even Nebraska. For example, in 1900, Indiana male teachers over age 45 numbered 54 out of 6,420, and in 1920 they accounted for 928 out of 5,176. From those figures one might hypothesize that a few men remained in the classroom for some time and that others elected to teach later in life. In addition, the relatively small number of professional categories for males, five in Nevada and nine in Vermont, produced low z scores (–1.46 and –.81, respectively). Thus, the lack of professional jobs for males in Nevada and Vermont may not have been a factor in men's avoidance of teaching as a career, because those states had low percentages of male teachers, as well.

The Second Generalization: Quality Education

Data derived from Leonard Ayres' (1920) total quality-of-education index score for all states and territories and the District of Columbia for the years 1890, 1900, 1910, and 1918 provide a means to investigate whether relatively large proportions of males taught in states where educational standards were low enough to provide easy entry into the field. Ayres' book describes in detail his calculations for his quality-of-education formula, but ultimately the total index score is comprised of ten different indices:

1. the percent of a school population that attends school daily;
2. the percent of high school attendance to the total attendance;
3. the percent of boys to girls attending high schools;
4. the average annual expenditure per student attending school;
5. the average annual expenditure per each school-age child, whether in school or not;
6. the average annual expenditure per teacher employed;
7. the average expenditure per pupil for purposes other than teachers' salaries;
8. the average expenditure for teachers' salaries;
9. the average days attended by each school-age child; and
10. the number of days schools were kept open (Ayres, 1920).

Another national survey (Foght, 1915) of the quality of education in rural areas and the percentages of male and female rural teachers reinforced the analysis. For the ten states, from Foght's study, z scores were computed from percentages of male teachers in rural areas and percentages of teachers without adequate training. A pattern was evident. By 1920 Arkansas, New Mexico, West Virginia, and perhaps Oklahoma provided a stereotypical climate for males to remain in teaching. For example, z scores derived from Ayres' total index for these states were predominantly negative throughout the late nineteenth and early twentieth centuries. A case in point was Arkansas, the z score of which descended from −1.08 in 1890, to −1.71 in 1918 (Ayres, 1920). Also in these states, the percentages and z scores of male rural teachers and especially of rural teachers without adequate training were high. All of the four states had a z score of over 1.45, with Arkansas (2.16) topping the list. Moreover, in Nebraska and Nevada the percentage z scores (−1.42 and −1.14, respectively) for the numbers of rural teachers without proper training were low, and most of those teachers were female (Foght, 1915). Therefore, it appeared that generally women in those states were more serious than men about their professional preparation.

Yet, emerging at this point was the absence of corroboration in Indiana and Utah for the assumption that men continued to teach because of these states' low standards. For example, although there was some fluctuation from 1890 to 1918, Indiana's and Utah's total index z scores were above average (z > 0) (Ayres, 1920). Conversely, in 1914, Vermont's 35.7 percent and Iowa's 65 percent of rural teachers without training produced z scores of .25 and 1.84, respectively. Moreover Vermont's (−1.32) and Iowa's (−.88) z scores for the percentages of rural teachers who were male indicate that a large amount of their poorly trained teachers were female (Foght, 1915). Finally, by 1918, Nebraska (.48), Nevada (.63), and Vermont (.02) reported lower total index scores than did Utah (.82), indicating that groups of poorly trained teachers were not always thronged with comparatively large numbers of men (Ayres, 1920). Such inconsistencies corroborate the work of Kaestle and Vinovskis (1980) who point out the pitfalls of making national generalizations about rural education.

The Third Generalization: Salary Differentials

In addition, z scores were derived from Ayres' (1920) salary index. These data and that of other federal salary reports for all states and the District of Columbia suggested that in some states men did teach in regions with small salary differentials between male and female educators and low average teachers' salaries. The relatively low salary differentials recorded in Table 1 substantiate that in Arkansas, New Mexico, Oklahoma, and West Virginia, school boards could afford to hire men, while the high salary differentials in Iowa, Nebraska, and Vermont, three of the comparison states, certainly could have priced men out of the teaching market. However, Nevada was the only comparison state that, from 1890 to 1918, had consistently positive salary index z scores (1.86, 1.16, .03, and .43), making it a possible exception to the supposed rule (Ayres, 1920). But, selected salary schedules reported in Table 1 show that even Nevada enforced higher pay differentials than many of the six states employing relatively large percentages of male teachers.

An exceptional pattern existed in Indiana and Utah. Particularly after 1910, school systems paid relatively high wages to both genders. Utah's salary index z scores rose consistently from .10 in 1890, to .81 in 1981 (Ayres, 1920). Moreover, Utah's male teachers were not cheap to hire, for this state consistently showed the highest male/female salary differentials of all the six states with relatively high percentages of male teachers (see Table 1).

The Fourth Generalization: Upward Mobility for Males in Education

Table 2 lists comparatively nation-wide data computed from U.S. Commissioner of Education reports on early twentieth-century teachers and administrators in cities with populations of 4,000 to 8,000 (shown as C 4–8, Table 2) and those with populations over 8,000 (shown as C o 8, Table 2). These data are important because the U.S. Census does not differentiate between teachers and administrators for a given state. Thus, Table 2 provides an opportunity, further, to scrutinize aggregate numbers of male and female educators and speculate about the generalization that males remained in teaching when the opportunity to move into administration was apparent.

In some cases, Table 2 reveals what appears to be the guaranteed upward mobility of male teachers. For example, in 1900, Arkansas and Oklahoma not only have relatively high numbers of male teachers but of administrators. And in 1900 and 1907, Iowa, Nebraska, Nevada, and Vermont hired few men to teach in any of their city schools, while in 1900, 100 percent of the administrators in Nevada and Vermont cities of 4,000 to 8,000 were male.

Indicating an emergent alternative pattern in the state of Indiana, a comparatively sizable number of male teachers seem to have remained in the classroom.

TABLE 1 Selected Monthly Teacher's Salaries in Dollars, by Gender in Ten States: 1880, 1910, & 1913

State	1880 M	F	1910 M	F	1913 M	F
AR	39.21	34.93	NA	NA	NA	NA
IN	38.40	33.20	72.40	62.20	75.46	69.45
NM	30.67	30.67	NA	NA	68.73	55.56
OK/IT	50.00	50.00	61.69	51.96	68.73	55.56
UT	35.00	22.00	94.49	71.95	92.06	75.08
WV	27.96	28.70	NA	NA	NA	NA
IA	32.56	27.25	79.23	48.14	83.22	49.91
NE	36.50	32.50	69.35	49.98	80.51	58.62
NV	99.50	74.76	122.02	77.00	125.92	81.91
VT	29.76	16.84	55.23	33.53	68.48	37.83

Source: U.S. House of Representatives. (1880). Executive documents of the House of Representatives for the 3rd Session of the 46th Congress. Washington, D. C.: U.S. Govt. Printing Office; U.S. Commissioner of Education. (1883). Report of the Commissioner of Education for the Year 1881. Washington, D. C.: U.S. Govt. Printing Office; Report of the Commission of Education for The Year Ended June 30, 1912, Vol. II. (1913). Washington, D.C.: U. S. Govt. Printing Office; Report of the Commissioner of Education, Vol. II. (1915). Washington, D.C.: U.S. Govt. Printing Office.

Diverging from the apparent norm, for both reporting periods in each city size, the relative numbers of male administrators in Indiana produced negative z scores. Referring back to Table 1 and to the discussion of rural teachers, although Indiana male teachers tended to work in urban areas where salaries were at least comparatively better than average, relatively small proportions of them went into administration despite the low wage differential between the genders' salaries.

Conclusions

In Oklahoma, Arkansas, West Virginia, and New Mexico historical assumptions that turn-of-the-century males continued to teach in areas where men had easy access into administration, standards and pay were low, and women were highly discriminated against in terms of salary and promotion seemed valid. But the inverse of these assumptions—that men would avoid teaching in states or regions where these conditions did not exist—was not always substantiated by data from Iowa, Nebraska, Nevada, and Vermont. Soon, nationally comparative data derived from U.S. Census reports will offer scholars a much more in-depth demographic profile of American teachers than current Census books can provide (Perlmann & Margo, 1989).

Yet, statistics can only point to patterns of relationships. The motivations of people who make up those trends must be determined through qualitative re-

TABLE 2 Percentage (%) and (z) of Male Teachers (MT) and
Administrators (MA) in Cities 4,000–8,000 (C 4–8) and Cities
Over 8,000 (C o 8), 100 and 1907

State	% MT in C 4–8	1990 z	% MA in C 4–8	z
AR	13.65	.34	100.00	1.31
IN	10.14	−.11	61.43	−.66
NM	44.44	4.27	NA	NA
OK	NA	NA	NA	NA
UT	33.36	2.89	66.67	−.39
WV	9.78	−.16	69.23	−.26
IA	6.41	−.59	67.74	−.34
NE	5.04	−.76	44.83	−1.51
NV	9.09	−.24	100.00	1.31
VT	6.67	−.55	100.00	1.31

State	% MT in C o 8	z	% MA in C o 8	z
AR	18.23	2.64	100.00	2.24
IN	12.21	1.04	48.36	−.43
NM	NA	NA	NA	NA
OK	12.31	1.07	80.00	1.21
UT	10.26	.52	65.62	.46
WV	9.74	.39	61.11	.23
IA	6.00	−.60	37.25	−1.00
NE	5.26	−.80	26.67	−1.55
NV	NA	NA	NA	NA
VT	4.64	−.97	60.00	.17

(Continued)

search that examines letters, diaries, and other documents. Such work in all states is needed to determine the reason why males may have remained in teaching.

Anecdotal sources about and from school masters and male teachers from various regions scattered across the United States suggest that some men may have taught for altruistic reasons not unlike those of their female counterparts—to help nurture students academically and morally (Alcott, 1856; Williams, 1900; Kennedy, 1940). Others may have chosen teaching to counteract what traditionalists feared was the "feminization" of American youth (Dubbert, 1980). More systematic qualitative research in each state could produce additional male-teacher prototypes, just as revisionist research sheds doubt on the old notion that female educators lacked professionalism and commitment to teach (Hoffman, 1981; Peterson & Vaughn-Roberson, 1988).

Utah and Indiana would be excellent places to begin. One might find that in Utah the patriarchal Mormon Church, which stressed male service to others, encouraged males to remain in teaching (Winget, 1969). The lack of any consistent argument for why Indiana males taught in comparatively large numbers suggests

TABLE 2 *(Continued)*

State	% MT in C 4–8	1907 z	% MA in C 4–8	z
AR	15.00	.98	71.43	.36
IN	19.08	1.99	52.53	−.55
NM	13.51	.61	100.00	1.74
OK	5.32	−1.42	69.23	.26
UT	20.93	2.45	57.14	−.33
WV	16.18	1.27	50.00	−.67
IA	6.24	−1.19	47.22	−.81
NE	6.42	−1.14	54.55	.45
NV	9.52	−.38	33.33	−1.48
VT	6.11	−1.22	40.00	−1.16

State	% MT in C o 8	z	% MA in C o 8	z
AR	15.19	1.91	78.57	1.67
IN	11.59	.84	49.49	−.13
NM	11.11	.70	62.50	.67
OK	20.47	3.47	57.14	.34
UT	10.38	.48	63.64	.74
WV	9.85	.33	56.41	.30
IA	6.29	−.73	39.41	−.76
NE	4.12	−1.37	28.21	−1.45
NV	NA	NA	NA	NA
VT	5.29	−1.02	25.00	−1.65

U. S. Commissioner of Education, Report of the Commissioner of Education for the Year 1899–1900, Vol. II. (1901). Washington, D. C., U. S. Govt. Printing Office; Report of the Commissioner of Education for the Year Ended June 30, 1907, Vol. II. (1908). Washington, D.C.: U. S. Govt. Printing Office.

that here and perhaps in other states male teachers were attracted to education for reasons other than those already examined in this study. There is much research to be done before we can make any blanket statements, nationally, about the motivations of turn-of-the-century male teachers. In fact, further studies will most likely indicate that the complex social structure of any state or locality, made up of males and females from a variety of ethnic groups and social classes, will rarely lead to generalizations about all teachers at any time.

References

Alcott, W. A. (1856). *Confessions of a schoolmaster.* Reading, PA: H. A. Lantz.

Ayres, L. P. (1920). *An index number for state school systems.* New York: Columbia Teachers College.

Census of the United States population, 1880, 1890, 1900, 1910, & 1920. (1883, 1905, 1914, & 1923). Washington, D. C.: U.S. Government Printing Office.

Dubbert, J. L. (1980). Progressivism and the masculinity crisis. In Pleck, E. H. & Pleck, J. H. (Eds.), *The American Man*, 303–320. Englewood Cliffs, NJ: Prentice Hall.

Elsbree, W. S. (1939). *The American teachers: Evolution of a profession in a democracy*. New York: American Book Company.

Foght, H. W. (1915). *Efficiency and preparation of rural school teachers*. Washington, D. C.: U.S. Government Printing Office.

Hansot, E. & Tyack, D. B. (1988). Gender in American public schools: Thinking institutionally. *Signs: Journal of Women in Culture and Society, 13*, 741–759.

Hoffman, N. (1981). *Women's "true" profession: Voices from the history of teaching*. New York: Knopf.

Hofstadter, R. (1963). *Anti-intellectualism in American life*. New York: Knopf.

Kaestle, C. & Vinovskis, M. (1980). *Education and social change in nineteenth-century Massachusetts*. Cambridge: Cambridge University Press.

Kennedy, M. F. (1940). *Schoolmaster of yesterday: A three generation story*. New York: McGraw-Hill.

Mattingly, P. H. (1975). *The classless profession: American schoolmen in the nineteenth-century*. New York: New York University Press.

Morain, T. (1980). The departure of males from the teaching profession in nineteenth-century Iowa. *Civil War History, 26*, 161–170.

Perlmann, J. & Margo, R. (1989). *Historical Methods, 22*, 68–73.

Peterson, S. C. & Vaughn-Roberson, C. A. (1988). *Women with vision: The Presentation Sisters of South Dakota, 1880–1985*. Urbana: University of Illinois Press.

Richardson, J. G. & Hatcher, B. W. (1983). The feminization of public school teaching, 1870–1920. *Work and Occupations, 10*, 81–99.

Rury, J. L. (1986). Gender, salaries, and career: American teachers, 1900–1910. *Issues in Education, 4*, 215–235.

Tyack, D. B. & Strober, M. H. (1981). Jobs and gender: A history of the structuring of educational employment by sex, 131–152. In Schmuck, P. A. Charters, Jr., W. W. & Carlson, R. O. (Eds.), *Educational policy and management: Sex differentials*. New York: Academic Press.

Williams, J. R. (Ed.). (1900). *Philip Vickers Fithian: Journal and letters, 1767–1744*. Princeton: The Princeton Library.

Winget, L. W. (1969). Utah, pp. 1225–1259. In Pearson, J. B. & Fuller, E. (Eds.), *Education in the states: Historical development and outlook*. Washington, D. C.: National Education Association.

Chapter 5

Sources of Data

This chapter defines and discusses the origins of data; discusses the importance of accuracy in data collection; explains the traditional links between truth-seeking and quantitative data and between perspective-seeking and qualitative data; and discusses variations from those norms. Also included is procedural information about how to locate and generate data.

As introduced in Chapter 2, data are what the researcher collects to answer the research question. They are always representations of the human phenomenon, belief, behavior, construct, or thought that the researcher intended to understand or measure. There are two means of obtaining data. One is to generate them through such things as instruments, surveys, questionnaires, interviews, or observations. The other is to locate them. Existing data may be housed in any number of international, national, state, district, or local depositories and may or may not be categorized or annotated. Other valuable data may exist almost in anonymity, in a person's home for example. Persistent questioning of those who are knowledgeable in a certain field and following all of their leads, are likely to lead the researcher to such uncataloged materials.

Coombs (1964) points out that quantitative *data* are the numerical or symbolic representations of the piece of a particular reality on which a study is focused. Their analysis could involve qualitative methods (patterning) or quantitative methods (measuring). For example, a researcher may ask the question: How did the editorial attention toward the topic of public schools change from 1970 to 1980 in major newspapers throughout the United States? After giving a good rationale for using selected newspapers (e.g., the five with the highest circulation or the one with the highest circulation from each region of the United States), the researcher might count the times certain words, related to schooling, were mentioned in all of the editorials and compute percentages for each of the years being studied. The numbers and percentages are examples of quantitative data that could be understood through patterning (qualitative) or statistical analysis (quantitative). (More about analysis is presented in Chapter 6.)

Generally, there are four types of quantitative data: nominal, ordinal, interval, and ratio. Because so many truth-seeking studies employ quantitative data, research books categorize them as such to be used in different types of statistical analyses: nonparametric (using nominal and ordinal data) and parametric (using interval and ratio data). Nominal data are created by naming a response. For example, to evaluate a citizenry's interest in the composition of its school board, a researcher might administer a paper and pencil instrument composed of questions involving voting behavior in local school board elections to which subjects respond "Yes" or "No."

In social science research quantitative data often represent concepts, so another researcher might examine the relative level of aggression expressed by a given sample of people. He could administer an instrument consisting of statements that are designed to provoke aggressive reactions, to which subjects record agreement or disagreement. The researcher would then compute a numerical score on the instrument, enabling him or her to rank the scores from lowest to highest. Such scores are an example of *ordinal* data. Together, they have an order and therefore have relative value to each other. In ordinal data, however, the difference between first and second is not necessarily the same as the difference between third and fourth. Rank in high school class is another example of ordinal data.

Interval data that may be generated have equal intervals between the ranks. The difference between first and second is equal to that between third and fourth. Temperature readings from a thermometer are interval data. The concept of zero, however, is arbitrary and, though it exists, as on a thermometer, does not mean the absence of the construct being measured.

Finally, a researcher or teacher could measure students' heights, creating ratio data (numbers that have a precise value on a scale from zero to some other number). The intervals are equal and zero means the absence of the construct. (See Borg & Gall, 1989, or other research texts for more detail about the different quantitative scales and their implications for appropriate statistics.)

In many perspective-seeking traditions, if numbers are used at all, their function is to identify patterns of human behavior. The Peshkin reading in Chapter 6 explains this process. He intended to determine how ethnicity affected the formal and informal operations of a particular high school. His first step was to administer a survey of questions or statements to record and map certain patterns of responses on a scale that ranged from "strongly agree" to "strongly disagree." Then he collected detailed qualitative data through interviews and observations. Thus, the numbers gave him an idea of what queries to pose in his interviews and what to look for in his observations.

When we speak of qualitative data we are referring to words, text, observations, ancient or newly created artifacts, maps, and illustrations. Both truth-seeking and perspective-seeking studies can utilize qualitative data. Usually, it is recorded within its contextual origin. For example, when understanding a participant's life history, the scholar must continually be aware of the total environment in which the participant was reared. Truth-seekers most often might generate qualitative data in the beginning stages of instrument formation (e.g., brainstorming with selected people to come up with statements that evoke a certain response or represent a construct) or when conceptualizing a topic (exploring an issue through interviews with experts in a given field, for example). Jensen (1984) explains that oral histories or interviews can be read to detect patterns for which quantitative variables might be named and tested to determine the precise nature of their relationships with other variables.

Some scholars believe that studies employing quantitative rather than qualitative data provide more precise answers to educational research questions. Others argue that qualitative, more than quantitative, data represent a more detailed or contextual portrayal of the phenomenon or behavior under investigation and therefore are better sources to answer complex research questions about human beings. Firestone points out, in the reading for Chapter 2, that both have useful purposes. Yet, both are only representations of the constructs or ideas to be measured, whether they are derived by scoring a test and counting the number of times certain students in a classroom raise their hands (quantitative) or reading a novel or diary and asking an interviewee a series of questions (Butler & Scott, 1992).

Validity, Trustworthiness, Contamination

Because all data are created by people, they contain remnants of human intervention. As noted in Chapter 2, validity addresses this issue by asking: Are data truly the reflection of what the researcher intends to study? Truth-seeking quantitative and some truth-seeking qualitative researchers use the term *validity*, other truth-seeking and perspective-seeking qualitative inquirers refer to the *trustworthiness* of data. A perspective-seeking quantitative researcher might use either term depending on the particular perceptions that the numbers in a study intended to symbolize. Also, as discussed in Chapters 2 and 4, the degree to which a researcher carries out all of the suggested ways to establish the validity and trustworthiness of data may depend on his or her ontological and epistemological beliefs. For example, the inquirer may contend that a person's self-knowledge is so cryptic and subconscious that an interviewee may not be able to tell an interviewer all of his or her thoughts on a particular subject, so the researcher can only take the words at face value.

Myriad suggestions exist in various methods books for checking the validity of existing quantitative data. For example, the United States Census Bureau issues reports every ten years that numerically describe the population. Becker discusses, in his Chapter 6 reading, problems with census data representativeness. Weiler (1992) also highlights this issue, writing that during different reporting periods the discrepancies between United States and state or county census records in California were dramatic. Often, United States Census records provide the only sources of quantitative data available, and this can pose a dilemma, as well. For example, in some decades those persons who categorized individual census data computed totals for various racial and ethic groups and added them together to make one category, such as "other," of non-white people. To remedy this discrepancy, Perlman and Margo (reading for this chapter) have obtained random samples of individual educators' census reports dating back to 1860 and are in the process of consistently organizing this information throughout the decades. When their work is completed we should be able to identify and compare educators within and between reporting periods. However, even in this process we must remember that when taking a random sample there is still a margin of error: the resulting sample will not perfectly represent the population from which it was derived. Also remember that the researchers, themselves, are constructing the categories in which certain individuals are placed. Thus, human intervention is occurring in the process, which prevents perfect validity of the data.

Other scholars offer insights when checking for the trustworthiness of existing qualitative data. For instance, you might locate biographies of educators written by historians working for the federal WPA program during the Great Depression of the 1930s. Although those interviewers personally spoke with teachers or administrators whose views might be crucial to answering your research question, the values of those who summarized the interviewees' accounts may have clouded the original statements' intended meanings. Faraday and Plummer (1979) call this *contamination of data*. The Thompson end-of-chapter reading contains some excellent instruction on how one might detect contamination in transcribed interviews. Moreover, autobiography scholars point out that autobiographies, interestingly enough, are not necessarily very revealing. It is likely that autobiographies are sometimes written to draw the reader away from the author's most painful or intimate memories and toward a reconstructed past, one that is easiest for the author to live with (Heilbrun, 1988; Earle, 1972).

There are five other specific types of validity, related largely to truth-seeking quantitative studies employing instruments such as tests to generate quantitative data. Remember, validity, in general, defines how well an instrument measures what it is supposed to measure. *Content validity* is usually based on professional judgments of a number of people. *Criterion-related validity* is assessed by comparing scores on an instrument with one or more external variables, called *criteria*. For example a new test of creativity could be administered at the same time as an accepted, established test is administered. The established test scores would be the criterion, and validity of the new test would be determined by how well the scores from it correspond to the scores from the established test. *Predictive validity* indicates the degree to which the score on a given test or survey is related to a subject's future behavior related to the test's content. For instance, do students with superior IQ scores make superior grades and show other evidences of academic success? If so, then IQ scores may have predictive validity regarding academic success. *Concurrent validity* indicates the extent to which the test scores estimate an individual's present standing on the criterion. For example, are students' scores on an achievement test similar to their current academic performance in school? *Construct validity* is the degree to which an instrument's scores measure what it is they are intended to measure, and establishing it can involve almost all of the above variants of general validity (Messick, 1988).

Validity or trustworthiness is also important to truth-seekers and many perspective-seekers who generate qualitative data. To establish validity or trustworthiness, qualitative researchers often return transcribed interviews to participants and informants to be sure that the investigator has accurately recorded what a person has said. Or a team of researchers might all listen to taped interviews and independently make tables of responses to see if each investigator detected the same themes (Lincoln & Guba, 1985).

Testing for reliability is crucial for the truth-seeker who must add a piece to the theoretical puzzle. He or she therefore must be relatively certain that her or his research produces the same results each time it is conducted. Only then can the researcher assert that the findings represent some sort of objective truth that exists outside of the subjective biases of those involved. If a study is reliable then it can be repeated by another researcher and the same or similar results will follow. To this end, an investigator may hire two or three people to conduct interviews with the same people, so that they can compare their qualitative data gleaned from those interviewed. For the sake of reliability, only those facts or perceptions recorded by all of the interviewers would be used. As Becker indicates in his reading at the end of Chapter 6, however, applying such a logical procedure to interviews is practically impossible.

Locating Data

Data are housed in any number of national, international, state, county, and district depositories. As you might expect, information available at the national and international levels may be more geographically comprehensive than that residing in a state or other more regional center. Most universities can provide a computerized search that pinpoints available data bases to assist in doing research. Also, university libraries contain many reference volumes indexed by subject or author that list and sometimes annotate a number of collections in various locations all over the world. These can be used to conduct a data search. Depending on the type of project selected one might also visit the actual depositories that one suspects, but cannot confirm, contain useful data. For example, when conducting research on education in the United States a researcher might visit certain states' capital cities. Here will be the state library, the historical society, the state superintendent's office, and a host of other city and state agencies that may contain all sorts of documents and figures. In addition, various branches of the National Archives, such as the Lyndon Baines Johnson Library in Austin, Texas, are located in capital cities. Talking to librarians in county libraries and historical societies may help uncover data not indexed in the reference volumes or flagged on the computer printout perused at the onset of a project. Such materials may be stored in a nearby company; denominational headquarters of a religious organization; local, state, and national offices of unions and professional association; or private homes. Hospitals often have libraries and archival collections, particularly if they are part of a medical training program. Convents and monasteries involved in educational efforts often have libraries that store special collections.

A wide variety of sources exist in these many storehouses. A few examples are numerical data, letters, diaries, records, oral history tapes or transcribed interviews (with teachers and other professionals, laborers, housewives, and retired individuals), and collections of the papers of certain individuals (typically including a multitude of artifacts and documents).

National and International

Along with the records that a country's government might keep, the Vatican in Rome holds useful information on education throughout the world and the Catholic Church. In the United States, various federal agencies, such as the Department of the Interior or of Education, publish a plethora of demographic data on citizens, much of which is related to education. For example, early in the twentieth century the government issued a number of reports on the quality and condition of education in each state (Fought, 1915; Ayres, 1920). A more recent example is the data bank of High School and Beyond (Horn, 1989). It contains numerical data on students, college student financial aid, course offerings, and enrollments of schools in the study, as well as transcripts for both high school and post-secondary schools, a language file, a parent survey, and a school file. There are several categories of information within each of these general areas.

Pamphlets and other written descriptions of data banks can be found in the government documents section of a university library. One such publication contains a description of twenty-two databases maintained within the United States Department of Education (Marshall & Rossman, 1989). Computer searches also can retrieve the citations for written research that has used any of these data.

Private Agencies

Various organizations, such as the Carnegie Foundation, also collect data and print national reports on education. For example, Feistritzer supervised the gathering and reporting of numerous descriptions of the teaching forces in each state and the District of Columbia (1985). This volume contains statewide numerical data on the nation's school population and enrollment trends, teachers, salaries of teachers, and teacher education and certification (1985). Data such as these are often fully indexed by a number of variables such as age, race, and socioeconomic status (SES).

University Archives

Universities often house nationwide samples of qualitative and quantitative data representing a number of topics relevant to social science and humanities research in education. The University of Syracuse has an archival collection of materials relating to the field of adult education. Radcliffe College supports the Henry A. Murray Research Center of Radcliffe College, for the study of women's lives. Radcliffe even sponsors fellowships to scholars interested in using its collection.

State Government

Government reports are also available at the state level. Particularly useful for educational research are the State Superintendent reports which have been issued over the years in various states since their territorial days. These documents often contain excellent narratives on the condition of rural education, of separate (non-white) education, or of special education programs. The reports also record numbers and percentages of teachers, students, and populations of various schools and school districts.

City, District, and County Levels

City libraries sometimes contain all sorts of potentially useful data. For example, the Denver Public Library has an extensive Western American history collection. In addition to many other materials, the collection has an annotated index for the Colorado Oral History Project conducted by the state's county library personnel and stored in those local facilities. Any number of transcriptions of tables or cassettes can be purchased or borrowed. School districts often have libraries and archives containing superintendents' papers, court cases, and many other records that document the history and present the status of education in a particular district.

Generating Data

As discussed in more detail in Chapter 7 on ethics in research, when generating data it is crucial to obtain participants' or subjects' permission to use the material obtained from them. Sometimes their actual names will appear, particularly in historical research, but more often than not one will need to provide them with written consent forms guaranteeing confidentiality of the source of the information they give and anonymity regarding the identification of particular people.

The process of generating data may sometimes seem overwhelming and never ending. Narrow the task by continuing to keep research question(s) or hypothesis(es) in mind. This avoids spending too much time gathering information that may never be used. Many doctoral students who are ABD (all but dissertation) or teachers who need to solve a problem involving their students have fallen into the trap of becoming perennial data collectors, and the research never gets done. On the other hand do not be too hasty. Before beginning the process, write or devise a carefully outlined plan that foresees as many sources of data as possible. As suggested, always show plans and work to other respected researchers. They will almost certainly think of points that were overlooked, thereby enhancing the validity or trustworthiness, as well as the comprehensiveness of all the data.

As noted earlier, generally the tools used to generate data are tests, questionnaires or surveys, interviews, and observations using instruments that already exist or that the researcher creates. (Some examples are described in this chapter's readings.) Instruments such as the Minnesota Multiphasic Personality Inventory (MMPI) and, sometimes, questionnaires or surveys that purport to measure or describe a specific construct, such as personality, and perhaps its various subcomponents can be used. For a list of many well-established ones and critiques of their validity (how well they measure what they intend to measure) and reliability (how consistently they are measuring it) see *Buros' Mental Measurement Yearbook* (1983). In the reference section of a university library one can locate numerous other theme volumes that contain documentation on instruments that examine a particular issue. One such work is *Gender Roles: A Handbook of Tests and Measurements* (Beere, 1990). Also the company that publishes a certain instrument may have available documents or monographs that discuss its use. The Educational Testing Service in Princeton, New Jersey, is one such example.

Tests and Other Instruments

If a reference book containing validity and reliability estimates for the instruments of choice is not available, you can initiate a computerized search, seeking the original article that explains how the instrument was formulated. For instance, in 1974 Bem published an article explaining how her sex-role inventory evolved. Bem's and other instruments such as the Piers-Harris self-concept scale for youngsters, are well known but have become controversial in recent years. Therefore, your computer search also might locate review articles such as one by Halote and Michael (1984) that critiques the Piers-Harris scale. In addition, while the Franklin et al. reading included in Chapter 4 validates that same instrument, the authors also caution that an instrument that uses self-reports is a questionable way to measure changes in children's self-esteem. For example, a statement on a self-concept scale may read, "I am generally well liked at school." The researcher may believe, after extensive pilot testing of his or her instrument, that a positive response to this statement reflects a subject's high self-esteem. Yet, a non-white child who attends a predominantly white or Anglo school may not feel well liked by his peers but still feel relatively good about himself. Thus, the instrument may not be a valid measure of self-concept for all children.

Debates about items such as the above concerning established instruments make it apparent that an inexperienced graduate student or other educator must be very cautious about generating his or her own instrument. It is not an easy task. A number of people who represent a variety of points of view should be involved in the creation of the initial items believed to define or identify a particular construct (i.e., items that have content validity). Pilot testing with a sample as similar as possible to the group that will be studied is essential. Various statistical analyses of the instrument will show which items subjects seem to answer similarly. For example, perhaps in a factor analysis there are groups of factors or subcomponents embedded within a particular construct. Factor analysis can contribute to an instrument's construct validity by revealing the factors included in a construct. (See, for an example, Langenbach & Aagaard, 1990.) A concern is that the novice researcher realize some scholars devote an entire career to developing a valid and reliable instrument that measures just one construct. Examples include creativity, intelligence, and leadership. Simply put, the beginning researcher cannot be cavalier about instrument development.

Surveys and Questionnaires

Collecting data through surveys or questionnaires is a bit easier, because they are generally constructed to obtain certain descriptive information about a particular topic or about the participants in the research. For example, a research question may be "What are the major values of a particular school system?" Initially, it might be wise to create and administer a values survey to produce a profile of the school and community, indicating percentages of people holding certain views on the purpose of religion, the family, government, and the schools, to name a few. When creating a survey, follow some of the same precautionary measures taken when creating a test or an instrument. As a content validity check, as in a pilot study, seek input from experts in the field when creating the original document. Such experts, for example, school administrators, teachers, and community officials, would not only help create items but also critique the overall document, looking for unclear statements or questions.

Interviews

An interview is another means of collecting data, either quantitative or qualitative. Many good books and articles describe the different types of research interviews and how they can be conducted (Brenner, Brown, & Canter, 1985; Schwartz & Jacobs, 1979). The Thompson reading at the end of this chapter contains some excellent suggestions for how to catalogue and store interviews to facilitate the analysis of data. Interviews range from the formal, the less-structured, the completely informal, to the nondirective interview. For example, in the Aagaard proposal included as a reading in Chapter 4, the author used all of these formats, depending on the informant. She had very specific questions for particular citizens of the community regarding their use of the facility. She first asked demographic questions to categorize the informant with regard to age, occupation, race, or ethnicity. Then she asked when they used the facility and why, in addition to any other questions that might tell her if the community center was being used for its intended purpose (directly related to her research question). When she interviewed Byers (the center's founder) she had some specific questions regarding his intentions and relative position in the community. Yet, because his motivations were crucial to answering the research question, she also allowed that interview to explore the participant's perceptions in a less-directive manner than she might have conducted other interviews.

The formal interview may use a number of different formats for recording data, such as tape recording, taking notes, or videotaping sessions. The interview schedule or protocol might read like a survey that could be, but is not, mailed. In an interview the researcher can record a participant's, respondent's, informant's, or subject's words and make note of body language as well. As a reminder of the unavoidably close connection between the data and researcher, perspective-seeking scholars use terms such as "participant" (phenomenology) or "informant" (ethnography), suggesting the contextual nature of these data. (See the Peshkin reading following Chapter 6 for excerpts from ethnographic interviews.) Truth-seeking quantitative researchers, who simplify data to numbers and try to maintain a distance between themselves and their data sources, more appropriately refer to their sources as "subjects." Moreover, any type of interview can focus on the interviewee's views or knowledge about a particular topic or the entire story of her or his life. This all depends on whether the information he or she gives describes another person or topic under investigation or contains variables that the researcher wishes to analyze or measure. In short, it depends on the question to be answered in the research.

Observations

Other means of generating data are through observations of social phenomena. One can record observations in a qualitative or quantitative manner. For an example of the former, one of our students, mentioned in Chapter 4, kept a journal as he wrote a novel for young readers. His intention was to record his thoughts and feelings throughout the novel-writing process in hopes of generating an individualized model describing the writing process (Wyatt, 1990). Other researchers have sat in a classroom throughout a school year in order to describe in a qualitative manner what occurred (Jackson, 1968; Peshkin, 1986).

Flanders (1970) devised an observational instrument and technique to generate quantitative data. A researcher would observe a particular educational setting to determine an educator's teaching style, for instance. During a classroom observation, the investigator would make a tally mark each time a student or teacher spoke. This might help him or her determine who was doing the most or the least talking in that teacher's classroom. Different types of tallies might also represent various kinds of talking such as lecturing, whispering, or answering questions. From these records patterns of interaction can be traced, and the researcher can begin to hypothesize about the relative degree of authoritarianism or democracy inherent in the teacher's style. Observing a child's behavior before, during, and after treatment, a common technique in single subject research, and recording the occurrence or frequency of, say, sharing with others, is another example of generating data from observations.

Videotaping is another means of recording observations, and it often provides a useful complement to self-reported data. For example, one might administer an instrument or survey or conduct an interview to ask administrators to describe their leadership style. If the research questions center round their actual rather than their perceived way of leading, then videotaping some of the respondents in action could provide a validity check on their self-reported data. One could then record any discrepancies between their self-perceptions and how the researcher and anyone else asked to view the tapes might perceive the administrators in the study.

Summary

In this chapter we have discussed the concept of data as a representation of some human phenomenon related to a research question. All data are merely representations of the "slice of life" that a researcher chooses to study, and his or her research project is an isolation of a particular event, feeling, or occurrence. Thus, a research project can never perfectly capture every aspect of whatever is being studied. This does not mean that research is futile, but that it must always be conducted and read carefully and critically.

This chapter has also outlined and given examples of a few of the myriad types of qualitative and quantitative data that might be identified or generated. Several of the readings in this book include samples of these. The next chapter builds on the introductions to design in Chapter 4 and your knowledge of the various types of data in this chapter to prepare you to answer research questions posed from truth- and perspective-seeking views of the world, as discussed in Chapter 2.

Discussion Questions

1. Explain with examples why data cannot be the actual behavior, thought, or construct that you need to examine to answer your research question.

2. Give an example of one kind of data and explain how you might go about establishing its validity.

3. Pose a research question and give examples of how you might locate or generate quantitative data to answer that question. Do the same with regard to qualitative data.

4. Why is the truth-seeking view of the world often associated with quantitative data? Find an example of a truth-seeking, quantitative study from a journal.

5. Why is the perspective-seeking view of the world often associated with qualitative data? Find an example of a perspective-seeking, qualitative study from a journal.

6. How can ideology influence the collection of data?

7. Find an example from a journal of a rating scale or other device designed to aid in observing a classroom. What are some advantages and disadvantages in using such an aid?

8. What are some advantages and disadvantages of having two observers collect quantitative data from the same setting at the same time? Would the advantages and disadvantages be the same regarding qualitative data?

Introduction to Readings

The Perlman and Margo reading, "Who Were America's Teachers? Toward a Social History and a Data Archive," explains a monumental project in quantitative data collection. The researchers intend to categorize random samples of census data on American teachers from the nineteenth century to the present time. When reading this piece note the plethora of quantitative data available that describe American teachers, even though the census routinely misses many individuals. The strength of the authors' contribution is that the census has not categorized its statistics in a uniform manner over the decades. For example, some years certain minority groups were totaled and listed in a race category called "other." Perlman and Margo's consistent categories will facilitate demographic comparisons of various groups over time.

Thompson's reading, "Storing and Sifting," gives some excellent suggestions on how to store and organize one type of qualitative data, oral histories. It would behoove anyone to expand on his advice and form a system to annotate, index, and file all of your materials, not only data, but also notes on other scholars' work. An office or work area could be arranged like a library, catalogued by topic and/or author. In this way you will save many weary hours of looking for information and have a manageable way to keep a growing collection of materials.

Who Were America's Teachers?
Toward a Social History and a Data Archive

Joel Perlmann

Robert Margo

This paper describes a research project designed to study the social origins, demographic characteristics, and labor market experiences of teachers in America from 1860 to 1940. To this end, we will collect, analyze, and make available to interested scholars a large body of machine-readable evidence, which will primarily include data on American teachers drawn from the manuscript census schedules and published school reports. In order to make more intelligible comparisons between teachers and the rest of the population in the years before 1900, for which no public use samples of the national population are currently available, we will also collect small national samples of all households from the 1860 and 1880 manuscript schedules of the United States census.[1] The sampling and data collection procedures we have developed can be transferred readily to the study of other occupations. Finally, these procedures are useful for many other research purposes because the procedures offer a way of drawing both national and local samples from the United States census manuscript schedules at relatively low cost.

The social and economic history of American teachers joins three strands of research: women's history, the history of education, and labor history. Historians of women have studied the early feminization of the teaching force and the importance of teaching as a source of employment for educated women.[2] Historians of education and labor have studied various aspects of the employment of teachers in the past, such as working conditions, salaries, teacher training, and early efforts at unionization.[3]

This valuable work to date has had to rely upon data restricted to particular geographic areas and brief periods of time, thus limiting the generalizations that can be drawn. Our project will contribute individual-level data that are national in scope and that cover a long period of time, a period that encompassed substantial educational change.[4]

Historical Methods, 22(2), Spring 1989, pp. 68–73. Reprinted with permission of the Helen Dwight Reid Educational Foundation. Published by Heldref Publications, 1319 Eighteenth St., N.W., Washington, D.C. 20036-1802. Copyright © 1989.

The Data

Census Samples of Teachers

National samples of teachers are being drawn from the 1860 and 1880 census manuscript schedules of population. For the years 1900, 1910, and 1940, we are drawing extracts of teachers from the Census Bureau's public use tapes, which constitute national samples. The samples for 1860 and 1880 will include approximately 3,500 teachers each. We anticipate that the 1900, 1910, and 1940 public use tapes will yield 500, 2,500, and 12,000 teachers, respectively. The total census data base will contain individual-level information on approximately 22,000 teachers and on the households in which they lived.

The information recorded from the 1860 and 1880 census manuscripts will include place of residence, place of birth, age, sex, race, marital status (1880), relationship to head of household (1880), parents' place of birth, unemployment (1880), health status, real and personal wealth (1860), literacy, and school attendance. For 1900–1940, information is also available on children ever born, years married, years of residence in the United States (1900–1910), home ownership, wage and salary income (1940), educational attainment (1940), and migration (1940).

Teachers are being located by scanning the occupation column of the census manuscripts.[5] Data are being collected for the teacher and for each member of the teacher's household. Research assistants are copying the information exactly as it appears in the census schedules.

The sampling of the manuscript schedules is being performed in two stages. Stage one is a simple random sample of 50 percent of census microfilm reels in 1860 and 1880. The primary advantage of sampling reels is that the sampling can proceed very quickly because comprehensive numbered lists of reels are available from the Census Bureau. The large number of reels to be sampled is necessary to ensure a geographically representative sample in both years.[6]

In stage two, we randomly select sets of pages from each reel to sample.[7] Enough pages in each set are included so that we can expect, on average, one teacher per set of pages. For example, in 1860, there were 110,000 teachers, approximately one for every 250 members of the free population. Since each page of the census schedules contains fifty persons, we would expect to find, on average, one teacher for every five pages of the census schedules. We wish to have a sample of approximately 3,500 teachers. To obtain this, we sample a set of five pages in every eighty pages of the schedules (on half the reels): 5/80 (pages sampled) × 1/2 (reels sampled) × 110,000 (teachers enumerated) = 3,438 (teachers expected in sample).[8]

The sets of pages sampled from the 1880 manuscript schedules were selected on a systematic basis (i.e., every n pages of the schedules were skipped).[9] The sets of pages sampled from the 1860 manuscript schedules were selected using a more complicated procedure in order to employ a simple random sampling of pages. That procedure relied on the availability of information on the number of pages on each reel (information that is not available in the same form for the 1880 reels). While a true random sample is always preferable, it is difficult to imagine how a systematic sampling of pages in 1880 could bias our results because the ordering of households on the schedules is determined by the routes chosen by the census takers.[10] (Note that the sampling procedure we have described could be modified for other research purposes to select particular households or lines on a page, rather than entire pages of the census schedules.)

We expect that our samples of nineteenth-century teachers will be large enough to provide information about the characteristics of teachers in different regions and even in the largest states. If resources permit, we will also collect some data from a few local areas in order to supplement our national perspective with in-depth local studies. We hope that others will collect more local data, using our national samples to place their studies of the social history of teachers in a wider perspective.

Finally, although the focus of this project is on the social and economic history of teachers from 1860 to 1940, we plan to extend the analysis to the post–World War II period, making use of the 1950–1980 census public use samples. Ultimately, it will also be possible to add samples to the data archive from the 1920 and 1930 manuscript census schedules and from public use samples from the 1990 and later censuses when they are released.

The use of census manuscripts to create national samples of teachers—or any occupation—has advantages and disadvantages. We know of no other source for the nineteenth (and for most of the twentieth) century from which national samples could be drawn.

Census Samples of All Households

We will need to know the extent to which any characteristic of teachers differs from characteristics of the population as a whole. Suppose, for example, that 20 percent of women teachers twenty to thirty years of age lived with only one parent. Is that proportion high for women in that age group, suggesting a distinctive characteristic of teachers, or is it typical for the age group? We can easily answer that type of question for teachers in 1900, 1910, 1940, and later years with the help of the public use samples (national samples of all households found in the census schedules). No such public use samples are currently available for 1860 and 1880, however. Consequently, we are collecting national samples of approximately 1,250 households from each census, in essence "mini public use samples." These samples will not merely allow us to compare the teachers with members of a national sample but will also permit the study of a national sample for its own sake, which allows the exploration of many other issues. These national samples of households were collected by exploiting the same procedures that were used for the samples of teachers: a subset of all the sampled reels and a subset of sampled pages used in the teacher sample were used in the national samples of households. The samples are too small to permit intensive study at the state level and will involve limitations even in studying regional patterns, but they can be used comfortably to explore national patterns. These samples will also be made available to interested scholars.

School Reports

Although the census schedules contain extensive social and demographic information on teachers, the information they provide on teachers' careers is quite limited prior to 1940. In the case of teachers, alternative and underutilized sources for career information are the reports of city school boards. In the late nineteenth and early twentieth centuries, such reports frequently contain lists of school personnel, and some provide extensive economic information on individual teachers, including name, street address, salary, educational background, teaching certificate held, years of teaching experience in current school system, years of total teaching experience, and position held.[11] Linking the personnel lists across years establishes a longitudinal file that documents the work careers of teachers in particular school systems.

To date, we have found personnel lists for nearly every city with populations between 100,000 and 500,000 in 1890. Not every report, however, contains the variables listed above. We are putting into machine-readable form the lists for Grand Rapids, Michigan (1880–1905); Paterson, New Jersey (1875–1910); and Portland, Oregon (1878–1930). (The lists for a fourth city—Houston, Texas [1892–1920]—were put into machine-readable form in 1981 by Robert Margo and Elyce Rotella.[12]) The lists for these three cities are the most comprehensive and complete that we have found, and they form the basis for the analyses described below. The total sample size for the three cities combined is approximately 10,000 teachers.

Collecting and computerizing the lists is a simple, if tedious, task. All of the relevant reports are available at major libraries or state archives. The lists are printed, so illegibility is not a problem. Creating a longitudinal file is straightforward because the files for particular years can be linked over time using standard software packages.

By surveying all state reports, we also discovered that the school reports of three [sic] states annually published the names of all public school teachers employed—Maryland (1871–1920 by county, district, and post office address), and Rhode Island (1874–1898 by town). We are drawing random samples of rural and urban teachers in these three [sic] states. The sampled teachers will be traced across time in order to establish the magnitude of the rural-urban differential in length of teaching experience in the states. Approximately 2,500 observations will be collected from Maryland and 1,500 from each of the other two [sic] states.

The Issues

The national samples drawn from the census manuscripts and the longitudinal files created from school reports will allow us to address a wide variety of questions concerning the social and economic history of teachers between 1860 and 1940. These are discussed below.

The Feminization of Teaching

Before 1840, most American teachers were men; after 1870, most were women.[13] The feminization of teaching is of considerable interest because few other occupations "feminized."

The feminization of teaching has received attention from social historians, but the data analyzed (typically from state school reports) are either local in nature or are state aggregates.[14] By contrast, our data will cover the country but will still allow analyses of individual teachers. For example, our data can shed light at the individual level on geographic patterns of feminization. Did feminization first appear, as many historians believe, in large urban areas? What about small or middle-sized towns? If rural areas lagged behind, what factors influenced the length of the lag? Did feminization vary by region, and, if so, why?

Age and Marital Status of Teachers

Teaching in the nineteenth and early twentieth centuries is usually thought to have been an entry-level occupation, not a life-long career. The extent to which this is true is related to the age distribution of teachers and other characteristics, such as marital status. What was the age distribution of the teaching force? To what extent did it vary by sex, and how quickly did it change over time? What fraction of male teachers were heads of households? Did married women teach? If not, did widows?

The answers to these and other questions might vary by geography. For example, the probability that a male teacher could raise a family was surely low in rural areas, but it may have been higher in urban ones. It is likely that very few married women taught in cities, but wives of farmers may have taught in summer sessions when older boys were not attending. Finally, substantial numbers of female teachers in urban areas may have taught until late in life as early as 1860.

Family Structure and Boarding

How common was rural boarding for teachers? How many young rural teachers lived with their parents? Both images are typical in the available literature, which is largely based on impressionistic evidence.[15] We will be able to clarify the prevalence of each type, as well as to investigate intensively the family structure of those who lived at home. We expect that living at home was the norm among teachers in urban areas.[16] Was the probability of becoming a teacher dependent upon family structure? For example, was teaching school more prevalent among daughters (still living with their parents) in large families or in families in which the father had died, as school authorities often argued?[17]

Ethnicity

We will know the ethnic backgrounds of teachers' parents and, for teachers living with their parents, of their grandparents.[18] To what extent did the probability that a person would become a teacher vary by ethnic origin? How quickly did the second or third generations of Irish, Germans, and Scandinavians enter the teaching force; how common, in particular, was the stereotypical Irish American teacher in the cities—by 1870, by 1900? The *Immigration Commission Reports*, for example, indicate that about a quarter of the teachers in the public schools were the children of Irish immigrants in Boston, Providence, and New York; data on the third generation, however, would probably raise this figure dramatically.

Social Class Origins

Little literature exists on the class origins of teachers before 1930.[19] We will be able to ascertain class origins (using the father's occupation as a proxy for social class origins) for those teachers who lived at home, particularly those in urban areas. Was teaching an engine of upward mobility into the middle class for relatively well-educated daughters of skilled workers and of low manual workers?

The South

Rates of illiteracy in the South, among whites and especially among blacks, fell sharply between 1860 and 1910. Historians have written extensively about northern teachers who came south after the Civil War, the so-called "soldiers of light and love."[20] Over time, however, the eradication of illiteracy in the South depended heavily on the efforts of southern teachers, about whom historians know very little, particularly about black teachers.[21] Our national samples will allow us to say much about the demographic characteristics of southern teachers.[22]

Educational Attainment and Earnings of Teachers

The 1940 census was the first to contain information on educational attainment and income (albeit from wages and salaries only). The attainment data can be used to study differences among teachers' educational attainments by age, region, rural-urban, gender, race, and marital status. Also, regression analysis will be used to estimate the economic returns from schooling among teachers, which will be compared with available estimates for the general population and for teachers at the turn of the century.

Work Careers

By linking the city and state reports over time, we can reconstruct the work careers of individual teachers. The linked sample will provide by far the best available evidence on how long teachers taught, how long they remained in a given school, their salaries, and their patterns of promotion into administrative positions. Furthermore, because we are following individual teachers through time, we can relate such outcomes to each other (e.g., promotion to length of teaching) as well as to various other personal characteristics (notably, length and type of education and gender).

The analysis of career length and promotion will illuminate the historical origins of gender discrimination in the teaching profession, or, as Myra Strober and David Tyack put it, "Why Do Women Teach and Men Manage?"[23] Women may have been less likely than men to persist in the teaching profession, but what of those who did have comparable lengths of service (even in the same school system) and comparable levels and types of education? Were such women really promoted less often than men? Myra Strober, David Tyack, and Laura Best have suggested that they were, as a consequence of cultural norms.[24] Such norms include supervisor expectations that women would quit, community expectations that the systems should be led by men, and a general lack of confidence in women's abilities to manage. We expect that these suggestions will be confirmed—that human capital characteristics alone will not explain why men managed, at least at the highest levels of management. At entry and middle levels of management (assistant principal and principal), however, the cultural norms may have mattered less. The critical point here is that previous studies have been unable to address this question because the data analyzed were cross-sectional and not longitudinal.[25]

The Determinants of Teacher Salaries

Although the determinants of teacher salaries have been studied extensively in the post-war period, evidence for the nineteenth and early twentieth centuries is scant.[26] An analysis of the determinants of teacher salaries is crucial for understanding the historical evolution of labor markets for teachers, particularly women. For example, what were the returns (in terms of higher salaries) from schooling and labor market experience among teachers in the nineteenth and early twentieth centuries? Did the returns vary by the type of education received as well as by length of schooling (normal school versus high school and, later, teachers' college versus other college)? Did the returns vary over time? Did they vary by gender? How did they compare with the returns in other occupations open to educated women, such as clerical work, and with more recent periods?[27] Our sample of teachers from the city reports will contain individual-level data on the relevant variables; thus, we can address these questions using regression analysis.

Conclusion

This paper has described a research project that will examine the social and economic history of teachers in America from 1860 to 1940. National samples of teachers will be drawn from the 1860 and 1880 manuscript census schedules and the 1900, 1910, and 1940 census public use samples. In addition, a national sample of all households will be selected from the 1860 and 1880 schedules. The census samples will be used to study various social and demographic characteristics of teachers during a period of rapid educational change. The procedure devised for sampling the manuscript census schedules is not specific to teachers and can be used to create similar samples for any occupation or to select efficiently other types of national samples. Also, the research design will permit scholars to add other samples to the data base in future work (see "Census Samples of Teachers"). A second source of material is the published school reports of various cities, which provide the basis for longitudinal files that document the work careers of individual teachers in particular school systems. Analysis of the school reports will focus on the determinants of teacher salaries, duration of employment in teaching, and promotion patterns.

Notes

We are grateful to Susan Carter, Thomas Dublin, Stanley Engerman, Gary Gerstle, Victoria Mac-Donald Huntzinger, Richard Murnane, Judith Singer, Daniel Scott Smith, Julie Juhon Sun, Stephan Thernstrom, Terrence Tivnan, and Maris Vinovskis for helpful comments. The project described in this paper has been funded by the Spencer Foundation and the National Science Foundation. Opinions expressed are our own and not those of the foundations.

1. All data collected from the project will eventually be deposited with the Inter-University Consortium for Political and Social Research (ICPSR) at the University of Michigan and will be available to interested scholars.

2. Sklar, K. K. (1983). *Catherine Beecher: A study in American domesticity.* New Haven: Yale University Press; Jones, J. (1980). *Soldiers of light and love: Northern teachers and Georgia blacks, 1865–1873.* Chapel Hill: University of North Carolina Press; Morain, T. (1980). The departure of males from the teaching profession in nineteenth-century Iowa. *Civil War History, 26,* 161–70; Carter, S. B. & Prus, M. (1982). The labor market and the American high school girl, 1890–1928. *Journal of Economic History, 42,* 163–71; Tyack, D. B. & Strober, M. H. (1981). *Jobs and gender: A history of the structuring of educational employment by sex.* In *Educational policy and management: Sex differentials,* edited by Schmuck, P. A., et al. New York: Academic Press; & Strober, M. H. (1986). The feminization of public school teaching: Cross-sectional analysis, 1850–1880. *Signs, 11,* 212–35.

3. Tyack, D. B. (1974). *The one best system: A history of American urban education.* Cambridge: Harvard University Press; Mattingly, P. H. (1975). *The classless profession: American schoolmen in the nineteenth century.* New York: New York University Press; Bernard, R. M. & Vonovskis, M. A. (1977). The female school teacher in ante-bellum Massachusetts. *Journal of Social History, 10,* 332–45; Strober, M. H. & Best, L. (1979). The female/male salary differential in public schools: Some lessons from San Francisco, 1879. *Economic Inquiry, 17,* 218–36; Oates, M. J. (1980). Organized voluntarism: The Catholic sisters in Massachusetts, 1870–1940. In *Women in American religion,* edited by James, J. W. Philadelphia: University of Pennsylvania Press; Murphy, M. (1980). From artisan to semi-professionalization: White collar unionism among Chicago public school teachers, 1870–1930. Ph.D. diss., University of California-Davis; Renner, M. (1981). *Who will teach? Changing job opportunities and roles for women in the evolution of the Pittsburgh public schools, 1830–1900.* Ph.D. diss., University of Pittsburgh; Urban, W. (1981). *Why teachers organized.* Detroit: Wayne State University Press; and

Cuban, L. (1984). *How teachers taught: Constancy and change in American classrooms, 1890–1980.* New York: Longman.

4. A national study of Canadian teachers has been underway for some time; see Laskin, S., Light, B. & Prentice, A. 1982. Studying the history of an occupation: Quantitative sources on Canadian teachers in the nineteenth century. *Archivaria, 14,* 75–92.

5. The work is not particularly arduous or time consuming because a large fraction of the population will have no occupation listed (for example, women and children not gainfully employed).

6. This is the principal cost disadvantage of sampling reels. Unless one has access to a regional branch of the National Archives, the reels must be purchased or rented. Experiments indicated that a substantially smaller fraction than 50 percent, however, is likely to yield unacceptable biases in the sample when analysis is undertaken at the regional or state level (for example, with respect to urban-rural differences).

7. Technically, by sampling sets of pages, we are creating a cluster sample. The clustering problem, however, is likely to be very small compared with, for example, randomly sampling townships or counties and taking every teacher within the township or county.

8. We excluded the slave schedules (which are also microfilm and are interspersed with the free schedules) prior to drawing the 1860 sample.

9. The page on which the counting began in the first reel was chosen randomly.

10. The number of pages on each reel of the 1860 census can be determined from a statement by the Census Bureau at the head of the reel. This information was not available in the same useful way on the 1880 reels. To obtain it, considerable preliminary work counting pages would have been necessary.

A brief description of the random sampling procedure used for the 1860 census pages follows. The sets of pages to be sampled are the same for every reel. For example, the tenth–fourteenth pages constitute the set to be sampled from the first eighty pages on each reel, and the eighty-fourth–eighty-eighth pages constitute the set to be sampled from the second eighty pages on each

reel. The particular starting page for each set of five pages (the tenth, eighty-fourth, etc.) was selected by random sampling. Unfortunately, the eighty-fourth page in order of appearance on the reel is likely to have a page number other than eighty-four because census microfilm reels were numbered at the Census Bureau independently of the microfilming process. The number on the page required for sampling can be determined, however, from the precise statement by the Census Bureau found at the head of each reel of the 1860 census concerning the pages to be found on that reel. We have written a computer program that identifies the numbers on the pages that must be sampled, using the particular reel's numbering system. More information about this sampling procedure, including the computer program, is available upon request. A fuller description of our procedure for sampling randomly chosen pages from the 1860 census is available upon request.

11. Unfortunately, we have yet to discover reports containing similar information for rural areas or for entire states. Thus, the generalizations drawn from the school reports will necessarily be more limited than those drawn from the census samples.

The data tell us about employment within one school system, not about the subsequent career of a teacher who left one system to teach in another. Also, the data are right-censored (the last year for which data are available precedes the last year that certain teachers in the data set taught in the system) and will therefore require use of standard techniques of duration analysis. On the other hand, the school reports do indicate the years of schooling prior to entering the school system in question, which should be useful in the analysis of salaries and promotions. (The data are not, therefore, left-censored, at least insofar as the length of teaching in the system and elsewhere is concerned.)

Finally, the data do not distinguish among the reasons for which one left the school system (death, outmigration, etc.). We therefore cannot explore reasons for leaving but only experience within the system.

There are also several standard technical problems raised when linked data of this sort are used. In particular, those teachers who are un-linked from one year to the next are assumed to have left the school system; however, they may simply not have been correctly identified by the linkage procedures, a bias that we, like everyone using linked data, will need to assess. One technical problem in record linkage with women is likely to have little relevance, however—the fact that women changed their name upon marriage. Very few, if any, married women worked in these systems during the period under study (with the possible exception of the World War I years). In any case, the married women would appear as having taught a certain number of years in the system, yet not be listed in earlier years (the sort of problem case to be examined by hand and compared with lists of earlier years).

12. Rotella, E. J. & Margo, R. A. (1981). *Sex differences in the market for school personnel: Houston, TX 1892–1923.* Paper presented at the Annual Meeting of the Western Economics Association, San Francisco.

13. Elsbree, W. S. (1939). *The American teacher: Evolution of a profession in a democracy.* New York: American Book Company; and Tyack and Strober, *Jobs and gender.*

14. Morain, *Departure of males;* and Strober, *Feminization.*

15. Eggleston, E. (1984). *The Hoosier schoolmaster.* Bloomington: Indiana University Press; Elsbree, *American teacher,* Kaestle, C. F. (1983). *Pillars of the republic: Common schools and American society, 1789–1860.* New York: Hill and Wang; and Tyack, *One best system.*

16. Huntzinger, V. M. (1984). *A portrait of late nineteenth century schoolteachers: The case of Providence, Rhode Island.* Seminar paper, Graduate School of Education, Harvard University; and Huntzinger, V. M. (1987). *Teachers, politics, and reform in Providence, Rhode Island, 1890–1900.* Seminar paper, Graduate School of Education, Harvard University.

17. Doherty, R. E. (1979). Tempest on the Hudson: The struggle for "equal pay for equal work" in the New York City public schools, 1907–1911. *History of Education Quarterly, 19,* 413–34.

18. The census obtained information on parents' places of birth. When the teacher lived with his or her parents, the information collected on the father includes his parents' (the teacher's grandparents') places of birth.

19. The major early survey, Coffman, L. D. (1911). *The social composition of the teaching population.* New York: Columbia University; (see also, Elsbree, *American teacher*) is seriously biased in coverage. For example, a third of its male teachers were from Indiana. In addition, the measurement of social class is crude and vague by contemporary standards. More recent work by social historians (when available at all) is local in coverage, unlike our proposed analysis. See Huntzinger, *A portrait,* and *Teachers;* Murphy, *Artisan to semi-professional;* and Renner, *Changing job opportunities.* On more recent periods, see Sedlack, M., & Schlossman, S. (1986). *Who will teach? Historical perspectives on the changing appeal of teaching as a profession.* Santa Monica: Rand.

20. Jones, *Soldiers;* Hoffman, N. (1981). *Woman's true profession: Voices from the history of teaching.* Old Westbury, CT: Feminist Press.

21. See Margo, R. A. (1984). Teacher salaries in black and white: The South in 1910. *Explorations in Economic History, 21*(3), 306–20.

22. See also note 3.

23. Strober & Tyack, *Why do women teach and men manage?*

24. Strober, *The feminization;* Strober & Tyack, *Why do women teach and men manage?;* Strober & Best, *The salary differential.*

25. Such data tell, for example, how long a male principal and a female teacher had been in the system in 1879, but not how long the male had worked at the time of his promotion nor what his previous position had been.

26. Strober & Best. *The salary differential,* is an exception.

27. On the returns to schooling in other female occupations, see Goldin, C. (1984). The historical evolution of female earnings functions in occupations. *Explorations in Economic History, 21*(1), 1–27, and the references cited there.

Storing and Sifting

Paul Thompson

The recording has been completed: but how then should the tapes be kept? And how can they be used to make history? We need first to consider the problems of storage and indexing, and then the stages in writing and presenting history with oral evidence.

Because magnetic tape recording is a relatively recent technique, it is far from certain how long it can last and what are the ideal conditions for its storage. The quality of tape has, moreover, been gradually improved, and with this the principal storage considerations have changed. Good modern tapes no longer have a backing which is likely to disintegrate. The chief problem now is the avoidance of 'print through', or sound echoes, which can develop during storage. Some experts recommend various means of reducing the risk of print through, such as running the tape through a recorder once a year so that it is re-spooled, but it is not clear that this is a worthwhile safety measure—indeed it may on balance create worse risks of other damage. For the moment, there are only two certain rules.

First, the quality of tape to be used for storage should be carefully chosen. It might be advisable to store on a different tape from that used for the recording itself. It is important that the original recording should use a tape with a high frequency range and low distortion, and also a low background noise, so that it reproduces sound as faithfully as possible. In addition, it must be recorded at a sufficient speed: for speech, on a reel-to-reel machine, no slower than 3¾ inches per second (i.p.s.), or there will be an audible loss of quality and some words will become difficult to catch on replaying. Obviously storage cannot make up for a bad choice of tape or other mistakes in the original recording. But in addition to the qualities essential in the field-work tape, the storage tape must have a low print through, and at present this means a thicker tape should be chosen. Thicker tapes are also less likely to suffer damage when in use on the machine.

Secondly, the place for storing the tape needs to be considered. The tape can be damaged by dust, or by excessive damp or heat. It should never be exposed to temperatures much higher than normal room temperatures by, for example, being stored up against a heating pipe. Modern tapes do not require artificially controlled temperatures or humidity, but the optimum for storage is now considered to be a temperature of 20°C. and a relative humidity of 50 to 60 per cent. Tapes can also be damaged, and even completely wiped of their recordings, by interference from a powerful magnetic dynamo. This risk needs to be taken into account in some buildings, as well as when travelling with them. But in practice, for most oral historians it will suffice to store tapes in a cupboard, stood on the shelf in their boxes on edge, away from the sun or fire or heating pipes, in a room comfortable for working in. And don't drop cigarette ash on them.

Every tape, as soon as used, needs to be well labelled. It is best to label the box, the spool, and with reel-to-reel the tape itself. The tape can be quite easily labelled on its red and green leads. Without these precautions you may lose tapes by accidentally winding them on to a wrong spool, or replacing them in a wrong box, and then perhaps even making another recording on top of the original. It is 'of course' much better if the original tape is kept as a master, and a copy made from it for normal use; and also if a machine is adapted so that it is possible to listen but not to record on it. For a public archive both precautions are essential.

Exactly what you put on the label will depend on how you develop your system of indexing. If you have only a few tapes, it is enough to put the inform-ant's name, 'Tape One, Side One', 'Tape One, Side Two', and so on. Corresponding to this, a box of cards can be kept in alphabetical order, each card with the name of an informant, and a list of the tapes made with them. It is a great time-saver, if you also have transcripts, to note on the cards which pages of transcript cover each side of tape. This box of cards then constitutes an index and catalogue of your collection, and you can easily check whether a tape or transcript ought to be there. The tapes and transcripts can themselves also be kept in alphabetical order to help finding. The disadvantage of this is that each new interview has to be inserted within the existing sequence, rather than added to it. After a while it becomes much easier to store the interviews in order of accession, giving each new informant a number, and adding the number to the index card. If you decide to put only the number on either the tapes or the transcripts, you will also need another index giving the name for each interview number. Similarly, if you decide it is more useful to keep your main index in number order because, for example, this conveniently separates two different parts of your collection, you will still find that you need an alphabetical index which at least gives the number of each informant's interview.

For a small project, one or two boxes of cards along these lines may be all that is necessary. A note of the place and date of recording, made at the time of the interview, can be left as it is with the tape; and the general subject matter suffi-ciently remembered to know whether it is worth looking up. But as the collection grows, and especially as more people contribute to making and using it, more information needs to be available in some systematic form.

First, either on the original cards or in a parallel sequence, it is desirable to add to the informant's name, when and where the recording was made, and by whom. It is also useful to note any important variations in the method or quality of recording. If we take a collection of reel-to-reel tapes normally recorded at $3\frac{3}{4}$, the entry for a somewhat botched recording might look like this:

Interview number

Address _____

_____

Recorded at above/elsewhere _____

_____

Interviewer _____
Dates of interviews _____

Tapes	*Sides*	*Transcript pages*	*Notes*

Restrictions of access _____

Secondly, it is worth extracting some of the basic background details about the informant which are essential for evaluating the interview and should thus be found within it. They will of course vary to some extent, depending on the focus of the project. Thus a political collection might include specific entries for elections fought or offices held; and the Imperial War Museum lists details such as 'service', 'arm of service', 'rank', 'decorations and awards', which would be inappropriate in a different context. But most historians need at least to know when an informant was born, his or her parents' occupations, where they lived, whether or not there were brothers and sisters, the informant's own education, occupational career, religious and political affiliation if any, whether he or she married, and if so, when, to whom, and whether they had children. All this can again be conveniently summarized on a card:

born _____
at _____
father's occupation _____
mother's occupation _____
brothers _____
sisters _____
education _____
occupations _____ *(dates)*_____

_____
_____
_____

politics _____
religion _____
lived at _____ *(dates)*_____

_____
_____
_____

date of marriage _____

husband/wife's occupations _____

_____

_____

children _____

_____

All this information can be condensed, and some of it codified, if this form seems too long. At the end of *Speak for England*, Melvyn Bragg has added a very helpful index of 'The People' set out in this form:

JOSEPH WILLIAM PARKIN LIGHTFOOT *b. Bolton Low Houses 13th December 1908 br. Two s. Two pl. Fletchertown 1938, Kirkland 1942, Wigton 1954 f.j. Coal Miner o.j. Retired, previously coal miner 1922, farm labourer 1924, labourer on pipe-tracks, part-time gardener 1930s, driver Cumberland Motor Services 1942–68, own shop in 1950s e. Bolton Low Houses until 14r. Methodist p. Labour m. Married ch. Two*

The abbreviations are self-explanatory, except perhaps for pl., which means 'places lived in.'

A third possibility is to create a series of content cards. For some projects, which are organized to follow a definite interview schedule, this may be superfluous; all the necessary clues will be in the basic background of the informant. But the larger and more diverse a collection, the more a contents card catalogue becomes necessary. One of the most fully developed examples is provided by the B.B.C. Sound Archives:

CAMPBELL, Beatrice, *Lady Glenavy (Wife of 2nd Baron Glenavy)*
D. H. Lawrence and His Circle: the first of two programmes in which she recalls some impressions of her friendship with Katherine Mansfield, John Middleton Murry, D. H. Lawrence, and Frieda Lawrence.
Producer: Joseph Hone
Copyright: PF
Annots: None
Trans: TP 30.3.64.
Script.
Note: This talk was recorded in Ireland, and is taken from her autobiography Today We will Only Gossip, published by Constable, 9.4.64.
/continued . . .

CAMPBELL, Beatrice, *Lady Glenavy (Wife of 2nd Baron Glenavy)*
LP28643
Recalls first meeting Katherine Mansfield and Middleton Murry, who were great friends of her future husband, Gordon Campbell: Katherine's appearance and manner; felt Katherine regarded her as an interloper into their circle, and tried

to shock her with daring conversation; Katherine's early struggles as a writer; sufferings from unhappy marriage and love affairs; devotion and care of her friend Ida Baker; how her hostility to Beatrice overcome by incident during visit to Paris; the 'psychological dramas' and discussions during evenings at Parisian cafes.

Gr.90: Through them met Lawrence and his wife, and Koteliansky, known as 'Kot'; qualities which made him a friend of Lawrence; Kot's first meeting with Katherine arising out of quarrel between Lawrence and Frieda, and their subsequent friendship; Katherine's association with Murry.

/continued . . .

CAMPBELL, Beatrice, Lady Glenavy (Wife of 2nd Baron Glenavy)
LP28643
Gr.145: Katherine's complex character and varying moods: two occasions when she 'put on acts'; a week-end the Campbells spent at the Murry's country cottage which was 'not a success'.
Gr.220: Reminisces about time Katherine and Murry spent on visit to Campbell's cottage in Ireland; Murry sorry to leave, but Katherine glad to return to London.

These cards provide a particularly full summary of the contents of each item in the archive, but they begin with a briefer heading. A contents index, depending on the time which is to be spent on it, can aim to be brief or full. But it ought at least to indicate the principal places, social groups, occupations or industries, political or other ideologies, personal or family matters, and (more clearly than these cards) time periods covered. Finally, especially with a large public collection, it may be necessary to create a general system of indexing leading to the other card series. Some public archives have had sufficient resources and ambition to experiment with computerized indexes. Most oral history collections will have to be content with a process closer to the name and subject indexing of an ordinary book. Thus all the places, persons, and organizations on the cards might be included. Important events could be similarly listed. And with more difficulty, a cross-referenced series of subject headings could be developed. There are at present no clearly established models to follow, so that it is important to use a system which allows for modification in the light of experience. And above all, it should be designed to help, rather than replace, human imagination, understanding, and intuition. In practice this means that the best cataloguing and indexing systems will tell the historian which parts of the collection will repay further investigation, and which will not. Ideally it should be made possible to eliminate, as quickly as possible, all those main sections, or individual items, which are concerned with a different time, place, or general subject-matter from the historian's own interest. Thus before proceding to a contents catalogue as full as that of the B.B.C. Sound Archives, it would be more valuable to break down the general index to this catalogue, so that 'Occupations'—'tin-mining' was further sub-divided to lead to 'Cornwall'—'1900–14'; or 'Folk Customs'—'harvest ceremonies' to 'East Anglia'—'1880s'.

Before a recording enters a public archive, another point needs to be clarified, as entries on two of our specimen cards suggest: that of control of the right to access and use. This is not, however, a simple issue, partly because the law of copyright is itself uncertain, but equally because it raises wider ethical questions of responsibility towards informants. The legal position is that there are two copyrights in a recording. The copyright in the recording as a recording is normally the property of the interviewer or of the institution or person who commissioned the interview. The copyright in the information in the recording—the informant's actual words—is the property of the interviewee. But normally some right to use this information is implied by a consent to be interviewed. Thus a person who, knowing that a historian is collecting material for a research study, agreed to be interviewed, would appear to have little ground for complaint if he found himself quoted in print. And in practice he would be very unlikely to attempt to prevent, or to seek compensation for, the publication of any quotation unless he considered it substantially damaging. A bona fide scholar is in fact unlikely to have committed an actionable libel, but it would be foolish anyway to provoke a publicized complaint. It is always important to consider carefully whether the publication of identifiable confidences could not cause local gossip or scandal. Equally, an informant could reasonably complain if information was used in a significantly different context from that suggested; and also, if it proved the making of a best-seller, could claim a share of the earnings. For most projects, there is much to be said for this balance of rights and the chief lesson to be learnt is that in explaining a project to an interviewee not only its immediate object, but also the potential value of their information to wider historical research, should be made clear. If the first approach is made in person rather than by post, this can at least be confirmed in a subsequent letter of thanks. An informal understanding of this kind has proved a satisfactory basis for the writing of innumerable sociological studies, as well as most of the oral history publications which we have discussed earlier. Similarly, the fact that in theory some copyright must also exist in most unpublished manuscript material, has rarely produced serious obstacles to the free access of scholars to the holdings of local and national record offices. It may well be that the best policy is normally to leave the issue unresolved. An insistence on a formal transfer of legal rights through explicit, written consent may not only worry an informant, but will actually reduce quite proper protection against exploitation.

There are, nevertheless, contexts in which a formal agreement has become the standard practice. This is the case in broadcasting, where observation of copyright has to be particularly careful because of the frequent involvement of public figures, and also due to the influence of the financial complexities of musical copyright. It is also advised by the Oral History Association of the United States, where standards were originally set for the recording of eminent public figures and a precise agreement was therefore necessary, not only as to copyright, but also as to whether particular pages of the transcript should be closed until a certain date, or accessible only by specific permission. In Britain the Imperial War Museum obtains a precise written agreement from its informants, who are often not merely eminent public figures, but especially security-conscious. The formula advocated in Willa Baum's booklet for American local historians is relatively simple:

> *I hereby give and grant to the Central City Historical Society as a donation for such scholarly and educational purposes as the Society shall determine the tape recordings and their contents listed below:*
>
> *(signed) _____ (informant).*
> *(signed) _____ (interviewer).*

> *The parties hereto agree that pages 14–16 of the manuscript and the portions of the tape from which these pages were transcribed shall not be published or otherwise made available to anyone other than the parties hereto until January 1, 1984.*

However, 'except in the few cases where sensitive material is really pertinent, it should be discouraged'.[1]

The Imperial War Museum, which has found that 'it is frequently more difficult to obtain assignments and settle other conditions of deposit and access with executors or heirs than with the informants themselves', seeks a quick exchange of letters 'to tie up all the legal loose ends' along the following lines:

> *I am now writing to formalize the conditions under which the Museum holds your recordings. The questions which I have already put to you verbally are listed below. I should be grateful if you would let me have your written answers in due course.*
>
> 1. *May the Museum's users be granted access to the recordings and any typescripts of them?*
> 2. *May the recordings and typescripts be used in the Museum's internal and external educational programmes?*
> 3. *May the Museum provide copies of the recordings and typescripts for its users?*
> 4. *Would you be prepared to assign your copyright in the information in the recordings to the Trustees of the Imperial War Museum? This would enable us to deal with such matters as publication and broadcasting, should they arise, without having to make prior reference to you. If you agree to this assignment it does not, of course, preclude any use which you might want to make of the information in the recordings yourself.*

Whether or not such a formal agreement is reached, there remains an ethical responsibility towards the informant which is probably more important. First of all, if the recording has been made with an implicit assumption of confidentiality, that must be respected. Any quotation from it which might embarrass the informant must either be made anonymously, or with subsequent permission. Similarly, permission should always be sought for its use in a different manner from that originally understood: for example, instead of a history book, a biographical collection, or an article in the local press, or a radio broadcast. Moreover, when informants have a right to a royalty fee, as for a broadcast, or a biographical collection, this should be secured for them. They should be warned of the broadcast time well enough in advance to tell friends. And if they are quoted at length in a book, they should receive their own free copy. As far as possible—and admittedly there are some legitimate forms of scholarly publication for which this might be counter-productive—informants' attention should be drawn to the use made of their material. Indeed, an oral historian who does not wish to share with informants the pleasure and pride in a published work ought to consider very seriously why this is so, and whether it is socially justifiable. There may perhaps be a case for publishing the material collected in a more popular form such as a local pamphlet as well as in some academic mode. One accepts that only the outstanding oral historian can reach the range of readership of a Studs Terkel with a single book. But it remains an over-riding ethical responsibility of the historian who uses oral evidence to ensure that history is given back to the people whose words helped to shape it.

It should be added that the depositing and preservation of tapes needs to be seen in the same light. They can be of interest and use to far more people than the historian who made the recording. All too many oral history tapes remain with the secretary of a local society, or in an academic's private study, effectively inaccessible to a wider public. This may be reasonable while they are being actively used for personal research, but commonly continues beyond this, partly because too few national or county record offices have organized facilities for storing and listening to tapes. But the offer of the original tapes, or copies, to a local record office or a public or university library, besides being desirable in itself, may stimulate the provision for those needs, and prove the seed for a significant collection—an asset which will find many different uses within the community.

For the same reason there is a strong argument, whatever the immediate use envisaged for them, for the full transcription of tapes as the first stage in the writing and presentation of history. Transcribing is undoubtedly very time-consuming, as well as being a highly skilled task. It takes at least six hours, and for a recording with difficult speech or dialect up to twice as long, for each hour of recorded tape. Yet unless the tape is fully transcribed, anybody but the person who made the recording—and so has quite a clear idea of what it contains—will be severely hampered in using it. A contents card is at best only a rough guide for the visiting researcher: listening to more than a few tapes takes several hours, where skimming through transcripts might take minutes. But the person who makes the tape is also best able to ensure that transcription is accurate. Because this task is so lengthy, and, apart from other claims on time, recording always seems more urgent, transcribing nearly always falls behind. In a research project supported by a grant, this can be avoided only by making a full estimate of the transcribing time and equipment needed at the start, and recognizing that the work can only be carried out by a person with particular skills, working on a regular basis. Part-time agency audio-typing will either be incomprehensible or prohibitive. A transcriber needs to be interested in the tapes, intelligent in making sense of them, especially in the key art of turning verbal pauses into written punctuation, and a good speller with an unusually quick ear. It is also isolated work. These are not necessarily the qualities which make a successful secretary. The only way to know whether somebody can transcribe well is to give them a tape and let them try.

Most oral history projects will not have the resources to pay for a transcriber, and will need to carry out the work themselves. If there is any money to spare, it is best spent on a tape recorded with a reverse foot-pedal for play-back, which will save them much time. For a very small group, or for a researcher's own tapes, the process can, however, be quite markedly shortened, even if at the expense of long-term satisfaction. The best 'shortened transcript' lies between the full contents card and the complete transcription. For the most part, the content is summarized in detail, but actual quotations are only used when the words are so well or vividly put that they are worth considering for extracts or quotations in the finished presentation. A finding device can be added in the margin, either by using the numbers in the counter-setting on the machine (although these unfortunately vary even between machines of the same make), or by listening through the tape after transcription and noting the time intervals every five or ten seconds (standard, but less quick to use).

Ultimately, however, there can be no substitute for a full transcript. Even the best shortened version is like an intelligent historian's notes from an archive rather than the original documents. Nor can the historian today know what questions will be asked by historians in the future, so that any selection will result in the loss of details which might later prove significant. The full transcript should therefore include everything, with the possible exception of diversions for checking that the recorder is on, having a cup of tea, or present-day chatting about the weather, illness, and so on. All questions should go in. Fumbling for a word may be left out, but other hesitations, and stop-gaps like 'you know' or 'see', should be included at this stage. The grammar and word order must be left as spoken. If a word or phrase cannot be caught, there should be a space in the transcript to indicate this. These are all quite straight-forward guidelines. But the real art of the transcriber is in using punctuation and occasional phonetic spelling to convey the character of speech.

The transcript is in this sense a literary form and the problems which it raises are inseparable from those of subsequent quotation. The spoken word can very easily be mutilated in being taken down on paper and then transferred to the printed page. Some distortion is inevitable in cutting out pauses and distracting hesitations or false starts in the interests of readability. Much more serious is the distortion when the spoken word is drilled into the orders of written prose, through imposing standard grammatical forms and a logical sequence of punctuation. The rhythms and tones of speech are quite distinct from those of prose.

Equally important, lively speech will meander, dive into irrelevancies, and return to the point after unfinished sentences. Effective prose is by contrast systematic, relevant, sparse. It is therefore very tempting for the writer, wishing to make a point effectively, to strip a spoken quotation, re-order it, and then, in order to make it continuous, slip in some connecting words which were never in the original. The point can be reached when the character of the original speech becomes unrecognizable. This is an extreme, but any writer, unless continually aware of this danger, may at times reach such a level of decadence in transcription.

The difficulties may be illustrated by taking as an example one of the first passages in Ronald Blythe's *Akenfield,* an old farm worker's account of a domestic economy in the years before 1914. The picture he gives is very bare, highly effective—but so terse in detail that one wonders how far the original interview has been tidied up:

> *There were seven children at home and father's wages had been reduced to 10s. a week. Our cottage was nearly empty—except for people. There was a scrubbed brick floor and just one rug made of scraps of old clothes pegged into a sack. The cottage had a living-room, a larder, and two bedrooms. Six of us boys and girls slept in one bedroom and our parents and the baby slept in the other. There was no newspaper and nothing to read except the Bible. All the village houses were like this. Our food was apples, potatoes, swedes and bread, and we drank our tea without milk or sugar. Skim milk could be bought from the farm but it was thought a luxury. Nobody could get enough to eat no matter how they tried. Two of my brothers were out to work. One was eight years old and he got 3s. a week, the other got about 7s.*[2]

There is in these lines an unremitting logical drive. Every word stands with evident purpose in its proper place. Every phrase is correctly punctuated. There are no ragged ends, no diversions to convey the speaker's own sense of a childhood home, or the bitterness or humour felt in poverty. Some phrases read like the author's own comments: 'skimmed milk . . . was thought a luxury'. There are no dialect words, no grammatical irregularities, no sparks of personal idiosyncrasy. The passage may convince but, unlike many others in the same book, it does not come alive. One wishes to know, but is provided with no indication of, where the interview has been cut, and what has been put in to sew it up again.

We can turn for a contrast to George Ewart Evans's *Where Beards Wag All,* also about Suffolk villagers, some of them from the same community. This is a book with more direct argument than *Akenfield,* but supported by substantial quotations in which we seem to hear the people themselves talking, even thinking aloud, in their own, very different style, as this old man:

> *It's like this: those young'uns years ago, I said, well—it's like digging a hole, I said, and putting in clay and then putting in a tater on top o' thet. Well, you won't expect much will you? But now with the young'uns today, it's like digging*

a hole and putting some manure in afore you plant: you're bound to get some growth ain't you? It will grow won't it? The plant will grow right well. What I say is the young'uns today have breakfast afore they set off—a lot of 'em didn't use to have that years ago, and they hev a hot dinner at school and when they come home most of 'em have a fair tea, don't they? I said. These young'uns kinda got the frame. Well, that's it! If you live tidily that'll make the marrow and the marrow makes the boon [bone] and the boon makes the frame.[3]

We have to pause here to listen, accept the difficult rhythm and syntax of his speech, ruminating, working round to the parable image which he has held all the time in store. This quotation certainly requires more adaptation by the reader. But that may be needed, and if so we will become generally learnt, as the qualities of speech become more understood.

George Ewart Evans is using artistry in his quotation as much as Ronald Blythe. Probably some hesitations, pauses, or repetitions have been eliminated from the recorded speech, and he has put in punctuation. But he has done this in a way which preserves the texture of the speech. Italics are used to indicate unexpected emphasis, and punctuation to bring the phrases together rather than to separate them. The syntax is accepted; the breaks in the passage left. And occasionally a word is spelled phonetically to suggest the sound of the dialect. Too much phonetic spelling quickly reduces a quotation (from whatever social class) to absurdity, but the odd word to convey a personal idiosyncrasy, or a key tone in a local accent like the Suffolk 'hev' and 'thet' used here, help to make a passage readable as speech without losing any of the force of its meaning.

In transferring speech into print the historian thus needs to develop a new kind of literary skill, which allows his writing to remain as faithful as possible to both the character and meaning of the original. This is not an art normally needed in documentary work. But the analogy with documentary quotation in other ways sets a useful standard. It is unfortunately not the usual practice in sociological studies quoting interviews to indicate cuts and other alterations. Historians can, however, insist on the care normal in their own discipline, showing excisions by a dotted line, interpolations by brackets, and so on. A re-ordering cannot be acceptable if it results in a new meaning, unintended by the speaker. And the creation of semi-fictional informants, by exchanging quotations between them, or dividing two from one, or creating one out of two, must always be by the standards of scholarship indefensible. An oral documentary which does this may gain in effect, but it becomes imaginative literature: a different kind of historical evidence.

Oral historians in the United States have introduced an additional standard in their practice. After transcription, typescripts are sent to the informant for correction.[4] This clearly has advantages in picking up simple errors and mis-spellings of names. It can also result in stimulating new information, and political historians who use the interview method often send transcripts for this purpose. But it has drawbacks too. Many informants find it impossible to resist rewriting the original conversational speech into a conventional prose form. They also may delete sentences and rephrase others to change the impression given from some particular memory. Since the original tapes are rarely consulted in American archives, and the transcript rather than the tape is regarded as the authoritative oral testimony, the process of correction weakens the authenticity of oral evidence in use. In addition, while some informants, like retired public figures, may have the time and confidence for correcting a lengthy transcript, there are probably many more for whom it would simply be a worrying imposition. For these it is much better to write asking only for a few clarifications of confusions, uncertain names, or vital details missing—which will usually be gladly supplied.

With transcription started, the sorting of the material for use can also be begun. It is best to make at least three copies of the transcript—and a fourth, if one is to go to an informant. The top copy can then be filed as a complete interview, a series parallel to the tapes themselves. The other copies can be re-sorted, and divided or cut up into different subject files (the third copy being used for cases where subjects overlap), depending on what use is in mind. Whole interviews could be put together by place, by social group, or by occupation. Alternatively, the passages within each interview about school, or church, or family could be cut out (marking the page in the transcript from which they are taken), and placed in a series of boxes. These boxes may well follow the sequence of the original schedule of questions. Then if a question has been asked, for example, about church attendance or how people met their husbands or wives, all the relevant material can quickly be found together in the same box. But the precise choice of method in re-sorting must depend upon the form of analysis and presentation intended.

Notes

1. Baum, pp. 41–48; the Oral History Association guideline is less precise, p. 46; she writes of the American legal situation generally concerning oral history, pp. 47–48, that libel is defined as the publication "of false utterance, without just cause, and which tends to expose the other to public hatred, contempt, or ridicule. Various court cases have progressively reduced the possibility of a court finding any historical effort either slanderous or libelous. First, the dead cannot be libeled. Second, libelous defamation of prominent living persons must include actual malice plus irresponsible disregard for truth.

"The researcher or interviewer may need to be a little more concerned if his questioning leads him into the purely private lives of prominent or not-prominent persons, although he still has a good defense if he can indicate this is truth published for good motives. Of course, there always exists the possibility of harassment in the lower courts through filing of suits for defamation. Such suits stand almost no possibility of ending in court award for damages but they could cost time and expense to the researcher in defending himself. But to all intents and purposes, slander or libel is a non-existent danger to an oral history project. It is the project's reputation for responsible work that needs guarding, not its legal liability."

The question of literary copyright in oral history recording remains as uncertain as in Britain. This statement is elaborated in an article by Truman W. Eustis III on American copyright law (*OHR*, 1976, pp. 6–18), with examples from cases including the important decision of New York State Court of Appeals in Ernest Hemingway's

Estate *v* Random House (1968) not to prevent publication by Hemingway's writer friend A. E. Hotchner of conversations which he had noted (not taped) with him. This decision, that "Ernest Hemingway impliedly licensed his rights under common-law copyright when he knowingly permitted Hotchner to interview him", brings the United States, according to James W. Wilkie, into line with the "common-sense position" which "appears to hold true throughout Latin America"—and certainly in Mexican procedure—that "intellectual authorship is held by the interviewer" (*Research in Mexican History*, p. 55).

2. P. 32.

3. P. 212. In the same spirit, the Aural History Institute of British Columbia, *Manual*, p. 40, advises the indication of local accent through spellings like "yeah," "huh," "must'a," "gonna."

4. With of course an explanatory letter which seeks to avoid some of the difficulties which follow. The Aural History Institute's example (*ibid.*, p. 49) includes this paragraph:

> Please read the transcript, remembering that it is a record of the spoken, rather than the written word. Change any incorrect dates, misspelled names or misinformation; correction of grammar is not recommended as it would distort the oral record. If you discover that you have omitted information concerning specific instances, add it in the margin or on additional sheets of paper. Similarly, if you wish to clarify statements that you have made, please add the information to the transcript.

Chapter 6

Data Analysis

Data analysis is what researchers do to answer their particular research question(s). The analysis is necessary because data alone do not yield very much useful information. In this chapter we offer a conceptual explanation for the major ways in which educational researchers analyze data. Primarily we focus on the manner in which truth-seekers analyze quantitative data through quantitative means and perspective-seekers analyze qualitative data through qualitative means. In fact the two descriptions of research projects detailed at the end of the chapter represent the two traditional types of studies. We do, however, discuss multidata, multimethod approaches employed by other truth-seeking and perspective-seeking researchers and cite examples from various readings that appear throughout the text.

Whether the researcher is working with quantitative data or qualitative data, it is important to remember that both have been acted upon before any analysis occurs. Qualitative data, especially words, texts, expressions, and statements, represent thoughts, feelings, and beliefs of people the researcher has observed or interviewed. These data have been abstracted by the user, as a result of his or her own perception of reality, and have been reduced or simplified to fit the particular definitions the user believes best represent his or her thoughts, feelings, and beliefs. Quantitative data, likewise, represent abstractions and reductions from some reality. Even observing and recording a behavior requires an abstraction (from all other behaviors) and a reduction (transforming the observation to a unit of data).

The validity of either type of data is a question that concerns all researchers. Becker, in his reading at the end of this chapter, makes this point about validity very well. Whether the data are quantitative or qualitative, questions will arise about their validity. Becker calls the assumptions, on which their validity rests, *theories of epistemology*. The differences, according to Becker, are irreconcilable. Each set of epistemological theories has strengths and weaknesses. Becker simply urges researchers to acknowledge the shortcomings of whatever data they are using and the methods by which they are analyzing them and get on with their project, that is, continue trying to make sense of whatever aspect of human behavior or thought the researcher addresses.

Perspective-seekers, because they assume multiple realities, are concerned with validity in terms of the data and their interpretations being in accordance with what the source of the data actually thought, sensed, or believed. Having the source of data read a transcription of an interview, before any analysis occurs, is one method by which perspective-seekers can approach validity. Some perspective-seekers have the source of data read the researcher's analysis and interpretation as well, to be more confident that the meanings are indeed those that were intended. Having a collaborator independently examine the data and assist in devising interpretations is another method by which perspective-seekers can assure readers of their research that the question of validity was addressed. Whatever methods the perspective-seekers use regarding validity are detailed in the methods section of the research proposal or report.

The validity with which truth-seekers deal is associated with the design of the study (see Chapter 4 for threats to internal and external validity) and the appropriateness of the method for analysis of the data. Truth-seekers also address the questions of validity in the methods section of their research proposals or reports.

Analyzing Quantitative Data

Many good quantitative data analysis books exist. We intend to provide a conceptual introduction to quantitative analysis; hence, our discussion here can only be general. It is followed by a description of a truth-seeking quantitative study that provides some illustrative detail.

The differences between analyzing quantitative data and qualitative data roughly parallel the differences between searching for truth and seeking perspectives. Remember, truth-seekers are interested in generalizing to other settings, conditions, and groups. They are concerned about objectivity and control of extraneous variables. Perspective-seekers are trying to make sense out of a relatively limited situation. Their primary intention is usually not in generalization to other settings—indeed, they place so much emphasis on context and peculiarities of the subjects (participants) they study that generalization beyond them is often a moot point. In effect, perspective-seekers claim the people and situations they study are unique, and because of their uniqueness, it is highly unlikely all the same conditions, circumstances, or motives discovered in their study could be found anywhere else.

Quantitative data analysis usually revolves around a hypothesis or other statement of expectation. The data are gathered from fairly standardized, or at least replicable, instruments chosen for the express purpose of yielding numbers that can be analyzed. Quantitative truth-seekers, because they have identified a specific gap in the puzzle they wish to fill, as indicated in Chapter 2, are quite certain about and focused on exactly what specific data they will collect and analyze. Once begun on their quest, they usually do not change direction or procedures in their collection or analysis of quantitative data.

Analyzing quantitative data is usually a separate function from the collecting or observing phase. One can muse over the data in the quiet of an office far removed from the source of the data without risking the loss of any meaning the data represent. In fact, it is often the case that a team of researchers will divide the tasks of the project such that some will collect the data and others will analyze the data. (By contrast, qualitative data analysis often is performed during the collection phase and by the same person who collects the data.)

Quantitative data analysis is guided by firm rules, often called *assumptions*, that must be adhered to in order for the results to be considered correct. When selecting subjects for a study, assumptions are made about the subjects' representativeness. For example, if quantitative data, say, math achievement scores, were collected from two third-grade classrooms, one that used a new technique for teaching math and one that used a more conventional technique, assumptions are made regarding how representative (similar) these two groups are of (to) all third-grade classrooms. The point is that the groups may or may not be similar to other third-grade classrooms. If dissimilar (not representative) then the generalizability of the quantitative data from them may be suspect even before actual analysis begins. By "suspect" we mean the researcher would have little or no confidence that the results of the analysis will be applicable to the larger group of third-grade classrooms in the school, district, state, region, or country. If the analysis of data yields conclusions that can apply only to the original two groups from whence the data came, the study would be considered to have a limitation. The severity or the limitation, that is, is it even worth doing the study, is a judgment that requires examination of the original intent. If the intent were to be able to generalize to more groups than the original two, in the typical manner of truth-seekers, then the limitation is sufficient to preclude carrying out the study.

In the Babad et al. study at the end of this chapter, the researchers used intact groups of teachers (preschool, remedial, and elementary), but were able to justify such use on the grounds that the groups were otherwise comparable. The study could proceed because all three groups were originally defined as being qualified for "senior teacher" status (i.e., all groups had been judged to meet the criteria associated with such status).

Once collected, quantitative data are analyzed through the use of procedures, formulas, and techniques that are rule bound. Entire books and graduate courses are devoted to the wide range of mathematical manipulations that can be made with quantitative data. Descriptive and inferential statistics, for example, enable the researcher to describe and make inferences about the groups being studied as well as the larger groups being represented in the study.

Other categories of statistical techniques are *parametric* and *nonparametric*. When the data represent a variable that is assumed to be normally distributed (i.e., plotting its occurrence would resemble a bell-shaped curve), parametric statistical techniques are used. When the variable being measured cannot be assumed to be normally distributed, then nonparametric statistical techniques are used. Understanding descriptive and inferential statistics is more important at this point than concerning ourselves with differences between parametric and nonparametric statistics. But being aware of the basic difference between them helps one to understand why the four types of quantitative data (nominal, ordinal, interval, and ratio) mentioned in Chapter 5 are so categorized.

Descriptive statistics simply describe the subjects or groups being studied. The common terms used in such descriptions are *mean, median, mode, range,* and *standard deviation.* The mean is the arithmetic average of whatever measures are taken. The median is the mid-point, the point on a list of ordered scores where half of the scores are higher and half are lower. The range is the difference between the lowest and highest scores from a list. The standard deviation is the average amount scores vary from the mean. While descriptive statistics relate to the sample or groups being studied, inferential statistics relate to the larger population represented by the sample being studied.

Inferential statistics are used when a sample is believed to be representative of a larger population, and findings about the sample are applied to the population from which the sample was drawn. As indicated in our discussion of experimental designs (Chapter 4), the best way to ensure that the sample is representative of the population is to randomly select the sample from the population. In group comparison studies additional assurance that bias will not enter into the study is achieved if members of the sample are randomly assigned to the treatment and control groups. Books on descriptive and inferential statistics that treat theory and methods of using such statistics include Moore and McCabe (1992), Ferguson (1989), and Winer (1990).

Usually quantitative data analysis can be carried out by different individuals and the same results will be obtained. When test scores are added together and divided by the number of scores, an average will be found. Anybody can find an average, and if the same scores are used, the same average will be found. Even when using the most complicated statistical techniques, the techniques are virtually "user proof." The findings from the analysis will be identical, irrespective of who does the analysis. One exception to the "user proof" rule in quantitative analysis is the case of factor analysis, in which judgments are made about forming and naming factors. But factor analysis is a specialized area within test theory and development and need not concern us here. Another instance when researcher judgment is used in quantitative data analysis is determining what variables will be considered for subsequent examination. As in the case of effective schools research, for example, choosing for subsequent study the variables that correlated highly with high-achieving schools was a value-laden decision.

Analyzing Qualitative Data

Several good books are devoted to the various methods of analyzing qualitative data. Some writers of research promote the use of tables and charts to graphically organize and display the data, almost as if they were quantitative in nature. If a study is couched within a truth-seeking qualitative research design, this may be particularly appropriate. Miles and Huberman (1984) and Goetz and LeCompte (1984) provide excellent guidance for proceeding in this quantitative manner. Our explication, by contrast, assumes that qualitative data should be treated qualitatively.

Our purpose is to illustrate some general guidelines that the beginning researcher can use to make sense out of the qualitative data that have been collected. We use Bogdan and Biklen's (1992) recommendations as our primary source. This posture assumes that one is operating within a more perspective-seeking qualitative research tradition. For more specific detail consult Bogdan and Biklen (1992) and consider our example at the end of this chapter. In addition, Peshkin's reading for this chapter reminds us of the complexity of the problems faced by perspective-seekers collecting qualitative data. His examples of data—both actual responses to interview questions and his descriptions of settings and participants—illustrate well the challenge of making sense of qualitative data.

Assuming you have a research question and a rationale for your study and have begun collecting data, say, for example, by interviewing participants in your study, adjust your interview questions in light of what your initial interview data revealed. Analysis of qualitative data begins as soon as the first bits of data are collected. Although you may have developed interview questions based on other sources and your own experiences, it is possible that the first person you interview will provide you with additional ideas and questions to pursue in subsequent interviews. These new leads may not produce anything you would otherwise miss, but there is no reason not to be responsive to the data as you collect them.

Making notes to yourself as you continue in your data collection is another practice that can aid you later when you analyze your completed data collection. Self-conscious notes—written to yourself—will help to remind you of the context of the data. For example, if the interviewee were particularly nervous or anxious about some response, make note of it after the interview is concluded. If you have been confused by responses or have different questions after the interview, write these thoughts and questions down for your own use later. (Bogdan and Biklen call these notes "observer's comments" and provide several good examples of them).

Also during data collection, when analysis has begun and preliminary ideas are occurring to you, it may be advisable to try out the ideas or themes on the people you have interviewed. They may not agree with your interpretations, but their disagreement does not necessarily invalidate your findings. More likely, once the interviewee realizes the kinds of themes or patterns for which you are looking he or she may be able to assist in some "fine-tuning" of your analysis.

Just because you are spending a lot of time collecting and beginning the analysis of your data does not mean you should stop reading in areas relevant to your inquiry. The analysis of your data may be considerably easier as you become more familiar with the conceptualizations others have used to describe or explain phenomena similar to those that you are studying. Even reading other accounts of perspective-seeking studies can assist you in your own study by providing insights about procedures and methods.

A final recommendation Bogdan and Biklen make for analysis during data collection is to review what you have collected so far and underline important words and phrases. Make the data you have collected and the notes you write to yourself more useful by marking them up to show emphasis, questions, insights, and whatever else that occurs to you as you proceed through data collection, reading, reflecting, and making notes throughout.

After all the data are collected—and there could be a large quantity of them—the researcher must decide how to analyze them. (Regarding quantity: Our experience has been that a thirty-minute taped interview, when transcribed, will equal fifteen to twenty typed, double-spaced pages.)

A principal rule in analyzing qualitative data is to use a coding system. The exact form, of course, will depend on the topic being examined. Bogdan and Biklen (1992) suggest eleven generic codes, eight of which are described below.

Setting or *context* codes are information you have collected that pertains to the setting or context from which you collected data. If you were studying teachers or administrators, for example, and had collected descriptive data about the school in which they work, such data would be separated from your other notes and placed in this category (or in some manner similarly coded).

Situation codes refer to how the participants view their setting. Their views may serve to explain some of their other perspectives. For example, if a teacher sees his school as a zoo or a prison, that perception may well affect the way he treats children. Such macro views of the setting would be placed in this category.

Process codes are commonly used in analyzing data from life history interviews. The categories could include early family, elementary school, middle school, high school, college years, first marriage, etc. The time periods are not uniform. The participant's responses will determine the specific categories.

Activity codes refer to the fairly routine activities of an organization. For example, the Wednesday teachers meeting would be classified with this code. Data that describe the nature of the meeting, numbers present, agenda, and so forth would be in this category.

Unlike activity codes, *event* codes derive from routine events that occur infrequently. Data that describe the event, for example, the unexpected death of a teacher, would be in this category. Even events that occurred before the study was begun, but are still talked about by participants, would be included here.

Strategy codes stem from the methods participants use to accomplish what they want and avoid what they do not want. How a teacher keeps students on a task is an example of a method or strategy that would be in this category.

Relationship and *social structure* codes are gathered from patterns of behavior you observe, or are reported by participants, that constitute friendships, romances, or hostilities, for example.

Methods codes come from all of the notes to yourself about the logistics of the procedures and reflections on such aspects of the study as whom to interview next, what other questions should be asked, and the like.

As indicated earlier, the nature of the study will help to determine how many and exactly what kinds of codes to use for the analysis. In addition, each code could have several categories within it and typically some data will fit in more than one category or code.

Once codes and their categories are tentatively identified, reread all of your notes and transcriptions and number as many of the entries as possible with the appropriate code. Typically paragraphs of interview transcripts will be the length of data entries you code, but sentences, phrases, or even some words could have different codes. The coding process takes time and careful consideration.

When all the data are coded, make a copy and put the original in a safe place. The copy can be cut up with scissors, according to the codes, and all like codes placed in appropriately marked file folders. Such classifications make further analysis easier because you can concentrate on more specific aspects all at once and not have to search through reams of paper to find them.

With your research question in mind (that which launched the entire project), reread the various coded materials to search for patterns or themes that characterize the data. You can locate at this stage of the analysis exact quotations you may want to use when you begin writing a report of your research. The quotations are to illustrate the pattern or theme and are provided so that the reader can see the justification for identifying the pattern or theme. The expectation is that the data you have collected will contain the answer to your research question. Chances are good that they will and, in addition, raise even more questions.

Multidata, Multimethods Approaches

Analyzing quantitative and qualitative data involves careful consideration of rules and guidelines for quantitative data, and responsible application of common sense for qualitative data. As noted midway in our comparison, both kinds of analyses require judgments. In the case of most quantitative data, certain decisions concerning the design of a study usually precede the analysis by virtue of their being related to reducing constructs—abilities, attributes, or motivations—to scores on some scale or instrument. Qualitative analysis requires judgment from collection time, when initial analysis begins, all the way through interpretation and reporting.

Thus far we have contrasted the two pure types of data analysis in order to highlight some of the differences. But different as they may be, we maintain that both quantitative and qualitative data or quantitative and qualitative analyses can be used together in a research project. We believe that a combination of quantitative and qualitative data can provide more information regarding a phenomenon than either one of them alone. Moreover, Brewer and Hunter (1989) promote a multimethods approach (of which data analysis is an integral part) to "attack a research problem with an arsenal of methods that have nonoverlapping weaknesses in addition to their complementary strengths" (p. 17).

The Fiske and Fogg reading following Chapter 8 is a truth-seeking study that employs both quantitative and qualitative data analyzed through quantitative and qualitative means. The authors begin by reviewing the existing knowledge about the content of the criticisms of those who screen articles submitted to various journals for publication. Much research has been done, they claim, about the editorial process, but little on the content of readers' responses. Because of the high rejection rate (98 percent) of first submissions, but the relatively good acceptance rate (20 percent to 40 percent) for revised manuscripts, they argue the need for a study to analyze the substance of reviewers' reports.

Providing you with an example of a content analysis which may be conducted either quantitatively or qualitatively, Fiske and Fogg used qualitative tools such as judgment to collect, code, and partially analyze their qualitative data text from reviewers' reports. In the process they transformed the qualitative text into descriptive categories (qualitative data) but also into frequencies of occurrence (quantitative data), displaying it all in a number of tables. Then Fiske and Fogg return to the content of several reviewers' reports, citing quotes to illustrate patterns that the numbers indicated. Several texts are available that further explain how these kinds of truth-seeking qualitative studies can be conducted (Bogdan & Biklen, 1992; Goetz & LeCompte, 1984; Jaeger, 1983; Miles & Huberman, 1984; and Shavelson, 1981).

The Vaughn and Liles reading following Chapter 4 and a subsequent study done by the authors provide another example of the multidata, multimethods approach. The researchers were interested in the perceptions of turn-of-the-twentieth-century male teachers who already seemed to be exceptions to various historical assumptions explaining why some men remained in teaching when so many others were choosing not to teach. The lack of theory to drive the project, the interest in perceptions, and the focus not on the mean but on outliers from the mean all made this study more perspective-seeking than truth-seeking. Yet, in Vaughn and Liles' first study they relied primarily on quantitative data analyzed through quantitative means such as computing z scores. However, in a follow-up study the authors used the first study to identify a particular state that seemed to employ male teachers whose motivations for teaching had never been alluded to in the literature. They then examined a selected group of male teachers from that state through a qualitative analysis of qualitative data such as oral histories, diaries, and letters (Farr & Liles, 1991).

Two Descriptions of Classic Studies

Now we offer two examples of research projects that we have conducted with our students to give you pictures of two different kinds of research from beginning to end. You might review Chapter 4 on design to refresh your memory concerning the early stages of conceptualizing and designing a research plan.

A Truth-Seeking Quantitative Data Analysis

Autry and Langenbach were both interested and had experience in elementary education. Owing to the large size of many elementary classrooms and of the importance of empowering children, enabling them to have some control over themselves and their behavior, the two researchers designed an experiment to determine whether it was possible to actually empower the students. The resulting study was entitled "Locus of Control and Self-Responsibility for Behavior" (Autry & Langenbach, 1985). In it the researchers examined how much, if at all, a sample of fourth, fifth, and sixth grade boys would change their locus of control regarding school achievement when trained in self-regulating procedures to control behavior. The study used three groups and had three expectations based on the theoretical and research literature:

1. Those who received training in self-regulation would become more internal (as opposed to becoming external or having no change in their locus of control for academic achievement);
2. Those who received training in self-regulation would increase their constructive classroom behavior and would maintain those behaviors longer than students who received external regulation of their behavior; and
3. Those who received training in self-regulation would decrease their disruptive behaviors and maintain the decrease longer than students who received external regulation of their behavior (Donaldson, 1978).

Forty students were selected to be subjects in the study. Selection was based on teachers' nomination and the notations, by trained observers, that each child contributed more than his share of disruptive behaviors. Male subjects were used in the study to control for gender-related differences. Subjects were randomly assigned to two experimental and one control group. The design was a variation of the pretest, posttest control group, discussed in Chapter 4, but with two treatment groups (self-regulation and external regulation).

Data collection included pretests and posttests with the *Intellectual Achievement Responsibility Questionnaire* (IRA) (Crandall, Katkovsky, & Crandall, 1965). This instrument was chosen because others had used it successfully to assess children's beliefs about locus of control in an academic setting. Scores on the pretest were averaged for each group and compared with each group's average scores on the posttest. Test scores from the instrument revealed statistically significant differences in the posttests for the groups receiving training in self-regulation and being externally regulated, when compared with a control group that received no training and were not regulated. The differences were as expected, except that even the externally regulated group improved with regard to the measure of internal locus of control.

Data for constructive and disruptive classroom behaviors were collected by five trained observers. This portion of the study was a variant of the single subject design, wherein baseline data are recorded, a treatment ensues, and subsequent behavior is compared with the baseline (A B A). Before baseline data were collected the observers were checked to see how well they agreed on their observations. Using a formula reported by Bijou, Peterson, and Ault (1968), observer agreement was calculated to be 91.5 percent, sufficient to assume the observers would reliably report both constructive and disruptive classroom behaviors. Behaviors were observed over a five-day period to establish a baseline; over the next thirteen days while the experimental groups were apprised of the token reward system that would be used; over the next fourteen days while the self-regulating group was trained in self-regulation; over the next fourteen days during which self-regulation was in effect for that group and finally, for ten days when subjects were told no more token reinforcements would be awarded.

The data for constructive behaviors and disruptive behaviors, recorded during a thirty-minute period each day, were graphically displayed to illustrate the comparisons of the self-regulated, externally regulated, and control groups. In addition, because graphs may be misleading, statistical tests were performed on the data to check on the possibility that differences did not occur by chance alone. (Statistics can be misleading as well, in which case graphs can illustrate information more revealingly.)

The expectations for the study, derived from the theory and previous research, directed the comparisons that needed to be made to consider the theoretical statements more or less credible. All but one of the statistical comparisons fulfilled the expectations. For a complete explication of all the procedures and results the reader should see Autry and Langenbach (1985).

A Perspective-Seeking Qualitative Data Analysis

A description of another study should give you some idea of the research process in a perspective-seeking qualitative study. Robinson-Hornbuckle (1991) became interested in studying women administrators. She was a pioneer in one state system, moving into school administration during the early 1970s. During her career, Robinson-Hornbuckle had noticed that the movement of women into school administration seemed to be more predominant in urban and suburban areas than in the many rural communities in that state. Thus Robinson-Hornbuckle began to read about gender variations among males and females in management and administrative positions and about women's history. She found an excellent book by Shakeshaft (1987) that synthesized the history of women in school administration and the current literature to date on the recent studies of women in those positions. (Such theoretical works are discussed in Chapter 3.) After reading many other studies, Robinson-Hornbuckle found that there were relatively few female administrators in rural areas throughout the United States and virtually nothing was known about them. So she decided to conduct an exploratory phenomenological study with a select number of female administrators. She confined her study to Euro-American women so as not to confound findings with issues of ethnicity and race. Her research question simply was, "Who are these women, and how did they obtain their jobs?"

According to Tesch's directions for phenomenological work, Robinson-Hornbuckle selected 12 participants and conducted in-depth interviews with each one (see Tesch's reading following Chapter 4). She selected two extra participants from the maximum of ten recommended by Tesch, so as to have enough participants in the event that someone canceled or was unable to give her a complete interview. She knew that family background and other demographic factors were essential data to answer her research question, so she conducted extensive life histories with each woman before asking her to tell the story of her professional life, as well. Robinson-Hornbuckle's interview style was very informal, allowing each participant to tell her own history, mentioning the things most important to her, rather than being asked to respond to prescribed questions. Robinson-Hornbuckle transcribed the interviews and coded and classified the data. Her advisor independently derived similar coding and classification schemes from the data, thus augmenting the trustworthiness of the analysis.

Robinson-Hornbuckle placed her findings within historical and current national context, showing their relevance to the larger field of gender studies in administration and management. She concluded that the rural female school administrators were much more conservative than their urban and suburban counterparts. Generally they shunned women's organizations, often behaved on the job in an authoritarian manner, and seemed to identify more with their male than female colleagues.

Summary

In this chapter we have discussed what might be called *epistemological theory*, the reason for certain sets of rules and regulations that enable you to answer your research question. Two standard procedures were broadly outlined and described in use through two particular studies. Also various multidata and multimethodological approaches were introduced and exemplified through readings from this text. You should now have a general concept of how to conceptualize and design a research study. Additional tools courses and involving yourself in actual research projects are the only ways to master the process, however; so get busy thinking of good ideas.

Discussion Questions and Activities

1. If all data are "abstracted and reduced," what are the implications for researchers? Explain your answers fully.

2. What does "valid data" mean? When are data not valid?

3. What differences, if any, exist between perspective-seekers' and truth-seekers' attempts to make their data more valid? Provide an illustration of each.

4. Find one recent study from a research journal. What steps were reportedly taken to ensure validity of the data? In what section of the report was this information found?

5. What are the advantages and disadvantages in having a collaborator assist in coding qualitative data?

6. Find an example from a research journal where qualitative data appear to be treated quantitatively (i.e., with tables, frequency charts, and other counting-like methods.)

7. Define and provide an example of nominal, ordinal, interval, and ratio scales. What implications would numbers from each have for statistical testing? (Consult an introductory statistics text for this.)

8. Locate two articles that utilize a multidata and/or multimethods approach. What function does each body of data and means of analysis serve in answering the research question?

Introduction to the Readings

Becker presented his paper, "Theory: The Necessary Evil . . . ," to AERA in 1991. In it he addresses theory two ways. The first is concerned with the philosophical and methodological underpinnings present in any project. In effect, he acknowledges the disputes present in views of the world and method and suggests that researchers proceed without being too distracted by them. More relevant to our discussion of theory is his second way of addressing it.

By implication, Becker is saying, "Find others who share similar interests and who have written about the topic in which you are interested and have their work inform your own." We read this admonition to mean that theories may conflict when used by those with dissimilar interests or ideologies, but that should not stop you. Seek out your kind and do not worry about the others. Chances are very good that someone, somewhere has addressed the same or a similar topic and that those efforts need to be incorporated in your rationale for proposing your study.

The reading by Babad et al., "Nonverbal and Verbal Behavior of Preschool, Remedial, and Elementary School Teachers," is a good illustration of a rationalistic effort to remove as much context as possible from the phenomenon being studied and reducing or simplifying the same phenomenon (teacher behavior) to numerical ratings on an instrument. Through the use of videotapes of teachers, the researchers used 15 judges to rate specific behaviors—face, body, audio, and so forth—on a nine-point scale. The results confirmed the conventional wisdom (for our purposes, read *theory*) that preschool teachers exhibited more positive affect than did elementary or remedial teachers.

The paper by Peshkin, "Understanding Complexity: A Gift of Qualitative Inquiry," addresses the issue of trying to understand the complexity of behavior, attitudes, and values associated with ethnicity. His setting is a California high school that has about an equal proportion of black and white students (33 percent of each), 20 percent Hispanic, 12 percent Filipino, and 3 percent others. Peshkin illustrates the use of a survey (a quantitative data-gathering device) to help him frame questions for the various participants in his study.

His log entries and verbatim reporting of interviews provide ample evidence of the complexity of the data that may be encountered. Peshkin's main point is that qualitative methods of collection and analysis are ideally (or at least better) suited to this task than are quantitative ones.

Theory: Necessary Evil . . .

Howard S. Becker

Epistemological Worries

Qualitative researchers in education have begun to question the epistemological premises of their work. Or at least, someone in the arena is questioning those premises, and the questioning worries the researchers who actually do the work of studying schools, students, and education close up. Attacks on qualitative [naturalistic] research used to come exclusively from the methodological right, from the proponents of positivism [rationalism] and statistical and experimental rigor. But now the attack comes from the cultural studies left as well, from the proponents of the "new ethnography," [some naturalists] who argue that there is no such thing as "objective knowledge," and that qualitative [some naturalistic] research is no more than an insidious disguise for the old enemy of positivism [rationalism] and pseudo-objectivity.

The attack can conveniently, if somewhat misleadingly, be as "theoretical." Convenient because it is not a question of empirical findings; misleadingly, because the theory involved is not substantive. These worries, which used to take the form of a concern with the theoretical bases of our substantive findings, now focus on the theory of knowledge [epistemology] that underlies the whole enterprise. What bothers qualitative [naturalistic] researchers in education, I think, is that they are no longer sure, as they once were, that they are doing things the "right way." They worry that the work they do may be built on sand; despite all their care and precautions, all their attempts to answer the multitude of criticisms that greet their efforts and all their attempts to still the qualms that arise from within, that the whole thing will count for nothing in the end. Not only that our work will not be accepted as scientific, but also that that model of scientific work we aspire to is now discovered to be philosophically unsound and in need of serious rethinking. Who are we kidding with all this science talk? Why don't we admit that what we do is just another kind of story, no better or worse than any other fiction?

How shall we understand all this? Are these realistic worries? Are we building on sand? Is what we do just another story?

Becker H. S. Theory: Necessary Evil. Paper presented at the American Educational Research Association Conference. Chicago, 1991. Reprinted with permission of the author.

Theory or Social Organization

We can take these debates at face value, worry over their content, and try to answer all the questions asked of us. That is the conventional way to deal with such problems. The literature discussing qualitative research in education parallels similar discussions in sociology, and especially anthropology. These discussions center on the relative merits of qualitative and quantitative research, on the problems or virtues of positivism, on the importance (or danger) of subjectivity and so on.

These are, of course, serious problems in the philosophy of social science. It is not clear how any of us, qualitative or quantitative, can justify what we produce as certified or warranted or credible knowledge. Whatever safeguards we take, whatever new tricks we try, questions can be and are raised. Qualitative research—we might better say, research that is designed in the doing, that therefore is not systematic in any impersonal way, that leaves room for, indeed, insists on individual judgment, that takes account of historical, situated detail and context and all that—research of that kind is faulted for being exactly all of those things and therefore not able to produce "scientific," objective, reliable knowledge that will support prediction and control. Research which tries to be systematic and impersonal, arithmetic and precise, and thereby scientific, is faulted for leaving out too much that needs to be included, for failing to take account of crucial aspects of human behavior in social life, for being unable to advance our understanding, for promising much more in the way of prediction and control than it ever delivers.

Epistemological issues, for all the arguing, are never settled, and I think it fruitless to try to settle them, at least in the way the typical debate looks to. If we have not settled them definitively in two thousand years, more or less, we probably are not ever going to settle them. These are simply the commonplaces in the rhetorical sense of scientific talk in the social sciences, the framework in which debate goes on. So be it.

Also, so what? Because I don't mean these remarks fatalistically. I don't counsel resignation, acceptance of an inescapable tragic fate. No. There is nothing tragic about it. It is clearly possible, on the evidence we have all around us, to find out things about social life in ways that are more or less good enough, at least for the people we are working with now. It has happened often enough in the past, and there is no reason to think it can't continue to happen.

In fact, this is exactly the import of Thomas Kuhn's analysis of science, as I understand it. Whenever scientists can agree on what the questions are, what a reasonable answer to them would look like, and what ways of getting such answers are acceptable [a paradigm]—then you have a period of scientific advance. At the price, Kuhn is careful to point out, of leaving out most of what needs to be included in order to give an adequate picture of whatever we are studying; at the price of leaving a great deal that might properly be subjected to investigation, that in fact desperately needs investigation, uninspected and untested.

That is all right. Because, though everything can be questioned, we needn't question it all at once. We can stand on some shaky epistemological ground Over

Here for as long as it takes to get an idea about what can be seen from this vantage point. Then we can move Over There, to the place we have been treating as problematic while we took Over Here for granted, and taking Over There for granted, make Over Here problematic for a while. It is John Dewey's point: Reality is what we choose not to question at the moment. (That is also Lily Tomlin's point, as it comes out of the mouth of Trudy the bag-lady, no mean philosopher herself: "After all, what is reality anyway? Nothing but a collective hunch." And she adds, "Reality is the leading cause of stress amongst those in touch with it.")

Any working scientist must have a position on such questions, implicit or explicit (and the better shape the science is in, the more the positions are implicit), just in order to get on with the work. Any working researcher's positions on these questions are likely—the chief fear of the philosophically minded—to be inconsistent, just because they have to be taken ad hoc, to deal with the immediate problems of getting the work done. Not only is inconsistency unavoidable, it is the basis of everyday scientific practice.

For instance, I am devoted to qualitative work, and I think that the criticisms made of "simple-minded counting" are often quite correct. But I also rely, whenever I can, on data from the U.S. and other censuses. I would be crazy not to. Any sensible analysis of social life will want to take into account the age distribution of the population studied, even though we know that people routinely misstate their ages. Why else are there so many more people who are 25 years old than there are 24 and 26 year olds? When we write and talk about schools and education, we routinely take into account the relative size of various ethnic and racial groups, as reported in the census, even though we know that those numbers simply report what people choose to put down as their race, which may have no relation at all to either biological or social fact. We use those numbers, even though we know they are riddled with errors the demographers themselves have exposed.

Similarly, the hardest-nosed positivists, if anyone will admit to being one of those anymore, routinely take into account, all sorts of knowledge acquired with the help of "soft" methods, without which they couldn't make sense of their data. They may not admit it, but the interpretations they make of "hard" findings rely on their own understanding of the less easily measured, though still easily observed, aspects of social life.

In short, we all, qualitative [naturalistic] and quantitative [rationalistic] workers alike, have to use methods that we disapprove of, philosophically and methodologically, just to get on with it, and take into account what must be taken account of in order to make sense of the world.

The Necessary Evil

So we all have to be epistemological theorists, know it or not, because we couldn't work at all if we didn't have at least an implicit theory of knowledge, wouldn't know what to do first. In that sense, theory is necessary.

But the questions raised about the justification for what we do, which is what these theories are, cannot be definitively answered. That is an empirical generalization based on the simple observation that we are still discussing the matter. To spend a lot of time on unanswerable questions is a waste of time, (see Stanley Lieberson's discussion in *Making It Count*) and quite paralyzing. If you have convinced yourself that what you are doing can't be justified reasonably, it is hard to get up the energy to do it. It seems better to continue discussing the problem in the hope of finding an answer that satisfies you and the people who are aggravating you about the warrant for your conclusions.

In that sense, the pursuit of epistemological and similar questions in the philosophy of social science is evil. If you are accustomed to this dilemma, it isn't a great trouble—you make a choice and go about your business. But some researchers—most especially graduate students—are especially vulnerable to the questioning doubts that paralyze thought and will and work. For them the evil is serious. To repeat, we still have to do the theoretical work, but we needn't think we are being especially virtuous when we do. Theory is a dangerous, greedy animal, and we need to be alert to keep it in its cage.

Social Organization

From a different vantage point, we can see that these debates over method and its justification as the kind of thing that happens in the world of social science, as a recurring social phenomenon to be investigated rather than a serious epistemological problem—in other words, to paraphrase the ethnomethodologist Harold Garfinkel, as a topic rather than an aggravation. And we can ask sociological questions about debates like this: When, in the life of a discipline, or of a researcher, as my remarks about graduate students suggested, or of a piece of research, do these questions become troubling? Who is likely to be exercised about them? How do such unresolved and unresolvable debates fit into the social organization of the discipline?

The Relative Specter

To ask such questions immediately raises the specter of a paradoxical situation in which *I* presume, on the basis of a social science analysis which is itself philosophically unjustified, to give *you* the social science lowdown on a critique of what I am at the moment doing. It is a kind of debunking, not unlike psychoanalytically inclined writers who respond to criticism with an analysis of the unconscious motives of their critics. That is just the problem that is giving some contemporary sociologists of science fits; because they understand perfectly well that their analysis of the workings of science is in some sense a critique of science.

If the critique is correct, then it applies to the analysis that produced the critique. You can see where that leads.

An alternative position is to accept the reflexivity this involves, indeed, to embrace it, and then use our knowledge of the social organization of science to solve the problems so raised. In other words, if it is an organizational problem, the solution has to be organizational. You don't solve organizational problems by clarifying terms or arguments. Organizations are not philosophies, and people don't base their actions on philosophical analyses. Not even scientists do that.

Science Worlds, Chains of Association

What does it mean to speak of the social organization of an intellectual or scientific discipline? We can speak here of scientific worlds in analogy to the analyses that have been made of art worlds. These analyses focus on a work of art—a film, a painting, a concert, a book of poetry—and ask: Who are all the people who had to cooperate so that that work could come out the way it did? This is not to say that there is any particular way the work has to come out, only that if you want your movie to have orchestral music in the background, you will have to have someone compose the music and musicians play it; you can easily, of course, have no music, but then it will be a different film than the one whose action is accompanied by a score.

An art world is made up of all the people who routinely cooperate in that way to produce the kind of works they usually produce: the composers, conductors and performers who produce concert music; the playwrights, actors, directors, designers and business people who produce theater works; the writers, designers, editors and business people who produce novels; the long list of everyone from directors and actors to grips and accountants and caterers and transportation captains who work together to make Hollywood films; and so on.

The cooperation that makes up an art world and produces its characteristic works depends on the use of conventions, standardized ways of doing things everyone knows and depends on. Some examples are musical scales, forms, like the sonnet or the three movement sonata; the Hollywood feature film, the pas de deux—a list that suggests the variety of elements that can be so standardized. When everyone in an art world recognizes and uses the same conventions, collaboration proceeds easily and economically, somewhat at the expense of originality and variety. If we all agree to use the 12-tone scale of Western music, we know that players and listeners alike will know and be able to deal with our music, but we give up the opportunity to use scales constructed differently.

That is an art world. A science world, by analogy, would consist of all those people who cooperate to produce the characteristic activities and products of that science. This means more than the people who make up the scientific community to which Kuhn called our attention. It includes, for instance, the people who provide the materials with which the science works; the experimental animals, the purified chemicals and water to experiment on them with, the carefully controlled spaces to do it all in. For social science it typically means, importantly, the people who provide us with data by gathering statistics, doing interviews, being interviewed, letting us observe them, collecting and giving us access to documents. Just as with art works, the kinds of cooperation that are available, and the terms on which that cooperation is available, necessarily affect the kind of science that can be done. A contemporary example is the conflict over the use of laboratory animals in biological research.

One of the distinctive characteristics of science worlds (as opposed, for example, to art worlds) is the emphasis on proof and persuasion, on being able to convince someone else by commonly accepted "rational" methods to accept what you say, even though they would rather not. Bruno Latour, the French sociologist of science, has made this the cornerstone of his analysis of "science-in-action." He speaks of scientists trying to get more and more people to accept their statements, doing that by enrolling "allies" with whom opponents of their statements will also have to contend. Footnotes and appeals to the literature serve to line up allies with whom people who disagree with you will also have to disagree. In Latour's analysis, people agree with each other not because there is a basic scientific logic which decides disputes, and certainly not because Nature or Reality adjudicate the dispute, but because one side or the other has won a "trial of strength," on whatever basis such trials are decided in that community. In a series of very provocative dicta, Latour says things like, (I will paraphrase here) "It is not that scientists agree when the facts require them to, but rather that when scientists agree, what they agree on become the facts."

A beginning on this kind of (what we might call) organizational epistemology, is to note that every way of doing research and arriving at results is good enough, good enough, for someone situated at some point in the research process. If it weren't good enough for someone, no one would be doing it. Who it has to be good enough for, and when it has to be that good, are empirical questions that depend on the social organization in which that bit of knowledge arises.

The most general finding here is that, though every scientific method has easily observed technical flaws, and is based on not-very well hidden philosophical fallacies, they are all used routinely without much fear or worry within some research community. The results they produce are good enough for the community of scientific peers that uses them. The flaws will be recognized and discounted for; the fallacies will be acknowledged and ignored. Everyone knows all about it, knows that everyone else knows all about it, and they have all agreed not to bother each other about it. So the census, with all the flaws I alluded to, is quite good enough for the rough differentiations social scientists usually want to make. But that is because the social scientists who use census data have made the collective hunch that these data are good enough for the purposes they will put them to, not because the flaws don't exist. Few enough people we would ordinarily think of as White say they are Black, and few enough people we would ordinarily think of as Black say they are White to change any conclusions we base on these numbers. And we don't think that the difference between 24 and 25 is large enough to invalidate the conclusions that we base on age statistics.

An interesting corollary of this is that what methods and data are acceptable depends on the stage of the scientific process at which they are used and presented and the purpose they are used for. At an early stage of the scientific process, for instance, we are mainly playing, exploring ideas for the further ideas or explorations they might lead us to. We don't really much care whether the results are valid or not, or whether the conclusions are true. What we really care about is that the discussion proceed, that we find something interesting to talk about. This stage may take place over a cup of coffee, in a seminar, in casual conversation with a colleague. I remember a seminar with Everett Hughes, in which a student interrupted one of his discursive explorations of a "fact" he had read somewhere to say that later research had shown that the fact wasn't true. Without breaking stride, Hughes asked what the new fact was, and then continued to explore *its* possibilities.

In fact, it is often seen as an intellectual mistake to dismiss ideas at this stage of work just because they might not be true. The worst thing that can happen to a research community, in some sense, is to run out of researchable problems. Yuval Yonay has pointed out that researchers will often accept all sorts of anomalies if the general position containing those anomalies opens up a lot of new researchable questions, whose exploration can produce publishable papers and the feeling of progress.

At a somewhat later stage in the research process, we are mainly interested in getting an idea that will be worth the time and effort we are going to put into it. At this point, not just any idea will do. We want some assurance that the idea we choose will bear the weight we are going to put on it, that the idea is not so unsupported in fact that taking it as a starting point will not leave us stranded, that taking it seriously will in fact produce a result. So we look in the literature to see what others have done and how it worked out. Before we go to the trouble of writing a research proposal or setting up a project—a more sizable investment than one makes in a casual conversation—we want to know that we are building on a solid foundation. We subject what we find in earlier reports to careful scrutiny, and bring more rigorous methodological standards to bear, because we don't want to waste our time. If there is something wrong with this way of working, we want to know it now. Putting down a larger bet, we want better odds.

We could pursue this analysis through a variety of steps. What kinds of rigor do we demand before we accept a journal article for publication or a paper for the annual meeting of the tribe? Here we might note the role of practical considerations. While everyone insists that only the highest standards are employed in choosing papers for these purposes, it is also well-known that scientific associations commit themselves to fill a certain number of rooms in the hotels in which they meet with paying customers; otherwise, they will be charged for the meeting rooms, the president's suite, and so on. The best way to ensure that a sufficient number will attend the meeting is to accept their papers for the program, and then require that everyone on the program register for their meeting. The people who organize these programs usually receive a nicely worded double message: maintain standards and maximize participation. It is not clear that those two are compatible.

A final stage has to do with what work receives the highest honor, which does not take the form of a prize, but rather of imitation. What research becomes paradigmatic in the Kuhnian sense, providing exemplars of the work that particular scientific community has standardized on, has taken as exemplifying the problems, methods, and styles of reasoning that everyone will work on? Oddly enough, at this stage we aren't really very critical, precisely because a whole community has accepted this work as paradigmatic. All the mechanisms of scientific training and community formation and professional socialization that Kuhn describes combine to convince people that what everybody already believes is what they had better believe too. Obviously, it doesn't always work that way, but of necessity it does work that way, every time a scientific community adopts a paradigmatic way of working.

Specialization (Philosophical and Methodological Worry As a Profession)

When intellectual specialties reach a size sufficient to support specialization (this is one of those demographic facts I spoke of earlier) they often (and in the social sciences, almost invariably) develop specialties in theory and methodology and philosophy of science (as those apply to their particular discipline). The specialists in these topics do some work which members of the discipline think is necessary to the entire enterprise, but which has become too complex and specialized for everyone to do for themselves.

The social sciences have probably (this is speculative intellectual history, and could be checked out in the appropriate monographs, although I haven't done that) developed specialized methodologists and philosophers of science because they have come under attack, in ways that hurt, from people who think that the enterprise is not philosophically (especially "scientifically") defensible. The attacks have frequently come from the natural sciences, and have had serious practical consequences in the struggle for academic recognition and advantages (faculty positions, research funds, etc.), so they have been seen as requiring answers. The job therefore must be done and, to be done right, must be done by people who can hold their own in that kind of argument, people who know the latest stuff and the most professional styles of argument.

One consequence of turning this part of our business over to specialists is that the specialists have interests which don't exactly coincide with ours. They play to different audiences. Philosophers of science, even if they come from our own ranks, have as at least part of their audience, the world of professional philosophy, at least that part of it which concerns itself with their topic. What makes them useful to us is also what makes them difficult. They know all the tricks of philosophers of science, in large part, because they have *become* philosophers, and are part of that world. In consequence, they are sensitive to the opinions of other philosophers of science, philosophers who do not have one foot in one of the social sciences, even when those people's opinions push them in directions that are not relevant to the concerns of working scientists.

Philosophers and theorists of knowledge, concerned to meet the standards of the philosophical discourse they are involved in, frequently follow their logic to conclusions which make the day-to-day work of science impractical or impossible. They seem to conclude that social science, as we now do it, can't be done. That always reminds me of Donald Campbell, the psychologist, and former colleague of mine at Northwestern, who used to say that these people are very convincing, but if they are right, then what have we been doing all these years? That is, to say that it can't be done is only to say that it can't be done in a way that meets some set of standards that is not extant in the research community in which the work is actually being done.

The same thing is true when we consider the specialists who deal with technical questions, claiming to derive the warrant for their structures from philosophical premises. Science is, remember, a cooperative enterprise, in which all the cooperators have something to say about what is done. That includes, to bring this down to some earthy and necessary considerations, the people who pay for what is done, and the people who are the objects (or subjects, since what term we use to describe them is contested) of our study.

A simple example: Some years ago a distinguished sociological methodologist reasoned that the newly invented technique of path analysis could be used to deal with measurement error in survey research. It was quite easy and straightforward: all you had to do was have the same interviewers interview the same respondents on three separate occasions, using the same interview guide. Easy enough, except that neither interviewers nor respondents would cooperate. The interviewers felt like fools asking the same people the same questions over and over again, and when they got their nerve up to do that, the respondents wouldn't answer. "You asked that twice already. Are you stupid or what?" The philosophical theory and its technical application were clear; the social logic was off.

Great advances in social science often depend on increases in funding. For years, most of what was known about fertility came from detailed analyses of the data of the Indianapolis study, in its time, the most detailed body of materials available on married couples' choices about how many children to have and when to have them. But it was all done in Indianapolis. A major step forward occurred when increased funding made it possible to use national samples to study the decisions of couples to have children. It had never, of course, been methodologically defensible to use Indianapolis as a surrogate for the entire United States, but what choice was there? So it was used. Once a "more adequate" sample became available, the ante was upped, to the point that when I asked a leading demographer what he would do if he could no longer finance national surveys of fertility, he looked thoughtful, and then after a while, he said, "Well, that is no problem. We will always be able to finance national samples." I said, "But no. Just imagine that for some reason it became impossible." So he thought about it for a while longer. He said, "No, no, that will never happen. We will always be able to have national samples." So he really couldn't consider the question seriously; you just had to have them and that was that. In the same way, Bronislaw Malinowski's enforced four-year stay (as an interned enemy alien) in the Trobriand Islands during World War I, set a new methodological standard for how long and in what degree of intimacy anthropologists had to be in contact with "their people." It is true. Before that, American anthropology consisted of what you could find out about the Navajo during the summer vacation.

In other words, general statements of what must be done to be scientifically adequate rely, usually without acknowledgement, on practical matters, and in this, they follow rather than lead everyday practice.

Audiences

Audiences (and especially the people whose lives and activities we study) react to what we say in variable ways and researchers worry about that. Some of our philosophical and epistemological and theoretical concerns have to do with justifying what we do to such "external" audiences.

Educational research is particularly vulnerable to problems of justification. Everything educational researchers do has some consequence for people in the education business. Do we find that one method of teaching is superior to others? The people who are committed to the others—not just "philosophically," but also by virtue of not knowing how to do the new thing, or of having built their reputations on the way they now do it—will want to find reasons why these results are not valid.

I don't mean that it is just mercenary. It is more complicated than that. If you have a reason to look for trouble, you are more likely to look. Every method having flaws, if you look, you will find. As I remarked earlier, every way of doing business is good enough—for someone at some time for some purpose. Conversely, no way is good for all purposes and all people at all times. So it is always possible to criticize how things are done if you are a different person, at a different time with a different purpose.

Finally

To come full circle, the reasons and the people and the times for research are organizational facts, not philosophical constructs. Epistemology and philosophy of science are problems insofar as we cohabit with the people who make those topics their business, and are thus sensitive to their opinions, questions and complaints. Educational researchers, poised uneasily as they are between the institutions of (mostly) public education, the scientific and scholarly communities of the university world, and the people who give money in Washington, who aren't sure which of those constituencies they ought to take seriously, have the unenviable task of inventing a practice that will answer to all of them more or less adequately. The difficulties are compounded by the splintering of the academic component of the mix into a variety of disputatious factions, which is mostly what I have been discussing. No amount of careful reasoning or thoughtful analysis will make the difficulties go away. They are grounded in different standards and demands based in different worlds. In particular, as long as theory consists of a one-way communication from specialists who live in the world of philosophical discourse, empirical researchers will not be able to satisfy them. In my own view, we (the empirical researchers, among whom I still count myself) should listen carefully to those messages, see what we can use, and be polite about the rest of it. After all, as Joe E. Brown remarked in the last scene of *Some Like It Hot*, when he discovered that the woman he wanted to marry was after all, a man, he said, "Well, nobody's perfect." Thank you.

Bibliographical Note

Thomas Kuhn's ideas can be found in his *The Structure of Scientific Revolutions* (Chicago: University of Chicago Press, 1962). The remarks of Trudy the Bag Lady appear in Jane Wagner, *The Search for Signs of Intelligent Life in the Universe* (New York: Harper and Row, 1986), p. 18. Stanley Leiberson's *Making It Count* was published by the University of California Press in 1986. I have analyzed the idea of an art world at length in *Art Worlds* (Berkeley: University of California Press, 1982). The fullest statement of Bruno Latour's views is *Science in Action* (Cambridge: Harvard University Press, 1987). I've discussed the idea that every way of presenting knowledge is good enough for someone in "Telling About Society," in my *Doing Things Together* (Evanston: Northwestern University Press, 1986). Yuval Yonay's thoughts about the utility of even bad ideas in opening up research questions are contained in his dissertation (in progress at Northwestern University) on the history of contemporary economics.

Nonverbal and Verbal Behavior of Preschool, Remedial and Elementary School Teachers

Elisha Babad

Frank Bernieri

Robert Rosenthal

Abstract

This paper presents a relatively context-free method of assessing teacher behavior. The context is removed through the use of extremely brief (10-second) clips of videotaped teacher behavior, separated into isolated nonverbal and verbal channels. This method makes it possible to trace subtle within-teacher differences in isolated visual and verbal channels, such as the face, the body, speech content, and tone of voice, as well as to compare teachers who work in disparate educational contexts. To examine a commonly held belief about the relatively high quality of Israeli preschool teachers, samples of preschool, remedial, and elementary school teachers were videotaped, and brief clips were rated on 10 scales by 15 judges. Following a principal component analysis, the 10 rating scales were reduced to three interpretable factor-based scores. The groups of teachers did not differ in their "active teaching behavior"—a composite score consisting of task-orientation, clarity, dominance, and activity/energy/enthusiasm. The groups differed in "nondogmatism" (ratings of teacher as democratic, flexible, and warm) and "negative affect" (ratings of teacher as hostile, condescending, and tense/nervous/anxious) manifested in their behavior. For these composite variables, a clear linear trend was observed, with preschool teachers showing least dogmatism and negative affect, elementary school teachers showing most dogmatism and negative affect, and remedial teachers falling between these two groups. Dogmatic behavior was detected in both the face and the verbal channels, whereas negative affect was detected only in the teachers' faces.

Parents, educators, pupils, and the general public often engage in subjective, intuitive assessment of teachers' quality. Frequently the assessment focuses on a generalized group of teachers rather than individual teachers, and assertions are

Babad, E., Bernieri, F., & Rosenthal, R. (1987). Nonverbal and verbal behavior of preschool, remedial, and elementary school teachers. *American Educational Research Journal, 24*(3), 405–415. Copyright 1987 by the American Educational and Research Association. Reprinted by permission of the publisher.

made about the quality or assets of a particular group of teachers (say, preschool teachers, kibbutz teachers, etc.) compared with other groups. Criteria for such assessments (e.g., teaching effectiveness, student achievement, classroom climate, student motivation, etc.) are usually undefined and almost never measured. But even if such criteria were operationally defined, it would not be possible to compare different groups of teachers, because they work in disparate educational contexts, and it is difficult to isolate the influence of the context and to assess the extent to which it determines particular patterns of teacher behavior.

Numerous observational instruments were constructed over the years to assess social behavior and to compare patterns of social interaction enacted in various contexts. Many of these instruments were based on, or at least influenced by, Bale's (1950) Interaction Process Analysis. With regard to teacher behavior in the classroom, Flanders (1967) constructed a widely used observational system, and Simon and Boyer (1967–1970) compiled a comprehensive anthology of classroom observation instruments. Most instruments are based on direct observations conducted in the classroom, where observers rate their impressions of teacher behavior on a variety of scales, such as: praises, accepts feelings, gives directions, criticizes, accepts ideas, and so forth. Most approaches try to reduce the influence of the context by recording the observed behaviors without consideration of when they occur, for what purpose, and under what conditions. Thus, although the actual behaviors are observed in the real-time setting of the classroom and coded in the classroom context, they are recorded without consideration of the context.

We maintain that such instruments are basically context-dependent: The observers are exposed to ongoing teacher behavior, and their judgments—even if specific and limited to defined aspects—are influenced by their overall impressions and interpretations of the global context of the interaction between teacher and students. In other words, the specific behaviors might be considered decontextualized to some degree, but the observational process itself is context-dependent.

Current conceptualization and empirical research on the mediation of teacher expectancies (Babad, 1987; Dusek, 1985; Harris & Rosenthal, 1985) repeatedly indicate the subtlety and elusive nature of the behaviors through which differential teacher expectancies are transmitted to students. We are only beginning to understand the substantial influence of very fine nuances in teacher behavior, most of which are nonverbal, uncontrollable, and often undetectable in natural observation. To isolate these fine nuances and to make meaning of the smallest elements of teacher behavior, research must aim at reducing the influence of the overall classroom context as much as possible in measurement of teacher behavior.

While educational researchers have used context-dependent measurement based mostly on natural observations in the classroom, investigators of nonverbal communication (e.g., Rosenthal, 1979; Rosenthal, Hall, DiMatteo, Rogers, & Archer, 1979) employed an opposite strategy—separating channels and eliminating most of the content—so as to be able to ascribe raters' judgments to particular channels and combinations of channels. In a recent study, for example, O'Sullivan, Ekman, Friesen, and Scherer (1985) tried to predict judgments based on combined channels (i.e., when a fuller context is available) from judgments based on separate channels, such as tone of voice, face alone, or body alone. Rosenthal, Blanck, and Vannicelli (1984) predicted therapists' tone of voice when interacting with their patients from their tone of voice when talking about these patients in brief (10-second) clips.

In this paper, we introduce a relatively context-free measurement method for assessing teacher behavior and illustrate its use in comparing Israeli preschool, remedial, and elementary school teachers. Two components of "context" are considered: (a) length of exposure and (b) separation of channels. In a natural classroom observation, exposure is very long, allowing the observer to follow events throughout their entire course, thus obscuring (and potentially biasing) the judgment of specific segments of behavior. In addition, the observer is exposed to multichannel information—visual and auditory, verbal and nonverbal. The use of film and VTR makes it possible to focus on the teacher alone without exposure to the students, to separate different verbal and nonverbal channels in teacher behavior, and to control the length of exposure of segments of teacher behavior to observers/judges.

It is commonly held by Israeli educators and parents that the preschool is the "best" part of the Israeli educational system, whereas the elementary school is valued less highly. It is hard to trace the antecedents of this belief. Possible explanations might include the relatively more flexible, creative, and free atmosphere of the preschool as compared to the more conventional and structured nature of the elementary school; the differences in the definitions of the teacher's tasks and the criteria for task effectiveness in preschool and elementary school; and/or the possibility of a natural selection process among prospective teachers. The validity and generalizability of this commonly held belief have never been examined empirically because of, among other reasons, the difficulty of comparing disparate educational contexts. Our goal is to demonstrate that through the reduction of context from raters' observations it becomes possible to compare teacher behavior despite great differences between their classroom environments.

In this method, very brief video clips of teacher behavior were recorded in the classroom. The clips consisted of the teacher's face, body, face + body, and speech. These clips were then processed in the laboratory, and nine clips were created, depicting 10-second samples of teacher behavior in separate channels (face alone, body alone, face + body, audio, transcript of words, and content-filtered tone of voice) or combination of channels (face + audio, body + audio, face + body + audio). These clips were shown to judges who rated each clip on a series of 10 behavioral scales. (We actually videotaped the teachers at three points in time and therefore showed the judges 3×9 clips.) This method made it possible to separate channels and to obtain different impressions from different channels. At the same time, it was also possible to examine the combined influence of all (or some) channels together while maintaining the relatively context-free nature of the measurement.

Method

Subjects

Subjects were 21 experienced teachers, in advanced training for a "senior teacher" certificate in an Israeli teacher training college. Nine were preschool teachers, five were elementary school teachers, and seven were remedial teachers.[1] All 21 teachers were female, married or widowed, and mothers of children. Their ages ranged from 27 to 55 years, with a mean and median age in mid- to late 30s. Their teaching experience ranged from 5 to 31 years, with a mean and median between 15 and 17 years.

With a sample of teachers as small as this, sample representativeness could not be ascertained. However, the fact that all teachers in this sample were accepted to a training program leading to a "senior teacher" status implies not only that they were sufficiently experienced but also that they passed selective screening and were positively evaluated—and recommended—by their supervisors.

The judges were 15 advanced undergraduate students in educational psychology at the Hebrew University of Jerusalem. All judges were Israeli females in their early to mid-20s. The judges were paid to rate the clips. They were not informed of the stratification of teachers in the sample.

Videotaping in the Classroom

This study was part of a larger project focusing on teachers' nonverbal and verbal behavior when talking about and talking to high- and low-expectancy students (Babad et al., 1987). The data base for this report was derived from the teachers talking to their entire classes. Subsequent videotaping of each teacher alone and in dyadic interactions with particular students constituted the data for the expectancy study.

The teachers were videotaped while addressing the entire class. The camera was positioned at the back of the classroom, and the teacher could not detect whether it was filming or not at a given moment. Following a few minutes of habituation to the presence of the camera in the classroom, three sets of clips were recorded for each teacher, from the beginning, middle, and end portions of the session. At each time point, three 10-second clips were taped, consisting (in random order) of the teacher's face, her body (from the neck down), and face + body (i.e., the entire person). The teacher's speech was recorded in all clips, and one was chosen at random to be used for the audio and transcript clips.

Preparation of Clips

Altogether, 27 clips were prepared for each teacher, 9 each for the three time points. The nine channels were: (a) *Face Only* (no speech); (b) *Body Only* (no speech); (c) *Face + Body* (no speech); (d) *Audio Only* (recorded speech, no video picture); (e) *Face + Audio*; (f) *Body + Audio*; (g) *Face + Body + Audio*; (h) *Transcript* (a written account of the words spoken in the 10-second segment, with neither video nor audio recording); (i) *Content-Filtered Speech* (a process that removes from the tape the high frequencies on which word recognition depends but preserves sequence and rhythm (see Rogers, Scherer, & Rosenthal, 1971; Rosenthal et al., 1984).

All 27 clips for each teacher were set in a fixed randomized order, to be viewed and rated by the 15 judges. The ninth channel (content-filtered speech) was later dropped from the analysis, because classroom noises and the children's speech blended with, and obscured, the teachers' tone of voice.

Four combinations of channels were analyzed after the judges completed their ratings of the randomized 27 clips: (a) *Video Only* (combination of face, body, and face + body); (b) *Verbal Present* (combination of transcript, audio, face + audio, body + audio, and face + body + audio); (c) *Face Present* (combination of face, face + body, face + audio, and face + body + audio); and (d) a combination of all eight channels (after the content-filtered voice was dropped).

Judges' Ratings

The 15 judges viewed all 27 clips of each teacher and rated each clip on a series of 9-point scales: (a) *Warm;* (b) *Dominant;* (c) *Task-Oriented;* (d) *Tense/Nervous/Anxious;* (e) *Condescending;* (f) *Hostile;* (g) *Clear in Communication;* (h) *Active/Energetic/Enthusiastic;* (i) *Democratic;* and (j) *Flexible.*

The judges were not given any information about the purpose of the research, its design, the stratification of the teachers, or the specific conditions under which the clips were collected. They were told only that the research dealt with verbal and nonverbal elements of teacher-student interaction in the classroom.

Clips were randomized within teachers. Judges rated all 27 clips for a given teacher before moving on to the next set of 27 clips. The method we chose was reasoned to increase the judges' precision in making finer distinctions among the clips for each teacher.

Principal Components Analysis and Composite Scores

The means of the judges' ratings, with each channel taken as a separate observation for each teacher, were correlated, and a principal components analysis was computed. This analysis yielded three clear and interpretable factors after varimax rotation: (a) *Nondogmatic Behavior* (consisting of flexible, democratic, and warm—with factor loadings of .91 to .93); (b) *Negative Affect* (consisting of hostile, condescending, and tense/nervous/anxious—with factor loadings of .80 to .91); and (c) *Active Teaching Behavior* (consisting of task-oriented, clear, dominant, and active/energetic/enthusiastic—with loadings of .69 to .94). This factor structure was fully replicated by a separate principal components analysis computed for subsequent behavior ratings of these teachers, recorded while talking about and talking to their high- and low-expectancy students. On the basis of these results and the homogeneity of the variances of all variables, three composite variables were created by averaging the relevant ratings. All results were reported for three composite variables only.

To explore the possibility of further reducing the data, time ANOVAs were computed. These ANOVAs yielded no changes over time for dogmatism and negative affect, and a trend of moderate, linear increases in active teaching behavior over time. We therefore decided to average the data across the three times, and present only the means of the three measurements for each channel.

Reliability of Judges' Ratings

Split-half reliabilities were computed for the three composite variables by correlating the mean ratings made by the first seven judges with the mean ratings made by the remaining eight judges. This type of correlation estimates the effective reliability of the mean rating by any randomly chosen group of eight judges with the mean of any of the randomly chosen group of seven. To find the effective reliability that any randomly chosen group of 15 judges would have, we applied the Spearman-Brown formula for correcting reliabilities to reflect the number of raters used (Rosenthal, 1982).

Reliabilities of the judges' ratings were computed separately within the three time periods mentioned earlier. Because reliabilities did not vary substantially across time periods, the median reliability of the three times was used. Effective reliabilities ranged from a low of .68 when judges rated the body for negative affect to a high of .95 when they rated the face for dogmatic behavior. Over all eight channels and for all three dependent variables, reliabilities were fairly consistent and quite high (Median $r = .90$).

Results

The judges' ratings, averaged over the three time points and averaged into composite scores representing dogmatism, negative affect, and active teaching behavior, were analyzed with a series of one-way ANOVAs for each channel and combination of channels. The results are presented in Table 1 and Table 2 for dogmatism and negative affect. In each table, the first three columns present the means for the three groups of teachers, and the last three columns present F-values of the omnibus ANOVA and the contrast analysis, as well as rs indicating effect magnitudes. Contrast weights were assigned to represent a linear trend from preschool (–1) to remedial (0) to elementary school teachers (+1).

Overall, the three groups of teachers did not differ in their teaching behavior (clarity, task-orientation, dominance, and activity/energy/enthusiasm) in the three educational settings. All ANOVAs yielded nonsignificant results, and the means and contrasts did not indicate any trend of differentiation between preschool, remedial, and elementary school teachers.

The groups of teachers did differ substantially, however, in dogmatic behavior (not flexible, not democratic, and not warm) and negative affect (hostile, condescending, and tense/nervous/anxious) in Tables 1 and 2. Strongly significant effects of high magnitude were found for both composite variables, showing a clear linear trend in which elementary school teachers were most dogmatic and showed the highest negative affect, whereas preschool teachers were least dogmatic and more positive affectively.

The results for dogmatic behavior are presented in Table 1. The main effects and the linear trend were evident in all channels and combinations of channels. Preschool teachers were rated as most flexible, democratic, and warm (mean of 4.34 for all eight channels combined); remedial teachers were rated more dogmatic (mean of 5.01); and elementary school teachers were rated most dogmatic (mean of 5.71). One should note that the contrast analysis yielded higher F-values than the omnibus Fs, because of the marked linear trend, which accounted for nearly all of the measured variance between teacher groups. The judges detected differences between the three groups of teachers in both visual clips (mostly

TABLE 1   Dogmatism ratings of preschool, remedial, and elementary teachers

	Preschool (M)[a]	Remedial (M)[b]	Elementary (M)[c]	Omnibus ANOVA (F)	Linear Contrast (F)	Effect Size (r)
Channels						
Transcript	4.43	5.07	5.71	4.37*	8.74***	.57
Face	4.28	5.07	5.89	5.59**	11.18***	.62
Body	4.78	5.18	5.53	2.14	4.27	.44
Audio	4.30	4.92	5.76	5.70**	11.31***	.62
Face + Audio	4.16	4.96	5.84	6.49***	12.97***	.65
Face + Body	4.26	4.96	5.71	5.91**	11.82***	.63
Body + Audio	4.36	4.91	5.51	2.83	5.66*	.49
Face + Body + Audio	4.17	4.98	5.75	5.68**	11.36***	.62
Combinations of channels						
All eight	4.34	5.01	5.71	5.71**	11.42***	.62
Verbal present	4.28	4.97	5.71	5.65**	11.30***	.62
Video only	4.44	5.07	5.71	5.09**	10.18***	.60
Face present	4.22	4.99	5.80	6.39***	12.78***	.64

The column headers include an *ANOVA results* spanning heading above *Omnibus ANOVA (F)* and *Linear Contrast (F)*.

[a]Sample size = 9; contrast weight = −1. *p. < .05.
[b]Sample size = 7; contrast weight = 0. **p. < .02.
[c]Sample size = 5; contrast weight = +1. ***p. < .01.

TABLE 2 **Negative affect ratings of preschool, remedial, and elementary teachers**

	Preschool (M)[a]	Remedial (M)[b]	Elementary (M)c	Omnibus ANOVA (F)	Linear Contrast (F)	Effect Size (r)
				ANOVA results		
Channels						
Transcript	1.92	2.08	2.36	1.59	3.10	.38
Face	1.83	2.16	2.87	6.18***	11.83***	.63
Body	2.10	2.29	2.63	2.13	4.15	.43
Audio	1.80	2.00	2.37	2.01	3.90	.42
Face + Audio	1.84	2.17	2.68	3.81*	7.51**	.54
Face + Body	1.69	2.06	2.35	2.93	5.83*	.49
Body + Audio	1.85	1.87	2.23	1.48	2.34	.34
Face + Body + Audio	1.77	.038	2.50	3.54	6.89***	.53
Combinations of channels						
All eight	1.85	2.08	2.50	3.75*	7.29**	.54
Verbal present	1.83	2.03	2.43	3.14	6.06	.50
Video only	1.87	2.17	2.62	4.29*	8.47***	.57
Face present	1.78	2.11	2.60	4.39*	8.67***	.57

[a]Sample size = 9; contrast weight = −1. *p. < .05.
[b]Sample size = 7; contrast weight = 0. **p. < .02.
[c]Sample size = 5; contrast weight = +1. ***p. < .01.

through the face) and verbal clips (including both audio and transcript components). Differences in dogmatic behavior were thus transmitted in a "multichannel" fashion, significantly detectable in nearly the entire range of separate channels investigated.

The results for negative affect are presented in Table 2. The main effect and the linear trend for all eight channels combined were similar to the pattern observed for dogmatic behavior. These effects were contributed mostly by the face and by channel combinations including the face, whereas the results for the body and for all verbal components were much weaker (and nonsignificant). Thus, the faces of elementary school teachers appeared to the judges to show more negative affect, and the faces of preschool teachers appeared to show the least negative affect, but their speech (both content and delivery) and their bodies did not indicate such differentiation among the three groups of teachers.

It should be noted that the judges' mean ratings showed a consistent pattern of differences between the three attributes across the three groups of teachers. Mean ratings for negative affect centered around 2, ratings of dogmatic behavior centered around 5, and active teaching behaviors were rated even higher, ranging from 5 to 6 on the 9-point scale. The consistency of this pattern was independent of the differences found between the three groups of teachers in dogmatic behavior and negative affect.

Discussion

If affective teacher behavior can be considered a criterion for evaluating teachers, the results tended to support the commonly held belief about the high quality of Israeli preschool teachers. Preschool teachers transmitted the least dogmatism and negative affect, elementary school teachers were most negative and dogmatic, and remedial teachers occupied a position between these two groups. The observed effects were strong and consistent, with high effect magnitudes.

Differences among the three groups of teachers were found in the affective domain (dogmatism and negative affect), but not in direct, actual teaching behavior. A further distinction in our findings concerned the differentiation of channels: Whereas differences in dogmatic behavior were found in both visual and verbal channels, differences in negative affect were detected mostly in the face.

This pattern—finding differences in affective variables but finding no differences in behaviors directly related to actual teaching—is quite interesting. Harris and Rosenthal (1985) reported somewhat similar findings in the mediation of teacher expectancy effects. In meta-analyses of 31 teacher behaviors, they found stronger expectancy differences in affective behaviors and emotional climate variables (e.g., positive climate, negative climate, eye contact, smiling), whereas smaller effect magnitudes were found for some direct teaching behavior (e.g., task-orientation, direct influence, work-related contacts). Teachers seem to be more balanced and equitable in direct teaching behavior than in affective behavior. We found similar patterns in our subsequent videotaping of teachers talking about and talking to their high- and low-expectancy students (Babad et al., 1987). It seems that in behaviors most directly related to actual teaching, teachers try harder to control and monitor their behavior. Sometimes they even consciously compensate weak students with more intensive learning-related behavior (Babad, 1987).

The major finding in this study—a strong differentiation between elementary, remedial, and preschool teachers in the quality of affective transmissions—is highly interesting, but it must be treated as suggestive at best. The findings indeed confirmed empirically a commonly held belief in Israel about the relative high quality of preschool teachers compared to elementary school teachers, but the small size of the sample and the fact that sample representativeness could not be ascertained limit the generalizability of these results. On the other hand, it must be remembered that all teachers in the sample were recommended and selected into a program leading to a "senior teacher" status, a fact that minimizes the probability that a top group of preschool teachers had been coincidentally sampled with a bottom group of elementary teachers.

The results provide no hint as to what might have caused the observed pattern. It might be that a process of "natural selection" operates to divide prospective teachers into the preschool, the special education class, or the elementary school, and that these natural dispositions might be reflected in the behaviors investigated here. On the other hand, it is equally conceivable that the types of educational contexts they experience lead teachers over the years to manifest differential patterns of behavior. Of course, it is equally possible that these factors interact with each other and with other factors to cause the differential pattern reported above.

The method we used in this investigation differed from the conventional context-dependent methods of measuring teacher behavior: It displayed only the teacher (and not the students) to the observers; it broke down teachers' verbal and nonverbal behavior into specific and isolated channels and combinations of channels; and the judgments were based on extremely brief samples of teacher behavior. Comparing three groups of teachers working in disparate educational contexts, we found that they differed in affective behaviors but not in direct teaching-related behaviors. We also discovered that, whereas some affective behaviors (i.e., dogmatism) were transmitted in both verbal and visual channels, other affective behaviors (i.e., negative affect) were mostly visual, detected from the teachers' faces.

Note

1. These teachers were selected from a larger sample of teachers to represent groups of unbiased and biased teachers (Babad, Rosenthal, & Bernieri, 1987). However, since all Bias X Type of Class interactions and bias main effects for each channel yielded nonsignificant and negligible effects, we omitted this variable from the present report.

References

Babad, E. (1987). *Social cognition, interpersonal behavior, and personality differences in teacher expectancy research.* Unpublished manuscript, Hebrew University of Jerusalem, School of Education.

Babad, E. Y., Rosenthal, R., & Bernieri, F. (1987). *Speaking to and about students: Diagnosing teacher expectations from verbal and nonverbal behavior.* Unpublished manuscript, Hebrew University of Jerusalem and Harvard University.

Bales, R. F. (1950). A set of categories for the analysis of small group interaction. *American Sociological Review, 15,* 257–263.

Dusek, J. B. (Ed.) (1985). *Teacher expectancies.* Hillsdale, NJ: Erlbaum.

Flanders, N. A. (1967). Interaction analysis in the classroom. In A. Simon & E. G. Boyer (Eds.), *Mirrors for behavior: An anthology of classroom observation instruments* (Vol. 1, pp. 1–49). Philadelphia, PA: Research for Better Schools, Inc.

Harris, M. J. & Rosenthal, R. (1985). Mediation of interpersonal expectancy effects: 31 meta-analyses. *Psychological Bulletin, 97,* 363–386.

O'Sullivan, M., Ekman, P., Friesen, W., & Scherer, K. (1985). What you say and how you say it: The contribution of speech content and voice quality to judgments of others. *Journal of Personality and Social Psychology, 48,* 54–62.

Rogers, P. L., Scherer, K., & Rosenthal, R. (1971). Content-filtering human speech. *Behavioral Research Methods and Instrumentation, 3*, 16–18.

Rosenthal, R. (Ed.) (1979). *Skill in nonverbal communication.* Cambridge, MA: Oelgeschlager, Gunn, & Hain.

Rosenthal, R. (1982). Conducting judgment studies. In K. R. Scherer & P. Eckman (Eds.), *Handbook on methods in nonverbal behavior research.* Cambridge, England: Cambridge University Press.

Rosenthal, R., Blanck, P. D., & Vannicelli, M. (1984). Speaking to and about patients: Predicting therapists' tone of voice. *Journal of Consulting and Clinical Psychology, 52,* 679–686.

Rosenthal, R., Hall, J. A., DiMatteo, M. R., Rogers, P. L., & Archer, D. (1979). *Sensitivity to nonverbal communication: The PONS test.* Baltimore, MD: Johns Hopkins University Press.

Simon, A. & Boyer, E. G. (Eds.) (1967–1970). *Mirrors for behavior: An anthology of classroom observation instruments: Vols. 1–12.* Philadelphia, PA: Research for Better Schools, Inc.

Understanding Complexity: A Gift of Qualitative Inquiry

Alan Peshkin

Introduction

Qualitative inquiry encompasses a broad band of practitioners who knowingly and willingly group themselves together, despite differences in the conception and practice of their research methodology. These differences necessitate locating oneself on a continuum of qualitative inquirers, so that onlookers have some idea of the specimen of practitioner in their midst.

Since 1972, I have been studying American communities and their schools, usually their high schools, in different settings—so far, in rural, fundamentalist Christian, and multiethnic settings. My data-collection means approximate those of the traditional ethnographer, including long-term fieldwork, with the usual participant observation, collecting of documents, and interviewing.

My approach to data collection enables me to be there, as anthropologists tersely characterize their research procedure. Being there is central to my point of understanding complexity. The "there" in the case that I draw upon for this paper is the California community I call Riverview, where I focused on Riverview High School, a multiethnic, grades 9 to 12 school of 1,600 students—33% black, 33% white, 20% Hispanic, 12% Filipino, and 3% others.

In methodological terms, ethnographers are there, as anthropologist James Fernandez puts it, "in the fullness and weight of their personal presence" (1986: 244). Now, not all matters we hope to understand in educational research require "the fullness and weight" of our "personal presence," but it is this way of relating to the objects of inquiry that largely distinguishes qualitative from quantitative research methodology. For in this manner of presence we bring first, the complete range of our senses to our investigations; second, the amplitude of time in which to be attentive; and, finally, the breadth of scope, that is, the fullness of what we are willing and what we are able to attend to. It is these three attributes that enable qualitative inquirers most notably to address and understand complexity.

The complexity I meant to explore in Riverview and Riverview High School relates to what I call the play of ethnicity. Simply put, I wanted to understand

Peshkin, A. (1988). Understanding complexity: A gift of qualititative study. *Anthropology and Education Quarterly, 19*(4), 416–424. Reproduced by permission of the American Anthropological Association from ANTHROPOLOGY & EDUCATION QUARTERLY 19:4, December 1988. Not for further reproduction.

what impact, if any, student ethnicity had on the formal and informal operations of the school. This entailed following ethnicity wherever it led me. "Quantities are *of* qualities," observes philosopher of science Abraham Kaplan (1964: 207), and one set of qualities of interest in the play of cross-ethnic group social interactions is specified by the terms "best friend," "most influential person," and "boyfriend/girlfriend." To explore these qualities, we administered a questionnaire to a stratified sample of several hundred students. I value the picture I can create by the resulting numbers. However, the larger part of my exploration of ethnicity proceeded by means of qualitative methods, particularly, but not exclusively, via open-ended, multi-session interviewing. These two aspects of interviewing—open-ended, multi-session—must be emphasized because they give shape to a type of interview that is particularly congruent with the intent of qualitative inquiry to get at complexity.

Qualitative and Quantitative Inquiry Contrasted

Before presenting the data obtained at Riverview, I will briefly contrast qualitative and quantitative inquiry in regard to the point of complexity.

Psychologist Lee J. Cronbach's 1954 presidential address for the Psychometric Society dealt with what he jocularly called the two worlds of Clinicia and Psychometrika. He compared and contrasted these worlds, basically in terms of their substantive and methodological orientation. Cronbach said,

> *Neither philosophy is more correct. The clinician's [read qualitative researcher's] passion for complexity is almost certainly a valid way to conceive of the universe. The Psychometrikan's passion for reduction is a practical compromise, to simplify problems enough so that scientific methods can come to grips with them. (1954: 266)*

Setting aside some moot points in these words, which Cronbach himself might see differently today, I focus on the two variant passions that Cronbach identified—for complexity and for reduction. The instruments that researchers devise in the name of reduction incorporate a purposefully narrowed order so that they can capture these aspects of the phenomena they have selected for investigation. The instrument's structure endows the outcomes with the promise of certainty, whether significant or not. The prespecified intent of quantitative inquiry is matched by the specificity of the instrumentation designed to fulfill or realize this intent. Thus are the gray and the ragged, the murky and the amorphous precluded. The instrument is adapted to a concrete and thus an abstracted or reduced diversion of a phenomenon. In the precision of this adaptation is the potency of the instrument's capacity to render.

The prespecified intent of quantitative inquiry contrasts with the relatively unprespecified intent of qualitative inquiry, which fastens on the ordinary, inexhaustible, awful, and enormous complexity of the circumstances of the social phenomena we investigate. Since qualitative inquiry is potentially responsive to the totality not the abstraction of an object, it is responsive to that which quantitative research is likely to preclude.

Quantitative inquiry finds its ultimate strength in the structure of the controlled experiment. Its findings are expressed in the disembodied, formal research report. Qualitative inquiry finds its ultimate strength in the vast opportunity that the holism of being there makes possible. Its findings are expressed in the multitude of forms that the qualitative research report is allowed to take.

In quantitative inquiry, researchers tend to look hard and to look once, seldom much more than once, as in the questionnaire or test performance, at least with respect to a given individual. In this fact is the trimness and orderliness that establishes the economy of this form of research. In qualitative inquiry, researchers tend to look again and again, and they look, moreover, in the varying moods and times of both researcher and researched. Thus, it gives credence to the contextual nature of social phenomena, that is, to the fact that they are protean, shaped by and embodying passions and values that are expressed variably in time and place. In these facts are its efficacy for capturing the surprise, disorder, and contradictions of a phenomenon.

Those who turn to qualitative inquiry deny neither the utility nor the necessity of finding regularities and of making generalizations and predictions. They are attracted more to a form of investigation that by considering the extraordinary variability of things is replete with ambiguity. By taste, talent, and personality, they are disposed to use the means of qualitative inquiry. These means allow researchers to bring to bear all the potency for learning contained in the full range of human senses.

It surely is the case that each mode of inquiry addresses different questions. For example, educational psychologist Lee Shulman identifies different levels of inquiry that one can direct to reading, each level associated with different data-collecting means. He ends with a level—found, for example, in reading, golf, human intelligence, etc.—which he illustrates with the question, "What is the underlying or explicit system of rules by which this complex activity is accomplished?" (1981: 7). Understanding these complex activities requires the methods associated with qualitative inquiry, as for example, in understanding not their elements or attributes but the *game* of golf, the *act* of reading, or the *play* of ethnicity, which is, as I have indicated, the particular complex focus of my research.

Shulman's observation is explicated by considering the research on dropouts done by Steinberg, Blinde, and Chan, who wrote,

> *It is not clear why being of Hispanic origin appears to contribute above and beyond socioeconomic disadvantage or language minority status to a greater risk of dropping out. . . . Unfortunately, we find no analyses that assess the independent contributions of socioeconomic status, language usage, and ethnicity to dropping out. (1984: 116–117)*

Yet, what if we had analyses which would allow us to assess the independent contributions of these three variables? What would these analyses tell us that would not be preliminary to further inquiry? For each of these variables truly incorporates an array of elements that for the purpose of instrumentation is operationalized into compact scales. Steinberg, et al., do not acknowledge the enormity of the task of disaggregating the variables, and locating other elements not embodied in their operationalization. Take ethnicity, just one of the three variables, whose blooming confusion I will momentarily illustrate: What do we really know when we know someone is Mexican?

Steinberg, Blinde, and Chan further wrote that because the finding that Hispanics' dropout "cannot be attributed solely to their greater economic disadvantage. . . . some other factor peculiar to Hispanic youngsters is at work" (1984: 118). Qualitative research is specially productive in finding "peculiar" factors.

Peculiarities of Ethnicity in Student's Social Interactions

Someday, somehow, I will have ploughed through the abundance of data I obtained for examining ethnicity among Riverview's high school students. At this point in time, and for the purposes of this paper, I will simply present a sampling of the data in raw form. The following segments will illustrate the type of data obtained by qualitative inquiry that illuminate complexity.

> *Log entry:*
> *Today I saw two sets of three girls standing within ten feet of each other. The first was of three black girls standing very close to each other and talking happily. The second was of one black, one white, and one Mexican girl standing no less close, and talking no less happily. Each set took no heed of the other.*

> *Log entry:*
> *Black female and Filipino male sitting in back of her play tic tac toe on the blackboard. They play game after game until the teacher gets the class to do a worksheet.*
> *Three black girls carry on the following talk during free time before class begins:*

Sarah: "You stole my lipstick."

Tammy: "No, I didn't. It just got into my purse."

Felicia: "That's your heritage coming out."

Tammy: "What do you mean, my heritage?"

Sarah (to Felicia): "What about your heritage?"

Felicia: "I'm Jamaican. My mom would slap my hand if I stole anything."

Segments of interview with Felicia, the girl above who said she is Jamaican, following a questionnaire she took:

AP: "I see that out of your three best friends, one is black, one is white, and one is Italian. If I'd given you five spaces, would you have included a Mexican and a Filipino?"

F: "Not a Filipino. I have Filipino friends, but they're not my best friends."

AP: "You say that influence of your ethnicity on what clubs you join is both helpful and unhelpful."

F: "I guess that question is asking me does it matter which groups I join because of my color. I guess, yeah, because I know next year I'm gonna join the Black Student Union."

AP: "OK, so that's an influence in a helpful direction, would you say?"

F: "Yeah."

AP: "And it's unhelpful . . . "

F: "Because it's like the club is set up for black people, right? But then it's unhelpful because I don't feel like I should be in a club just because of color. I think it would be helpful to me, like telling you that there's no limitations to what you can do because of your color, and learning about black people, something that can help me better myself."

AP: "Several things occur to me, Felicia. One is that you are very, very open to having the closest relationships with people who are not black. Two, that you are strongly conscious of being black and it is important to you, as I see from your questionnaire where you said that if I wanted to know you, the second most important thing, after your ambition to work in law enforcement, is your black identity. I would have guessed that someone who felt as you do would have blacks as best friends."

F: "I guess I'm pretty unusual. It's just real important to me that you would know that I like being me. I'm proud to be me. It's just like saying that I have to be me. My friends, they're from different ethnic groups, but they know how I feel."

AP: "But who you are does not seem to influence who your choice of friends is."

F: "Right. Because people are people. It doesn't matter to me what color they are."

Summary of interview with white, sophomore male, Chuck Kenton:

Chuck tells me that his dad does not mind if he has as friends black males and females, but he draws the line at romantic involvements. "To me," Chuck says, "It doesn't matter." He explains that he feels no prejudice toward any group, just toward individuals within a group who are mean to him.

Overheard in the teacher's room:

A white teacher tells other white male colleagues about his son, a junior at Riverview High School, who had been referring to fellow black students as "niggers." This got to his father, who then asked his son, "What about Ron Tally and Carl Patton?" These are other Riverview students. His son answered, "They're not niggers; they're my friends."

Segment of interview with Ron Tally, black, senior male:

"I think most whites realize blacks are OK, but not all blacks. Same as us. We realize whites are OK, but not all whites. I think people are OK, but not all people. Then, they just happen to put that racism in there and put a little color to it. I never really experienced harsh racism. I think everyone is starting to realize they're in the same boat. They're just treating people as people. Like when someone gets bad and says, 'Fuck you, nigger,' I don't think they really mean it in a racial sense. It's just your color's the obvious thing, just something a person can refer to. I put that word in the same class with asshole or jerk. Just another word; instead of saying asshole, they say nigger. I think maybe only 10% of the people say nigger really mean it in a racial sense."

Conclusions

What do I make of all this? To begin with, the this I have presented here is a very small portion of my data that pertains to the play of ethnicity; furthermore, it is premature to try to get at its meaning. But, tentatively, I see in student behavior a recoding of the meaning of color, a recoding that says: black and white are colors of people I like and of people I do not like. Black and white do not automatically translate into danger, avoidance, or revulsion. And I see in student behavior a secularization of ethnicity. It remains sacred primarily in the sense that one must willingly and proudly proclaim one's ethnic origins. Beyond this, ethnicity operates as a semipermeable membrane that permits the transgress of other cultures' values and behaviors.

From exploring the nature of ethnicity among Riverview's adults, I postulate that Riverview High School is like Brigadoon, Brigadoon being the fantasy community that in the play by that name appeared to mortals only one day every hundred years. In the Brigadoon-like multiethnic Riverview High School, which appears in the life of its adolescents for four years, students are disposed to be just people, like any other people. However, given the general persistence of ethnic identity in American society, I suggest that the adolescent view that being ethnic is not cool is likely to be replaced when, as adults, they find solace and company among those they designate "my people."

As I see it, qualitative inquiry is a wonderful meld of opportunity—which relates to what is possible; personality—which relates to what we like to do; and actuality—which relates to what we perceive of the phenomena under study, and to what, following our perceptions, we should do about them. Given the unpre-specified or vaguely prespecified [emergent design] nature of the qualitative inquirer's scholarly intentions, and given the immensity of the means we bring to data collection—no less than the fullness of ourselves, I suggest that qualitative inquiry resists standardization. It is, therefore, idiosyncratic in regard to our ends, our means, and the forms we adopt to present our findings. Such idiosyncrasy is in keeping with the complexity of the social world we choose to study.

For now, I can better point to complexity as the right perception to hold about the play of ethnicity at Riverview High School, than I can set forth the outcomes of my understanding of ethnicity. Clearly, perceiving that things are complex precedes understanding their complexity, which notion Hamlet might have had in mind when, in the presence of Marcellus and a ghost, he said, "There are more things in heaven and earth, Horatio, than are dreamt of in your philosophy." What I hear Hamlet saying is, "Horatio, my man, the things of this world, both at Elsinore and beyond, are damnably involved, convoluted, obfuscated, nonlinear, and downright 'mutatious.' So, if you hanker to do qualitative inquiry, there's no limit to the good work to be done. Heed, though, a word of warning: have no truck with ghosts. The other side will never believe you."

Notes

Acknowledgements. A version of this paper was presented at the 1987 Annual Meeting of the American Educational Research Association in Washington, D.C. It benefited from the critical comments of the Fat Data Group (Illinois Branch).

The illustrative data on ethnicity were collected by fieldwork supported by the Spencer Foundation and the University of Illinois' College of Education, Bureau of Educational Research, and Research Board.

References

Cronbach, L. J. (1954). Report on a Psychometric Mission to Clinicia. *Psychometrika, 19*(4): 263–270.

Fernandez, J. (1986). *Persuasions and Performances: The Play of Tropes in Culture.* Bloomington, Indiana: Indiana University Press.

Kaplan, A. (1964). *The Conduct of Inquiry.* Scranton, Pennsylvania: Chandler.

Shulman, L. (1981). Disciplines of Inquiry in Education: An Overview. *Educational Researcher, 10*(6): 5–12, 23.

Steinberg, L., Blinde, P. L. & Chan, K. S. (1984). Dropping Out Among Language-Minority Youth. *Review of Educational Research, 54*(1): 113–132.

Chapter 7

Ethics

A discussion of ethics in research is essentially a discussion of the values of the researcher. Earlier we talked about the proposition that research is a value-laden undertaking; nowhere is this more true than in the area of ethics. Personal values will determine what one considers unethical in the conduct of his or her daily life and in the conduct of his or her research. In an attempt to standardize ethical behavior, many professional societies (e.g., American Psychological Association, American Sociological Association) have established and published guidelines for researchers. The guidelines are taken seriously; a breach on the part of the researcher may result in expulsion from the profession. This chapter discusses the major issues involved in maintaining ethical standards of research.

In 1992, the American Educational Research Association published a set of ethical standards for educational researchers ("Ethical Standards," 1992). These standards were designed "not only to guide the behavior of researchers but also to protect them from the questionable demands and pressures of employing agencies and sponsoring institutions" (p. 23). The standards offer guidelines with regard to six major areas: responsibilities to the field; research populations, educational institutions, and the public; intellectual ownership of research products; editing, reviewing, and appraising research; sponsors, policy makers, and other users of research; and students and student researchers.

In this chapter we will not refer to those guidelines as such, but rather will outline some of the ethical quandaries which are present at each stage of the research process. Some of these quandaries are spoken to by the various published guidelines but many are not. We do not have answers for all of the questions we will raise in this chapter, but we believe it is crucial to be aware of the questions themselves. For those gray areas it comes down to you and your particular situation: what do you think is wrong and what do you think is right?

Choice of Research Question

As indicated in Chapter 4, the first step in the research process is the choice of a question to investigate. Ideally, a research question should flow from some interest on the part of the researcher. However, as Smith (1990) points out, in the real world of finishing degree programs, tenure, publish or perish, and grant-grabbing, questions may well be chosen because they can be answered quickly or have a good chance of being funded.

This raises an ethical issue: is the researcher committed to a study of the question or to the idea of promotion or grant money? Does it matter? We think so. It is our belief that this issue of commitment can influence the remainder of the research process, from data-gathering and analysis to reporting the results. If you have no real interest in the topic under study, you may not be as thorough with your analysis or as careful with your participants as you might be were you intellectually committed to the research question. There may be cases where shoddy research is better than none, but they are few and far between.

Data Gathering

There are many ethical issues related to data-gathering and we cannot discuss them all in this chapter. (However, we recommend your further perusal of the references we cite and of those cited in the end-of-chapter readings.) Primarily, of course, the researcher has a responsibility to collect honest data, and not simply make them up as Cyril Burt did in his infamous twin studies of the 1950s in order to show that intelligence was hereditary. Besag (1986) calls this injunction the Great Commandment: "Thou Shalt Not Fake Thy Data." Other than that very obvious ethical violation, the three issues that we touch on here concern the safety of the research participants, the researcher's relationship to the participant, and the researcher's reaction to knowledge of illegal behavior. In the readings at the end of the chapter you will find some other issues dealt with as well, such as the use of other researchers' test items, the improper use of measuring instruments, and some of the special problems in conducting historical research.

Participant Safety

By safety of the participants, we are referring not only to an absence of physical harm, but to the protection of the participants from emotionally, psychologically, and socially adverse effects as well. Most institutions such as universities, hospitals, and public school districts have a committee that reviews proposed research for human subjects violations. These committees are variously called Human Subjects Committees or Institutional Review Boards. You as researcher must submit a plan of research to the committee members if you wish to do a study under the auspices of their institution. Master's research projects, theses, and dissertations should receive clearance from the university's review board. They may require you to revise your plan to solve some ethical problem they find, and they almost certainly will require that you have every subject sign an informed consent form.

Informed consent means that the participants know (at a minimum) the purpose of the research, what is going to be required of them, how the data will be stored, and what harm or benefits they might receive from participation in the study. For those studies where explaining the purpose of the research to the participants ahead of time would interfere with the collection of data, the committee might require that the participants sign an abbreviated consent form and that the researcher explain everything to them after the study is over. (That is commonly known as *debriefing* or *dehoaxing* the subjects.)

In those situations where the purpose of the research is hidden from the participants lies the greatest risk of harm to the participants resulting from the research process. The most infamous case is probably that of Milgram (1963— before the days of human subjects committees), who studied reaction to authority by having unwitting subjects administer "electric shocks" of increasing strength to accomplices who were acting as though they were in pain. Of 40 subjects, 26 obediently administered (they thought) the full dose of 450 volts. Needless to say, the "shocking" participants were unaware of the real purpose of the research.

Clearly it was more ethical to deceive the participants than to actually inflict pain on the accomplices. However, imagine your state of mind had you been one of those who pushed the 450-volt button. How would you feel about yourself afterward when you were dehoaxed and told that the study was about response to authority? What emotional harm would have been done when you realized that you had been willing to inflict a lot of pain on another human being based solely on the word of someone in a white lab coat? Certainly a modern Milgram would not be extended permission by any institutional review board to conduct this kind of study today.

A related concern is with studies in which there is a control group as well as a treatment group. The medical field has many examples of giving a possibly beneficial drug to one group while withholding it from a control group to ascertain the benefit of the drug therapy. The ethical problem inherent in such studies is whether it is right to withhold a beneficial treatment from people who need it. Several times in recent memory, for instance with aspirin's effect on preventing heart attacks, medical researchers have halted the study because preliminary data indicated a large enough benefit from the drug that they could no longer in good conscience continue to withhold treatment from the control group.

Education has few such life-and-death research topics, but we do conduct studies of new educational techniques or technology. Here the quandary is not that one group will die without the new technique but that its members will be deprived of some educational benefit. Often this ethical (and political) problem is remedied by switching the control and experimental groups midway in the study to give the treatment to the original group of controls. The length of the study might have to be increased to accommodate the switching, but the comparisons could still be made between experimental and control groups. That way everybody receives whatever benefit was associated with the new technique.

Much of educational research deals with children, and this raises a unique ethical question regarding participant consent. Consent forms may alleviate some of the ethical difficulties in gathering data from adult participants, but as May (1987) points out, the same may not be true if you wish to study children. Even if there are ten layers of consent from the school district, parents, and the children themselves, the students are still on the losing end of an unequal power relationship with any adult researcher. Some children might feel that if an adult wants them to do something then they have no real say in the matter, but must go along with the adult and consent to answer questions or submit written work. May indicates that any creative adult may be able to overcome children's resistance by offering rewards for answering questions or participating in the study, but that this might be ethically unacceptable because of its coercive nature.

Researcher Relationship to Participant

Ideally, the participants in a research study should be on an equal footing with the researcher, that is, fully informed and free to participate when and if they choose. Given the nature of people, however, this clarity of relationship between researcher and researched is rarely maintained, especially in qualitative studies or collecting qualitative data.

In a study that uses qualitative methods, the researcher typically spends a great deal of time observing or interviewing the participants. As the study progresses, the nature of the relationship inevitably changes from researcher and researched to something more like a friendship (although one of the friends asks an awful lot of questions!). Field researchers (Everhart, 1977; Peshkin, 1984) say that it is at this point that they obtain their best data, yet at the same time they are the most ethically vulnerable. Although the participant may forget for a time that the researcher is conducting a study, the researcher never forgets. Everything is grist for the analytical mill, even comments made only because the researcher is regarded as a friend.

In some cases, to gain the rapport and trust necessary for collecting valid qualitative data, the researcher has (in the words of Peshkin, 1984, p. 258) "donned masks in order to remove the masks of those I wanted to observe and interview." These deceptions allow a researcher to gain more and better data, but leave her or him in an ethical dilemma and feeling vaguely disreputable. (The Peshkin reading at the end of the chapter discusses this in much more detail.)

A more serious problem arises with covert research, in which the researchers do not reveal themselves as such at all. Rather, they simply blend in with the group of people they wish to study and observe them on the sly. One example of this sort of study is *When Prophecy Fails* (Festinger, Riecken, & Schachter, 1956), in which covert researchers joined a group of people who believed the world was soon coming to an end. At the predicted time there were as many researchers assembled as there were actual believers. (Perhaps that is why "prophecy failed." As it turned out, the covert research activity was not only an ethical problem, but may have seriously affected the nature of the group behavior of the actual believers.) The ethical question is whether or not it is right to invade people's privacy to study them without their permission.

There are other, less extreme types of covert activity, however. Imagine an observational study of teachers' methods of motivating students in the classroom. Obviously the researcher cannot blend into a class full of younger students, so the teacher is definitely aware of the researcher's presence. However, if the researcher explains the true purpose of the research to the teacher, the teacher may feel uncomfortable and his or her behavior regarding motivation of students may well change. Instead, the researcher is more likely to offer a general explanation such as, "I just want to see what a year in a fifth grade classroom is really like." This may be enough to gain access to the classroom, but you should be aware that it is not completely honest.

Knowledge of Illegal Behavior

In some studies the researcher comes into unforeseen possession of knowledge about illegal activities, or may actually participate in the illegal behavior. The ethical questions are what to do with the "guilty knowledge" (Polsky, 1967), and whether or not a researcher ought to have "dirty hands" (Klockars, 1979).

There are many examples of guilty knowledge and dirty hands among naturalistic researchers or those who collect qualitative data. Fetterman (1984) reports being involved in buying marijuana (dirty hands) while studying high school dropouts. The fact that he was not arrested by two policemen who observed the exchange brought him further guilty knowledge regarding corruption in the police force. Whyte (1984) reports voting four times for the same candidate during a congressional election in order to conform to the standards of a group he was studying at the time.

Survey returns can also result in guilty knowledge if the researcher has coded the surveys so that individuals can be identified from them. Consider a questionnaire that investigates how teachers handle standardized achievement testing in their classroom. What if the school district is using a standardized test that has mandated elaborate security measures, but the teachers are reporting that they opened test packets a week early to look at the items and give practice tests to their students? What would you as the researcher do with that knowledge? To whom is your responsibility? Is it to the subjects of your study, the teachers? Or is it to a wider audience of some sort? Taken to an extreme, the ethical questions of illegality and researcher responsibility could imply that some topics simply cannot be studied ethically. Take the following as examples:

1. axe murders in action;
2. the lifestyles of active child pornographers;

3. the teaching styles of mentally and emotionally abusive classroom teachers; and

4. the ongoing political corruption of a school district superintendent.

Can a researcher observe what is going on without any responsibility for those who are victimized by the subjects of the study? In the above cases there is real harm being done to the murdered individuals, the abused children and students, and to the operations of the school district. Could you as the researcher justify such studies? Do the ends in any way justify the means? That is the critical concern, and it involves a balancing of the benefit of the study against the ethical violations inherent in its design. We would not feel justified in conducting any study in which we tacitly had to condone murder or abuse. On a smaller scale it is our opinion that if a study involves clear ethical violations of any sort and has no wider benefit than your own professional accomplishment, that study should not be conducted.

Analysis of Data

The primary issue during analysis is summed up by Besag (1986) as the Sort of Great Commandment: "Thou Shalt Follow Thy Data Wherever [They] Lead Regardless of Whether They Agree With What Thou Thought Previously Or Not." Many quantitative researchers have had to face the temptation to round a probability value either up or down to make their results conform with their expectations. And all beginning statistics students are (or should be) cautioned that it is not ethical to change their hypotheses to fit their results. (In the readings, Brookover touches on another analysis issue: whether increasing computer technology leads to inappropriate analysis of data.) Naturalistic researchers or those who collect qualitative data are not immune to problems in this area, either. They have a duty to search relentlessly for evidence that is contradictory to their foreshadowed theories.

Your ideology can be an ethical problem in some sense during the data analysis stage of research. If you embark on your study with an avowed intent to reform society, it is incumbent on you to diligently seek out data that support the status quo as well as those which indicate the need for reform. Of course, the same can be said for researchers who support the status quo; their ideology may prevent them also from seeing the other side of the issue. This can be true regardless of the methodology you are using. It is possible to word questions on a survey so as to gain only information that is favorable to your hypothesis or expectation. Likewise, interview questions can be slanted and the responses taken out of context to conform to a particular ideology. (If you are skeptical, confirmation can be found by watching the nightly news or reading any newspaper.)

As an example, we know of a student who wished to do a historical study of the life of Hitler to "prove" that he (Hitler) was a bad man. We do not wish to imply that we believe Hitler was a good man, only that the strong ideological statement the student was making before he even began to gather data indicated that he might not be able to consider alternate theories. Ideological convictions are not necessarily a hindrance, but beware that they do not blind you to other interpretations of your data. And, as indicated in Chapter 3, never try to "prove" anything through research.

Reporting Results

The question of to whom the researcher is ultimately responsible is of primary importance during the reporting phase of research. Participants generally are provided anonymity or at least confidentiality regarding their participation in the research study. For most analyses of quantitative data this is easy to do, because when you average a string of numbers no person's name is attached to the average. Questionnaires can be handled so that nobody knows who returned them. With quantitative data there is more concern with protecting the identity of the subject from anyone who might have access to the raw data rather than the final research report.

Reporting qualitative data, however, is another matter. Often collecting qualitative data, for example through interviews, involves fewer participants and they are often fully described as individuals. Even if participants are assigned pseudonyms in the report, anyone familiar with the school or the community in which the study took place may be able to identify them. The participants should be told at the outset (in the informed consent form) that this is the case, so that they can decide whether or not they wish to take the risk of social harm or embarrassment that may result from being identified in the final report.

There is a related problem unique to the reporting of historical research. Suppose that you are doing a research project on the life of an eminent educator who is no longer living. Whatever you discover and report will not affect the dead person in any way, but what about his or her friends and relatives? They could suffer a great deal of social harm and embarrassment if you indicate that the educator in some way did not really live up to his or her reputation. Do public figures give up not only their own but also their family's right to privacy?

Another quandary during the reporting phase involves who has legitimate rights of access to your data. Suppose you are doing a study of classroom teachers and you have assured them confidentiality. At the end of the study the principal asks to see your data on one particular teacher because there have been parental complaints regarding that teacher's classroom behavior. What do you do? To whom is your responsibility? Is it to the teacher, to whom you promised confidentiality? Is it to the principal, who allowed you to do the study in the school in the first place? Or is it to the students, who may not be learning all they could because of their poor teacher? If you as researcher think about such issues ahead of time, you can clearly state in your informed consent form precisely who will or will not have access to the data.

As a way of handling the dangers inherent in the ideological issue brought up in the previous section, Peshkin (1986) has suggested that researchers owe it to their readers to examine and clearly report their own biases in the research write-up. In this way, the readers can make up their own minds about whether or not the researcher sufficiently considered alternate explanations or pursued contradictory data. Unfortunately, few researchers are as self-aware and willing to disclose themselves as is Peshkin. (If you read *God's Choice* [Peshkin, 1986] you will find that at the end you know almost as much about Peshkin as you do about Bethany Baptist Academy.)

Summary

Developing an awareness of the ethical issues inherent in educational research is an important part of your education in research methods. This involves investigating your own values and perhaps those of your sponsoring institutions and professional associations as well. Each stage of the research process has attendant ethical dilemmas, some of which are addressed by written standards, but many of which are not. In the end, much depends on the individual integrity of the researcher.

Discussion Questions and Activities

1. Individually or in groups, look up more information on Cyril Burt and his purported twin studies, Festinger's study of the prophecy that failed, Milgram's shocking studies, and perhaps Humphreys' tearoom trade study. Report back to the class and discuss the ethical violations involved in each study.
2. Go over your institution's informed consent requirements and forms. How would the wording vary for the following two research projects?
   a. A study in physical education that required an experimental group of fifth graders to exercise for thirty minutes every day for a month, with the researcher monitoring their pulse and blood pressure. A control group did no exercise for the month.
   b. A naturalistic study of active PTA members in a small community, with researchers interviewing the subjects.
3. How can you do research with children and be sure that they really are consenting and are not being coerced or intimidated into participation?
4. Can the following topics be researched ethically? Why or why not? Would not it be helpful to understand how these things develop? Do the benefits outweigh the costs?
   a. teaching styles of emotionally abusive classroom teachers
   b. political corruption of the district superintendent
5. Is it ethical to be sole author on a research report where you sought help, for example, because the statistical analysis was more complicated than you are capable of doing or understanding by yourself?

6. How would you feel if you were the principal of the Bethany Baptist Academy and had just finished reading the Peshkin article? A parent? The host family of the researcher? Is it likely that school, or any other like it, will ever allow another researcher in? Was Peshkin justified in his deception?
7. Discuss class members' ideas for their own projects (or studies they have found in the literature of their field) and examine them for ethical problems or issues.
8. Critique the ethical guidelines from the American Educational Research Association cited in this chapter.

Introduction to the Readings

The first two readings, "A Half Century of Educational Research Ethics: Developments and Failures," by Brookover and "The Ethics of Historiography and Why It Doesn't Work," by Button, were paper presentations at the same session on the ethics of research at the annual meeting of the American Educational Research Association in San Francisco, California, in April 1986. The session included Wilbur B. Brookover's overview of educational research ethics, H. Warren Button's discussion of ethics specific to historiography, as well as presentations on the ethics of quantitative, qualitative, and applied research. The Brookover and Button readings have points in common with our chapter on ethics, but they also include additional issues that we did not cover. Brookover touches briefly on a number of ethical quandaries that he believes have not had enough attention in the past, while Button discusses the nature of truth and the role of ideology in doing historical research.

The third reading, "Odd Man Out: The Participant Observer in an Absolutist Setting," is Peshkin's account of his ethical concerns with the role deception he practiced in his 18-month study of a fundamentalist Christian school. Although lengthy, it is included because we believe that Peshkin's introspection can acquaint beginning and experienced researchers who collect qualitative data and are concerned with capturing the perceptions of participants with important issues that they may face while doing research in the field.

A Half Century of Educational Research Ethics: Developments and Failures

Wilbur Brookover

Although I have been involved in educational research for approximately 50 years, I did not find writing this paper an easy task. The most difficult part was trying to find a way to organize the paper so that it focused on the topic, but, at the same time, said some things that I wanted to say other than a history of educational research ethics. It is appropriate to indicate at the outset what the paper *is not* and to give a brief introduction to what it *is*.

I could have focused on the philosophy of research, but this is not my forte. You will find, however, that a bit of philosophy of science creeps in here and there. Neither is this a review of the literature on research ethics. I have read, however, considerable of the social science research ethics literature over the past few months. There is very little literature focused specifically on educational research. Much of the social science literature is applicable, and the paper reflects considerable of that, but it certainly is not a comprehensive review.

I was tempted to follow the suggestion of a colleague to review and describe the unethical cases of which I am aware either from the literature or personal knowledge. This is not my approach, but it will be noted that I have used a number of cases to illustrate points that I want to make. A discussion of the known cases of unethical research behavior, however, raises the issue of how common are these practices. Are known and unknown unethical practices the norm or are they only a few cases?

Hopefully, this will not be viewed as an inventory of my personal experiences, but some have been used to illustrate existing practices.

The paper is organized in three sections: first, the developments in social and educational research ethics over the past 50 years; second, the identification of the major issues in contemporary research ethics; and third, a discussion of some ethical issues that are in my opinion unresolved and insufficiently recognized in educational research.

Brookover, Wilbur. *A Half Century of Educational Research Ethics: Developments and Failures.* Paper presented at AERA, 1986.

Developments in Social and Educational Research over the Past 50 Years

My analysis of the developments over the past 50 years is based primarily on two sources: first, my personal knowledge and recollection and second, a cursory review of the most extensive bibliography that I have found (Diener and Crandall, 1978). Diener and Crandall refer to approximately 400 sources in their "Ethics in Social and Behavioral Research."

Prior to 1940 there was little discussion of social-behavioral science research ethics. I have no recollection of a discussion of research ethics in my graduate education in the late 1930s. I distinctly recall, however, a conversation with a fellow graduate student who subsequently became an eminent sociologist, in which he expressed the opinion that the way to get ahead and become famous in sociology was to climb on the shoulders and destroy if possible the work of the prominent pillars in the field. We did not at that time discuss the ethics of this approach but some of the subsequent research behavior of my fellow student clearly reflected this position which he apparently considered quite ethical.

There are two references prior to 1940 in the Diener and Crandall bibliography. The first is a 1919 comment in the *Nation* on spies as scientists (Boaz, 1919). The second is a 1938 paper dealing with adult conversation (Henle and Hubbell, 1938). This like many of the other 400 references illustrates the problems of accurate and objective information gathering. There are seven references in the Diener and Crandall bibliography from the decade of the '40s. Some are not concerned with ethics directly but are reports of research in which problems may be illustrated. There are, however, articles on participant observation and in the late '40s articles on bias and on dishonesty in interviewing. I recall some suggestions concerning interviewing in the instructions provided by the National Opinion Research Center for their interviewers in the early '40s. More dramatically however, I recall a discussion of an alleged tampering with the study of a Southern town. Allegedly a manuscript by Hortense Powdermaker reporting the study entitled "After Freedom" was held up by reviewers and possibly used in part for John Dollard's "Caste and Class in a Southern Town." The latter was first published in 1937. The Powdermaker book, which reportedly was in manuscript before the Dollard book, was later published in 1939. References to the sequences of manuscript and publication dates are made in the preface and introduction to a 1968 edition of "After Freedom." So far as I know no investigation or determination of the exact facts of this affair was carried out by the Anthropological Society, the Psychological Association, or the American Sociological Association. But rumors about it were disseminated widely.

Seventeen publications during the decade of the '50s are listed in the Diener and Crandall bibliography. A number of these focus on interviewing bias and deception in the research process. This is the beginning of considerable literature and the development of codes of ethics concerning subjects being deceived and potentially harmed by the research process. Only one of the seventeen references is concerned with educational research.

One of the celebrated cases of this decade concerned with deception and other ethical problems was the famous case study of the cult that predicted the end of the world (Festinger et al., 1956). The researchers infiltrated the group which believed the world was coming to an end and assembled with members of the group for the coming. On this occasion when "Prophesy Failed" as many or more researchers were assembled to observe the occasion as believers of the group. The report of this research, "When Prophesy Fails," reported the deception and discussed the problems of participant observers affecting the nature of the group behavior.

It was during this decade of the '50s that an unpublished study of opinion leadership and opinion networks was discovered to be based on completely faked data. The well known sociologist who had prepared this report was released from his association with the research agency that had sponsored the study. Although the data-faking was not revealed until much later, some of the presumed twin studies in Great Britain by Sir Cyril Burt were reported during the decade of the '50s.

The remaining 375 or so references in the Diener and Crandall bibliography were published between 1960 and 1978. The rate and amount of concern no doubt continued into the '80s. The problems of participant observation, interviewing bias and objectivity, and deceptions of subjects all continued to be subjects of concern in the '60s and '70s. Honesty and accuracy in reporting research, the use of appropriate methods, the researcher's role and the use of research in public policy received increasing attention during this period.

Concern with various aspects of research ethics in the social-behavioral sciences has resulted in the development of codes of ethics by the Anthropological Association, the Psychological Association, the Political Science Association, and the Sociological Association. Also related to educational research are ethical standards for Research in Child Development and standards for evaluation projects by the Joint Committee on Standards for Educational Evaluation (Krathwohl, 1985). Generally these involve some professional ethics as well as specific research ethics. We know of no evidence one way or another whether the adoption of the codes has resulted in more ethical patterns of behavior among social and behavioral scientists.

Until quite recently there has been no significant movement toward the adoption of an ethics code in the American Educational Research Association. The Women's Committee of the Association developed guidelines for the consideration of race and gender issues and a committee is now at work on a code of research ethics. Most educational researchers are aware of one or more of the several discipline codes. There are, however, some issues that are peculiar to educational researchers.

The extensive involvement of educational researchers in educational policy development and the dependence of educational policy makers on research findings greatly enhance the need for clear definitions of researcher and policy maker roles and for understanding the ethical issues involved in each of these roles.

Some Common Foci of Contemporary Ethical Concerns and Codes in Social and Behavioral Research

Time and space does not permit a comprehensive examination of all the concerns and issues identified in contemporary ethical codes. The identification of the more common ones seems appropriate however. A cluster of concerns in the behavioral science and education areas involves issues of informed consent, harm to experimental subjects, balancing the benefits to society against potential harm to subjects, and deception of subjects. The issues in this area have not all been resolved. In some respects the problems are exacerbated in cross-cultural research. The problems of informing host country subjects and the uses that may be made of cross-cultural research become particularly significant when research may be used as a cover for intelligence activities. Project "Camelot" highlights a number of these issues (see Horowitz, 1967).

The responsibility of the researcher to report honestly and accurately to fellow scholars and students and to the public continues to be a major focus of concern in our research. This, of course, encompasses the whole series of some-times unrecognized issues involving research methods as well as misinterpretation and faking of the findings. There are numerous illustrations of inappropriate research methods, interpretation, and data collection. We will not attempt to identify these, but I can testify to an early temptation in my research career to try to have the findings support my desired conclusions.

Another area that has received much attention in recent years is the relationship of the researcher role and the public policy advocate or social reformer role. It is easy and tempting for the researcher to consciously or unconsciously over-interpret research findings in supporting particular policy positions. Warwick and Pettigrew (1983) have discussed these issues comprehensively and suggested some guidelines for researchers dealing with matters of public policy. These issues are particularly relevant in educational program evaluation. Researchers have often exploited their research role and interpreted findings in a questionable professional manner. This may be more prevalent in legislative and court testimony than in other situations.

Another set of issues concerns the identification of research sponsors and the freedom to report research findings in various research settings. Universities generally protect the right to publish, but there are many instances in which restrictions may be applied by various means. We have not yet defined adequately the parameters of freedom in reporting versus the pressures to supply particular interpretations or suppress research findings.

There are, of course, issues of common honesty in the use of research funds and in the representation of the researchers plans and competencies in research proposals. Exaggeration and questionable practices are not uncommon in these areas.

Although there is a long history of the following set of issues there remains the necessity to have fully understood ethical practices in regard to recognition of research assistants' contributions, credits for all persons contributing to the research, plagiarism from students' papers, or extended plagiarism from other sources. I was somewhat astounded some years ago to discover while in Puerto Rico that the first edition of my *Sociology of Education* had been published in Peru in Spanish with no permission from either the publisher or me. I was pleased that somebody thought it important enough to translate and to publish in Latin America, but I would have liked to have known about it and negotiated at least a modest royalty. I am currently involved in another situation in which the rights of the authors and the possible questions of public domain are involved. Are public agencies such as the State Department of Education privileged to reproduce and distribute research and related reports that were supported by funds provided by other public agencies?

A final issue of ethical concern to behavioral scientists, although much more to biological medical researchers, is the appropriate use of animals. Most readers are aware of the contemporary public debate concerning this issue.

Some Issues That Are Unresolved and Require Further Attention in Educational Research Ethics

Although apparently some progress is being made in defining ethical behavior in educational research, it appears to me that there is much that remains to be done in all the social sciences, but particularly in education. I would like, therefore, to identify some areas in which we have unresolved problems that warrant particular attention by both educational researchers and educational policy makers.

The first of these involves the process of research proposal evaluations. The competition for limited resources to support research makes the decision-making process extremely important to the life chances of many researchers and the development of the science. We have instituted peer review processes to objectify the evaluation process, but this does not guarantee that the best research proposals are awarded support. The composition of review panels with varying knowledge, competence, and personal interests may predetermine the nature of the research supported. The power to select peer review panels and also to accept or reject recommendations is highly subject to political considerations. Politics in proposal evaluation is the process of determining who gets what, when and how.

I could recite several personal experiences in which questionable ethics in proposal evaluation prevailed. My first experience was with a foundation whose president had encouraged me to summit a particular research proposal. It appeared that the grant would certainly be forthcoming. Shortly, after it was rejected, however, an announcement was made that a member of the foundation staff would undertake a research project in the area. A review of that proposal revealed that major portions had been lifted directly from the one I had written. That researcher's inability to obtain the cooperation of schools resulted in complete failure of the project. Another research proposal that was rated very highly by the peer panel was rejected by the agency's director who had a personal preference for research in another area irrelevant to the RFP [request for proposals]. In another case a person with competing interests and some influence acquired access to the review panel and injected false or distorted information into the proposal evaluation process.

I would not want to leave the impression that my experience has been characterized by the cases mentioned. I probably have received my share or more of grants during the past 25 or 30 years, but I cite these cases to illustrate that the system of proposal evaluation and funding does not always work in a highly ethical fashion.

The second area that I would like to discuss is the use of questionnaire or test items. Are the individual items in copyrighted or uncopyrighted tests, scales and other research instruments public property? Our copyrighted "Self-concept of Academic Ability Scale" has been used in literally hundreds of studies, some with our permission and some without. On occasion, the items have been modified and the scale has been used in an inappropriate fashion. It is possible that in some instances there has been essentially independent development of test or scale items. A recent experience involves an attempt by my colleagues and me to develop and validate an instrument to assess effective school learning climates. I cannot honestly identify the sources of some items used over a period of five or more years. We developed an extensive pool of items that have been tried and discarded or kept, depending upon their validity in distinguishing between effective and ineffective schools. The current composition of the instrument contains some items that are identical to those instruments put together by others. I do not know whether or not they were originally formulated by our staff. There are obviously differences of opinion about how this issue should be resolved. Since I have had experience with both sides of the question, I find it difficult to indicate what I think are proper practices.

To me, a more important issue involving tests or other instruments is the use of such instruments to measure and to control variables that are clearly not measured by the instrument. For example, hundreds of educational research projects have used some measure of "intelligence," aptitude, or previous achievement as an indicator of a student's ability to learn. Frequently such instruments are used to "control" some fixed ability to acquire knowledge, skills, or other behavior. This common practice is followed, even though it is well established that such instruments measure only a sample of what students have learned prior to taking the test rather than the ability to learn. Such measures are frequently so highly correlated with the measure of educational outcomes that their use as controls in studies intended to measure the effects of teaching or educational programs destroys the possibility of identifying such effects. Probably a pervasive belief in wide differences in "ability" to learn impels researchers to use instruments to measure "it" that clearly do not do so. In a similar fashion, the socioeconomic composition of schools has frequently been used as a measure of school learning environments with the conclusion that there are no other school environmental characteristics that affect student outcomes. Our failure to accurately measure such variables and our belief systems concerning them have resulted in highly inappropriate use of instruments and decidedly questionable research findings.

Another area in which we have done little in the definition of research ethics involves the fact that some social or behavioral experiments are impossible in our society. Our society's ethical restraints on the treatment of human beings prevents the design of many controlled human experiments. Although the few instances of extreme isolation provide some near experiments in the learning of language, for example, our society would not knowingly permit a researcher to carry out a controlled experiment in which a child's isolation from human language interaction would occur. In similar fashion we would not knowingly permit researchers to deny children the opportunity to learn to read, for example, in order to test an experimental instructional program. We are unlikely to ever be able to solve the nature-nurture question for this reason. In our attempts to do so we have frequently used completely inadequate measures and methods. The importance that we attach to this question has sometimes resulted in entirely inappropriate and, as demonstrated by the Sir Cyril Burt case, faked data. I suggest that the ethical position to take is that we simply will not do the necessary kinds of research to answer certain questions. The social and behavioral sciences do not have the license to manipulate human subjects as we do physical objects.

Moving to a different area, I want to indicate that the availability of computer technology and extensive data banks has provided the opportunity to misuse data, the likelihood of nonverification of the validity of the data, and, in many instances, the inappropriate analysis of data. This calls for the careful development of ethical practices for this new arena of research. My own identification of inaccurate analyses and data use which have resulted from computer processing of unknown and/or unverified data suggests the necessity for a new set of ethical standards in social and educational research.

The last area that I wish to call to your attention is the unrecognized bias in research resulting from the researcher's social values and position in society (see Pratt, 1978). The typical educational researcher's position as a high status member of society and the prevailing belief in great differences in innate ability to learn, believed to be associated with meritoriously acquired status, provide the bases for biased research methods and biased interpretation of research findings. Such interpretations in turn provide support for educational policies that maintain the established social system. There is little evidence that we have recognized this bias resulting from dominant social values. Certainly we have not developed ethical standards to overcome such bias. All our research dealing with questions of equality of educational opportunity, differentiation of educational programs for presumedly different types of students, and many other areas of research are subject to bias resulting from social status, norms, values and practices.

I trust all recognize that I have no easy solutions to the ethical issues which I have tried to identify. I simply want us to recognize that we have not solved the ethical problems in the 50 years of educational research with which I am acquainted.

References

Boaz, F. (1919). "Correspondence: Scientists and Spies," *Nation, 109,* 797.

Diener, E. & Crandall, R. (1978). *Ethics in Social and Behavioral Research,* Chicago: University of Chicago Press.

Dollard, J. (1937). *Caste and Class in a Southern Town,* Garden City: Doubleday, 3rd Edition (1957).

Festinger, L., Riecken, H. & Schachter, S. (1956). *When Prophecy Fails,* Minneapolis: University of Minnesota Press.

Henle, M. & Hubbell, M. B. (1938). "Egocentricity in Adult Conversation," *Journal of Social Psychology, 9,* 227–34.

Horowitz, I. L. (ed.). (1967) *The Rise and Fall of Project Camelot,* Cambridge, Mass.: M.I.T. Press.

Krathwohl, D. R. (1985). *Social and Behavioral Science Research,* published by Jossey-Bass: San Francisco.

Powdermaker, H. (1939). *After Freedom: A Cultural Study of the Deep South,* New York: Viking Press; republished with preface by Elliot Rudwick (1968).

Pratt, V. *The Philosophy of the Social Sciences,* London: Methuen and Co., Ltd., Chapter 12.

Warwick, D. P. & Pettigrew, T. F. (1983). "Toward Ethical Guidelines for Social Science Research in Public Policy," in Daniel Callahan and Bruce Jennings, *Ethics, The Social Sciences and Policy Analysis,* New York: Plenum Press.

The Ethics of Historiography and Why It Doesn't Work

H. Warren Button

My great-grandfather was a bishop in some obscure New England religious sect. For him there were no ethical problems, since the way to goodness was in the Word of God. (Occasionally I envy that stern, bearded man, whose portrait frowns at me as I pass it by.) His son was a master mechanic at the Springfield Armory, I am told. He made rifles, but did not shoot anyone. For him ethics had no place in technology, or in science. They were ethically neutral, and occasionally I envy him too. My father was a matter-of-fact man, but I suspect he sometimes puzzled over what we could call ethical issues. If ethics was puzzling to my father, ethical problems are downright confusing to me, personally and professionally. I have what may be the grave misfortune to live and write at the end of the twentieth century. But I will put the matter more formally, and as a historian sees it.

History as a discipline did not exist in the United States during the life of my great-grandfather, and the Revealed word has not figured much in the discipline here. I will start my story a little later.

Once upon a time—as a proper historian should say, circa 1900—there was a world in which professional academic historians lived. It was a world in which history was the scientific search for factual "truth." With sufficient accuracy in detail, history would be infallible in its conclusions. History, being both factual and scientific like science generally, was neither ethical nor nonethical, but above all that. What the historian was to do was in principle straightforward, though enormous in scope. Events were to be described "as they really were," truthfully. In hindsight this was too good, too simple, to be true.

It was too good in several ways. It was too good because "truth" as a concept became more complex as more thought was devoted to it. Was "truth" a manifestation of divine law? Was it some preexistent entity awaiting discovery? Was "truth" to be judged, as William James somewhat crassly put it, by its "cash value," its utility? Purely historical "truth" was not logically demonstrable, as a Euclidian proposition was. And truth was not simply factual, although facts could be true, that is verifiable.

The nature of truth became more complex upon examination, and the nature of history became more perplexing. That onetime dream of a universal "social

Button, H. W. The Ethics of Historiography and Why It Doesn't Work. Paper presented at AERA, 1986.

science," explaining all human affairs and being the base for global and accurate prescriptions, faded away. If history was to be factual, which facts, however well verified, would convey "truth"? Obviously, not all facts were retrievable, and not all facts were of equal significance. Taken one by one, facts, the historian's data, were trivial, as any single datum is.

Scientism was outlived. Factualism was discarded. Ethical neutrality was no longer plausible. The historian's subject and its treatment of it were shaped by matters which were in another sense historical only. They were and are shaped by nationality and nationalism, by political convictions, by historians' concern for public policy, and by their devotion to good causes and laudable reforms. For my purposes here, whether "pure" science or quantitative science is ethically neutral is not pertinent. History and historians cannot be ethically neutral.

Most historians write history which is in a sense national history. To begin with an old example, in the times of Caesar, Tactitus wrote an admiring account of Germans' freedom and democracy. Tactitus was of great interest to German and other historians with teutonic leanings. One cannot imagine, for instance, that French historians were as enamored by Tactitus' account. As another example, an Englishman writing on the history of India in the past two centuries naturally treats events as seen through the eyes of Englishmen; An Indian historian sees and describes events quite differently. For most of us here the treatment of Puerto Rico by the United States may be seen as benign and generous, if not entirely productive. But from the point of view of a Cuban, the United States' occupation of Puerto Rico was and is imperialist exploitation. As historians of American schooling we begin our accounts with the establishment of the Boston Latin Grammar School and Harvard College. The preceding centuries of English universities and Latin schools are only prelude. Our nationality, like it or not, often shapes our views and interests.

Political views also shape historians' views. President Roosevelt's actions at the Yalta Conference are under attack, again or yet, by "neo-conservative" historians. Reform minded historians saw Rockefeller and Morgan at the end of the 1800s as "robber barons." Other historians saw them as "captains of industry." Concerning schools, the traditional conservative view of the early nineteenth century common school revivalists has been that they were pure-hearted reformers, solely interested in the welfare of society and of pupils. But it is possible to see and portray the common school reformers as incipient bureaucrats whose actions would protect the status quo, and were intended to. A kind of political judgment seems to have a part in reaching either of these conclusions. One cannot deny the right of the historian to have political convictions. But the historian with such convictions cannot maintain that he is ethically neutral.

Less generally, the historian may deal with particular governmental policies. Again, examples may clarify. The financial crises of farmers are given considerable attention these days, and rightly so. Therefore, it would be of interest to examine governmental agricultural policy, perhaps since the enactment of the AAA—Agricultural Adjustment Act—of the 1930s. Have these policies been appropriate, and if not why not? The presence of United States marines in Nicaragua through the 1920s has seemed unimportant until now. But in today's controversies about the Sandinistas and the Contras, there are almost certainly historians looking again at those earlier military presences.

There is no lack of concern or debate about school policies. Has the centralization of control of public schools been a net gain? Have gains in expertise and economy outweighed loss of local control? You will remember debates of a decade or so ago concerning the interpretation of the history of the Black family. That interpretation was important because history shed light, supposedly, on what policies would be appropriate. It would give reasons why Head Start might or might not be of value. We hear now discussions of school vouchers, and of the more general question as to whether the state monopoly, or near monopoly, of schooling is advantageous. Historians interested in bilingual-bicultural schooling, as still another example, have convictions on policy. Again, they are entitled to their convictions. Not to have them may be in another sense unethical.

Like most other educators and scholars, historians hold near to their hearts some causes and some reforms. It is still difficult, or maybe impossible, to be evenhanded when talking or writing about John Brown. Was he a saintly martyr or a demented megalomaniac? It is terribly difficult to find some compromise position between these extremes. Considering schools, was Prudence Crandall, who opened her school in Canterbury, Connecticut to Black girls, a foresighted idealist? Usually, though not always, she is treated that way. But could she have been an agent provocateur for William Lloyd Garrison and abolition? The two were acquainted, and Miss Crandall shared Garrison's convictions. Or, consider the academies, nonpublic secondary schools that provided most of the secondary education available in the century following the Revolution. Were the academies most of all a hindrance to the establishment of publicly supported high schools? Or were they useful in severing the connection between the church and schools? How would they be seen by those now advocating a voucher system? Thinking in something like the same way about the Committee of Ten, which established the college preparatory curriculum as the standard one in high school. Was this useful in preserving the integrity of the high school? Or is one inclined to see it as limiting even more the usefulness of the high school to children of the workers? There would be differences of opinion, depending upon the cause that was favored.

The history we write, then, is shaped by any or all of several factors: our nationality, our politics, the causes we support—or the causes we oppose. We cannot be objective. If we reflect on the matter we must make choices, and those choices will sometimes be ethical choices. It is not that we look for ethical problems, but that we cannot avoid them.

No matter what the basis of our ethical standard is, there are two or three areas in which the ethical position is nearly categorical. We must not misrepresent by intent: We must be honest. Plagiarism is dishonesty and a deadly sin, which I wish was to be punished in purgatory. And probably we should not degrade or belittle, at least without good cause.

History written with intent to deceive is relatively rare. It is not true that George Washington chopped down the cherry tree, but the fabricator of that fable was not a historian, and standards were different when Parson Weems wrote his best seller. No counterpart of Sir Cyril Burt or of his fudged data come to mind. One must go back at least to the last works of Charles Beard on the eve of World War II to find even the suspicion of counterfactualism of such magnitude. Partly, this is because historians are, generally speaking, honest. Partly, pragmatically, we know we cannot get away with it. C. P. Snow pointed out that the nature of science makes it self correcting, and that holds true of history also.

Misrepresentation is of course dishonesty. Another sort of dishonesty is plagiarism. This too is rare, though not as rare as I wish it was. Now and then a probably desperate doctoral candidate plagiarizes—I know of three or four such cases. Of course that is entirely too many cases, but for several decades now I have read dissertations written at my own university and at others. Now and then one sees a part of a book that is not above suspicion. To plagiarize is to steal the work of another.

If benevolence or kindness is a commendable ethical value, then the writing of history which degrades, derides, or belittles is unethical, unless there are overriding reasons. One could ridicule Horace Mann's conviction that smoking cigars was unspeakably sinful, but unless it makes a point—as I hope this does—the foible is irrelevant. More seriously, the attacks on John Dewey a few years ago did come close to vindictiveness, and served no reason apparent to me.

A more subtle and more pervasive shortcoming, I maintain, is failure to admit to bias, or possible source of bias. Occasionally—far too seldom—history is funded. The source of funding surely could affect the historian's view. Some years ago Alan Nevins wrote his biography of John D. Rockefeller after receiving a substantial subvention fund from the Rockefellers. That biography is generally favorable, for whatever reason. But an earlier derogatory book by Ida Tarbell could have been affected by her father's having been bankrupted by Rockefeller. Either book is best read in the light of such knowledge.

We take it almost as a given that most histories of colleges and universities have been written by their loyal and devoted supporters. Probably that is why so few professors have been described as less than learned, and why the feet of clay of so many otherwise distinguished college presidents are so well draped. I maintain that the historian is ethically obligated to state his biases so far as he is aware of them, and the source of possible biases.

Honesty, decent benevolence, a kind of toleration, hope for benefit for schools or for society: This is the briefest of lists of ethical principles. Nevertheless, they lead to ethical dilemmas. One or two of these demonstrate the difficulty. First, there was the matter of the Civil War colonel. He is a local hero, still admired. A village is named after him, and he has prominent descendants. But every official record and every biography by his contemporaries demonstrated that he could have been the model for General Jubilation J. Cornpone of "Lil Abner" in the comic strips. My tentative subject lost every battle with two exceptions. Once he successfully avoided the battlefield. Another time he surrendered on the eve of a battle. He suffered an undignified wound at the hands of his own enlisted men. There were court martial charges against him. He was forced to resign. The kindest thing his superiors ever said about him was that he was utterly obscure. Should I have written and published my revisionist essay? Truth is better than fiction, better than legend. But the long gone colonel still had admirers, and proud progeny. The choice seemed to be between honesty and kindness; a real dilemma, a conflict of ethical principles. It seemed better to remain silent. I did not want to be like the man who shot Santa Claus.

Or consider the dilemma of one of our graduate students. He believed passionately in an educational revisionist thesis or theory, not as an infatuation but with lifelong allegiance. He located information which might support the beloved thesis. The evidence was not perfect, but it was usable. It seemed, after a few weeks of working with it, to contradict that beloved theory, most regrettably. Thereupon he changed the topic of his dissertation. The theory seemed to promote a good cause. The information was factual, that is to say truthful. I was inclined to disagree, but I did recognize the quandary. Other examples come to mind, but two serve the purpose. Our ethical principles are too often mutually contradictory.

The kind of a panacea a historian could hope for cannot be found. The history of ethics offers me little help, although it is to be wished that it was not so. From Aristotle to Bentham and beyond are contradictions, hazy words and misty phrases. This is, after all, the end of the twentieth century. I listen today hoping to hear described an ethical base which will resolve my quandaries.

Odd Man Out: The Participant Observer in an Absolutist Setting

Alan Peshkin

Introduction

The time has long past since fieldwork was done primarily in remote, preliterate societies. Today's fieldwork is frequently located close to home, at least in a geographic sense (see Messerschmidt, 1981). This proximity usually precludes the need to learn a new language, to puzzle through exotic belief systems and political structures, or to learn how to participate in the life of a community with few important points in common with one's own.

Nonetheless, fieldworkers may be culturally distant from the people and institutions encompassed by their field site. When this is the case, they are still strangers despite their proximity to home, and they must be alert to the requisites of gaining access, on the one hand, and of maintaining it, on the other. In both instances, proper role behavior is essential.

Behaving properly, generally speaking, is the primary focus of this article. The several issues I will discuss were generated by my recent eighteen months of research in a fundamentalist Christian school and church. As a Jew, both at the time of my entry in and departure from the pseudonymous Bethany Baptist Church and Bethany Baptist Academy, I was, and indeed remained, the odd man out. This was the basic fact affecting my relationship and response to the world of Bethany.

Bethany Baptist Academy is a K-12 school with approximately 350 students, 70 percent of whom are from Bethany Baptist Church families. At the time of my study, it was eight years old and financially viable. It had established itself as a respectable educational institution in the community of Hartney, the city of 50,000 people in which it is located. Based on the relatively low turnover rates of both students and teachers, I judge it to be a stable school. In short, Bethany Baptist Academy gives every indication of having a secure future.

The issues I will explore in this article are (1) the nature of the participant observers' deception, (2) the limits of the role deception they practice to advance their work, and (3) the limits of the human participant observers' role. In this third point, I am using Freilich's distinction between the human and the research

Alan Peshkin, "Odd Man Out: The Participant Observer in an Absolutist Setting," *Sociology of Education* 57: 254–264 (1984). Reprinted by permission.

participant observer. The former refers to behavior and outlook that characterize researchers in general, as human beings, unrelated to the requirements of their research projects. The latter refers to behavior fashioned to be effective for research purposes (Freilich, 1970:535–36).

Before discussing these issues, I will describe the background of my study, the fieldwork procedure, and my role in and reactions to Bethany.

Background of the Present Study

Following two studies that documented the close relationship between school and community in a rural setting (Peshkin, 1978, 1982), I organized a third study of school and community in a fundamentalist Christian setting where the fit would be extremely close. Bethany Baptist Academy belongs to the doctrinally conservative, 1,000-member American Association of Christian Schools, which aspires to build schools based on Scripture. As fundamentalists, the Academy's sponsoring church and its national education association see the Bible as the word of God; it contains nondoctrinal sections (for example, Revelations, Acts, and most of the Old Testament) and doctrinal sections. While respecting all of Scripture, the Academy's instructional activities are particularly devoted to doctrine, which they perceive as absolute truth.

"Christian" is used in this article as it is used by Bethany's Christians: It refers only to born-again Christians who share their view of Scripture. Under the particular doctrinal circumstances that characterize Christian schools, I planned to explore those elements common to all schools—educational purpose, authority, the control system, teaching methods, instructional materials, teacher-student and home-school relationships, student culture, etc. Specifically, I planned to learn what form these elements take when a school is shaped by educators who are chosen for their full allegiance to a monolithic doctrine.

Procedure

Gaining Access during the Pilot Study

Gaining access in previous studies was straightforward and simple. In the midwestern village of Mansfield, I had the blessings of an introduction from a respected resident of a neighboring community and the entree provided by a much-beloved superintendent who took me under his wing. In Mansfield, I was the urbanite who was naturally uninformed about rural life and wanted to learn all about it; Mansfielders were pleased to tell me. In the five-village school district of Unit 110, I studied a school-closing controversy, the latest incident in more than twenty-five years of discord over consolidation. Everyone was deeply involved and upset; everyone wanted to tell his or her story. The disputants found it therapeutic to speak to the dispassionate outsider, who saw the point of everyone's story and never interrupted its telling. Successful contact was no more complicated than a telephone call.

In preparation for my Christian-school study, I organized nine months of preliminary fieldwork in Catholic, Lutheran, Seventh Day Adventist, and Christian schools. The purpose of this year was to see Christian schools within the context of traditional parochial schools and to become informed about the nature of Christian schools and the process of collecting data in them. We were welcomed into the parochial schools and readily obtained consent to observe classrooms and interview teachers. I was not prepared for the response from Christian schools. Two of them flatly denied us access. A third allowed us in for two weeks and told us not to bargain for more time. A fourth gave us unrestricted access that lasted almost one full semester. It ended with a long-distance call from the pastor that aborted my plans to be there for two semesters and raised my anxiety level for the next two years. We had to leave, he explained, because my research assistant made several of his teachers nervous; he said it would be better if my assistant was a Christian. What he meant to say was that as long as we were not Christians, our presence in his school would be intrusive.

Despite gaining access to Bethany's church and school, our fifth effort and the one Christian school that never denied us entry or gave us qualified access, the experiences in the previous four alerted me to the Christian educator's sensitivity to one's religious identity. I was soon to learn why: They felt besieged by a hostile federal government (particularly by the Internal Revenue Service) and by those state legislatures that tried to regulate Christian schools. They also felt that the media misrepresented them. Accordingly, Christian leaders developed a paranoid disposition, and because of my access problems during the pilot year, I developed some paranoia of my own.

In any event, after one semester of pilot work at Bethany Baptist Academy, we requested permission from Pastor Muller, the Academy's superintendent, to attend his church's activities and study his church's school for at least one full year. He knew from our first contact three months earlier that I was not a born-again Christian; this was the important fact to him. He did not ask what I was. From my entry commitments, he learned and accepted that I planned to write a book, that my ignorance and the ignorance of my fellow educators about the Christian-school phenomenon motivated my inquiry, and that my research assistants and I would respect Bethany's prevailing behavioral guidelines. To me, this meant refraining from any speech or deed that contravened the behavior expected of Bethany adults. Even if we were not Christians, we meant not to act in un- or anti-Christian ways; we never promised to act in pro-Christian ways.

Data Collection at Bethany

In the course of eighteen months of fieldwork (one year proved to be too short), I obtained data by a variety of means. I moved into a small apartment in the home of charter members of Bethany Baptist Church and became, in time, a member of the family: I ate meals, celebrated birthdays, and went to church with them. I attended all regular church and school activities. Two research assistants joined me only in the school aspect of the study; they observed classrooms and attended school activities scheduled during the school day. We interviewed all teachers, about one-third of the high school's 120 students, and some parents. The interview results became the basis for questionnaires administered to students, teachers, and parents; the questionnaires provided data for quantitative analysis. I also collected all available school and church documents. Finally, my experiences were clarified by both students and teachers who related to me as informants, albeit within limits set by Bethany's doctrine.

My Role in and Response to Bethany

My role at Bethany had no explicit label. I spent most of my time at school, but I never became one of the several types of people who staff a school, such as teacher, counselor, and custodian. To the students, I was Dr. Peshkin or Doc; to the teachers I was Alan. To both, I was the professor from the University of Illinois who came to learn about Christian schools so he could write a book. In no other way was I covered by a role that could disguise that I was a researcher always collecting data. I tried to look as much as possible like any other Christian adult when I attended church and school activities, ate lunch in the dining room, and rode the school bus to a basketball game. I wanted my non-Christian identity to be forgotten because I believed that to the extent it was palpable, I would not have the invisibility necessary for Bethany's people to be themselves. Furthermore, I feared that if they were continuously conscious of me as a non-Christian, they would become uneasy about the unrepentant intruder in their midst and see grounds for my dismissal. Despite the security their doctrine provides them in sacred and secular matters, Bethanyites feel threatened by what they see as a hostile society. Beyond the towering walls of their doctrinal fortress, danger is rampant. I felt like the enemy within, and feared discovery and dismissal.

The general role I meant to establish was, in Gold's terms (1969), participant-as-observer, although during each school week I moved to the role of fairly complete participant in church services (with the paraphernalia of data collection seldom visible) and of fairly complete observer when I sat in the back of classrooms and meetings and took notes or tape recorded.

During the first year of my intensive fieldwork, I employed two graduate student research assistants—an ex-Catholic male and an ex-Lutheran female. Both of them joined me in being "odd men out." We were outsiders, stuck with the stigma of what we were not—born-again Christians. The environment that Bethany had shaped to fit its view of Scripture contained no one—custodian, secretary, bus driver, cook, or teacher—who at the time of hiring was not already a born-again Christian and fully willing to join Bethany Baptist Church. Moreover, all students and teachers signed a pledge committing themselves to right conduct everywhere, at all times. The headmaster called this his "twenty-four-hour umbrella."

My interview and questionnaire data clearly document that (1) student life centers around their church and school; (2) doctrinal standards govern their choice of friends, reading matter, and television programs; and (3) both the ordinary persons and the significant others in their lives are overwhelmingly born-again Christians. Viewing their doctrine as "Truth" with a capital T, Bethany, within its day-school limitations, logically establishes a total institution. Although unlike Goffman's (1961) total institutions in major respects (for example, it is the preferred voluntary, not the rejected coercive, choice of most students), Bethany Baptist Academy has managed the means to encompass its students' lives—that is, their contact with information, ideas, and people. The headmaster's twenty-four-hour umbrella is basically reality. In this setting, the non-born-again Christian is and remains fully marginal.

Proselytizing is an invariable commitment of Bethany's Christians. Since it is mandated by Scripture, they are obliged to actively and energetically bring the unsaved to salvation. In classroom, chapel, and church service, children are instructed in the nature and strategies of salvation and learn to ask non-Christians the basic question, "If you died right now, do you know for sure if you would go to heaven?" They hear and exchange success stories among themselves. In this setting, we three non-Christians were not just unsaved others whom they were obliged to bring to their Lord, we were also friendly unsaved others whom they knew and liked. Wanting us to join them, they gave us explicit invitations, which we took care never to reject forthrightly. "We appreciate your sharing what you treasure," we would say, "but it is a decision we can't make now." We hoped to avoid appearing as antagonists who might lead astray their youth.

As long as we remained unconverted, we were "they" to the born-again's "we," part of the humanist crowd regularly railed against in whatever forum the Bethany educator chose to speak. We were from the world that students were taught, with about as much emphasis as they were taught anything, they had to live in but were never to become part of. We participated at Bethany under increasingly cordial, if not warm, circumstances (the consequence of our successful presentation of selves) at the same time that we endured the anomaly of being their Jesus-rejecting "they." If at church and school we were never treated with reserve, let alone disdain, we were also not the recipients of the sort of hospitality I had come to expect as fairly routine in previous studies. The students were as friendly as those in any school I have studied; the teachers were friendly but kept a distance, virtually confining their friendliness to the numerous public church and school events that dominated their lives and, therefore, my life.

The other side of the coin, that is, how we (the three outsiders) felt about them, is important to examine for its possible influence on our participation and on our collection, analysis, and interpretation of data. Although each of us was most moved by different aspects of Bethany's doctrinal stance, we rejected all of their central theological positions (for example, those on the nature of life and death, God, and Jesus Christ), on the one hand, and its applications (for example, to ERA, homosexuality, welfare, gun control, and acceptable art, literature, and music), on the other. In short, if we were their aliens, they were no less ours. Since we did our best to obscure our beliefs and ordinary behavior, they knew only in the most general way that we were alien; we, however, striving to know them better and better, became increasingly aware that except in relatively trivial matters—an interest in the same sport, author, vacation spot, etc.—we could not have been more unlike them. Thus, we needed to hide both our research purpose and ourselves.

I reasoned that since Bethany has gone to such considerable lengths to create an institution shaped totally by Scripture, we could not signal by word or deed the least overt alternative to their structure of belief and control. They overlooked the possibility that simply by our presence as likable, non-born-again Christians, we might be seen as alternatives. Therefore, we could never appear to be encouraging students or teachers to relate their doctrinal reservations and misdeeds, however valuable it was both to obtain them and to probe their meaning.

It was easy to separate the people from their beliefs and behavior. They were not automata driven by Scripture; their devotion to fundamentalism did not preclude their being warm, spontaneous, and responsive to humor. Moreover, they were cooperative and generous with their time, and they answered any questions we asked. The headmaster monitored our data collection procedures (what we observed and whom we interviewed) but never rejected a single request. Both he and Bethany's pastor, the school's superintendent, gave me many hours of interview time. I enjoyed the people, but I rejected their doctrine and its educational concomitants. While I am fully untroubled by their school's legal right to exist (established by the famous 1925 Supreme Court decision in Pierce v. Society of Sisters), I would feel threatened by a society dominated by the true believers it aims to develop, which I believe would reject people like me. I do not think we are near to such a society; indeed, Bethany's brethren believe that such a society is unattainable before Christ returns.

Questions Regarding Fieldwork

Notwithstanding the idiosyncrasies of every fieldwork setting, there are generic issues that crosscut these varied settings. Researchers react to these issues with varying personal values and assessments of fieldwork realities. In this section, I will discuss my responses to three such issues within the context of the fundamentalist setting I have just described.

The Nature of the Participant Observer's Deception

The relative ease with which I gained and maintained access in my previous studies placed me in the humanistic camp regarding the development of rapport. I believed, as Freilich does, that "rapport can be achieved by anyone who is a good and humane human being" (1970:540). I thought of rapport in terms of trust: If researchers appear good, honest, and decent, then they are rewarded with trust. If trusted, they have the open sesame to meetings, documents, interviews, etc.

This simple notion may approximate the researcher-native interaction at some research sites, but only in the roughest sense. Indeed, the humanistic view may be held by those who suffer the distortions of self-deception. Although there is an element of truth in the humanistic perspective, it is what Freilich calls the "engineering view" that more aptly characterizes the fieldworker's behavior: "The research [in contrast to the human] participant-observer manipulates situations and people to get data, and he manipulates himself to gain rapport, so that more . . . and better . . . data are collected" (1970:540). In this Machiavellian outlook, not everything goes, but deception surely does. To respond generally to the issue under discussion, deception is a sine qua non of fieldwork, varying among participant observers only to the extent that it is practiced (and to the extent that they are aware of and acknowledge practicing it).

Deception, defined here as incomplete or untrue statements of research purpose and the calculated use of masks and roles, begins at the time of first contact with the field. In changing forms, it continues throughout the period of research. Obliged to communicate their research purpose, researchers engage in deceptions, falsifying by omission and commission. For example, though he planned to study apartheid in South Africa, van den Berghe told authorities he intended to investigate the economy (Glazer, 1972:30); Whyte told Cornerville residents he was preparing a community history (Glazer, 1972:106); and Douglas, a most unapologetic manipulator, informed TV news people that he and his colleagues were studying a political convention. "What we did not say was that . . . [t]his was part of our way of worming our way in" (Douglas, 1976:171). I told Bethany's superintendent and headmaster that I thought Christian schools were a significant and unstudied aspect of American education and that I planned to write a book informing educators and the public about them. Later, when I heard a distinction made between man-centered and God-centered schools, I incorporated this distinction in what became my cover story: I had spent years learning about man-centered schools and now I wanted to learn about God-centered schools. This proved to be the salient point Bethany leaders mentioned when they introduced me to other Christian educators at meetings and conventions.

Fieldworkers, of course, present more than false accounts of their goals: They present false fronts, as well. That is, they play roles remote from any they would play under nonresearch circumstances. Douglas refers to his "saintly submissiveness" and to being a "spineless boob": "As soon as we left their office," he writes about his study of a political convention, "we spent some time venting our anger, but our servile and cowardly attitude did pay off. They later let Lum into the planning department" (1976:169). Humphreys, in his famous study of homosexual encounters in public places, claims that he had to pass himself off as a deviant in order to observe the phenomenon of interest to him. "I am convinced," he writes, "there is only one way to watch highly discreditable behavior and that is to pretend to be in the same boat with those engaging in it" (1976:103). Daniels, a woman studying the military about twenty years ago, when men dominated even more than they do today, mitigated the resistance she faced by learning "to smile sweetly, keep [her] eyes cast down, ask helplessly for favors, and exhibit explicitly feminine mannerisms" (1967:275). Fieldworkers are clear about the ordinariness of their duplicitous behavior. Douglas, for example, notes that "field research is inevitably a partly traitorous activity" (1976:139), and Gans notes that the "participant observer is acting dishonestly; he is deceiving people about his feelings" (1968:314).

Because I feared losing access at Bethany, I was more conscious of my behavior there than anywhere else I had been. Feeling alien, I was unusually aware of the personas I created to be an effective (i.e., data-collecting) presence at Bethany and of the resulting discrepancy between my research self and my human self. This awareness was the basis for my eventual understanding of how consistently and meaningfully I manipulated my behavior, blending in like a chameleon when invisibility was in order and appearing in this or that posture when I needed to produce a particular effect. In time, I realized that I had couched my trust-building demeanor within the general role of an as-if Christian, a part that required accommodations of appearance—short hair, no beard, suit and tie; language—no minced oaths ("gee whiz," "gosh," etc.) or profanity; and behavior—regular attendance at all church activities expected of Bethany members.

I also realized that by designating my accommodations as part of my efforts to create rapport, I obscured what I was doing with a euphemistic term. After all, is rapport not a good thing? We want it with our in-laws, our bosses, our colleagues, our natives, ad infinitum. Lurking behind this good thing are the imposters we become in order to pursue our research goals most efficaciously. To be sure, rapport induces trust; and I want trust because I want to obtain the natives' naturalistic behavior. Without it, my study fails. What I had not appreciated before was the mask-stripping dimension of my rapport-promoting process: I donned masks in order to remove the masks of those I wanted to observe and interview. Since the normal protectiveness of people vis-á-vis strangers is dysfunctional to my work, I need to make them drop their masks so I can achieve purposes that I have never fully disclosed to them. Accordingly, they are uninformed about what they have let themselves in for when, by the impact of my artifice, they reveal themselves to me.

The wearing of masks and the playing of roles are not moot aspects of the fieldworker's behavior. Unmasking others, the natives whom we wish to investigate shorn of their variety of defenses, is mentioned less frequently. Perhaps the self-inflicted guilt and anxiety (Gans, 1968) that accompany the researchers' consciousness that they strip masks, and the image of pain and embarrassment that this conjures up, suffice as their punishment.

In any event, though we carry differential burdens of guilt and anxiety in response to our deceptions and though we express our deceptions in different terms, for example, as "an expedient device" (Gold, 1969:38), as "exploitative" (Daniels, 1967:290), or as the jargon-laden "phenomenon of synthesizing discrepant identities" (Johnson, 1975:99), we must accept deception—in some form, to some degree—as an inevitable concomitant of the participant observer experience. Few researchers join Erickson in his concern for deception, which he expressed in his reaction to concealed—that is, fully secret—observation: "The practice of using masks in social research compromises both the people who wear them and the people for whom they are worn, and in doing so, violates the terms of a contract which the sociologist should be ready to honor" (1970:253). The consensus in the literature clearly attests, however, that without deception, things of value are lost: Participant observers deceive because they have "no other alternative" if they are to be granted access (Gans, 1976:56, see also Glazer, 1972:32), and they need the "freedom to observe meaningfully" (Yancey and Rainwater, 1970:254). More than this, we snake-oil peddlers serve not only our own ends but also the natives' to the extent that our deception gains us a fair measure of their behavior so that we can portray them accurately. Deception helps to minimize distortion.

Limits to the Role Deception Researchers Practice to Advance Their Work

Both Junker's (1960:35–37) and Gans's typologies of the participant observer's roles have the extreme point of complete or total participant. This point is tantamount to going native, a polar position in anyone's typology. The issue of going native arose for me in the following way.

Throughout the first six months of my research at Bethany, I accommodated to the realities of their world by acting, as I have said, as if I were a Christian. My accommodative role was not planned; it was the only role I could play to remain acceptable there. Since Bethany's Christians operate by a single set of rules, there is only one game in their town, so to speak, and everyone has to play in it. Notwithstanding my persisting strain of paranoia, everything went well.

That is, for six months everything went well. The situation changed when we began to interview students and teachers, using open-ended questions for depth probes. Our interviewer's role, most emphatically that of the dumb stranger or outsider, elicited a new response from Bethanyites: proselytizing. Our as-if Christian posture was a suitable cover when we were mainly observers; our actual non-Christian status did not seem to be provocative. But when we inquired about the nature of their beliefs and practices, this cover wore thin. We changed our behavior, they changed theirs. By calling attention to our non-Christian selves, we evoked the fundamentalist's commitment to go forth to all nations and spread the word of God (Matthew 28:18–20).

I fully understood the evangelizing efforts of students and teachers. Thus, I could not expect to avoid their attempts to convert me. Yet, since the human participant observer was also always present, I was bothered by the arrogance of their belief that failing to adopt their Truth placed me in eternal jeopardy. As the proselytizing continued, I became more annoyed, at least the private "I" did.

Annoyance is not a felicitous state of mind either for collecting data about a group or for writing it up. But the question here is, could I have avoided these conversion attempts? Had I gone too far with my as-if Christian and my dumb stranger roles, or to the contrary, had I not gone far enough? As part of the participant experience, should I have converted so that I could have more truly understood the natives?

To convert for the sake of the exploitative researcher's role is tantamount to becoming Gan's and Junker's total participant; I would have gone native. However, I could not have done so intermittently as long as I remained at Bethany, because once they identify a person as Christian, Bethanyites naturally expect him or her to conform to the particular requirements of that status.

Evans-Pritchard (paraphrased by Freilich) makes a distinction between culture, "which includes rules for living, thinking, and acting," and society, "which is a collectivity whose capital includes the assignment of membership" (Freilich, 1970:531). He advises fieldworkers to endorse the cultural aspect of a community and live like the natives to the fullest extent possible. In addition, he urges them to avoid the societal aspect, its membership, because this entails going native and, thereby, losing one's perspective as an anthropologist and the purposes that brought one to the field in the first place (Gold, 1969:34). Freilich uses this culture-society distinction to identify the researcher's position as a "marginal native"; he joins many writers in rejecting the over-identification or "over-rapport" (Miller, 1969), which tends to impair the researcher's objectivity.

At Bethany, I could live as the natives lived, but given their evangelizing proclivities, my as-if posture did not satisfy them. They wanted me to go native. In contrast with what is found in the preponderance of field settings, they invited and urged me to do so. They never asked me to stop being a researcher; they never called my as-if behavior into question; they wanted me to become one of their brethren. Moreover, there was no "romantic pluralism" (Nash, 1970:482) at work here on my part, no going too far in search of genuine experiences; there was little danger of developing "over-rapport." I had gone as far as I could with the deception of my fictive Christian role—farther, often, than I felt comfortable going. Though they wanted me to go all the way, I had gone as far as I could. I could neither extend my deception and indicate I was a Christian nor truly accept Christ as my personal savior and genuinely become a Christian.

Clearly, going native has different meanings in different settings. When it involves Evans-Pritchard's cultural commitment, it may mean going the long way of a Cushing, who was pressed by the Zuni to live like them (Georges and Jones, 1980:15) or the shorter way of a Whyte, who was told by Doc, his extraordinary informant, not to swear as he and his pals did (1955), or of a Liebow, who did not participate in the sexual side of the life of his street-corner men (1967). When it involves societal commitment, some researchers can go the covert participant route (Sullivan, Queen, and Patrick, 1970) and approximate membership to a most significant extent; others can refuse the offer of membership, as I did and as Ethel Waters did. She was invited to participate in homosexual activities in the course of her study of lesbians (Yancey and Rainwater, 1970:258). She was not a lesbian and she rejected activities that would have cast her in a personally unwanted role. Thus, there are limits to the extent of one's deception. Signing a pledge that he would not drink when he studied the Women's Christian Temperance Union represented Gusfield's limit (1960:106). Becoming a born-again Christian, as I have indicted, represents mine. This role exceeds the boundaries of my capacity for dissimulation. The annoyance I might have avoided and the insights I might have garnered by virtue of conversion could not overcome the feeling of personal violation this act represents.

I concede that I conclude my study of Bethany not fully understanding what it means to Bethany's Christians that God "speaks" to them, that He never fails those who truly accept Him, and that salvation guarantees eternal life. However, this would not have been revealed to me if I had pretended to be born-again. More than this, such pretense, if exposed, would have offended my Bethany hosts. If, as Wax notes, they did not resent my 'acting like them' or 'learning their ways'" (1971:49), I am nonetheless convinced they would have rescinded my access had I feigned conversion.

This discussion brings me to the final issue of this article. It also relates to the fieldworker's role, going native, deception, and successfully maintaining access.

Limits to the Researcher's Human Participant Observer Role

`Freilich's distinction between the human and the research participant observer (1970:529) reminds us that we bring two general categories of selves into the field. At times, the interests of these two sets of selves are at cross purposes, as when, for example, some situation invites behavior from the human participant that would endanger the purposes of the research participant. In this regard, Lofland writes, "People everywhere tend to need help . . . But one is the observer . . . To what degree should he—would-be neutral observer—respond to the pain and difficulty he must inevitably observe . . . ?" (1971:97). The human participant's conscience and commitments are the antagonists of the research participant's calculated appearance of neutrality—surely calculated in that he or she constantly makes judgments that must remain unmentioned and go unacted upon.

During the course of my fieldwork at Bethany, a friend presented me with a hypothetical problem. Though I never actually faced this problem, given the circumstances of Bethany it is not a farfetched one to consider. Suppose, my friend said, a Bethany student wanted to discuss his doubts about religion. Suppose he came to me, because I was the only adult he knew who was not wed to his school's prevailing orthodoxy and who, therefore, would not give him predictable responses to his distressing uncertainty. "Would you," my friend asked, "counsel this student?" I said I would not because I perceived the student's need as one that could require me to hear and, possibly, comment on the rationality of his apostasy. Her response was, "Peshkin, aren't you ever a human being when you're doing research?" In short, she wondered if I could not spare a moment for an untailored human self to intrude among the research selves I fashioned for exploitative purposes.

This exchange did not end my reflections on this problem. For many months, I daily interviewed students, may of whom volunteered detailed accounts of their deviations from the doctrinal obligations and behavioral code they pledged themselves to observe. My friend inadvertently prepared me to respond to student requests for counseling help, which, I am pleased to add, I never received. But why not counsel? Why not be human when I am doing research?

There may indeed be few occasions to be human in a field such as Bethany. There are those "work-break" times, described by Freilich (1970:533–36), when participant observers set aside the tools of data collection and seemingly act human. At these times, they resonate with what is human in both themselves and the natives.

> *At prayers, parties, marriages, and deaths a working anthropologist would stand out as an incongruity . . . . Ostensibly he is there out of neighborliness, respect for the deceased, friendship for the host, or whatever, but he really is working (Freilich, 1970:535).*

Riding back from a basketball game on the school bus, I talked to the gym teacher. We discussed our families. I ate fried peanut butter and jelly sandwiches with the Bible teacher; we shared childhood tastes not yet outgrown. I discussed the agonies of adolescent children with the speech teacher—mine of the past and hers of the present. I took no notes and asked no business questions. It was a work-break time, but I was nonetheless working. For all the humanness of the encounter, I was mindful of working.

To be sure, fieldworkers cannot remain remote from all activities that engulf them: They may help out, both volunteering and recruited to be of service in numerous human ways that may be much appreciated. By remaining aloof, they not only call attention to themselves but also risk offending their respondents, who may expect them to do their share in an "exchange of services" (Lofland, 1971:97). English sociologist Frankenberg, for example, during research in the village of Glynceiriog, was elected to the Football Club's governing committee, became its assistant secretary, and even served as its chair (1982:51). As we learn from his account, though his own initial sense of the limits of participation would not have included accepting these positions, he felt that the circumstances of the situation left him no choice but to accept them.

But researchers make judgments about the consequences of their human participants' behavior, ascertaining its impact upon their continuing need for access. Gans deftly characterizes participation observation in regard to the researcher's human role:

> *Participant-observation . . . is the taking of a formal participatory role in a social situation without the emotional involvement that normally accompanies participation; it requires the surrender of any personal interest one might have in the situation in order to be free to observe it . . . (1968:304).*

Thus, when Gans prepared to leave Levittown, his neighbors, knowing he was a liberal, concluded that he would sell his house to a black family. "They were right about my feelings," Gans recalls, "but wrong about my intentions; I wanted to do so, but because I feared it would endanger the field work I still planned to conduct . . . I did not do so" (1968:307).

In response to the previous issues, I discussed the possibility that fieldworkers may excessively identify with the natives such that they approach membership in their society. In the present discussion, I want to note the converse case and its attendant pitfalls. By their persistent inability or unwillingness to surrender their personal interests, fieldworkers risk excessive attachment to their human participant observers' role. In this case, rather than becoming too native, they remain too human. They fail to control their normal, out-of-the-field behavior sufficiently to prevent its intrusion into their research participant observer needs. This handicap precludes successful use of those fictive roles that are necessary for the fieldworker's success. Guided by their human dispositions, researchers may take the high road of minimal deception; but, I believe, the rewards received at this road's end are correspondingly minimal, although I do not mean to suggest that high deception and substantial research rewards are directly and positively correlated.

I have indicated before that Bethany is a doctrinally monolithic setting. To appear to endorse any but its single authorized position is to place oneself beyond the pale. In other settings where various factions exist, one pays a price for overidentification with any one faction; the polyvalent situation may require researchers to walk a fine line. However, if they overstep it, the results need not be fatal, especially if the values held by the contending groups are not absolutist, like those at Bethany.

Yet, to not be for Bethany's fundamentalism is to be against it. They clearly sort out people as believers and nonbelievers, as children of God or of Satan. I believe, therefore, that by counseling a Bethany student who had doubts about his faith, I would have exceeded the bounds of behavior that Bethany authorities could condone. A counseling relationship with such a student would have given me "guilty knowledge" that could have been valuable to my research, but at a price not worth paying. When I obtained such information in the course of my normal interviews, I may have been culpable in the eyes of Bethany authorities. It would have been a different case if I had knowingly entered a counseling relationship that was likely to provide me such knowledge and, worse yet, likely to contribute to the undermining of the student's faith. By this offense, I would certainly have risked losing access.

Refusal to aid the student with the wavering faith is one more manifestation of deception, because I am refraining from behavior that I actually favor. I like to help people; I feel it is important to do so. Since adolescence is a troublesome period for many American youth and since Bethany's codes of conduct and their doctrinal beliefs are unusually demanding, I can easily understand the anguish of ambiguity some Bethany students experience. To withhold counsel when capable of providing it is to be irresponsible and, moreover, to model reprehensible behavior. But—of course, there is a but—I obscure who I am in the interests of other obligations to my hosts and to my research. I avoid those human acts, as I see them, that bear short-term personal gains and long-term professional losses;

and I endure the ambiguity, with its concomitant guilt (see Georges and Jones, 1980:9; Glazer, 1972:65; and Metz, 1983:406–7), of my juxtaposed selves vying for ascendancy as I wonder if there really are occasions to be human when I am doing research. By this time, however, having grown accustomed to playing roles that maximize my data collecting capacity, my research participant observer self takes the upper hand.

Finally, in good faith, one should not undermine the work of the people under study. If, by some reckoning, their work deserves to be undermined, then researchers should cease being researchers, taking care to distinguish their researcher and reformer roles. Higher principles and overriding considerations may justify the researcher's intervention as a "human being." I do not deem the case in point to be such an instance.

Conclusion

The absolutism of fundamentalist Christian doctrine determines the nature of Bethany Baptist Academy. It demands that teachers be the most perfect instruments possible of this doctrine, that instructional materials and library books offer no alternatives to it, and that students' lives be controlled in ways approximating the control of total institutions. Doctrinal and behavioral diversity are anathema at Bethany; the true believer's absolute Truth tolerates no competitors within its confines.

For eighteen months I lived and worked within its confines, a member of the secular humanist world that Bethany's educators constantly attack, one of those with whom they were not to be yoked, according to the much quoted 2 Corinthians 6:14: "Be ye not unequally yoked with unbelievers; for what fellowship hath righteousness with unrighteousness? and what communion hath light with darkness?" My public behavior, encompassing almost the entirety of my association at Bethany, also had to conform to Bethany's single, acceptable register. Bethany's leadership consistently enforced its doctrinal and behavioral imperatives, so its affiliated adults and youth knew what to expect. So did I: Conformity was my necessary standard within the limits of my status as a known non-Christian—limits that provided me some leeway in religious behavior (for example, I did not take communion) but not otherwise in my routine, daily conduct at church and school. I clearly invited attention to my religious status by the continuing interest I showed in the particulars of their religion and their religiously oriented educational practices.

Bethany's special combination of single-minded devotion to Truth and scripturally required commitment to disseminate this Truth established the unusual conditions within which I conducted my fieldwork. I refused to follow their preferred path to salvation and go native. Thus, I had to affirm their general behavioral orientation while rejecting the doctrinal foundations that established the rationale for their entire church and school undertaking, indeed for their entire life. In fundamentalist ideals, there are no part-time Christians.

My research behavior was set in relief by the exceptionally direct behavior of Bethany's Christians. In most ways, it was rewarding to be engaged with these straight arrows; however, seeing myself in their light compounded the guilt that accompanies one's ordinary, deceptive fieldwork practices. I was odd man out in a number of ways, unreassured by the thought that I had perfectly innocuous research goals—I did not; that I could reciprocate in an exchange of services that had me doing my bit as a volunteer for the cause—I did so minimally; or that my ordinary research behavior as an as-if Christian (combined with my mask-stripping personas) did not spur Bethanyites to acknowledge unorthodox behavior and beliefs—it did.

Nonetheless, the bipolar orientation of Bethany's world, one of clear truth and clear falsehood, left little margin, so I believed, for error. I felt I was "in" on good behavior that was at variance with my own norms. Except for a handful of student informants and fewer parents, Bethany's Christians did not relate to me from the edges of their subgroup culture; for absolutist doctrine leads logically to absolutist behavioral expectations, tempered but never altered by the belief that we are sinners all, imperfect, and periodically lured by the devil's temptations. I never fully avoided the anomalous sense of being wily Satan's man of darkness and unrighteousness in this milieu that was deliberately fashioned to epitomize Christian light and righteousness.

To end on a note that bridges from this article's methodological considerations to their implications for writing up the data, I have decided to devote most of the book I plan to write, entitled "God's Choice: The Total World of a Fundamentalist Christian School and Community," to the depiction of Bethany in a way that persuades Christians that Christian schools are fine places for their children while persuading non-Christians that such schools are a menace to theirs. My characterization will be drawn from an orientation I share with Bethany—that its church and school must take the form of a total institution in order to inculcate its absolutist doctrine. Bethany's success in fashioning a total institution is the basis both for their well-being—to present this understanding I must see the world as they do—and for my distress—to present this understanding as more than pique, I must place Bethany within other convincing contexts. By these understandings I will discharge what I see as my responsibility to Bethany and to myself and the larger society.

I intend to do full justice both to the extraordinary confidence and comfort Bethanyites derive from knowing their school is God's choice and to the discomforting reaction I have to this extraordinary view.

References

Daniels, A. K. (1967). "The low-caste stranger in social research." In G. Sjoberg (ed.), *Ethics, Politics, and Social Research*, 267–96, Cambridge, MA: Schenkman.

Douglas, J. D. (1976). *Investigative Social Research.* Beverly Hills, CA: Sage.

Erikson, K. T. (1970). "A comment on disguised observation in sociology." In W. J. Filstead (ed.), *Qualitative Methodology*, 252–60, Chicago: Markham.

Frankenberg, R. (1982). "Participant Observers." In R. G. Burgess (ed.), *Field Research*, 50–52, London: George Unwin and Allen.

Freilich, M. (1970). "Toward a formalization of field work." In M. Freilich (ed.), *Marginal Natives*, 485–585, New York: Harper and Row.

Gans, H. J. (1968). "The participant observer as a human being: Observations on the personal aspects of field work." In H. Becker et al. (eds.), *Institutions and the Person*, 300–317, Chicago: Aldine.

Gans, H. J. (1976). "The West End: An urban village." In M. P. Golden (ed.), *The Research Experience*, 40–59, Itasca, IL: Peacock.

Georges, R. A. & Jones, M. O. (1980). *People Studying People*. Berkeley, CA: University of California Press.

Glazer, M. (1972). *The Research Adventure*. New York: Random House.

Goffman, E. (1961). *Asylums*. Garden City, NY: Anchor.

Gold, R. L. (1969). "Roles in sociological field observations." In G. J. McCall and J. L. Simmons (eds.), *Issues in Participant Observation*, 30–39, Reading, MA: Addison-Wesley.

Gusfield, J. (1960). "Field work reciprocities in studying a social movement." In R. N. Adams and J. J. Preiss (eds.), *Human Organization Research*, 99–108, Homewood, IL: Dorsey.

Humphreys, L. (1976). "Tearoom trade: Impersonal sex in public places." In M. P. Golden (eds.), *The Research Experience*, 85–114, Itasca, IL: Peacock.

Johnson, J. M. (1975). *Doing Field Research*. New York: Free Press.

Junker, B. (1960). *Field Work*. Chicago: University of Chicago Press.

Liebow, E. (1967). *Tally's Corner*. Boston: Little, Brown.

Lofland, J. (1971). *Analyzing Social Settings*. Belmont CA: Wadsworth.

Messerschmidt, D. A. (ed). (1981). *Anthropologists at Home in North America*. Cambridge: Cambridge University Press.

Metz, M. H. (1983). "What can be learned from educational ethnography?" *Urban Education*, 17, 391–418.

Miller, S. M. (1969). "The participant observer and 'over-rapport.'" In S. McCall and J. L. Simmons (eds.), *Issues in Participant Observation*, 87–89, Reading, MA: Addison-Wesley.

Nash, D. (1970). "The ethnologist as stranger." In J. E. Curtis and J. W. Petras (eds.), *The Sociology of Knowledge*, 468–87, New York: Praeger.

Peshkin, A. (1978). *Growing Up American: Schooling and the Survival of Community*. Chicago: University of Chicago Press.

Peshkin, A. (1982). *The Imperfect Union: School Consolidation and Community Conflict*. Chicago: University of Chicago Press.

Sullivan, M. A., Jr., et al. (1970). "Participant observation as employed in the study of a military training program." In W. J. Filstead (ed.), *Qualitative Methodology*, 91–100, Chicago: Markham.

Wax, R. H. (1971). *Doing Fieldwork*. Chicago: University of Chicago Press.

Whyte, W. F. (1955). *Street Corner Society*. Chicago: University of Chicago Press.

Yancey, W. L. & Rainwater, L. (1970). "Problems in the ethnography of the urban underclass." In R. W. Habenstein (ed.), *Pathways to Data*, 245–69, Chicago: Aldine.

Chapter *8*

Writing

The importance of writing is often undervalued. Some researchers think that because conducting a study is the real substance of the entire project then the presentation is incidental. This belief is misleading, because no matter how important your findings are they will not receive the attention they deserve if they are not clearly discussed and well presented in writing. In fact, if your work is poorly written, no one may ever read it at all. In addition, unclear writing can introduce another kind of contamination issue into the project, because it stands between the reader and a clear understanding of the phenomenon, thought, or construct being studied. For this reason, the best writing might be considered invisible writing.

This chapter discusses the format and content of a research report and how these may vary depending on an author's view of the world and methodology. Four different written projects and research reports are introduced and outlined. In addition, a number of other kinds of documents you may write as a graduate student or professional educator are discussed. After reading this chapter you should be on the road to becoming a more informed critic and producer of the written report.

After having read most of the readings in this book, you should be aware of the many ways in which a research report can be organized and written. Whether the tone is conversational or formal depends on the audience you wish to address. Moreover, there is no one set formula to follow, no outline format that fits all research studies. Generally the major aspects of design addressed in Chapter 4 constitute a logical manner in which to present the content of your study:

1. Introduce the topic;
2. state the rationale and background for the study (often, but not always, this includes a review of literature);
3. state a research question(s) or hypothesis(es) or expectations;

4. indicate subjects or participants and other sources of data;
5. describe how the data will be analyzed;
6. present the findings; and
7. conclude with an emphasis on the most important evidence to support the answers to the question.

This last section returns the reader to the rationale for the study. It shows either how the results affect the theory that launched the study or the new beginnings of theoretical work the study helped to initiate.

Four of the readings provide good illustrations of organizational format for various kinds of studies: truth-seeking quantitative (Franklin et al.), truth-seeking qualitative (Palmieri), perspective-seeking qualitative (Sims), and perspective-seeking quantitative (Vaughn & Liles) research.

Truth-Seeking Quantitative

Characteristic of the traditional truth-seeking quantitative write-up, researchers personally detach themselves from the work by avoiding the first person and employing the passive voice. For example, truth-seekers rarely if ever write, "I found that . . . " They also include few if any quotes from subjects because in the truth-seeking quantitative study the subjects' words or responses usually have been simplified (reduced) to a number. Also, when specific constructs are defined and "tested," word repetition is common because certain words refer to a particular construct such as "aggression" or "self-concept." Sentence structure is simple, and specific sections such as the review of literature, hypothesis(es) or question(s), description of data, method(s) of analysis, results, and discussion of the findings outline each aspect of the research.

The Franklin et al. reading is a good example of truth-seeking quantitative writing. The article begins with an abstract that summarizes what was done and what was found. An introduction follows which includes a discussion of the theoretical positions concerning the value of the Piers-Harris Children's Self-Concept Scale. "Procedures" outlines the research questions which stem directly from the literature review, revealing the theory-driven aspect of truth-seeking research. As Firestone points out, the "Results" section receives special emphasis, because this is a crucial aspect of truth-seeking quantitative design. Franklin et al. weight this section heavily. They describe the subjects and the population from which they were drawn. This is crucial, because the authors need to be able to generalize their findings to a group other than their subjects. They also explained how they tested the instrument's validity. The "Summary" restates the results—that the instrument was valid, but that the results of the experiment conducted within the study suggest that there are better ways to evaluate changes in self-esteem.

Truth-Seeking Qualitative

As noted in Chapter 4, the Palmieri piece is theory-driven and primarily qualitatively analyzed. As is more common in truth-seeking qualitative and perspective-seeking qualitative work, fewer if any headings are used, but different sections of the article can still be discerned. The first three paragraphs provide a rationale for the study of Wellesley College professors and summarizes the existing theory which the study tests—that the women were relatively non-assertive. Rather than state a research question, Palmieri writes what is known as a *thesis statement* (hypothesis without the "hypo"), the corollary to what at one time might have been a hypothesis. This could very well be an example of *reconstructed logic*, the process of writing one's report as if the study proceeded deductively when in fact it may have been an exploratory process (Worthen, 1985). As is sometimes the case with historical writing, Palmieri's narrative does not have a methods section. Truth-seeking qualitative ethnography almost always has a methods section or refers to methods in an endnote referenced early in the report. Palmieri used an endnote for methods. Checking the notes, you will see how she selected her subjects through a statistical procedure and that the author used a variety of qualitative and quantitative data such as faculty autobiographies, letters, and newspapers, and census reports. As is important with any qualitative research, the next section describes the selected, but not necessarily representative sample of professors in context. Palmieri uses the first person, which is somewhat unusual in truth- seeking writing, although anthropologists conducting ethnological or ethnographic work have been known to do this as well. She notes such things as her subjects' rebelliousness, attachment to nature, their research accomplishments, unconventional relationships with other women, and their social activism, always substantiating the points with specific examples of data. However, she uses shorter quotes than those typically found in perspective-seeking work. In truth-seeking historical studies the scholar employs her or his own reasoning and judgment, along with contextual corroboration, to interpret rather than merely report data. The conclusion section stresses the points in the paper that substantiate the thesis statement.

Perspective-Seeking Qualitative

Perspective-seeking researchers place heavy emphasis on writing. When explaining the phenomenological research process, for example, van Manen (1984) discusses the importance of writing and rewriting to capture the best description of the phenomenon under investigation. For readers to fully understand interpretations and analyses of data your writing must be vivid enough to draw readers into the research setting and take them through the same logical processes that you went through when conducting the study. Also, the researcher may refer to herself or himself in the first person to alert the reader to the researcher's opinion as opposed to that of the participants or informants.

Often, therefore, perspective-seeking research is presented through some inductive means of *logic-in-use,* reflecting the manner in which the research was actually conducted (Worthen, 1985). Such a piece might consist of an introduction that includes a rationale for the study, based either on the lack of theory in a given field or the inadequacy or narrow focus of a particular theory base. Then the research question(s) is mentioned, along with a section describing the data that will be collected to answer it (or them) and what method of analysis will be used. Depending on the academic discipline from which a study derives, the particular requirements of the audience, and the need for contextualization, the narrative, analysis of the results, and even theoretical implications may be written together or in separate sections.

A theoretical discussion might suggest one or several bodies of literature that inform, corroborate, or are reinforced by the study. Often, this section is written in a way to allow the reader, rather than the researcher, to make generalizations concerning the findings. This is accomplished through the use of verbs and phrases such as, "While these results pertain only to this study, they do indicate that . . . could be true for. . . . Further research into . . . might clarify this suggestion."

The Sims reading following Chapter 3 exemplifies a perspective-seeking qualitative study. In many respects Sims presents the research as it actually happened. In her introduction she references various sources showing that children's racial attitudes may or may not be changed by reading books about African-Americans. In view of the inconclusive evidence, Sims suggests that an exploratory study is in order. She therefore proposes to look at one child (Osula) to examine her response to children's literature for and about African-Americans. In "Response to What?" Sims gives the reader an idea of what truth-seeking quantitative researchers would call the *treatment,* what they would apply to one group while leaving a control group alone, thus determining the effect of the treatment. In "Osula and the Books" Sims presents Osula's response to the books that she read, couched in illustrative quotes. In "Discussion and Implications" Sims makes three connections between her results and existing theory: how children identify with characters in books; that readers must be of appropriate developmental ages to appreciate certain books; and that characters must be appealing.

Perspective-Seeking Quantitative

As noted earlier it is difficult to imagine a perspective-seeking quantitative study that is as personal as that of Sims. Because quantitative data are so symbolic we must speculate more in a perspective-seeking quantitative study about the perceptions of the people whose perceptions the numbers represent. Having said that we offer the Vaughn and Liles reading as an example of perspective-seeking quantitative writing. As in all research the authors conceptually introduce and defend the need for the study. They note that there is little theory on men teachers that deals with their motives to teach. In a series of sections defined by the particular assumption being investigated, they explore the motivations for turn-of-the-century males to remain in the classroom. The conclusion, as in Sims's study, speculates about links to existing knowledge and suggests questions for future study.

Manuals of Style

One of the most important rules for any kind of writing is to be aware of your audience. This will guide you in selecting a writing style, means of organizing your material, and particular citation format. Everything you write should follow a manual of style or a derivation of it employed by a particular graduate college, journal, or publisher. Manuals of style contain detailed information concerning how to organize and write your research. They are helpful, particularly to the beginning author, because they answer numerous questions about such things as form and citation procedures. Also, by following a manual, your paper will be uniform and consistent in style. In general, two are common to educational research, that of the American Psychological Association (APA) and of the University of Chicago. Also Turabian and the MLA (Modern Language Association) style book (both more akin to the University of Chicago style) are sometimes used.

A lot of educational research journals use APA style. The best thing about APA style is that it does not require any footnotes or endnotes. Rather, references are cited in the text by the author's last name, date of publication, and page number (if the citation is a direct quote). The APA manual also includes standard ways to present figures, tables, charts, and graphs. An alphabetized list of references used appears at the end of the manuscript. Only occasionally is an explanatory endnote deemed appropriate in APA style.

The University of Chicago style is quite different, and usually humanities-oriented educational research (e.g., studies in historical and philosophical foundations) follows this format. Sentence structure is more complex, and the document reads more like a piece of literature than a research report. For example, word repetition is avoided where possible. The sources and methodology sections often appear in a footnote or endnote or perhaps are not mentioned at all. The notes are often voluminous, including lengthy explanations of several citations.

Writing Specific Types of Documents

Now we turn to specific discussions of the various kinds of documents that you may write. Although we will explain some general rules that you might follow when writing each of these, it is always advisable to locate models of documents similar to yours before beginning your research. They may include more specific details about organizing and explicating your work than we mention in the general discussion that follows.

Prospecti and Proposals

Probably in no other capacity will you be required to write such a self-consciously explicit document as when constructing a proposal, particularly for a thesis or dissertation. We require our students to follow one of two flexible outlines, one reflecting a perspective-seeking, inductive and the other a truth-seeking, deductive approach. As discussed in other chapters, qualitative or quantitative methods, along with varying ideological perspectives, may be a part of either of these outlines.

The perspective-seeking proposal does not follow a specific outline of categories to address; the entire format for its proposal is highly dependent on the specific study. However, some elements that we consider essential are: a rationale, purpose and/or problem statement(s); question(s); and sources of data and possible means of analyzing them. This prospectus might also speculate on theoretical links to the study's findings.

Although the inductively written prospectus does not necessarily flow from any particular theory base, the rationale and purpose or problem statements may contain references to research that support the need for the proposed work. (See, for example, Becker's suggestions following Chapter 6.) Thus, the introduction of an inductively designed study is just as conceptual as that of a deductive one. Moreover, in preparing to conduct any research project, you will almost always discover various theoretical bases that are at least tangentially related to your own project and can therefore be used to argue for your research and perhaps indicate how to conduct it. For example, one of our students studying the dilemmas of an interim college or university president found that the United States military had conducted numerous studies of interim leadership and that the United States Army Research Institute would provide these studies to researchers. We and the student concluded that although the military provides a unique setting, some insights from their findings could inform a study of interim presidents in colleges and universities.

The deductive, hypothesis-driven proposal consists of a rationale, purpose or problem statement, discussion of the literature that includes all of the related known pieces of a particular puzzle (see Chapter 2), research question(s) or hypothesis(es) that, when answered, will add another piece, and methods of analysis. Because this proposal takes a truth-seeking approach, your literature review must uncover every defensible conceptual point made to explain the phenomenon under investigation so as to show how your work will add to what is already known. The literature review can be overdone. We recommend that at least the seminal work be reviewed as well as a good sampling of current research (i.e., conducted in the last five years).

Other types of proposals are those that request funding for a particular project. When writing a grant proposal to a local, state, national, or international funding agency, you will use similar components of either the deductive or inductive styles mentioned above. However, it is most important that you strictly follow the format and style suggested in the request for proposals (RFP) issued by a particular agency. In general, a point that seems to benefit grant writers is to avoid jargon common to a particular academic discipline. As is beneficial in all writing, give copies of drafts to both experts and nonexperts on the topic to check for factual errors and for clarity of thought.

Master's Projects

If you are in a program of study that requires a culminating or capstone experience—often called a master's project—and you (or others) want it to be a research project, we recommend you heed the advice we have offered. First and foremost, the specific topic you want to investigate either should be derived from theory (deductive) or should lead to new or existing theory (inductive). You may take a truth-seeking approach or one that seeks perspectives. (A large enough project could use both—one for the first phase and another for the next phase.) Your data and your analysis may be quantitative or qualitative or both. And your ideology could be status quo or reform.

By choosing a research project, which means you will make an explicit link to theory, either before you collect data or afterward, you connect your work with the work of others. Your findings will have greater impact because they will make existing theory more credible, possibly suggest revision of such theory, or begin to create new theory (i.e., working hypotheses) that can serve to describe and explain the phenomenon you choose to study.

Many of the readings we have attached to the chapters and studies we have described within the chapters can serve as models for your research project. The major difference between a master's research project and a thesis, in our opinion, is the scope or magnitude of the study. The size of the sample, the number of participants, and the length of time to collect data are all negotiable aspects of a project. What is not negotiable for a research project is the connection with theory.

Theses and Dissertations

Directions for organizing and writing your thesis or dissertation stem directly from your prospectus. For example, if your proposal were deductive and quantitative then your finished product will merely fill in the separate sections already outlined, adding a chapter on results (findings) and one on discussion, conclusions, and recommendations. If you have proposed an inductive project and written your proposal accordingly, then the results should reflect the means with which it was conducted. Such a dissertation or thesis should employ as little reconstructed logic as possible. The introduction might merely expand on the proposal's rationale and background for the study, then pose the question(s) that you asked. Something to consider here might be, "Were the questions renegotiated as the research process progressed?" Other sections would include a description of participants, informants, or respondents and the materials that you generated from them or found elsewhere and how you analyzed them. Finally, you should discuss the study's links to one or more theoretical bases and pose questions for further study. Whereas a master's project may or may not be linked to theory, depending on whether or not it is a research project, theses and dissertations must have theoretical connections.

As a final note, we suggest that you copyright your thesis or dissertation. Although there are many ethical people in academe, there are those who are not. There have been instances of students and other researchers or scholars who have plagiarized the work of others. It is particularly tempting for unscrupulous people to prey on older theses or dissertations that have not been copyrighted, because of the debatable illegality of such an act (see the George reading following this chapter), and the fact that fewer people would recognize the plagiarized work of a thesis or dissertation than of a highly recognized published work. Today, University Microfilms of Ann Arbor, Michigan, holds the copyright for dissertations, if the author does not request it personally.

Thought Pieces, Opinion Pieces, and Theoretical Essays

Thought or opinion essays are usually written by experienced scholars whose reputations as researchers are well-documented. Such writing presents an informed thesis about a certain professional topic such as tenure, or a point of debate in a certain academic field such as the efficacy of intelligence testing in the public schools. The author's opinion is substantiated by experience and by citations from other works. *The Chronicle of Higher Education*, the *Phi Delta Kappan* and *Educational Leadership* are publications that feature thought and opinion pieces.

Book Reviews and Book Review Essays

A book review or book review essay is not merely a report on a certain book or books. Rather, it is a critical analysis of a certain work or works. The main point or thesis of your review reflects your informed reaction to the book(s). The remainder of your writing should support this statement.

Writing and publishing book reviews and book review essays are excellent ways for you to remain current in your chosen field(s) and to begin building a resumé. Journal editors often have difficulty locating published scholars willing to take the time to review books. Write to several editors of journals and magazines in your field, sending a vita and a letter that explains why you are qualified to review books in certain academic areas. It may surprise you to find that you will be contacted, particularly by the regional and state publications. Not only will you get to review the book but also you will receive a free copy for your library.

If you are asked to review a book, solicit help from your advisor or mentor or from some other faculty member whose work you respect. Ask for suggestions on how to approach the topic and see if that person will edit your review before you polish it for the final draft. Typically the book review is only three to five pages long, and it does not contain citations to other works. One paragraph of summary is usually enough. The remainder of the review supports your reaction to the book with a defense of that assessment. For example, "The book is well documented as shown in the many citations to manuscript sources."

A book review essay usually hinges on one book, but it could be a general critique of several related works. Again your task is to create a thoughtful response to the book and to defend it with a longer essay. This writing will contain citations to other sources that substantiate your points. For example, if your major reaction to a work is that it represents a significant contribution to a particular academic field, it would be necessary for you to describe the current knowledge base in the area—what researchers know and what they do not know. The *Review of Education* and *Educational Studies* are two journals that specialize in publishing essay reviews.

Poster Presentations, Papers, and Articles

Master's research projects, theses, or dissertations can provide the basis for a presentation or article. Particularly if you are working on a doctorate, it is advisable for you to seek a forum for your research before you begin the dissertation. In so doing you can receive valuable critiques and comments that will help you produce a quality piece of research by the time you have completed the degree. If you accomplish this, you should be able to publish parts or all of your dissertation research. There are a number of national, regional, state, and local conferences in all of the educational research fields that sponsor graduate-student sessions or consider graduate students' work for inclusion in paper, roundtable, and poster sessions. The latter two are particularly conducive to the graduate student participant, because neither one of them requires that you submit it to critics who will point out its flaws (and sometimes its merits!) to your conference audience.

Particularly pertinent to fifth year teacher education and master's students is attending and presenting at state and local research conferences. Here you can meet many people in your field with whom you are or will be working as a teacher. Not only can you begin to make contacts with other professionals such as curriculum directors and administrators who will assist you in conceptualizing and planning your lessons, but also if you give a presentation to other educators who are responsible for planning school curricula, one of them may ask you to consult his or her school district regarding your area of expertise. And the pay for such activities is usually good!

Roundtable sessions are held in rooms that, literally, contain several round tables. You come to the conference with several copies of your paper and are seated at one table. Any persons interested in your topic will visit you at your table, ask you questions, and offer suggestions concerning your research. Each of these people will probably want to have a copy of your paper. Be sure to type on the cover sheet that no one should quote you or use your material without written consent. Most likely you will not have your paper copyrighted, so the statement on the cover gives you some protection against anyone who might refer to your work without giving you credit for it.

Poster sessions are perhaps an even better forum for beginning researchers to present their research, because you are not required to have written an entire article summarizing your study. Instead, you outline the research project and findings on a large poster or several smaller ones that will be displayed in a room along with other researchers' posters. As in the case of the roundtable you stand by your poster at the time of your scheduled sessions and visit with persons interested in your work.

Although you will inevitably encounter someone whose comments are based on personal rather than professional reactions to your work, when presenting your research you will no doubt receive many useful suggestions from colleagues throughout the United States, and perhaps, abroad. After you have revised a completed paper for an article that incorporates any critiques from others that you may or may not have solicited, have someone with good writing skills and a knowledge of your subject read your paper to check the substance and clarity of your writing. This kind of peer review is exactly what happens when you then submit your work for possible publication.

Some researchers believe that you should select the journal to which you will submit your work before you even begin the project. This way you can be sure to follow certain prescribed procedures when conducting and writing up the work. If you do not choose to do this, after completing a study you might review journal articles similar to yours, particularly ones that relate to the theoretical implications for your study. A number of reference volumes, such as *Cabells' Directory of Publishing Opportunities in Education* (1989), contain a good deal of information about numerous journals that publish educational research. You would be wise to follow the instructions of a particular journal (listed and outlined in *Cabells'*) when putting your article in its final format and even to look at actual articles that a particular journal has published to make sure that you have correctly used a desired format and writing style.

Most journals that publish educational research consider it unethical to submit a completed article to more than one journal at a time. This can be frustrating, because some journal reviewers are notoriously slow. If two or three months pass, and you have received no word about your article, write the editor a polite inquiry concerning the current status of your piece. As is the case with articles submitted for publication or with papers that you submit to present at conferences, the worst that could happen is that your work will be rejected. However, even if your work is rejected, you will usually receive substantive critiques that might enable you to rework the presentation of your research so that it will eventually be published in another journal. (Included in the readings after this chapter is an article by Fiske and Fogg that discusses the role of opinion and perspective in the evaluation process.)

Books

Possibly, one of the first books that you publish will stem from your dissertation. Many presses, whether university or commercial, consider it unethical to send a completed work to more than one potential publisher at a time. But it is acceptable to send proposals for a book simultaneously to several publishing houses. Because you will need to revise your dissertation before submitting it anyway, rework your introductory sections or chapter(s); eliminate many of the self-conscious details that explain how and why you went about devising and conducting your study. While your graduate faculty advisor or committee needed such information to evaluate your ability to conduct your research, you are now a researcher and scholar in your own right, and it is unnecessary to include all of the information that constituted a defense of your graduate work.

Again, for models, collect recent copies of books published by presses that specialize in your academic field. From those samples (if you used a chapter format) recast the first and perhaps second chapters of your dissertation and then write paragraph summaries of the additional chapters. You might then send this proposal to as many publishers as you wish and let them compete for your work.

Be patient with yourself when learning to organize and write your research. Good writers write constantly, but even they complain that sometimes they correct one problem such as wordiness, only to develop another, such as oversimplification. Depending on the way your cognitive processes operate, you may always need to go through several drafts of a paper so that you can see it unfold and shape it almost as a sculptor might sculpt a bust. Or you may be able to outline and envision a finished product in your head, and thus have to write it out only once. Experiment. Give your writing to respected colleagues so that they might critique it, learn to take criticism, and be willing to revise.

Summary

This chapter provides examples of the many types of documents that you might produce. The discussion also stresses how various research and other projects may be written. Through examples from four of our readings by Franklin et al., Palmieri, Sims, and Vaughn and Liles, we illustrate the variety of ways in which the content and organization of specific projects is written up. Throughout the chapter helpful tips are included that, if followed, should enhance your professional career.

Discussion Questions and Activities

1. Compile a list of journals that publish articles on one or two topics you wish to study.

2. Locate two very different types of research reports. Evaluate each of them for clarity and content. Then compare the two reports.

3. Submit a paper to your classmates for them to critique.

4. Present a research paper or book review to the class.

5. Do some investigation and compile a list of local, state, regional, and national research meetings of interest to you.

6. Examine a program from a recent American Educational Research Association conference. Use the index to find paper presentations related to a topic of interest to you.

7. Write or call a presenter from a recent AERA conference (or other national conference) and request a copy of his or her paper. How does the research report contribute to current theory on the topic it addresses?

8. Attend a research conference. Take note of the various styles of presenting and responding to papers.

Introduction to the Readings

George's article, "The Fight over 'Fair Use': When Is It Safe to Quote?" discusses the issue of fair use of quoted material from either primary sources (raw data) or secondary sources (published works). The piece serves to show that the issue of how much material may be quoted without violating laws is a highly debatable question. It is always wise to check with the editorial board or other agency that might be printing or publishing your work to get guidelines.

Fiske and Fogg, in "But the Reviewers Are Making Different Criticisms of My Paper!" ironically, find in this truth-seeking piece that, in the minds of reviewers of written research, truth rarely exists. The lesson for you as a fledgling writer is that although various critiquers of your work will not make the same comments, it may be that they all are contributing thoughtful, but different remarks or suggestions. Do not expect uniformity from them. They are all people with different experiences, strengths, and weaknesses. But as Fiske and Fogg instruct, it can always be beneficial to ask a colleague or two to critique your manuscript before submitting it for publication.

The Murray piece, "Write Research to Be Read," makes several important suggestions that should assist you in writing clearly and concisely. Often, the novice mistakes wordiness for a sign of intelligent-sounding research. Murray assures us that this is not true. Although your writing must discuss your major points with specific examples, it need not belabor any of them. And often highly complex sentence structures are more confusing than elucidating.

The Fight Over "Fair Use": When Is It Safe To Quote?

Gerald George

Let us say you are a historian sitting in a special-collections library. You are reviewing an exciting letter you have turned up in research for an article or book. It perfectly makes your new point about its author. It also illustrates his or her colorful style. It will give both vivacity and veracity to your manuscript. You must quote it—how can you do without it?

But wait a minute—what will your publisher say? Do you have express permission to quote the letter? No, and you are not likely to get it. For one thing, the letter sheds negative light on your subject, whose heirs may want to protect his or her angelic image. They may even want to review your entire manuscript. Moreover, it may be hard to find your subject's heirs, or even determine who owns the copyright. The library can identify only the donor of the letter, who was the heir of a recipient of it. Even if you find an unprotective heir, will that heir get greedy ideas just from knowing that you value the letter? Will he or she try to get a stiff fee out of you for permission to quote it, or even try to sell it for publication to someone else?

So what? You can quote it without permission, can you not? You are protected by "fair use": At least limited quoting without permission may be done for purposes of "criticism, comment, news reporting, teaching, scholarship, or research," right? You call your publisher to doublecheck.

"Forget it," your publisher advises. "Get unequivocal, written permission. Otherwise do not quote the letter. Do not closely paraphrase it. Be careful about even photocopying it to show other scholars or your students. Let's not get sued."

What Is Your Publisher Talking about?

Your publisher, in that hypothetical scenario, is talking about a series of court opinions that some scholars and publishers charge are making it dangerous to rely on the doctrine of fair use for anything. Last year, the Organization of American Historians joined several other national organizations of scholars, authors, and publishers in support of an appeal to the U.S. Supreme Court to overturn those opinions. Last February, without comment, the court refused to respond, thus letting the restrictive opinions stand.

George, G. (1990, August). The fight over 'fair use': When is it safe to quote? *OAH Newsletter, 10*, 19.

Subsequently, Robert Kastenmeier (D-WI), in the House, and Paul Simon (D-IL), in the Senate, have introduced legislation to amend the copyright law. [See "Capitol Commentary," *OAH Newsletter,* May 1990.] Their bill is intended to make clear the intent of Congress that fair use may be made of copyrighted work "whether published or unpublished." They have been listening to scholars recount actual experiences not unlike the one above. In *The Chronicle of Higher Education* (April 18, 1990), political scientist David J. Garrow goaded scholars to write their Congressional representatives in support of the bill. But historian Michael Les Benedict, who also has been prominent in sounding the alarm, does not believe that even the proposed legislation is enough to stop what he calls the "erosion" of fair-use principles by the courts.

What Exactly Have the Courts Decreed?

In a lead article in *Perspectives* (April, 1990), Benedict asserted that scholars won new protection from the Copyright Revision Act of 1976. It provides, among other things, that fair use may be made of unpublished as well as published materials. In 1985, however, in the case of *Harper & Row v. National Enterprises,* the U.S. Supreme Court ruled that under "ordinary circumstances, the author's right to control the first public appearance of his undisseminated expression will outweigh a claim of fair use." Two years later, in *Salinger v. Random House,* the federal Second Circuit Court of Appeals, in New York, set forth specific prohibitions. The use of direct quotes from unpublished material to make a biography more vivid or readable would not be fair use. Neither would close paraphrasing. In 1987, a federal court ruled in *Craft v. Kobler* that, without permission, even published material could not be quoted for just stylistic purposes.

In 1988, in *New Era v. Henry Holt & Co.,* a district judge said an author could quote without permission from unpublished, as well as published, sources to prove points about character. But on appeal, the Second Circuit seemed to overrule even that. It declared that "fair use is never to be liberally applied to unpublished copyrighted material," which "normally enjoy[s] complete protection," and warned that violators could be stopped from publishing even if their fair-use infractions were few. The U.S. Supreme Court let that decision, too, stand without comment, making it currently the law on fair use.

Results of these decisions include the following: Publication by Holt of Russell Miller's sharply critical biography of L. Ron Hubbard, founder of the Church of Scientology, would have been stopped except for a court finding that an injunction had not been sought early enough. Ian Hamilton had to revise substantially his Random House biography of fiction writer J. D. Salinger to reduce use of unpublished letters from Salinger to others. The courts' critics, including Arthur Schlesinger, Jr., as well as Professors Benedict and Garrow, have cited a dozen additional instances in which suits have been filed or threatened, or fair-use worries have led publishers to shy away from books, or authors have amended them significantly.

Prominent among pending cases is that of Victor Kramer of Georgia State University. Fair use is one of five grounds asserted by Professor Kramer in his suit against the estate of author and film critic James Agee, whose trustee denied permission to use material Kramer says will illustrate a study of Agee's literary development. (The same trustee is disputing ownership of some Agee materials now held in the University of Tennessee's library.) But the case is unlikely to counter the trend of recent court decisions. Even if it is not decided on other issues, it will be heard in the same federal circuit (southern New York), where the earlier cases were decided. Kramer's lawyer, Kirsten Lundergan, is not aware— "unfortunately," she says—of any fair-use cases pending in any other circuit.

In the meantime, scholarly publishers seem little alarmed—even little aware—of potential danger. Certainly they are not panicking. Editors of the *Journal of American History* and the *Journal of Southern History*, for example, report no unusual problems yet for authors in consequence of the court cases. Nor have they changed previous policies on quoted material. "Maybe we are too comfortable," says Clyde Milner, editor of the *Western Historical Quarterly*. "But let's get clarification in the courts and the Congress. My bottom line is, we don't want [scholars] to get too nervous, to start censoring themselves."

Among scholarly presses, the University of Tennessee Press was to have been Kramer's publisher, and Professor Benedict cited fair-use concerns at his own university, Ohio State. But some other scholarly publishers continue to rely on policies they have traditionally followed. John Drayton, editor in chief of the University of Oklahoma Press, directs authors to the Chicago *Manual of Style*, which he says encourages getting permissions to quote but discourages "excessive caution." "We all deplore the erosion of fair use of published and unpublished material," says Kate Torrey, editor in chief of the University of North Carolina Press. But "it has not changed the way we operate—not yet."

Among documentary editors who collect and publish primary source material, the degree of worry seems inverse to how remote in history one's subject is. The University of Tennessee, for example, houses editorial projects on the papers of three former presidents—Jackson, Polk, and Andrew Johnson. Polk editor Harold Moser reports no new difficulties and hopes to be able to continue relying on the principle that "letters written to a public figure in his public capacity are in the public domain." Editors of papers of non-presidential, more recently prominent figures are less comfortable. Robert Schulmann is struggling to obtain access to some papers of Albert Einstein from the Hebrew University of Jerusalem. Publication-permission difficulties could come next: "We anticipate having problems." Megan Maxwell says that editors of the Martin Luther King, Jr. papers have been using "some pretty incredible means" to try to find obscure writers of letters to King who seem "to have disappeared." The fear is that upon publication they might reappear to assert rights.

Among commercial publishers, Byron Dobell, editor of *American Heritage* magazine, tends to regard the whole thing as a tempest in an inkwell. "People are suckers for stories about their own business," he observes, and this may be just another case of journalists and other writers overreacting to controversies that concern them; less publicized issues probably seem just as alarming "to doorknob manufacturers." Dobell doesn't expect problems at *Heritage*, which he says tends to deal with long-deceased historical figures: "We haven't really had any problem and haven't been sued . . . Teddy Roosevelt is not about to descend on me."

Commercial presses, however, where big money as well as reputations may be at stake, are more concerned. Fearing that publicity might put lawsuit ideas into someone's head, editors there refuse to cite specific recent examples of putting pressure on authors to get permissions to quote or of delaying publication for want of them. "I am not aware of anybody I deal with being frightened off by these [fair-use] cases," says James Mairs, a vice president of W. W. Norton and Company. But he acknowledges that publishers may become more shy if only to avoid increased likelihood of "nuisance suits." Senior Editor Ashbel Green of Alfred A. Knopf, Inc., is more emphatic: "Our consciousness was raised on the Salinger case. We are asking authors for permissions more carefully now." Another New York publisher who declined to be identified described plans to go ahead with a biography of a controversial figure despite some possible fair-use exposure: "We're taking a lot of risks."

Why, in the view of such a concerned person as Professor Benedict, will the newly proposed legislation not end the riskiness and uncertainty? Because, he contends, the Supreme Court already has agreed that fair use applies to unpublished as well as published documents. The new legislation does not say that it applies "equally" to both kinds. Professor Benedict himself is among those who are not at all sure that published and unpublished material should be treated exactly alike, which could raise financial and privacy issues. In Benedict's view, a better solution would be more liberal judicial interpretation. "The whole doctrine of fair use was developed by the courts . . . the real problem is that the courts have defined it unrealistically.

Effects on scholarship will continue to unfold, he predicts, and obstacles to the use of documents increase. "It is a question of when, not if, owners will copyright unpublished materials," he declares. But he hopes scholars and publishers will not react in fearful self-censorship. "I hope they will go on waiting" to see what happens—"there isn't any reason yet to do anything else."

But the Reviewers Are Making Different Criticisms of My Paper!
Diversity and Uniqueness in Reviewer Comments

Donald W. Fiske

Louis Fogg

Abstract

This research studied the critical points made in 402 reviews of 153 papers submitted to 12 editors of American Psychological Association journals. The diverse
criticisms dealt not only with the planning and execution of the research but also
with the presentation in the report, spreading fairly evenly over all steps in
research activity from early conceptualizing to final writing. The modal category
is Interpretations and Conclusions. In the typical case, two reviews of the same
paper had no critical point in common. It seemed that reviewers did not overtly
disagree on particular points; instead, they wrote about different topics, each
making points that were appropriate and accurate. As a consequence, their recommendations about editorial decisions showed hardly any agreement.

   An author receiving the editor's letter about a submitted paper is apprehen-
sive not only about the editor's decision but also about the paper's weaknesses
as alleged by the editor and the reviewers. The knowledgeable author is little
comforted by the fact that no more than 2% of initial submissions are accepted
(Eichorn & VandenBos, 1985), although 20 to 40% of revised manuscripts are
accepted.

   But what do the reviewers and the editor say about the author's cherished
paper? It is certain that most of the perceived weaknesses will surprise the author.
Perhaps the receipt of such painful feedback would be more tolerable if the author
knew more about the contents of reviews received by other authors.

   A survey of reviewers' and editors' criticisms can also provide indirect evidence on the methodological sophistication of authors and of reviewers and
editors. What types of defects are reported? What kinds predominate? Are the
improvements proposed by reviewers ones that a colleague might have suggested
or ones known only to methodological specialists?

Fiske, Donald W., & Fogg, Louis. (1990). But the reviewers are making different criticisms of my paper:
Diversity and uniqueness in reviewer comments. American Psychologist, 45(5), 591–598. Copyright ©
by the American Psychological Association. Reprinted by permission.

Most papers are sent out to two or more reviewers. Are multiple reviews replicative or independent? Although their wording may differ, are the reviews saying much the same thing about a given paper? Do reviewers agree on the editorial actions they recommend to editors?

Many articles have been written on the editorial process. Largely critical, they often propose changes. Yet almost nothing has been reported on the free-response comments of reviewers. Smigel and Ross (1970) presented reasons given by associate editors for recommending acceptance or rejection of submissions to one journal. Daft (1985) classified the major problems he had found in 111 of his own reviews. Agreements between reviewer recommendations have often been studied—the reported correlations converging around .3. Aside from some instances given by Smigel and Ross, and some general statements made by Spencer, Hartnett, and Mahoney (1986), we have found no comparisons of the specific comments made by reviewers of the same paper.

The editorial process has many stages, from the author's selection of the journal to which a paper is submitted to the editor's final decision about that paper. At an intermediate stage is the work of the reviewer, reading the paper one or more times, thinking about it, and writing a report giving a general recommendation, a list of weaknesses noted by that reviewer, and perhaps a sentence or two on the paper's strengths and contributions. This article considers just the products of that stage, as reported back to the editor and author: What irremediable errors did the author make in planning and executing the research? What corrigible faults are there in the exposition, the presentation of the research? Do the several reviews report the same errors and faults?

Method Used

We have studied the reviewers' reports and the editors' decision letters for 153 papers submitted for the first time to American Psychological Association (APA) journals in late 1985 or in 1986. (The project was approved by the APA Publications and Communications Board.) At our request, editors sent these materials from their files to a consulting editor for an APA journal who painstakingly deleted the names and institutions of all authors and reviewers. Sampling widely in the spectrum of APA journals, we encountered one editor who refused to assist us and two others whose reluctance was respected. The final list included seven journals or sections and 12 action editors: For five journals, separate sets of materials were obtained for an associate editor as well as the editor. We used materials on 7 to 16 papers per editor. The journals were these: *Developmental Psychology, Journal of Abnormal Psychology, Journal of Comparative Psychology, Journal of Experimental Psychology: Human Perception and Performance, Journal of Experimental Psychology: Learning, Memory, and Cognition, Journal of Personality and Social Psychology: Attitudes and Social Cognition,* and *Journal of Personality and Social Psychology: Personality Processes and Individual Differences.* We were impressed by the amount of time and effort that reviewers put into their work. Some of the submitted reports ran three or four single-spaced pages, lending credence to statements that manuscripts had been reread several times.

Coding

Each review, consisting of the reviewer's report to the editor and author, together with any comment directed only to the editor, was searched for statements about weaknesses identified in the submitted manuscript. Each critical point was coded separately. In each review, the number of such points ranged from 0 to 37, with a *mean* of 8.6. The brevity of the two reviews with no criticisms suggests a rapid if not cursory reading of the paper.

Each point was coded into the category in the research process to which it referred. The categories form a rough temporal sequence, from prior conceptual formulation to interpretation, conclusions, and writing (see Table 1). In addition, the defect was coded as having occurred during Planning and Execution of the research itself or later, during the Presentation, the preparation and writing of the submitted paper. We coded only weaknesses because reviewers focus on them; they make only broad statements—if any—about the positive features of papers.

The coding was a long and difficult task. After some practice coding and the development of a preliminary manual, each of us independently coded reports, and then we discussed our judgments and reached consensus on the final coding.

TABLE 1 Distribution of Weaknesses as Reported by Reviewers for APA Journals by Percentages

Category	Weakness attributed to		
	Planning and execution	Presentation	Total
Conceptual:			
Pre-execution	4.9	10.3	15.2
Conceptual:			
Linkage to execution	3.0	2.0	5.1
Design	6.9	3.9	10.8
Procedures	6.0	6.3	12.3
Measurement	3.4	3.9	7.3
Statistical analyses	5.8	2.7	8.5
Results	4.1	9.1	13.2
Interpretations and conclusions		16.1	16.1
Editorial and writing		8.5	8.5
General	0.3	2.6	2.9
Total	34.4	65.4	99.8

Note. For 153 submitted papers, 3,477 weaknesses were coded from 402 reviews.

The agreement between our independent judgments was only fair. After efforts to improve it had very limited success, we decided that, with the ambiguities in the reports and in the coding system, higher agreement was not feasible. Of all the segments identified as codable by either of us, we agreed on 79%. For 73% of the agreed-on points, we agreed on which of the 11 categories in the research was involved in the criticism (kappa = .69). Many disagreements involved adjacent categories or steps. Agreement was 85% (kappa = .67) on whether the problem occurred in the Planning and Execution of the research or in the Presentation of the manuscript.

Because the critic's judgment of the seriousness of just a single defect can play a major role in the reviewer's or editor's overall evaluation of a paper, the reader may wonder why we did not code the severity of each point. We did have such a scale for points referring to the Planning and Execution of the research, and seriousness was implied in some subcategories for Presentation points. Our agreement, however, was lowest on this aspect of the coding. Although a reviewer would sometimes write that the paper should not be published because of one or two specified points, more commonly the reviewer did not weight the points, or at most classified them as major or minor. It must also be recognized (as a thoughtful reviewer has reminded us) that the same weakness may be judged as fatal or as troublesome but acceptable as a function of the substantive context and the research area. In a well-developed research area in which the nature of the appropriate controls is generally accepted, overlooking one control could make a paper unpublishable. In a new area or a socially important one, the omission of a reasonable control—especially an expensive one—might be tolerated.

Note also that a criticism can be serious in several diverse ways. A critical flaw in the design may (in the eyes of the reviewer) make the paper worthless. An omission or ambiguity in exposition may make the reviewer uncertain about the soundness of the research plan. Departing from current practice in a research area may cause the reviewer to infer that the author is not sufficiently qualified in background and experience to attempt such a research study. These several types of seriousness could not be captured readily in a single scale.

Results

Loci and Weaknesses

Weaknesses were associated with activities in all the categories or stages of the research and with the presentation of all activities (see Table 1). Over all the reviews coded, the most frequent locus for weaknesses was in the Interpretations and Conclusions made after the research was completed. (This finding rebuts the proposal by Kupfersmid, 1988, that editorial decisions be made without seeing the Results and Discussion sections of submitted papers.) The next most common type was in the presentation of the conceptual work that was done before the empirical research was started. After these come the categories in which most authors probably expect to receive criticisms: Results, Procedures, and Design. Note that the proportions for Presentation are large for the first two of these.

Of all criticisms, two thirds were coded as Presentation problems. Although this accumulation is due largely to defining the Interpretations and Conclusions stage as occurring subsequent to the research execution (along with the Editorial and Writing category), it is impressive that the reviewers saw as many problems in the presentation—exposition and description—as in the actual research activities (the categories in the first seven rows of Table 1). Moreover, these data slightly understate the actual frequencies of presentation problems because we had the convention of coding each type of minor problem, such as typographical errors and poor sentences, only the first time it was mentioned. Criticisms of presentation are corrigible. Many of them could have been prevented by more careful review by the authors themselves and also by frank critiquing from a number of colleagues.

Types of Weaknesses

But just what criticisms were made? How were the categories in Table 1 defined? Table 2 provides answers to these questions by showing the types of contents subsumed under each grouping. The labels for the subcategories are almost paraphrases of reviewer comments. The reviewer would write something similar to one of these headings and then, typically, specify more concretely the nature of the difficulty. Thus, the reviewer might devote several words, a sentence, a paragraph, or a whole single-spaced page to a difficulty that was coded as one point.

How was Table 2 produced? Forty papers were arbitrarily selected for analysis, 4 from each of 10 editor-journal sets. (At the request of one editor, materials from one journal were not included in this analysis.) For each of the subcategories in Table 1, all reviewer points about these papers were assembled and inspected. Types perceived by one of us were reviewed by the other, and the final types listed in Table 2 were derived by consensus. The number in the right-hand column gives the frequency of reviewer criticisms falling in the preceding grouping. A frequency of 39 means that there were 39 criticisms falling in, say, the Conceptual: Pre-execution, Planning and Execution subcategory. In this case, 39 of the 40 papers were likely to have received such a criticism, assuming that a given point about a paper is not made by more than one reviewer. This assumption was rarely violated (as shown subsequently). This estimation also neglects the fact that a paper with more reviewers, and hence more criticisms, would be more likely to have a criticism of a given type.

From inspection of Table 2, it is obvious that hundreds of different kinds of criticisms are made by reviewers. Even within the individual subcategories of the table, there are from 3 to 13 types. The fact that there are no types with large frequencies is purely a consequence of our approach to the categorizing: We wanted our types to be reasonably specific in order to maximize their potential usefulness to authors.

TABLE 2 Classification of Weaknesses Reported by Reviewers for APA Journals

Category	No. of Criticisms
Conceptual: Pre-execution	
Planning and execution	**39**
Does not seem to know current state of the field	7
Other poor scholarship	4
Poorly differentiated concepts or issues	
Concepts poorly defined	3
Conceptual basis for study poor or incomplete	7
Other poor conceptualizing	3
Reviewer disagrees with author's statements	8
Presentation	**87**
A body of literature is slighted or left out	11
A reference or author is left out	5
Report of prior research is erroneous	8
References to the literature are out of date	2
Theoretical presentation incomplete, needs expansion	4
Omissions in Introduction	6
Concepts or issues not clearly described	6
Overall theoretical presentation poor or unclear	5
Conceptualizing is erroneous or poor	6
Introduction or theoretical discussion too long	10
Introduction is inadequate	4
Terminology in Introduction is incorrect, confusing, etc.	9
Other problems in writing of Introduction	5
Conceptual: Linkage to execution	
Planning and execution	**27**
Poor basic rationale for study	8
Experiment or task does not test the theory	9
Rationale does not justify the measure used	3
Measures are poorly chosen	3
Presentation	**18**
Conceptualization or hypotheses unclear	6
Rationale for experiment unclear	2
Predictions are not justified	2
Design	
Planning and execution	**61**
Design is defective, incomplete, or inappropriate	9
Design should be within-subject (or within-group)	4
Variable, condition, or manipulation missing	4
Faulty procedure	3
Sample is too small	11
Sample is too restricted or not appropriate	4
Sample is poor or contaminated	5
Sample is too heterogeneous	3
No control or comparison group	4

Table 2 (continued)

Category	No. of Criticisms
Poor control group	6
Variables not controlled	5
Presentation	**25**
More information about subjects is needed	6
Explain selection or elimination of subjects	7
Number of subjects is unclear	3
Design or experimental protocol unclear	5

Procedures

Planning and execution	**58**
No or poor controls	5
Confounding, nonindependence, or lack of counterbalancing	11
Poor task	4
Poor instructions	3
Poor experimental procedures	8
Poor choice of stimuli	10
Manipulation defective or not checked	5
What are the processes in subjects	3
Effects of demand characteristics	3
Presentation	**45**
General lack of clarity	8
Procedural detail missing	12
Give justification for procedure	3
Clarify the stimuli	10
Were there order effects?	4

Measurement

Planning and execution	**34**
Measure is indirect, superficial, not the best	11
Measure does not cover the construct	3
Potential bias in the measure	4
Problems with recall and self-report	4
Measure is not validated	6
Reliability poor or unknown	3
Presentation	**35**
Describe item characteristics, format	5
Explain development and scoring of measure	5
Describe administration of measures	3
Reliability or validity data not given or unclear	8

Statistical analyses

Planning and execution	**48**
A statistical error is specified, and a better statistic is suggested or implied	9
A statistical error is specified, but no remedy is suggested	5

(Continued)

Table 2 (continued)

Category	No. of Criticisms
The statistical analysis is performed incorrectly	5
General, unspecified criticism of the analyses	6
A specified statistical analysis should be added	12
Some additional analysis is needed	5
Presentation	**23**
Rationale or justification for the analysis is faulty	14
Unclear how an analysis was done	5
A statistical procedure is described poorly	4
What data were used?	3
Statistical results are not given	3
Report of statistics is incorrect	3

Results

Planning and execution	**50**
Results are inconsistent	6
Results are inconclusive, incomplete	7
Results are puzzling, difficult to interpret, confounded	7
Results are weak	6
Results are chance	3
Results are obvious, expected, not surprising	6
Results replicate prior work	7
Results give little or no new information	8
Presentation	**63**
Unreported relationships	6
Other results not given	7
Tables and descriptive data are needed	7
Present the results more succinctly	8
Delete some tables or figures	4
Tables or figures need clarification	8
General presentation of results unclear	5
Specific clarifications are needed	6
Inconsistencies in presentation of results	5

Interpretations and conclusions

Presentation[a]	**121**
Interpretations or conclusions are not warranted by the data	17
Statement is unacceptable, unconvincing	19
There are alternative interpretations	7
Findings or results are not interpreted or not explained	10
Their meaning or theoretical relevance is unclear or not shown	8
Their implications need to be worked out	6
Discuss or elaborate on a point	10
Discussion is too long	6
Discussion is generally poor or unclear	8
Inaccurate statement about the literature or does not know it	7
Prior literature should be cited or discussed	7
Methodological matters pertinent to findings or conclusions	10

Table 2 (continued)

Category	No. of Criticisms
Editoral and writing	
Presentation	**44**
Generally poor writing	10
Bad sentence	5
Poor or wrong word or phrase	5
Specific suggestions to improve writing	3
Paper is too long	6
Make it a short report	3
Citations missing, unclear, or inappropriate	4
Typographical errors	3
Not in APA format	2
General	
Planning, execution and presentation	**25**
Contribution is of little or no importance	8
Paper is premature; not enough work or studies	3
Paper replicates previous research	2
Paper should be submitted elsewhere to a more appropriate (e.g., specialized) journal	4
Paper should be submitted to a less demanding journal	5

Note. For each cell, the items not accounted for by the stated category frequencies were placed in a "miscellaneous" category not listed here.
[a]Also included here are nine points originally coded as overinterpretations.

The types in Table 2 are empirical, being derived from the recorded examples. After the fact, it looks as though kinds of weaknesses, as opposed to contents, could profitably be classified as follows: something not done or omitted, something done incompletely, something done poorly, and something done wrong. That classification is applicable to Planning and Execution points as well as to Presentation points. For the latter, "done poorly" has two subtypes: The exposition can be either unclear or too long.

For the methodologist, the types in Table 2 suggest that the typical reviewer is aware of standard methodological considerations and also of the special problems in each given type of research. Most of the criticisms concerned methodological matters that are fairly well known and generally accepted; they were not arguments for specialized or unusual techniques lacking consensual endorsement nor were they objections to the failure to use methods only very recently developed and disseminated. Note, however, the frequencies of diverse conceptual problems in planning the research and the numerous criticisms of interpretations and conclusions.

We also coded each letter communicating the editor's decision to the author, using the same coding scheme as that for reviewer reports. These data were not subjected to intensive analysis for two reasons. First, editors varied greatly in the length of their letters: Some simply said, "Given these reviews, I must reject your paper," whereas others wrote two- or three-page independent reviews of papers before discussing the points made by reviewers. Also, the majority of points noted in editors' letters were restatements of reviewer points.

The Relative Uniqueness of Each Review

In principle, the several reviewers for each paper could make the same or similar points, and that set of points might have little overlap with the set for another paper. Instead, as we coded, it became clear that reviewers were not making the same points—in fact, rarely did one reviewer make the same point as any other reviewer of that paper. To elucidate this perception, we made a number of exploratory analyses, using various criteria for a match or correspondence between points made by different reviewers. In no analysis did we find a suggestion of more than a quite minimal degree of overlap between a pair of reviews.

To demonstrate this state of affairs, we carried out an analysis using eight papers per editor (only seven were available in one case). For each paper, we compared two reviewers chosen a priori. We looked for instances in which the two reviewers had points coded in the same cell of the original coding scheme. Points in the same cell were in the same row (category) and the same column—one of three degrees of seriousness for Planning and Execution points or one of five types of inadequacy for Presentation (defective, unclear or incomplete, missing, excess length, and weak or other). Whenever the two reviewers made criticisms falling in the same cell, we went back to the original reports to see if the points were identical. For example, here are quotes from two reviewers making the same point: "On page 12 the author states that the relation between [X] and [Y] was not examined but Footnote 3 reports such an analysis," and "On p. 12, it says that the relation between [X] and [Y] will not be examined, but it is in Footnote 3." In contrast, here are two statements making similar but different points: "There seems to be no particular reason for interest in specific [items] so Tables [X and Y] are unnecessary," and "The discussion in places reiterates the results by listing . . . items showing significant effects. . . . Because the individual items are not derived from a tight rationale . . . these types of conclusions do not help the reader get the big picture of what happened in the study."

In order to evaluate the agreement between a pair of reviewers, we determined the level of agreement that might occur by chance. Two reviews of different papers can make the same point, such as not having enough subjects or having too lengthy a discussion section. We generated an estimate of chance agreement by comparing, systematically, one reviewer of each paper with one reviewer of the next paper in our set. Because the two papers had different content, the criteria for a match had to be relaxed a bit: For example, "Figure 1 is unclear" was

TABLE 3 Correspondences between Points Made by Two Reviewers

Count	Same paper	Different papers
Number of pairs of reviewer reports compared	95	95
Maximum possible correspondences	585	538
Number of pairs of points similarly coded (same cell)	156	113
Number of exact matches:		
Same point is made by both reviewers	42	11

judged to match "Figure 3 is confusing." Note also that some points can be made only about a specific paper: See the earlier example, "On page 12. . . . "

The results of this analysis are given in Table 3. For each of 95 papers, a pair of reviewers were compared. The number of possible correspondences, in which cells would have a point from each reviewer, is obtained from the smaller of the two reviewers' total numbers of points (e.g., if one made five points and the other nine, there could be no more than five correspondences). For reviews of the same paper, there were 585 possible correspondences. Among these, there were 156 instances of a point from each of the two reviews being coded into the same cell. Finally, among these, we judged that in 42 instances, the same point was being made by both reviewers. So, for these 95 papers, there were 42 instances in which the two reviewers made the same point—0.44 instances per pair of reviewers for a paper.

To estimate the rate of chance agreement, we carried out a similar analysis for pairs of reviews for different papers. There were 113 instances of a pair of points being coded into the same cell, but only 11 of these involved the same point (e.g., "How many did not agree to participate?" and "How many patients declined [to participate]?" So, at this level of analysis, some correspondences are found between the points made by a pair of reviewers, but similar matches sometimes occur in reports on different papers. In these data, out of 585 possibilities, there were only 31 matches beyond the number expected by chance.

To permit exact comparisons, the preceding analyses required strict criteria for matches. Perhaps those criteria were too strict. Given the modest reliability of the coding, it was possible that the same point made by two reviewers of a paper might have been coded into adjacent cells rather than the same cell (e.g., because of the point's different contexts in the two reports). An analysis testing this possibility included all possible pairs of reviewers (361 instead of 95). In this way, we identified 125 different points on which two or three reviewers agreed. Thus, this looser criterion for matching of points did not increase the low rate of occurrence of matches.

Of these 125 points, 51% concerned Planning and Execution—which had only 34% of all points. In contrast, for the same categories (Conceptual through Results), Presentation matters had 38% of all points but only 22% of the matches. (The greater proportion of agreed-on points for the Planning and Execution area is highly significant by chi-square.) Relatively high rates of correspondences were also found for the Editorial and Writing (e.g., "The paper is too long") and for the General (e.g., "The paper is not appropriate for this journal") categories.

Finally, it should be noted that when two reviewers make the same point about a paper, it does not necessarily mean that they have much the same overall impression about the paper. Comparing pairs of reviewers making the same point with pairs not making any common point, we found reviewers' overall recommendations to the editor showed similar disparities in both sets of pairs.

It was of course possible that even though reviewers reported different points, their general evaluations of papers agreed fairly well. As mentioned earlier, the prior literature did not encourage that hope. Nevertheless, we computed intraclass correlations for the several reviewers' overall recommendations to the editor. Using both the reviewer's checkmark on the brief multiple-choice item furnished by the editor and the general tone of the reviewer's broad qualitative appraisal (especially in any note directed to the editor alone), we coded each reviewer's recommendation onto a 15-point scale. That scale was developed from the alternatives in the items used by the several journals for obtaining reviewer overall judgments and from standard editor phrases in their letters to authors. The scaling of the statements and phrases was based on the judgments of 15 colleagues. Although the intraclass correlations varied from −.23 to +.68 because each of the 12 samples per editor journal was small, the mean was .20—a little lower than other studies have found.

Not reported earlier were our analyses looking for differences between journals and between editors. The data are messy—several points per review, several reviews per paper, but not very many papers per editor. We focused primarily on profiles of category means: Did the reviewers for a given editor produce a profile of points per category (stage of the research) that differed from that for other editors? We applied our primary criterion: Were the results consistent? In our judgment, the answer was negative. For example, clusters of editors for the Planning and Execution side differed from those for the Presentation side. Similarity between areas covered by journals was not matched by correspondence between profiles. The editor and associate editor for the same journal might or might not fall into the same cluster. It was our impression that the basic unit was each editor and that editor's choice of reviewers.

Discussion

It is possible that our failure to find consistency in those analyses comparing editors was due to the unreliability of our coding, but we do not believe that unreliability was a major factor. Because our data were pooled codings, they are more reliable than the figures given earlier. Typically, when one of us found that he had missed a point noted by the other, he would accept his oversight. Similarly, one of us would usually agree that the other's case for his coding was better than his own.

What are the possible effects of our limited coder reliability on the findings reported earlier? We believe that another pair of judges, using our coding manual, would generate data like those in Table 1. Similarly, they would find the same weaknesses we found, and so their table would look like our Table 2, with some differences in the frequencies and perhaps some variations in the locations of some subcategories. Finally, with more reliable coding, the number of exact matches in Table 3 would presumably be larger although the basic finding would remain intact. More generally, the relative independence of the comments made by separate reviewers would still be evident: Any author who has available the reviews for a submitted paper can confirm this finding by taking each point in one review and searching for its replication in another review.

As an anonymous reviewer of a prior draft of this article pointed out, one's interpretation of our findings depends on one's conception of the reviewers' role in the editorial process. The points we coded from each reviewer report included all the weaknesses noted by that reviewer, and hence provided the basis for the reviewer's overall judgment of the quality of the paper. But what does the editor want from each reviewer? Does an editor want merely the overall recommendation, with the comments of the reviewer being primarily for the edification of the author? It seems likely that most editors want to know what weaknesses each reviewer saw, as an aid to the editor's own evaluation of the quality of the paper. But each additional reviewer contributes one more list of weaknesses. Is an author's paper at greater risk of rejection with more reviewers? We cannot provide a clear answer because the number of reviewers is a multiply determined variable. The analysis of editors' decisions and their precursors must be left for a later article.

Saying that two reviewers typically do not agree does not necessarily mean that they disagree. An attempt to locate explicit disagreements turned up only a few instances in which one reviewer said a given aspect of the paper was satisfactory but another found a problem: For example, "As for the methods, they are clearly and sufficiently described," and "The methods presented are insufficient to reproduce the study in another lab." Of course, because the typical review devotes little space to positive statements about the paper, there are undoubtedly many hidden disagreements of this sort.

Given the low degree of manifested consensus between reviewers, it is reasonable to ask whether the reviewers' criticisms were appropriate. Although we cannot give a definitive answer to that question, we believe that they generally were. We very rarely saw any criticism that we were inclined to question, on the basis of internal or other evidence, such as the reviewer's stating that a statistical test had a particular assumption. Also, in instances in which we consulted the original manuscript, we found no reviewer criticisms with which we disagreed. (We obtained some censored manuscripts to see whether we could code more reliably with their aid. We could not.) Finally, it was very uncommon for an editor to indicate disagreement with a point made by a reviewer.

Our evidence for the relative independence or uniqueness of reviewer reports will not surprise many editors. (See Roediger, 1987, for a judicious discussion of this and other aspects of the editorial process.) Editors are familiar with such nonoverlap, and of course they pick reviewers with different kinds of expertise, reviewers who will be likely to emphasize different kinds of defects.

These data raise questions for editors and reviewers. First, given the limited agreement between reviewers and the sizable but finite population of weaknesses that can be identified for any one paper, are two reviews sufficient? Don't the editor and the author need to have a larger set of points called to their attention? Second, should editors ask reviewers to consider more explicitly the positive features of each paper? Perhaps a bipolar scale could be used to indicate the overall positive or negative balance between strengths and weaknesses. One question that editors and reviewers might (or perhaps do) ask themselves is this: Assuming that the authors prepared a revision that successfully dealt with the reported problems in exposition or presentation, would the remaining weaknesses outweigh the paper's potential positive contribution from its ideas and findings?

Everyone who has submitted manuscripts for publication knows that reviewers always can and do find some weaknesses to report. An author's aim should be to minimize the number of such reported defects, thereby reducing their negative influence on the overall evaluations of the paper by the editor and reviewers. One can only do so much alone. One needs to get a number of colleagues to help by reading one's paper as carefully and critically as possible. Scientific research is a community activity. As von Bekesy (1960) reported in his own experience,

> Another way of dealing with [potential research] errors is to have friends who are willing to spend the time necessary to carry out a critical examination of the experimental design beforehand and the results after the experiments have been completed. An even better way is to have an enemy. An enemy is willing to devote a vast amount of time and brain power to ferreting out errors both large and small, and this without any compensation. The trouble is that really capable enemies are scarce; most of them are only ordinary. Another trouble with enemies is that they sometimes develop into friends and lose a good deal of their zeal. It was in this way that the writer lost his three best enemies. (pp. 8–9)

References

Daft, R. L. (1985). Why I recommended that your manuscript be rejected and what you can do about it. In L. L. Cummings & P. J. Frost (Eds.), *Publishing in the organizational sciences*, 193–204. Homewood, IL: Irwin.

Eichorn, D. H. & VandenBos, G. R. (1985). Dissemination of scientific and professional knowledge: Journal publication with the APA. *American Psychologist, 40*, 1309–1316.

Kupfersmid, J. (1988). Improving what is published: A model in search of an editor. *American Psychologist, 43*, 635–642.

Roediger, H. L. III. (1987). The role of journal editors in the scientific process. In D. N. Jackson & J. P. Rushton (Eds.). *Scientific excellence: Origins and assessment*, 222–252. Newbury Park, CA: Sage.

Smigel, E. D. & Ross, H. L. (1970). Factors in the editorial decision. *American Sociologist, 5*, 19–21.

Spencer, N. J., Hartnett, J. & Mahoney, J. (1986). Problems with reviews in the standard editorial practice. *Journal of Social Behavior and Personality, 1*, 21–36.

von Bekesy, G. (1960). *Experiments in hearing*. New York: McGraw-Hill.

We are indebted to the several editors and their editorial assistants who sent us copies of materials in their files and to Susan T. Fiske who deleted all identifying contents. We are also indebted to the Biomedical Research Support Program of the Division of Social Sciences, University of Chicago, for a grant that enabled this research to be started. We are grateful to Lois Creer and Diane Hawkins for their careful work in preparing this article and its tables. Finally, we were greatly helped by the incisive criticisms of Alan P. Fiske, Barbara P. Fiske, and Susan T. Fiske on an earlier version of this article: They made an average of 13 critical points about it. Three anonymous reviewers also gave us thoughtful and helpful reactions.

Write Research To Be Read

Donald M. Murray

The results of educational research might reach classroom teachers, school administrators, school board members, parents, legislators, and taxpayers if researchers would learn from journalists and other non-fiction writers how to write for the general public.

Educational research reports are too often written in a private language and an academic form which obscures their conclusions and excludes those people who might implement the research results.

The craft of clear writing is not a mystery. Writing is a process which can be learned, and the principles of writing for a general audience are clear and simple. They are, in fact, deceptively simple, and that very simplicity is often rejected by the academic mind which confuses complexity with intelligence. Simple writing is easy to describe, hard to perform, yet it can be learned and practiced by persons who have something to say and the courage to communicate.

The obscurity of research writing may not be critical—although I think this could be debated—in certain of the sciences, where a few members of a private club write for other members of the same club. But educational research must reach the classroom. Educational researchers must be able to communicate with those who control the classroom if educational research is to have significant impact on our educational system.

There are ten basic principles which should be understood and practiced by the researcher who has the commitment and the courage to write for a general audience. They are:

You Can't Write Nothing

The amateur believes a professional writer writes with words, that the pro can erect a solid piece of writing out of rhetoric, grammar, vocabulary and a magic called talent. The writer writes with information. Words are the symbols for information, and if there is no information there will be no effective writing, no matter how graceful or correct the arrangement of the words upon the page. The raw material from which a piece of effective writing can be constructed is knowl-

Murray, Donald M. (1982). Write research to be read. In D. Murray, Learning by teaching: Selected articles on writing and teaching (pp. 760–768). Montclair, N.J.: Boyton/Cook.

edge—solid, specific, concrete pieces of information which can be built into a meaning.

The ghostwriter or ghost editor doesn't start with the text but with the subject. The subject is first learned, and the professional must be a quick study. Content precedes form, in fact, content predicts form. Accurate information arranged in a logical and meaningful order will produce writing which will stand up to a reader. As Ernest Hemingway said, "Prose is architecture, not interior decoration."

Write to Think

Teachers frequently say, "Know what you want to say before you say it." Writers know that is often false counsel. The professional writes to discover what will appear on the page. Language leads the writer toward meaning. We are all familiar with the process of talking out a problem with another person to find out what we mean and how we feel about it. The writer talks to himself or herself through writing.

Many writers put their notes aside when the time comes to complete a first draft and dictate or write as fast as they can to see what appears on the page. Experience reveals to them that much of what is forgotten needs to be forgotten, and what is remembered is what is important. The subconscious is a good editor. And, of course, if memory fails, what is forgotten can be recovered from the notes later, for the writer assumes that any piece of writing will evolve through a series of discovery drafts, which first explore and then clarify the subject. The writer knows rewriting is not punishment, but an essential part of the process of using language to discover meaning.

Look at what is happening in these sentences from successive drafts.

The teachers observed in a succession of schools within this one system seemed both comfortable and competent with the curriculum, which seemed to this observer to repeat much of the Language Arts material year after year.

The observer thought the curriculum was repetitive, with an excessive overlap from year to year, and it was surprising that there seemed little evidence of boredom on the part of the teachers and their students.

The observer realized that both teachers and students were comfortable within this curriculum for they were learning little that was new.

The observer began to realize the resistance to change within the school system when he saw that both teacher and student were comfortable within a traditional curriculum.

One of the principal reasons for resistance to change was the fact that teachers were teaching what they had taught before to students who had learned it before. Everyone knew what was expected of them. Classrooms had a comfortable feeling. There was efficient performance but little learning.

There are many things going on in those sentences, but the most important thing is that the writer is moving towards meaning, is thinking on the page. The writer works from an observation toward an understanding of its cause. The writer, during the process of writing, is not looking at a handbook, a dictionary, or thesaurus, but is looking through the page at the classroom. The writer is looking at information, symbolizing it with words, and then examining what is on the page to discover what it means. Writing is thinking.

Write in Terms of People

The general reader is far more interested in people than in ideas, theories, or concepts. Academics may resent or deplore this, but they must accept it as a condition of work if they want to write for a general audience. Educational researchers, at least, should be comfortable writing about people, for although we need more basic research in learning, in chemical-electric brain functions, still most educational research is, by its nature, research which has direct implications for students and teachers. It should be able to be reported in terms of people.

Writers who achieve a large audience populate their pages with individual persons whose actions reveal the ideas the writer wishes to communicate.

There are two principal techniques of putting people onto a page of writing:

- The basic building block of the popular magazine article is the anecdote, or little story, which reveals a point in terms of people. As an editor once told me, "Your article should be written in parables, the way the Bible is." I laughed, but I learned.

The researcher might write:
"The omission of conventional verbalization is often an effective technique of classroom management."
The magazine article writer might write:
"It was a typical after lunch class at Inner City High School. Roscoe gave a peanut-butter belch and Jed, Tom, and Theodore clapped in appreciation. Marianne giggled. Herbert knocked Joan's books on the floor. Hannah flipped a paper clip into Jody's soft drink.
Then Miss Gooch came into Room 212. She was elderly—at least forty years old and four feet eleven inches tall. She wore last year's dress. The observer knew this would be a disaster.
Miss Gooch marched to the exact center of the wall, in front of the obscenity on the blackboard and looked right at Hannah. When she caught her eye she turned to Jody, and then Herbert, and then Theodore, Tom, Jed, Roscoe and, one by one, they grew quiet. The silence grew louder and louder until she said in a soft voice, 'My name is Lucinda Gooch.' No one laughed.

Research has documented what Miss Gooch knew. Silence can be an effective tool in classroom management."

- The other technique is simply to perk up a general statement by populating it with people when it can clarify the meaning.

The researcher might write:
"It is dysfunctional educative practice to postulate on-site, in-service, participatory sessions when school practitioner fatigue has multiplied the tri-administrative managerial inter-face malfunctions."
The writer might say the same thing this way:
"At 2:50 the bell rings and students stampede from the school. They are released for the day, but the teachers aren't. Clutching paper cups of instant coffee, juggling armloads of papers to be read that night, muttering threats of a yawn-in, they slump off to an in-service training session."

Obviously a piece can be made too perky, cluttered with people or filled with anecdotes and descriptions that obscure what is being said. But most research in education never lets the reader see what has been studied in terms of the individuals examined and show what it means to individuals in the classroom. And that is one reason educational research is rarely read and rarely implemented.

Say One Thing

An effective piece of writing has focus. There is a controlling vision which orders what is being said. The writer writes drafts to establish the priority of meaning, and then eliminates all that doesn't follow. In this article the dominating idea was that educational researchers could and should learn the principles of writing for a mass audience. When that idea is established, every page, every paragraph, every sentence, every word must advance it.

A successful research project usually will give off many ideas. A new technique in teaching math may have implications for using statistics in social studies and language acquisition. The way the math approach was successfully introduced to a resisting math department may have a lesson for school administrators. This may also produce a design for the retraining of teachers in a union-dominated school system. The method itself may have some implications for teachers of advanced students and quite different ones for brain-damaged students. It may incorporate a team-teaching technique and a new variation on evaluation. Most of all, it may clarify how we think through certain problems. The tendency is to jam everything into one article. The editor experienced with reaching a large audience would advise the educational researcher to publish a series of short articles, each one developing and documenting a research finding for a specific audience.

Emphasize the Positive

Inexperienced writers usually assume that the reader does not know the problem—classes are too large, teachers need retraining, there are students with learning disabilities in the classroom—and preach, telling the reader there is a problem. In fact, most of the time the reader knows the problem—Johnny can't spell "smel"—but doesn't know what to do about it.

The writer will reach a large audience if solutions are presented as well as problems. Spelling may not be learned in 284 schools, but it may be in Bear Paw School. The professional writer will concentrate on Bear Paw School. Writing which attracts readers shows a problem and its solution. It tells the reader what can be done. It leaves the reader with something to do—try the techniques which work in Bear Paw School.

Short Is Harder—and Better

Many writers apologize for writing a long letter by saying they didn't have time to write a short one. It takes time—and courage—to produce a short piece of writing, because brevity is achieved by selection. Meaning is not jammed into a bullion cube to produce brevity; the writer selects what is most important and develops each of those points efficiently but fully.

This requires an executive turn of mind. The writer must decide what is important and what can be left out. Brevity, of course, exposes the writer. It allows the reader to see just what the writer means, and academics, too often, are trained to play it safe. This results in communication—and exposure.

The influential readers that educational researchers must reach are busy. They simply will not read long, involved pieces of writing. Perhaps they should. The most responsible—and most guilty—will purchase, clip, copy, and put aside long, profound pieces to be read during Christmas break, or next summer, or on a sabbatical some time in the future. While those pieces grow into Alps of good intention, short, disciplined pieces of writing which get to the point in a hurry are read and have an impact.

Answer Your Readers' Questions—Especially If You Don't Want Them Asked

The writer must assume an intelligent ignorance on the part of the general public. The writer believes the reader does not know the subject but is capable of knowing it.

Probably the best way of anticipating what the audience needs to know is to write down the questions—the toughest questions—an uninformed but intelligent reader might ask.

The kinds of questions which the writer must ask of his own piece of writing might include:

- What are the results of this experiment with using computers to teach language?
- Who chose the sample? Did that load the dice?
- Is the school typical?
- What does it mean for high school students?
- What needs to be done now?
- What are the problems teachers will have using the system?
- What will it cost?

These may not be the questions the writer wants asked, but they may be the questions an intelligent and skeptical audience will ask.

The writer often finds it helpful to ask these questions during the prewriting process before the first draft. These questions can become an outline or an organizational plan for the article or book, since the effective writer anticipates the reader's questions and answers them at the point they will most certainly arrive in the reader's mind.

Edit for Simplicity

The goal of writing should be simple clarity. The writer should not be visible. As George Orwell said, "Good prose is like a window pane." The reader's attention should be focused on the subject, not on the person presenting the subject. Not all ideas, of course, can be expressed with elementary simplicity. But each idea should be presented as simply as possible if the writer wants to achieve a general audience. Some of the tricks of the editor's trade include:

Write Titles, Not Labels

A label simply says what it is: "A Test to Evaluate Mathematical Skills of Creative Writing Students." A title focuses, clarifies, and draws the reader in, "Killing a Myth: Poets Can't Calculate." Obviously the title, far more than the label, helps the reader, but it also is of great importance to the writer, for each title is, in a sense, a draft. Often I will write a hundred titles during the prewriting process. Each one limits the subject, helps me focus on it, and may even establish the voice with which the piece will be written. Of course the title must be honest; it should not promise what the writer can not deliver.

Write Leads, Not Introductions

The introduction tells the reader what you intend to say. The lead draws the reader right into the subject. The introduction gets between the reader and the subject; the lead is the subject evolving. If you do not see the importance of writing effective leads, then have a friend go through a newspaper, magazine or journal and tell you when the decision is made to read on or turn to another article. In my experience that decision will be made in less than five seconds, in most cases less than three. Clearly the writer must realize that he or she has ten lines or less in which to capture and hold the reader.

The discipline of the lead, however, is not only a service to the reader, it is an opportunity for the writer. As the title helps the writer focus on the subject, so does the lead. The lead eliminates much of what might intrude upon the subject. It focuses, it establishes the dimensions of the piece. It often identifies the audience, and it sets the voice.

Skillful lead-writing is what makes it possible for the journalist to write clean copy in a brief period of time under pressure. The experienced journalist usually writes the lead on the way back to the office, and once the lead is set, the piece of writing flows. The hard news journalist's lead is built on who, what, when, where, and why (or how). As the journalist becomes the magazine writer, the lead becomes even more important. I often write fifty leads, fifty first paragraphs, before starting the first draft. Sometimes the lead will come quickly, other times it will emerge only after a great deal of struggle. But most nonfiction writers find they must establish the lead before they go on. The lead gives them the approach to the piece of writing.

Let us see how a lead might evolve:

"It was established that the parameters of the writing program were less withdrawn than might have been predicted at the beginning of the testing program. One saw written communication in contextual situations in which it had not been hypothesized."

"The experiment was designed to show when students wrote within the Language Arts curriculum. Data revealed that students write as much or more during other elements of the learning experience."

"Writing isn't owned by Language Arts teachers. Writing is taught, learned, and practiced in all parts of the curriculum and outside of school as well. That was the result of a test program . . . "

"Muriel wrote a book report on Monday for her Language Arts teacher, a science report on Tuesday, and an imaginary explorer's account in Social Studies on Wednesday. After school on Wednesday, Muriel helped write a new class constitution. On Thursday she described a turtle trying to escape a tank. That night she wrote a thank-you note to her grandmother and then worked on a skit with four children from church. On Friday Muriel wrote a description for her Language Arts teacher. She said that was Muriel's second writing assignment for the week.

The Language Arts teacher thought she was the only writing teacher in the school. Research shows that writing is taught more by Social Studies and Science teachers than Language Arts teachers, perhaps even more in the home and the community than in the Language Arts classroom."

That last lead doesn't tell you what is going to be said, it draws you right into what is being said. It informs and attracts. And note how much it helps the writer. The subject of the article and, therefore, its dimensions, its order, its development, its audience, its tone, pace, and voice are all made clearer by the lead.

Build with Paragraphs

The paragraph is the basic unit of nonfiction. Each paragraph should be short, and it should move the piece of writing forward by developing a piece of information which the reader needs when the reader needs it. It is helpful to remember that the point of greatest emphasis is at the end of a paragraph, and the next most important point at the beginning. Information in the middle of the paragraph is not emphasized.

The greatest enemy to vigorous and effective paragraphs is the topic sentence (even though this is one). English teachers teach that a flat statement topic sentence must always be used. But this statement of what is to be said tends to get between the reader and the subject. Each paragraph should have a topic, but in most cases that topic should be implied, not stated.

Writers who are having difficulty organizing a piece of writing often find it helpful to draft a single paragraph to the page. This helps the writer develop each paragraph fully. Then, when all the paragraphs are drafted, the writer can spread them out on a desk, table, bed, or floor, and move them around until the writer discovers the simplest, most effective organization, the one which answers the reader's questions at the time that the reader asks them.

Respect the Subject-Verb-Object Sentences

The simple sentence seems too simple for many academics, but good writing for a general audience is constructed of sentences which are direct and vigorous. Of course, the effective writer varies the length and design of the sentence so that the sentences march before the reader in a pleasing and clarifying order. But the key points should be made in short, declarative sentences, and not hidden behind a hedgerow of clauses.

Avoid Jargon

Jargon is the private language spoken between specialists. Specialists may argue that they use jargon because it is precise. But such precision—if it exists—is lost unless it is spoken between specialists in the same narrow area of knowledge. And, more and more, we can not stay within our narrow specialties. One group of computer programmers may speak the same jargon, but they deal with statisticians from psychology, sociology, political science, education, forest resources, and their jargon is blurred until it becomes meaningless. And when these people attempt to speak to the public the jargon becomes incomprehensible.

Most jargon is used to impress, not to communicate; to establish a professional club and exclude everyone else; to complicate, not to clarify. We all have
our special pet hates—*parameters* instead of *limits, school practitioners* instead of
teachers, interface, finalize, interpersonal relationships, software, viability—each day
seems to bring a new horror.

Language should be a precision instrument, and it can be if the writer looks
at the subject and seeks the simplest, most direct word which communicates
information. The important thing for the writer to remember is that he or she is
writing with information, and that each word must carry information to the
reader as efficiently as possible.

Write with Verbs and Nouns

Verbs are the machines that make writing move. The effective writer for the
general public will write principally with active verbs and specific nouns. The
writer feels that adverbs and adjectives imply failure, failure to find the right verb
or the right noun.

Writers also seek the active voice rather than the passive. "John was hit by
Jim," uses two more words but says no more than, "Jim hit John."

Cut Everything That Can Be Cut

A paragraph E. B. White quoted from William Strunk, Jr. in *Elements of Style* was
framed over my desk for many years:

> *"Vigorous writing is concise. A sentence should contain no unnecessary words,
> a paragraph no unnecessary sentences, for the same reason that a drawing should
> have no unnecessary lines and a machine no unnecessary parts. This requires not
> that the writer make all his sentences short, or that he avoid all detail and treat
> his subjects only in outline, but that every word tell."*

The writer should have no greater joy, perhaps, than pruning a piece of
writing, cutting out every word that can be cut out, changing constructions so
that they are clearer, simpler, shorter, making the abstract concrete, the general
specific, the complex clear.

Each writer will develop a personal list of editorial enemies. Mine includes
quite, that, -ings, would, the verb *to be,* transitional phrases. This list will change as
the writer changes. Of course, these are stylistic choices (and, of course, *of course*
should be on my list) and, of course, there will be times when they are appropriate, but they tend to clutter my page. You will have to identify your own clutter
and then eliminate it.

Listen for Your Own Voice

Writing for a mass audience is still an individual act—one person speaking to another. Write as much as possible as you would speak. At least give the illusion of speech. And when you have a question about how to write something, read it aloud. Even the most prolific writer speaks far more than he or she writes. The ear is an effective editor.

A piece of writing which appeals to a general audience usually has a human, consistent voice. Effective, memorable writing is usually not impersonal and general, but specific and personal.

Break Any Rule

George Orwell's final rule in "Politics and the English Language" was "Break any of these rules sooner than say anything outright barbarous." The purpose of clear writing is clarity and communication, not etiquette. Any rule can and should be broken if it helps to clarify and communicate the meaning. And no rule should be followed if it impedes the clarification of meaning.

One of the greatest impediments to effective writing is the way writing has been taught by English teachers. Language is alive. It changes with the seasons. Grammarians try to contain it, but they cannot. Language can't be imprisoned in any rule book. There is, in fact, little agreement between some of the principal rule books and between the teachers who use them. The writer should not follow rules, but follow language towards meaning, always seeking to understand what is appearing on the page, to see it clearly, to evaluate it clearly, for clear thinking will produce clear writing.

As in ice skating, it's easier to say how to write than to write. Educational researchers can, however, learn to write clear prose which will be read by classroom teachers, principals, superintendents, taxpayers, parents, and school board members. Writing for the general public is not an art, but a craft; not a mystery, but a discipline which can be understood and learned if it is practiced. Then the results of educational research may reach the classroom and improve the education of our children.

References

Agnew, N. M., & Pyke, S. W. (1987). *The science game: An introduction to research in the social sciences.* Englewood Cliffs, NJ: Prentice-Hall.

American Educational Research Association. (1992). *Encyclopedia of educational research.* M. C. Alkin (Ed.). New York: Macmillian.

Argyris, C., Putnam, R., & Smith, D. M. (1987). *Action science: Concepts, methods, and skills for research and intervention.* San Francisco: Jossey-Bass Publishers.

Autry, L. B., & Langenbach, M. (1985). Locus of control and self-responsibility for behavior, *Journal of Educational Research, 79*(2), 76–84.

Ayres, L. P. (1920). *An index number for state school systems.* New York: Columbia Teachers College Press.

Baird, J. C. (1988). *The inner limits of outer space.* Hanover, NH: The University Press of New England.

Bannister, R. C. (1987). *Sociology and scientism: The American quest for objectivity, 1880–1940.* Chapel Hill: University of North Carolina Press.

Bar-On, D. (1991). Try to understand what one is afraid to learn about. In Schon, D. A. (Ed.), *The reflective turn: Case studies in and on educational practice,* (pp. 321–341). New York: Teachers College Press.

Barnes, H. L. (1963). *A history of historical writing.* New York: Dover Publications.

Beere, C. (1990). *Gender roles: A handbook of tests and measurements.* New York: Greenwood Press.

Bem, S. L. (1974). The measurement of psychological androgyny. *Journal of Consulting and Clinical Psychology, 42*(2), 155–162.

Berkhofer, R. F. (1983). The two new histories: Competing paradigms for interpreting the American past. *Organization at American Historians Newsletter, 11*(2), 9–12.

Besag, F. (1986). *Research ethics and why they don't work.* Paper presented at the annual meeting of the American Educational Research Association, San Francisco, CA.

Bijou, S. W., Peterson, R. F., & Ault, M. H. (1968). A method to integrate descriptive experimental field studies at the level of data and empirical concepts. *Journal of Applied Behavioral Analysis, 1*(2), 175–191.

Bogdan, R. C. & Biklen, S. K. (1992). *Qualitative research for education: An introduction to theory and methods.* 2nd ed. Boston: Allyn & Bacon.

Brenner, M., Brown, J., & Canter, D. (Eds.). (1985). *The research interview: Uses and approaches.* Boston: Academic Press.

Brewer, J., & Hunter, A. (1989). *Multimethod research: A synthesis of styles.* Newbury Park, CA: Sage Publications.

Buros, O. D. (Ed.). *Mental measurement yearbook.* (1983). New York: Gryphon Press.

Butler, J., & Scott, J. (Eds.). (1992). *Feminists theorize the political.* New York: Routledge.

Cabell's directory of publishing opportunities in education. (1989). Beaumont, TX: Cabell Publishing Company.

Campbell, D. J., & Stanley, J. C. (1966). *Experimental and quasi-experimental design for research.* Chicago: Rand McNally.

Cohen, L., & Manion, L. (1989). *Research methods in education.* New York: Routledge.

Commager, H. S. (1965). *The nature and the study of history.* Columbus, OH: Charles E. Merrill.

Coombs, C. H. (1964). *A theory of data.* New York: John Wiley & Sons.

Crandall, V. C., Katkovsky, N., & Crandall, V. J. (1965). Children's belief in their own control of reinforcement in intellectual academic achievement settings. *Child Development, 36*(1), 91–109.

Donaldson, M. (1978). *Children's minds.* New York: W. W. Norton.

Earle, W. (1972). *The autobiographical consciousness.* Chicago: Quadrangle Books.

Eisner, E. W. & Peshkin, A. (1990). *Qualitative inquiry in education: The continuing debate.* New York: Teachers College Press.

"Ethical standards of the American Educational Research Association." (Oct., 1992). *Educational Researcher, 21*(7), 23–26.

Everhart, R. (1977). Between stranger and friend: Some consequences of "long-term work in schools. *American Educational Research Journal, 14*(1), 1–15.

Faraday, A., & Plummer, K. (1979). Doing life histories. *Sociological Review, 27*(4), 773–798.

Farr, C. A., & Liles, J. A. (1991). Male teachers, male roles: The Progressive Era and education in Oklahoma. *Great Plains Quarterly, 11*(4), 234–248.

Feinberg, W., & Soltis, J. (1985). *School and society.* New York: Teachers College Press.

Feistritzer, C. E. (1985). *The condition of teaching: A state by state analysis.* Princeton: Princeton University Press.

Ferguson, G. A. (1989). *Statistical analysis in psychology and education.* New York: McGraw-Hill.

Festinger, L., Riecken, H. W., & Schachter, S. (1956). *When prophecy fails.* New York: Harper & Row.

Fetterman, D. M. (1984). Guilty knowledge, dirty hands, and other ethical dilemmas: The hazards of contract research, 211–236. In D. M. Fetterman (Ed.), *Ethnography in educational evaluation.* Beverly Hills: Sage Publications.

Flanders, N. (1970). *Analyzing teaching behavior.* Reading, MA: Addison-Wesley Publishing Co.

Ford, J. (1975). *Paradigms and fairy tales: An introduction to the science of meanings.* Boston: Routledge & Kegan Paul.

Fought, H. W. (1915). *Efficiency and preparation of rural school teachers.* United States Bureau of Education Bulletin, 1914, no. 49. Washington, D. C.: Government Printing Office.

Gage, N. L. (1963). *Handbook of research on teaching: A project of the american educational research association.* Chicago: Rand McNally.

Gilligan, C. (1982). *In a different voice: Psychological theory and women's development.* Cambridge: Harvard University Press.

Gilmore, J. B. (1971). Play: A special behavior. In R. E. Herronard & B. Sutton-Smith. (Eds.), *Child's play* (pp. 343–355). New York: Wiley.

Glaser, B., & Strauss, A. (1967). *The discovery of grounded theory.* Chicago: Aldine Publishing Company.

Goetz, J. P., & LeCompte, M. D. (1984). *Ethnography and qualitative design in educational research.* Orlando, FL: Academic Press.

Goldenberg, C. (1989). Parents effects on academic grouping for reading: Three case studies. *American Educational Research Journal, 26*(3), 329–352.

Grob, G. N., & Billias, G. A. (1992). *Interpretations of American history: Patterns and perspectives.* Vols. I & II. New York: The Free Press.

Guba, E. G. (1981). *Toward a methodology of naturalistic inquiry in educational evaluation.* San Francisco: Jossey-Bass Publishers.

Halote, B., & Michael, W. (1984). The construct validity of an exploratory academic self-concept subscale derived from the Piers-Harris Children's Self-Concept scale. *Educational and Psychological Measurements, 44*(4), 993–1007.

Hatch, J. A. (1985). The quantoids versus the smooshes: Struggles with methodological rapprochement. *Issues in Education, 13*(2), 158–167.

Heilbrun, C. G. (1988). *Writing a woman's life.* New York: Ballantine Books.

Horn, L. (1989). High school and beyond: National longitudinal study of 1972. Washington, D.C.: U.S. Dept. of Educ. Office of Educational Research and Improvement.

Howe, K. R. (1990). *Getting over the quantitative-qualitative debate.* Paper presented at the annual meeting of the American Educational Research Association, Boston, MA.

Jackson, P. W. (1968). *Life in classroom.* New York: Holt, Rinehart & Winston.

Jaeger, R. M. (1983). *Statistics: A spectator sport.* Beverly Hills: Sage Publications.

Jensen, K. (1984). Oral histories of rural western American women: Can they contribute to quantitative studies? *International Journal of Oral History, 5*(3), 159–167.

Kerber, L. K., Greeno, C. G., Macoby, E. E., Luria, Z., Stack, C. B., & Gilligan, C. (1986). In a different voice: An interdisciplinary forum. *Signs, 11*(2), 304–333.

Kerlinger, F. (1973). *Foundations of behavioral research.* New York: Holt, Rinehart, & Winston.

Klockars, C. B. (1979). Dirty hands and deviant subjects. In C. B. Klockars & F. W. O'Conner (Eds.), *Deviance and decency: The ethics of research with human subjects* (pp. 261–282). Beverly Hills: Sage Publications.

Kruglanski, A. (1989). *Lay epistemics and human knowledge: Cognitive and motivational bases.* New York: Plenum Press.

Kuhn, T. S. (1970). *The structure of scientific revolutions.* Chicago: University of Chicago Press.

Langenbach, M., & Aagaard, L. (1990). A factor analytic study of the adult classroom environment scale. *Adult Education Quarterly, 40*(2), 95–102.

LeCompte, M. D., & Goetz, J. P. (1982). Problems of reliability and validity in ethnographic research. *Review of Educational Research, 52*(1), 31–60.

Lincoln, Y. S., & Guba, E. G. (1985). *Naturalistic inquiry.* Newbury Park, CA: Sage Publications.

Lincoln, Y. S. (1988). *The role of ideology in naturalistic research.* Paper presented at the annual meeting of the American Educational Research Association. New Orleans, LA.

Maguire, P. (1987). *Doing participatory research: A feminist approach.* Amherst, MA: University of Massachusetts Press.

Marshall, C., & Rossman, G. (1989). *Designing qualitative research.* Newbury Park, CA: Sage Publications.

May, W. T. (1987). *On the potential to be an unethical researcher of children.* Paper represented at the annual meeting of the American Educational Research Association, Washington, D. C.

Merriam, S. B. (1988). *Case study research in education: A qualitative approach.* San Francisco: Jossey-Bass Publishers.

Merriam, S. B., & Simpson, E. L. (1984). *A guide to research for educators and trainers of adults.* Malabar, FL: Krieger Publishing Company.

Messick, S. (1988). "Validity." *Educational Measurement.* New York: Macmillian.

Miles, M., & Huberman, A. (1984). *Qualitative data analysis: A sourcebook of new methods.* Beverly Hills: Sage Publications.

Milgram, S. (1963). Behavioral study of obedience. *Journal of Abnormal and Social Psychology, 67*(4), 371–378.

Moore, D. S. & McCabe, G. P. (1992). *Introduction to the practice of statistics.* New York: W. H. Freeman.

Moustakas, C. (1990). *Heuristic research: Design, methodology, and applications.* Newbury Park, CA: Sage Publications.

Olson, J. S., & Wilson, R. (1984). *Native Americans: In the twentieth century.* Chicago: University of Illinois Press.

Packer, M. J. (1985) Hermeneutic inquiry in the study of human conduct. *American Psychologist, 40*(10), 1081–1093.

Peshkin, A. (1978). *Growing up American: Schooling and the survival of community.* Chicago: University of Chicago Press.

Peshkin, A. (1982). The researcher and subjectivity: Reflections on an ethnography of school and community. In G. Spindler (Ed.), *Doing the ethnography of schooling* (pp. 48–67). New York: Holt, Rinehart, & Winston.

Peshkin, A. (1984). Odd man out: The participant observer in an absolutist setting. *Sociology of Education, 57*(4), 254–254.

Peshkin, A. (1986). *God's choice: The total world of a fundamentalist Christian school.* Chicago: University of Chicago Press.

Piaget, J. (1969). *Science of education and the psychology of the child.* New York: Grossman Publishers.

Pike, K. (1954). *Language in relation to a unified theory of the structure of human behavior.* Vol. 1. Glendale, CA: Summer Institute of Linguistics.

Polsky, N. (1967). *Hustlers, beasts, and others.* Chicago: Aldine Press.

Proposed ethical standards for AERA. (1991). *Educational Researcher, 20*(9), 31–34.

Rist, R. (1980). Blitzkrieg ethnography: On the transformation of a method into a movement. *Educational Researcher, 9*(2) (February), 8–11.

Robinson-Hornbuckle, M. (1991). *Female administrators in rural schools: Who are they? What are their leadership styles?* Ed.D. dissertation. Norman, OK: University of Oklahoma.

Rotter, J. (1966). Generalized expectations for internal versus external control of reinforcement. *Psychological Monographs: General and Applied, 80*(1), 1–28.

Salomon, G. (1991). Transcending the qualitative/quantitative debate: The analytic and systemic approaches to educational research. *Educational Researcher, 20*(6), 10–18.

Schornick, S. (1992). *Learning through a play-based curriculum: How does free play behavior facilitate cognitive growth within a developmentally-appropriate environment?* Master's Project. Norman, OK: University of Oklahoma.

Schwartz, H., & Jacobs, J. (1979). *Qualitative sociology: A method to the madness.* New York: The Free Press.

Shakeshaft, C. (1987). *Women in educational administration.* Newbury Park, CA: Sage Publications.

Shavelson, R. J. (1981). *Statistical reasoning for the behavioral sciences.* Boston: Allyn & Bacon.

Smith, J. K. (1990). *Are there differences that still make a difference?* Paper presented at the annual meeting of the American Educational Research Association, Boston, MA.

Smith, L. M. (1990). Ethics in qualitative field research: An individual perspective. In E. W. Eisner & A. Peshkin (Eds.), *Qualitative inquiry in education: The continuing debate* (pp. 258–276). New York: Teachers College Press.

Spindler, G. (Ed.). (1982). *Doing the ethnography of schooling: Educational anthropology in action.* New York: Holt, Rinehart & Winston.

Tawney, J., & Gast, D. L. (1984). *Single subject research in special education.* Columbus, OH: Charles Merrill.

Tesch, R. (1984). *Phenomenological studies: A critical analysis of their nature and procedures.* Paper presented at the annual meeting of the American Educational Research Association, New Orleans, LA.

Tesch, R. (1990). *Qualitative research: Analysis types and software tools.* New York: Falmer Press.

Trigger, G. G. (1982). Ethnohistory: Problems and prospects. *Ethnohistory, 29*(1), 1–19.

Urban, W. J. (1982). Historiography. In H. E. Mitzel (Ed.), *Encyclopedia of educational research,* Vol. 2. New York: The Free Press.

Van Kaam, A. (1959). Phenomenal analysis: Exemplified by a study of the experience of "really feeling understood." *Journal of Individual Psychology, 15*(1), 66–72.

van Manen, M. (1984). Practicing phenomenological writing. *Phenomenology and Pedagogy, 2*(1), 36–69.

van Manen, M. (1990). *Researching lived experience: Human science for action sensitive pedagogy.* New York: The State University of New York Press.

Vaughn-Roberson, C. A. (1984). Sometimes independent but never equal—women teachers, 1900–1950: The Oklahoma example. *Pacific Historical Review, 53*(1), 39–58.

Weiler, K. (1992). *"Yes I'm a pioneer teacher": California teachers' narratives.* Paper presented at the Western Women's History Association Conference. Lincoln, NE.

Werner, O., & Schoepfle, G. M. (1987). *Systematic fieldwork: Ethnographic analysis and data management.* Vols. I & II. Newberry Park, CA: Sage Publications.

Whyte, W. F. (1984). *Learning from the field: A guide from experience.* Beverly Hills: Sage Publications.

Willis, P. (1981). *Learning to labor: How working class kids get working class jobs.* New York: Columbia University Press.

Winer, B. J. (1990). *Statistical principles in experimental design.* New York: McGraw-Hill.

Wolcott, A. F. (1982). Mirrors, models, and monitors: Educator adaptations of the ethnographic innovation. In Spindler, G. (Ed.) *Doing the ethnography of schooling* (pp. 68–95). New York: Holt, Rinehart, & Winston.

Worthen, B. R. (1985). *The unvarnished truth about logic-in-use versus reconstructed logic in educational inquiry.* Paper presented at the annual meeting of the American Educational Research Association, Chicago.

Wyatt, R. L. III. (1990). *The role of the writer in the writing process: A look at a composer's journal for evidence of writing stages.* Ph.D. dissertation. Norman, OK: University of Oklahoma.

*Glossary**

A priori is a Latin term which indicates that an idea or thought is evolving from cause to effect. In social sciences *research,* the term is usually used to indicate an assumption derived from *theory* rather than experience. It is occasionally used as a synonym for the word "before," to indicate preexisting *theory.*

Action research is the use of *theory* and *research* to implement and establish a program or behavior. Researchers collect *data* from initial change efforts, assess problems with the procedure, and then refine or change their strategies. *Action research* is usually reform oriented, and would be placed in that portion of the *ideology* continuum of the *conceptual cube.*

Action science is inquiry into how human beings design and implement action in relation to one another. It is a science of practice that calls for basic *research* and *theory* building that are intimately related to social intervention. Its reform orientation would place it in the back half (reform portion) of the *conceptual cube.*

Activity codes are classifications of *qualitative data* that include recurrent behavior.

Aesthetics is a division of the philosophical area of *axiology.* It is the study of art and beauty.

Analysis of variance (ANOVA) is a statistical method by which the *means* of three or more groups can be compared regarding their similarities or differences.

Anonymity is the assurance that *data* will not be traceable to the *subject* or *participant* who provided them.

Applied research is the use of *theory* and *research* to solve a problem, usually in a localized area.

Artistic approach is a *research tradition* or *design* that seeks to show the personal experience of the subject. It typically analyzes narratives that stand alone and must be evaluated on the basis of their own internal consistency or coherence, much as any piece of art.

*Italicized words are also to be found in the glossary.

Axiology is one of three major philosophical areas of study. It is the study of values, usually divided into *ideology*, *ethics* and *aesthetics*.

Behaviorism is a *school of thought* within psychology that assumes human behavior is the result of external reinforcement, either before or after the behavior.

Blitzkrieg ethnography is a term used to highlight the use of *ethnographic* methods (mostly interviews) without the consideration or inclusion of such basic structures as a reason for the study, current *research* in the field, what existent *theory* the work is related to, or how perspective or *theory* may be generated from the *research*.

Bracketing is the process of setting aside the researcher's beliefs when analyzing *qualitative data*.

Case site is the localized boundary of a *research study*. Although the site can range from individual behavior to group behaviors, it is usually limited to a geographically small area, such as a classroom, school, or business. *Case* and *site* may also be used synonymously.

Case study is a *research design* focusing on one person or thing to be analyzed (n = 1) or a small *sample* of people. Case studies are designed to provide limited information that focuses on a single issue, individual, or organizational behavior, or on one outcome within a narrow context containing limited *variables*. Because of the small *sample*, a case study researcher, ultimately, must relate her or his findings to *theory* in order for the work to be considered *research*.

Chi-square is a statistical procedure used with *nominal data* to determine if patterns or characteristics are different across populations.

Cognitive anthropology is the study of people's mental processes as they are related to their culture's knowledge and beliefs.

Conceptual cube is a visual framework for distinguishing certain *ontological, epistemological*, and *axiological* positions of a *research* project. Two or more *research* reports can be plotted on the cube and compared to the other(s).

Conclusion-bound study is any project that has connection(s) to *theory*, either through *theory* testing or *theory* generating.

Concurrent validity indicates the extent to which the test scores estimate an individual's present standing on the criterion. For example, are students' scores on an achievement test relatively similar to their current academic performance in school?

Confidentiality is the understanding between researcher and *participant* (*subject*) that the *data* from the *participant* will not be shared in a manner that would aid in the identification of the *participant*.

Confirmability is the ability to validate *data*.

Conflict theory, at one time referred to as Marxian analysis, is an interpretation of collective human behavior that does not use the conventional or normative explanations of the prevailing *ideology* of a given culture. For example, in the United States the popular *ideology* of capitalism might attribute the cause of poverty to the inability of poor people to use their assets to produce capital.

A conflict theorist, on the other hand, maintains that capitalists structure society to create an underclass and prevent it from obtaining assets by erecting barriers to prevent its children from obtaining an equitable education.

Consistency is the likelihood that the same or similar *data* would be collected from the same *participants* in a *naturalistic* study. Its corollary in *rationalistic research* is *reliability*.

Constant comparative method is the process of continuously checking and cross-referencing new *data* with *data* previously obtained, other sources, and with the categories developed in *qualitative analysis*. This provides a method whereby the *consistency* and *trustworthiness* of the *data* can be maintained.

Constitutive ethnography is a *research tradition* that focuses on how peoples' minds translate or process information as they interact with their culture or environment.

Construct is a complex idea or image that is not directly observable or measurable. Examples include motivation, intelligence, creativity, and social class.

Construct validity is the degree to which an *instrument* measures the construct it purports to measure.

Constructivism is a philosophical position or world view contending that reality does not exist independently of people's perceptions. Rather, reality consists of how individuals perceive, create, and construct it.

Contamination of *data* occurs when an external factor affects the observations (*data*) and interpretations of them.

Content analysis is the examination of *qualitative data* by *quantitative* or *qualitative* means; for example, counting how frequently words or phrases appear in a text and determining what they mean or what impact they might have on a reader.

Content validity involves judgments that the words of an item or an *instrument* will indeed measure what the item purports to measure.

Context in language is the part of a sentence before and after a word or phrase that determines the meaning of the word or phrase. In *research*, it is the information that surrounds the object of study, such as history, socioeconomic status, or even the researcher himself or herself.

Control group is, in a *true or quasi-experimental design,* one of two similar groups selected from a *population*. One becomes the *experimental group* and receives the treatment. The other, the control group, does not.

Conventional research is often used as a synonym for *rationalism* and *positivism*.

Convergent refers to moving from the general to the specific, as in logic. See *deductive procedures*.

Correlational research examines the relationship(s) between two or more *variables*. The intent is to show that one is associated with change in another. If one increases when the other increases, the correlation is positive. If one decreases when the other increases, the *variables* are said to be negatively or inversely correlated.

Covert participant is a researcher who participates in the activities of the *subject* under inquiry without letting anyone know research is being conducted. Although information may be uncovered that may not have been obtained if the researcher had revealed his or her real interest in the participation, the process does have a number of potential difficulties. These include the ability of the researcher to maintain a dispassionate frame of mind, that a researcher may not be subject to the same penalties or rewards once her or his identity is revealed, and that the *research question* might be obtained by deception.

Covert research is a study in which the researchers do not reveal themselves as such at all.

Credibility is a synonym for believability.

Criterion-related validity is assessed by comparing scores on an *instrument* with one or more external *variables,* called criteria. For example, a new test of creativity could be administered at the same time as an accepted, established test is administered. The established test scores would be the criterion, and *validity* of the new test would be determined by how well the scores from it corresponded to the scores from the established test.

Critical realism is a philosophical position that agrees with *realism*, in that there is an objective reality, but disagrees that this can be known simply by experiencing *data* through the senses. For example, although two people may see the same car, this bit of knowledge also contains both persons' interpretations of the car. The critical realist insists that meaning must, therefore, be determined by a process of analysis.

Critical theory is a *school of thought* in education that developed in response to the inability of *functional* or *normative* (*status quo*-oriented) explanations to expose the subtle manner in which schools perpetuate the values of those in positions of political and economic power. For example, *functionalist theory* explains women's place in United States society as serving a necessary role, that of the second-class citizen, and recognized no sexism. Critical theory offers the explanation that there is no rational reason for this; rather, that sexism simply serves the interests of a few in a patriarchal society. Moreover, normative theorists explain the underrepresentation of minority groups as the natural result of inferior racial characteristics and therefore do not recognize racism. Critical theorists view racism as a means by which Euro-Americans identify and maintain an underclass to serve them.

Data are the information collected and analyzed in a *research* project.

Data reduction is the process of deciding what *data* to include, remove, or change in the *research* process. With *qualitative data* it may happen in site selection, a narrowing of the research question, or the sorting of information collected. With *quantitative data,* examples include reducing responses by offering only certain choices, transforming responses to numbers, and removing *outliers.*

Data saturation is the point at which the information received, *data,* becomes redundant, or simply begins to repeat what are now common patterns in the *research* study.

Debriefing is informing a *participant* or *subject* in a study of the nature of the study at the conclusion of his or her participation.

Decision-bound study is any project that proceeds or culminates without connection(s) to *theory*. Most evaluations of projects or programs are decision-bound studies.

Deductive procedures are means of reasoning from the general to the specific, typically from an existing premise to a logical conclusion.

Demographics is the science of vital statistics. In the social sciences, demographic *data* include compilations of numbers relating to race, ethnic background, income, gender, occupation, and so forth.

Dependability, sometimes referred to as *consistency,* is the likelihood that the *data* are reliable indicators of the phenomenon or construct being studied.

Dependent variable is, in a *true experimental design,* the *variable* that the experimental treatment is intended to affect. In a *quasi-experimental design* the *dependent variable* is also the one that is intended to change, but any change can only be inferred to be a relationship or association, not the result of cause and effect.

Descriptive statistics are those used to describe how a particular characteristic is distributed among a group. *Mean, median, mode,* and *standard deviation* are descriptive statistics.

Descriptive theories are related *generalizations* that purport to represent phenomena as they are, not necessarily as they should be.

Design is the arrangement of procedures and methods of a *research* project that typically includes *case site, sample, data* collection, and analysis. Within *naturalistic* studies *research tradition* is used as a synonym for *design.*

Dialogical reflection is a special kind of discussion that is specifically designed to expose and analyze the ideological component of attitudes and feelings, in an atmosphere of safety, so as to expand the awareness of the participants about how *ideology* shapes their thought and behavior.

"Dirty hands" belong to researchers who commit an illegal or unethical act during the course of their research.

Divergent describes a thought process that evolves from the specific to the general. See *inductive procedures.*

Educational anthropology is the study of educational phenomena that considers the context, typically determined *inductively,* to play an important role in fully understanding the phenomena.

Emergent design is the change in the *design* of a *research* project during the course of the project that facilitates *data* collection and/or reframing of the *research question.*

Emic is an anthropological term meaning *native description,* that is, the words and language used by the natives of a culture.

Empirical anarchy is the use of *quantitative data* and means of analysis to overshadow or displace the value of *qualitative data* and means of analysis.

Empiricism is a belief in experience and the physical results of experimentation, as opposed to any information that cannot be identified by the physical senses.

Empowerment is the attainment of personal and collective power, after becoming aware of one's oppression and ability to overcome it.

Epistemology is one of the three major areas of philosophical study. When applied to *research* it is concerned with the nature of knowledge necessary to answer a *research question* and the methods of obtaining and understanding that knowledge. Within the *conceptual cube* the epistemological continuum or plane includes only the methodology used to derive, elicit, and analyze *data*.

Error is an incorrect assertion or prediction about the behavior of the *subject(s)*. In rationalistic research the concern about *internal* and *external validity* has to do with reducing error from the *research design*.

Ethics is the study of standards of conduct and moral judgment, how they are derived and applied, and, in the case of *research*, how these standards affect all those concerned with a particular project.

Ethnography is a *research tradition* or *design*, typically that collects and analyzes *qualitative data*. Ethnography usually seeks perspective about the culture of individuals, groups, or systems. *Data* obtained by interview or other methods is often placed within historical, cultural, and sociological context.

Ethnohistory is a *theory-driven research tradition* or *design* that focuses on a particular culture (often one that has been abused by another) and how it has attempted to maintain its cultural integrity throughout a given period in its history.

Ethnology is a generic term that describes a *research tradition* or *design* that is characterized by a belief in the inseparability of history, culture, and language from any empirical *data* in the pursuit of a *research question*. The work done in this area tends to be *truth-seeking* because ethnologists ultimately hope to determine through culturally comparative studies what human attributes seem to be characteristic of all people and which are culturally determined.

Ethnomethodology is a *research tradition* contending that all people are actors and redefine themselves continuously in their interactions with others. Ethnomethodologists study the manner in which people create their rules and negotiate for how they are identified relative to their culture.

Ethnosemantics is the study of how systems of classification are created and understood from the point-of-view of the subject, through his or her language.

Ethnoscience attempts to classify the cultural information of a society using that society's criteria and rules. Linguistic mapping is a common procedure in ethnoscientific research.

Etic is the characteristic way in which an outsider observes a culture—its rules and the life of its natives—using her or his criteria to try to understand *emic* perspectives.

Evaluation studies determine to what extent, if any, existing programs are working as planned. When *theory* is tested or developed in such studies they become *evaluation research*.

Event codes are classification of *qualitative data* that include infrequently occurring events, such as failing a grade, being suspended, or receiving an award.

Experimental design   includes the selection and assignment of *subjects, data*-gathering, and analysis to achieve *internal* and *external validity*, thus permitting inferences of relationships between experimental treatments and *dependent variables.*

Experimental group,   in *true* or *quasi-experimental designs,* is the group to which an experimental treatment is applied. It is used as a synonym for *treatment group.*

External validity   is an estimate of the degree to which results demonstrated in a *research* project are generalizable to the population.

Extraneous variables   are those *variables* that are not controlled and have the potential for affecting the results of a study.

F-Value   is a statistic produced by performing an *analysis of variance*. It is the size of the F-value that indicates whether or not differences in *means* occurred by chance.

Factor analysis   is a statistical method of determining a small set of *variables* from a larger set. For example, a general intelligence test usually has at least two factors that are named verbal and quantitative.

Factualism   is a philosophical belief or world view that involves the discovery and pursuit of what are seen as facts; that is, objective *data* that would be perceived as being the same, and having the same meaning, by all who would be exposed to them. It is roughly synonymous with *truth-seeking* and roughly the opposite of *perspective-seeking.*

Fair use   is a legal term related to copyright law, which refers to the legal use of unpublished material in published material.

False consciousness   is lack of awareness that keeps the oppressed in their position below the oppressor, and the oppressor bound by the same relationship. It is through dialogue and praxis (a combination of action and reflection) that a new awareness can develop in the oppressed, which will lead them to restructure society so that it leads to a more just existence for both the oppressed and the oppressor.

Feminist research   involves investigations that have developed in response to the need to expose the values and practices that maintain a patriarchal and materialistic society.

Field notes   are written notes taken while in the field doing observation or interviewing. They may include the researcher's comments and interpretations of what was seen and heard.

Fieldwork   is the gathering of *data* at the location of the *research site*. Usually *data* are gathered in the field and then taken to another location for further analysis and organization.

Foreshadowed theories   are the theoretical implications one anticipates the *data* to have before the *research* project is completed.

Functionalism   is primarily an anthropological and sociological *school of thought* maintaining that all of a social system's social events and institutions further the survival of the society as a whole.

Generalizability   is the ability to extend the conclusions of a *research* project to the *population* from which the *sample* was drawn.

Generalizations can be made from a *research* project's *sample* to the *population* when threats to *internal* and *external validity* have been sufficiently minimized in a *rationalistic* study. In a *naturalistic* study, generalizations can be made when the results corroborate existing *theory*.

Grounded theory is a *research tradition* related to *naturalistic* philosophy. It derives models or explanations (generates *theory*) from patterns in the *data*, rather than testing *a priori* or preconceived *theory*.

Guilty knowledge is knowing something incriminating about someone or something in a *research* study.

Hegemony is the domination of certain values or beliefs that are typically not even questioned by members of the culture.

Hermeneutics, originally referring to Biblical analysis, is in modern educational *research* the science of discovering what *participants* believe or perceive they have experienced. Hermeneutic researchers believe nothing can be understood apart from the context within which it was experienced.

Heuristics or *heuristic research* is a *research tradition* or *design* in which the central focus is to study the experience of the individual, seeing this as unique and not *generalizable*.

Historical research is the telling of a story, beginning at some point in the past, within the local, state, and national context of a given time period.

Hypothesis is a statement that predicts the result of manipulating one or more *variables* in a *research* study. The realization of this prediction is the beginning of *theory* for the *truth-seeker,* as truth consists of theoretical statements *generalizable* across all *populations*. The *truth-seeker*'s search for a generalizable *theory* is what drives the continual construction and testing of hypotheses.

Hypothesized relationship is an assertion or statement that there is some relationship between two characteristics or phenomena. A relationship, however, does not necessarily refer to cause and effect, just that there is some affiliation or *correlation* between two *variables* such as age and maturity.

Idealism is a philosophy propounding that truth or authority exists within each person, and is knowable only through reflective thought, rather than through what you can see or touch.

Ideology is a person's point of view or sociopolitical belief. For educators and researchers *ideology* plays an important part in guiding educational practice and *research*. Ideology may not be easily recognizable to those who hold or experience it. This is known as *paradigm*-blindness.

Independent variable is, in an *experimental design,* a characteristic or quantity that, when manipulated, produces a change in one or more *dependent variables*. The *independent variable* in *quasi-experimental designs* may be seen to be related to or associated with the *dependent variable,* but not the cause of it.

Inductive procedures are thought processes that derive conclusions from particular facts and individual cases, moving from specifics to *generalizations*.

Inferential statistics are used to draw inferences from the *sample* being studied to the larger *population* the *sample* represents.

Informants are the people in an ethnographic *research* project from whom *data* are gathered. The term *informant* is used to indicate both that the researcher is gathering a person's viewpoints and that the researcher is an investigator interpreting the *data*.

Informed consent is an agreement between researcher and *participant* or *subject* that the *participant* understands the nature of the *research*, what, if any risks are involved by participating and that the *participant* may withdraw from the *research* at any time without penalty.

Instrument is a generic term used to describe any survey, questionnaire, mechanical instrument, picture, or ink-blot test that is used to gather *data* in a *research* project. The most frequent use of the term is to describe the tests designed to gather *quantitative data*.

Internal validity is an estimate of the degree to which a *design* controls for *variables* that might account for the changes in the *dependent variable* that are not attributable to the experimental treatment.

Inter-observer reliability is the degree to which two or more observers agree on their observations.

Interpretivism is a *research tradition* or *school of thought* in educational sociology maintaining that an external truth does not exist. Rather, what we know is what we interpret or translate, based on our language, thinking patterns, or other cultural or biological characteristics.

Interval data are *data* that have equal intervals. A thermometer is an example of a scale that uses interval data.

Logic-in-use is a form of writing, often appearing in studies that have an *emergent design*, wherein the evolution of the *design* is described.

Longitudinal study is one that examines a phenomenon over a relatively long period of time.

Mean is the arithmetic average of a group of numbers. For example, given the results of a group of tests, the scores are totaled, and then divided by the total number of tests. The result is the mean.

Median is the point at which a group of ordered test scores is divided so that half of the scores are above and half below the median.

Methods codes in *qualitative data* analysis include the researcher's notes about the procedures used in obtaining, classifying, and analyzing *data*.

Mode is the score that appears most frequently in a group of scores. For example, if the most frequent score in a group of tests is a 90, this is the mode.

Naturalism is a *research* philosophy that structures studies to seek perspectives of *participants* or *informants*, usually by collecting *qualitative data* analyzed through *qualitative means*.

Nominal data are *data* that indicate classification. For example 0 = male and 1 = female. Although numbers are used, amount has no meaning in nominal data.

Nonparametric statistics are used when *data* from a *sample* cannot be assumed to be normally distributed in the *population* from which the *sample* was drawn.

Normal distribution is the assumption that a characteristic of a *population*, when plotted on a graph, will be bell-shaped.

Objectivism is a belief that bias-free information can be generated, given proper attention to *design*.

Ontology, also known as, or related to, metaphysics, is one of three major areas of philosophy. It seeks to understand what reality is and/or of what it consists.

Ordinal data are *data* ranked according to order. First, second, third, etc., are ordinal *data*, but unlike *interval* and *ratio*, the difference between ranks cannot be assumed to be equal.

Outliers are *data* from a given project that do not conform to the common patterns found in the study.

Paradigm, as described by Kuhn (1970), is that set of beliefs under which a group of researchers chooses to operate. It includes a *research* philosophy and the *theory* that results from *research* in a given area.

Parametric statistics are those statistics appropriate for use when it is assumed that the *data* represent a *normal distribution* in the *population*.

Participant observer is a researcher who both collects *data* from and becomes involved in a certain *case site*.

Participatory action research is a *research tradition* or *design* in which people (the *participants*) investigate their own reality. They, rather than an independent researcher, act as decision makers regarding the reason for the *research*, its focus, methods, and interpretation.

Path analysis is a statistical means by which different *variables* are estimated to be associated with the *dependent variable*. Typically, path models are drawn showing the nature and strength of the relationships.

Perspective-seeking refers to the *ontology* or view of reality that a *research* study takes. It presumes that no one reality exists. Rather the phenomenon under investigation can be as varied as the number of persons who interact with it.

Phenemonology is the search for understanding how *participants* experience and give meaning to an event, a series of events, a concept, or phenomenon.

Phenomenography is a *research tradition* that seeks to study and represent the subjective experience of the *participant* or *informant* for analysis and understanding.

Pilot study is a scaled-down version of a study to test the logistics and manageability of the procedures.

Policy research or *policy studies* investigate the formulation, implementation, and consequences of public policies and law.

Population is the larger number of people about which the researcher intends to discover theoretical knowledge. Frequently the *population* is too large to study, so that smaller groups (*samples*) are selected to focus on.

Positivism is a philosophy that is grounded in the absolutism of *data*, typically numerical, which lead to the ability to "know" an objective reality.

Post-constructivism maintains that people can change the social structures that helped create their beliefs. This is seen as building on the ideas of *structuralism*.

Post-Modernism refers to the time period that followed the modern age—an era in which the distribution of work, the progress of science, and the accumulation of power and wealth increased for a portion of the world, but mainly for the Western-European white men. Post-Modernism is the transcendence of that age.

Post-positivism (also *anti-positivism*) is a *research* philosophy that rejects the belief that human behavior is regulated by general laws and that one can objectively understand any human behavior. Instead, post-positivists contend that understanding behavior requires subjective involvement with another person's perspective.

Posttest is a test that occurs after a treatment is administered to a *subject* or a *sample*.

Predictive validity indicates the degree to which the score on a given test or survey is related to a subject's future behavior related to the test's content. For instance, do students with higher IQ scores make higher grades and show other evidences of academic success? The extent to which they do is the extent to which the IQ test has predictive validity.

Prescriptive theories are general statements that contain "should" or "ought," seeking to prescribe behavior.

Pretest is a test that occurs before a treatment is administered to a *subject* or sample.

Process codes in *qualitative data* analysis include changes over time, for example, within a school career, a professional career or the entire life history of a *participant*.

Qualitative data are pieces of nonnumerical information collected to answer a *research question*. They are frequently textual, typically used in association with a described context, and can be historical, sociological, or anthropological.

Qualitative methods are techniques by which *qualitative data* are obtained and analyzed. Examples are interviews and *participant observation* (obtained) and seeking patterns or themes within textual *data* (analyzed).

Quantitative data are symbolic or numerical representations of the phenomenon or construct under analysis in a given *research* study.

Quantitative methods are the systematic and mathematical techniques by which quantitative *data* are collected and analyzed.

Quasi-experimental design is one that approaches but does not achieve the features of the *true experimental designs*. Usually, the inability to randomly select *subjects* from a *population* and/or randomly assign *subjects* to groups is what makes a *design* quasi-experimental.

Radical theory maintains that extreme change in or restructuring of existing social structures must be achieved to create an equitable society.

Random sample is a smaller number of subjects chosen from a larger *population* in such a way that all relevant characteristics of the *population* are represented in the *sample*.

Randomness is a quality sought in a representative *sample* from a larger *population*. *Subjects* must be selected completely by chance to create a random *sample* from a particular *population*.

Ratio data are *data* that have equal intervals and a zero point signifying an absence of the construct being measured.

Rationalism is a *research* philosophy that assumes the existence of objective, knowable truths and includes well-structured *research designs* that typically collect *quantitative data* that are analyzed quantitatively. This research philosophy is based on the general philosophy of *realism*.

Realism is a general philosophy that presumes a knowable, objective reality exists.

Reconstructed logic is the process of recreating a *research* study when writing the report to reflect a *deductive* path of reasoning and logic.

Reductionism is the process of simplifying a phenomenon or *construct* into words or numbers, for example, to create *data* around which *research* studies are designed and carried out.

Reform ideology maintains that the *status quo* is not satisfactorily meeting the needs of all people in a given society. See *critical* and *radical theory*.

Regression coefficient is a number between 0 and .99, derived from a statistical treatment known as regression analysis, which indicates how well one characteristic can predict another.

Relationship and social structure codes in *qualitative data* analysis are those classifications that include informal associations, for example, friendships, coalitions, etc., that may not correspond to formal organizational relationships.

Relativism is a belief that reality consists of the interpreted, and therefore relative, point of view of individuals and groups. See *phenomenology* and *interpretivism*.

Reliability is an estimate of the degree to which an *instrument* or other observation will produce similar results time and time again.

Replicability is the practice of attempting to reproduce the results of a *research* project in another place or with a different group of subjects.

Research is the act of seeking understanding of or perspective on a problem, concern, or area of interest. It includes *design*, methodology, and dissemination, all of which are influenced by *ontology* (view of the world), *epistemology* (type of knowledge), and *ideology* (support for *status quo* or *reform*), although these may not be explicitly stated in a given *research* report.

Research methods are techniques or means by which *data* are elicited, compiled, or analyzed. *Qualitative data* might be generated from interviewing or reviewing original source material. *Quantitative data* are often derived from paper and pencil test results, survey responses, or recorded observations.

Research problem is a broad, general delineation of the limits of an academic area of concern or interest, typically arrived at by a study of how existing *research* has or has not addressed an area of concern or interest.

Research question is a relatively narrow, specific delineation of what the proposed *research* will address. This is frequently determined after the development of a thorough understanding of how existing *theory* or *research* has or has not addressed an area of concern or answered the question.

Research tradition is, within *naturalistic research,* synonymous with *design* in *rationalistic research.*

Review of literature is a written report of at least the seminal and most recent *research* and *theory* that is relevant to the *research question.*

Sample is the portion of a *population* that provides the *subjects* of a *research* study.

School of thought is a particular view of phenomena that influences the kinds of questions a *research* project will attempt to answer. Within the natural sciences (e.g., biology, physics, and chemistry) a well-established school of thought is called a *paradigm.*

Scientism is a belief that the results of empirical, scientific procedures can improve the human condition.

Semiotic research assumes that a literal or surface interpretation of human behavior consists of a series of signs that exist within an overarching system of understanding.

Semistructured interview is one in which the researcher guides the *subject* or *informant* by asking questions within broad categories. Open-ended questions are also asked.

Setting or context codes are classifications of *qualitative data* that include descriptions or characterizations of the setting or context within which the study is taking place.

Single subject (case) design is a *research design* for the in-depth, extended study of a single individual or group, in which the goal is understanding or change of the current situation.

Split-half reliability is a technique of dividing a test in half and comparing one half with the other, as if each half were a separate test. The more the two halves yield similar scores, the more reliable the test.

Standard deviation is an average measure of how individual scores vary from the group *mean.* The more spread out the scores are, the larger is the standard deviation.

Status quo is the *hegemonic* social or political conditions of a group, an organization, or a nation.

Strategy Codes in *qualitative data* are classifications of ways in which *participants* get things done.

Structural functionalism is often used by educational sociologists and anthropologists as a synonym for *functionalism.*

Structuralism is a philosophical position or world view in which the whole of the subject under study, usually institutions or society, is seen as consisting of various "structures" (i.e., ideology, school curriculum) that influence the behavior of those who come into contact with it. The individual is seen as rational, and thus freely chooses to be or not to be influenced by those structures.

Subjects are those studied or under investigation in a *truth-seeking research* project. In *perspective-seeking* studies the same individuals would be called *participants*.

Subjectivism refers to the researcher's personal interest or political beliefs and their influence on a given *research* project. This is seen as an intervening *variable* by *truth-seekers* and an inevitable part of *research* by *perspective-seekers*.

Symbolic interactionism is a *research tradition* or *school of thought* in sociology in which individuals' identities are seen as being continually shaped by their interactions with others. Moreover, their behaviors are symbolic or representative of the culture to which they are a part. Symbolic interactionist studies, therefore, delve beyond literal explanations of narratives or human behavior in an attempt to understand a culture and its people.

Systematic approach is a *research tradition* carefully constructed to reduce the probabilities of gathering or analyzing *data* inappropriately for the type of *research question* to be answered.

Systematic sampling is a technique to systematically select *subjects* from a particular category of a *population*. For example, given a study of 100 college students, the researcher may simply choose a proportionate number of subjects from predetermined groups of students based on race, religion, or grade point average.

t-Test is a statistical test that compares the *means* from two groups.

Theory, used within a *truth-seeking* study, is a statement that predicts a causal relationship between two or more *variables*. It frequently begins with a *hypothesis,* tested by experimentation. From the *perspective-seeker's* point of view, *theory* is a statement of description or explanation that provides understanding of a phenomenon under investigation or to which a *research* study's results add insight.

Theory-driven research seeks to add another piece of the puzzle regarding a particular field of education. Theory-driven *research* begins with the premise that existing knowledge on a certain topic comprises a body of facts that will be augmented by conclusions from the current study.

Theory-generating research begins with the assumption that *hypotheses* for further study cannot adequately be derived from existing *theory*. Thus, the researcher designs a theory-generating study that collects and analyzes *data* from which hypothetical *theory* is generated.

Thesis statement is a statement near the beginning of a report that concisely states what the report is about.

Transferability in *naturalistic* studies can be achieved if enough thick description is available to permit some application of results to other like settings. This concept is similar to *generalization* in rationalistic studies.

Treatment group in *true* and *quasi-experimental* designs is the group that receives the treatment. This group is also called the *experimental group.* See experimental group.

Triangulation is a technique in which at least three independent sources are used to verify the *trustworthiness* of *qualitative data*.

True experimental designs are *truth-seeking, quantitative* studies structured to minimize both *internal* and *external* threats to *validity*. Randomization (i.e., randomly selecting *samples* from *populations* and randomly assigning *subjects* to groups) is a necessary condition for achieving a true experimental design.

Trustworthiness is, in *naturalistic research*, the determination that the *data* are consistent, credible, *transferable, dependable,* and *confirmable*.

Truth is the end product of a *research* method designed by a person who believes that there is a definable and distinguishable reality that is the same for everyone, and that the purpose of scientific *research* is to find these *generalizable* statements or mathematical theorems.

Truth-seeking research proceeds on the assumption or world view (*ontology*) that reality is external, objective, and knowable.

Unstructured interview is used when the researcher does not want to sensitize the interviewee as to the nature of the research question, for example, asking an interviewee to recount important events in his or her life history or professional career, without asking specifically about the role of a particular individual.

Validity is a determination of the credibility of the *data* being measured or understood in a *research* study.

Variable is, in a *research* study, an identifiable characteristic of a person, group, place, or inanimate object.

Variance means the extent to which a group of scores vary. For example, given a test with a possible 100 points, and a majority of the test scores over 90, the variance would be relatively small. If, instead, the scores include many different scores from 10 to 100, the variance would be larger.

Verstehen is the subjective understanding gained by being a *participant* in a society or culture. This is seen as the perspective of a potential *research participant* or *informant* and the goal of a researcher is to know and understand this point of view.

Working hypothesis is, in *naturalistic* inquiry, a statement, developed from study about the problem, current *theory*, and *fieldwork*, that acts as an explanation of perspective. It is likely to change as more is discovered and will never be validated completely.

z-Scores are standardized scores with zero as a *mean* and 1 as a standard deviation.

Index

The abbreviations t and f stand for table and figure, respectively.